WORLD RELIGION AS A CONTEXT FOR OUR DIVERSITY

WORLD RELIGION AS A CONTEXT FOR OUR DIVERSITY

RECLAIMING VALUE IN A TIME BETWEEN STORIES

• • •

The Evolution of Outrageous Love and the Universal Grammar of Value

*One Mountain, Many Paths: Oral Essays
Volume 17*

With Special Section on Prayer

DR. MARC GAFNI

Copyright © 2025 Center for World Philosophy and Religion

All Rights Reserved

No part of this book may be used or reproduced in any manner whatsoever without written permission except in the case of brief quotations embodied in critical articles or reviews.

No part of this book may be reproduced, or stored in a retrieval system, or transmitted in any form or by any means, electronic, mechanical, photocopying, recording, or otherwise, without express written permission of the publisher.

All brand names and product names used in this book are trademarks, registered trademarks, or trade names of their respective holders.

For additional information and press releases please contact CWPR Publishing.

Author: Marc Gafni
Title: World Religion as a Context for Our Diversity
Identifiers: ISBN 979-8-88834-021-9 (electronic)
ISBN 979-8–88834–020–2 (paperback)

© 2025 Marc Gafni

Edited by Talya Bloom, Rachel Keune, Jeffrey Malecki, and Elena Maslova-Levin

World Philosophy and Religion Press
St. Johnsbury, VT

in conjunction with

IP Integral Publishers

https://worldphilosophyandreligion.org

CONTENTS

EDITORIAL NOTE ABOUT AUTHORSHIP, EDITING, AND THE RADICAL CONTEXT FOR THIS SERIES	XVIII
LOVE OR DIE: LOCATING OURSELVES	XXVIII
ABOUT THIS VOLUME	XLIV

CHAPTER 1 "I AM GLORIA"

Oh My God! A Direct Apprehension of Spirit	1
Reality Is Made Manifest in Love	2
Reality's Intention Is the Evolution of Love	3
Reclaiming the Glory of God	4
The Glory of the Physiosphere	5
The Glory of the Biosphere	7
The Glory of the Noosphere	8
The Glory of *Homo Amor*	9
Tribute to Ram Dass	12
The Second-Person Face of Gloria	13

CHAPTER 2 GLORIA: RECLAIMING RELIGION AT A HIGHER LEVEL OF CONSCIOUSNESS

Gloria: The Gravitas of Reality, Lined With Love	14
Towards a Cosmocentric World Religion	15
Praying to the Divine in the Second Person: The Infinity of Intimacy	18
Evolutionary Love Code: Reality Needs Your Service	20

CHAPTER 3 HOMO AMOR, WE ARE ALL NEEDED

The Dangers of a Partial Story	21
Reclaiming the Evangelical Spark	23

To Be an Evangelist Is to Be an Outrageous Lover	26
Outrageous Love: We're Outraged	28
Evolutionary Love Code: For True Evangelism We Need Both Ecstatic States and Developmental Stages	29
In Every Great Tradition There's an Intimate Incarnation of the Divine	31
Passover: For the First Time, I'm Going to Find That Hidden Dream	33

CHAPTER 4 RELIGION NEEDS TO BE PART OF THE REVOLUTION: EVOLVING THE UNIQUE SELF OF THE GREAT TRADITIONS

No More "Business As Usual"	36
Becoming *Homo amor*	37
The Source Code Move	39
Honoring Islam: *Allahu Akbar*	40
Evolutionary Love Code: Every Religion Has a Unique Self	42
Eye of the Senses, Eye of the Mind, Eye of the Heart	44
The Interpretation of Revelation Through the Prism of Consciousness	46
Liberating the Experience of Revelation	49
Participating in the Evolution of Great Traditions	52

CHAPTER 5 REWEAVING CHRISTMAS: FROM BIOLOGICAL FAMILY TO HOMO AMOR FAMILY

Weaving a New Cloth of Outrageous Love Into New Visions of Value	56
Silent Night: Son of God, Love's Pure Light	58
On the Other Side of Guilt Is Our Second Innocence	59
Outrageous Love Knows No Boundaries	61
Level One of Love: Biological Family	62
Level Two of Love: Romantic Love	62

Level Three of Love: Evolutionary Family and Outrageous Love	64
Articulating the Interior and Exterior Sciences of Love: Outrageous Love Drives Cosmos	66
We Are Evolutionary Lovers Looking Deeply Into Each Other's Eyes and Together at a Shared Horizon, Ready to Lay It All Down for the Sake of the Whole	67
Evolutionary Love Code: Evolutionary and Soul Root Family	69
In Excelsis Deo: Liberating the Exiled Energy of Gloria	70
The Practice: Birthing a New Structure of Intimacy	71
Gloria: Feel Your Innocence Slipping Away	72
Gloria: In Excelsis Deo in the Field of Love's Pure Light	73

CHAPTER 6 RECLAIMING THE EVOLUTIONARY TECHNOLOGY OF CHANT FOUND UNIQUELY IN EACH RELIGION

Setting Our Intention in This Time Between Worlds, This Time Between Stories	75
How Do We Know Anything? Accessing the Field of Value	77
Accessing the Eye of Value By Becoming the Music	78
Entering the Practice of Chant: Let the Chant Enter You	80
Evolutionary Love Code: The Path of Chant—Each Great Religion Is a Different Quality of Intimacy	81
Kashmir Shaivism: Devi Prayer	81
Cathars—Lo Boièr	82
Gyuto Monks—Mandala Offering	84
Native American—Sacred Spirit	85
Wisdom of Solomon Chants	85
Mizmor Shir Le'yom Ha'shabbat	87
Ki Atah Hu Ba'al Ha-Yeshuot: For You Are the Master of Liberation, For You Are the Master of Transformation	87
My Unique Self Is My Unique Chant	88

CHAPTER 7   THE NEW WORLD CALLS FOR A NEW WORLD RELIGION AS A CONTEXT FOR OUR GLOBAL DIVERSITY

What Would It Mean to Articulate a Vision of a New World Religion?	92
A Collapse of Value Is a Collapse of Eros	97
In the Absence of a Genuine Story of Value, Humans Create Pseudo-Stories of Value	98
Existential Risk Is a Direct Result of Pseudo-Stories of Value	100
Trialectics of Religion: We Need to Transcend and Include the Premodern and Modern	101
The New World Religion Can't Be Local, and Compassion and Kindness Are Not Enough	103
A Shared World Needs a World Religion	104
Building a Foundational Framework of First Principles and First Values	105
Spirituality Without Religion Is Not Enough	106
New Life Conditions Demand a New Language of Value	107
"Until Philosophers Are Kings… Cities Will Never Have Rest From Their Evils" —Plato	109
Powerfully Addressing the Rigorous Critiques of Value	110

CHAPTER 8   TAKING THE NEXT STEP IN THE URGENT NEED FOR A NEW WORLD RELIGION: CELEBRATING BARBARA MARX HUBBARD

A Shared Grammar of Value for a Global Conversation	115
We Live in a Conversational Cosmos	118
Evolutionary Love Code: New Need Generates New Emergence	120
A Planetary Awakening in Unique Self Symphonies	122

CHAPTER 9 SEDUCING HOMO SAPIENS INTO HOMO AMOR: THE MORAL OBLIGATION OF A NEW WORLD RELIGION

The Root Cause of Existential Risk Is a Global Intimacy Disorder	124
The Modern Word for Armageddon Is Existential Risk, The Modern Word for Messiah Is *Homo amor*	126
First Values and First Principles Are at the Center of It All	127
Evolutionary Love Code: Holy and Unholy Seduction	128
Practice: Clarifying Your deepest heart's desire	128
Screaming the Name of God: The Sacred Mystery of Erotic Explosion	130
Seduce Me and I Will Run After You	131
Seduction, Unique Self, and Unique Self Symphony	134
The Distinction Between Holy and Unholy Seduction	135
Articulating a World Religion That Can Seduce Reality Towards the Highest Version of Itself	136
Prayer: Draw Me After You	136

CHAPTER 10 RESPONDING TO THE THREE GREAT QUESTIONS OF COSMOEROTIC HUMANISM

Two Kinds of Existential Risk	139
Evolving the Source Code of Consciousness and Culture	141
What Are Evolutionary Love Codes?	144
Evolutionary Love Code: The Three Great Questions	146
Principle One: Outrageous Love Is Our Response Both to Pain and to Beauty	147
Principle Two: Outrageous Love Is the Heart of Existence Itself	148
Principle Three: I Am a Unique Configuration of Outrageous Love	149
Principle Four: Outrageous Lovers Commit Outrageous Acts of Love	152
Principle Five: Outrageous Acts of Love That Are Mine to Commit Are a Function of My Unique Self	154

Principle Six: Find the Others to Play
    in the Unique Self Symphony 157

Prayer: *Hallelujah* 161

**CHAPTER 11   FROM PERENNIAL PHILOSOPHY TO WORLD
RELIGION AS A CONTEXT FOR OUR DIVERSITY:
IN RESPONSE TO THE META-CRISIS**

Outrageous Love Is Reality 163

Every Religion Has a Unique Self 166

Evolutionary Love Code: Every Religion Has a Unique Self . . . 168

The Perennial Philosophy 168

The Name of God Is the Infinite Intimate 173

Every Unique Self Participates in the Name of God 176

The Seamless Coat of the Universe Is Seamless
    But Not Featureless 179

We Need Shared Universal Rituals to Bind Us
    in a Global Intimacy 181

Prayer: When I Speak, the Field of LoveIntelligence
    Listens and Responds 184

**CHAPTER 12   RESPONDING TO THE META-CRISIS THROUGH
THE EROTIC GNOSIS OF TEARS**

Evolving the Source Code of Consciousness 186

Rosh Hashanah Is the Portal to Transformation 188

When God and Goddess Are Brought Together,
    Blessings Flow Into the World 190

Tears Are an Expression of the Eros of Cosmos 192

God Is the Infinity of Intimacy 195

Rosh Hashanah and Yom Kippur Are Days of Tears 196

The Language of Mothers Is the Language of the Sacred 198

Tears That Shatter Our False Identity 201

The Gates of Tears Are Never Closed 205

I Am a Unique Desire of the Infinite 207

Tears Tell a Story About the True Nature of Self and Reality . . 208

CHAPTER 13 TEN PRINCIPLES OF OUTRAGEOUS LOVE: CLOSING THE GAP BETWEEN FEELING AND HEALING OUTRAGEOUS PAIN

Crossing to the Other Side	212
The Dharma Is the Psychedelic of Reality	214
The Evolution of Tears on the Side of Joy and on the Side of Pain	215
Deepening Our Commitment to Rebuild the New World With "Monogamous Polyamory"	218
When God Is Dethroned, Our Solutions Become the Great Tragedy Itself	221
Prayer Is One of the Most Powerful Medicines	223
We Are the Influential and the Powerful	226
Evolutionary Love Code: Healing What's Uniquely Yours to Heal	228
The Ten Principles of Outrageous Love	229

CHAPTER 14 HOW BIG IS YOUR HEART? FROM THE AGONY CRUCIFIXION OF THE CROSS TO THE BLISS CRUCIFIXION OF THE CROSSING

To Be Non-Intimate With Reality Is to Be Lost in the Drama of My Own Life	237
We Have to Face the Pain—But With Radical Joy!	239
We Have to Articulate a New Politics of Outrageous Love	241
We Live in an Intimate Universe and the Intimate Universe Lives in Us	243
We Are Coming Together from Around the World to Write a New Constitution	245
Forgive Yourself! Forgive All The People Who Betrayed You!	248
From the Cross to the Crossing	250
We Desperately Need Each Other	253
Infinity Needs Your Service	256
My House Is Your House	258
We Are Not Alone in Cosmos	260

CHAPTER 15 LIVING THE DREAM IN RESPONSE TO THE META-CRISIS: LIBERATING THE SPARKS OF CELEBRATION FROM ANCIENT TRADITIONS INTO A NEW WORLD SPIRITUALITY

Only a New Story of Value Changes the Vector of the Real	264
The World Itself Pulses With Joy	268
We Are Welcome	270
Evolutionary Love Code: The Unique Self of Every Religion	272
Liberating the Sparks from Hanukkah	272
The Miracle of the First Day	274
Capacity to Celebrate Partial Victories	277
The Way We Decide to Tell the Story Defines Everything	278
Liberating the Sparks from Christmas: The Birth of God as Human Being	280
We Need the Democratization of the Christed One	283
Gloria In Excelsis Deo ("Glory To God In The Highest")	285

CHAPTER 16 TELLING THE EVOLUTIONARY STORY OF CRUCIFIXION AND RESURRECTION

Evolving The Source Code, the Inescapable Frameworks in Which We Live	287
We Cannot Evolve the Source Code Without Religion	290
Weaving Easter and Passover Into the New Story	292
Evolutionary Love Code: Hope Is the Ontology of Reality	293
Redemption Is a Political and Economic Event	294
Everything Is About the Story We Decide to Tell	297
Life Is a Series of Love Stories	301
The Evolution of Love Is the Source of Hope	304
This Lifetime Is a Chapter in the Story	306
Choosing to Tell the Most Accurate Story	309

CHAPTER 17 A HERETICAL BLUEPRINT FOR A WORLD RELIGION AS A CONTEXT FOR OUR DIVERSITY

We Don't Wait for the Prophets	312
From *Homo sapiens* to *Homo amor*	315
Evolutionary Love Code: We All Stand Together on the Side of Love	319
A Shared Story of Value Is a Cosmic Anthem	319
"Show Me Something Real, Tell Me Something True"	322
The God You Don't Believe in Doesn't Exist	327
"What's Real Is That You're Loved"	331
"What's True Is That You're Not Alone"	333
Tenets of the World Religion	335

PRAYER AND WORLD RELIGION

CHAPTER 18 ANSWERING THE CALL OF PROPHECY: ENVISIONING NEW POSSIBILITIES & THE DIGNITY OF PRAYER

We Become the Voice of the Next Iteration of Evolution	341
The Universe: An Evolving Love Story	343
We Are All Connected: Invisible Lines of Non-Locality	345
In the Separate Self, We Have Lost the First Principle of Personhood	346
Being a Prophet Means Accessing Your Unique Voice and Seeing New Possibility	348
Slow Down, Listen Deeply, Fill Up With Eros	351
The Prayer You Thought Was Prayer Is Not Prayer	353
Evolutionary Love Code: Prayer and Prophecy	353
Second Person: The Pan-Interiority of Cosmos	355
Third Person: All Fields Are Interpenetrating and Are an Expression of the Larger Eros	357
Prayer Is When I Turn to the Field of Infinite Personhood	358
Third-Person Realization In Prayer	362

CHAPTER 19 PRAYER: THE PERSONHOOD OF COSMOS— RESTORING THE DIGNITY OF PERSONAL NEED

We Are Allured to Each Other In a New Configuration of Intimacy	364
You Are the Radiance of the Big Bang Incarnate	366
Prayer: The Seven Steps of the Stairway to Heaven	368
Step One: Faces of God	369
Step Two: Realizing the Personhood of Divinity	371
Step Three: Prayer Is Always Heard By Divinity	371
Step Four: The Movement of Prayer	373
Step Five: Feeling the Infinity of Power	374
Step Six: The Infinity of Power Is Right Here With You	374
Step Seven: The Feeling of God	375

CHAPTER 20 PRAYER: THE PERSONHOOD OF COSMOS— RESTORING INTIMACY THROUGH PRAYER AS PROTEST

The Urgency of a World Without First Principles and First Values	377
It's a Fucking Revolution	380
Evolutionary Love Code: The God You Don't Believe in Does Not Exist	382
Reality Is the Progressive Deepening of Intimacies	382
Prayer Itself Is a Form of Protest	383
Protest, Laughter, Mysticism and Paradox	384
The Paradox of Choice and Choicelessness	385
Laughter Holds Paradox	387
When Will You Come Already? We're Waiting for You	388
God, Show Up, Be Here	389
Getting Beneath the Space-Time Continuum and Reconfiguring the Past	390

God, I'm Done—Let Me Know If We Have a Deal	391
The Paradox of *Hallelujah*	393
In Genuine Intimacy With God There Is Protest	393

CHAPTER 21 PRAYER AWAKENS US TO THE APPROACHABILITY OF THE INFINITE

Intention Setting: Ratzon and Holy Seduction Into Outrageous Love	397
Evolutionary Love Code: Prayer Is Intimate Communion With the Infinity of Intimacy	399
Prayer: Turning to the Infinity of Intimacy	399
Personhood of Prayer: First Person	401
Personhood of Prayer: Second Person	402
The Butcher's Prayer	404
Personhood of Prayer: Third Person and Second Person	406
Prayer: Tenderness and Fierce Passion Exponentialized	409

CHAPTER 22 THE THREE FACES OF GOD = THE THREE FACES OF LOVE—REWEAVING THE UNIVERSE: A LOVE STORY

Existential Risk Presses Us Into the Realization That the Evolutionary Impulse Is Living in Us	410
The Narrative Arc of the Story of Reality	411
I Participate as the Universe in Person, in the Field of Love	413
We're Here to Tell the Best Love Story Ever Told	414
Outrageous Love Code: In the Greatest Love Story Ever Told, No One and Nothing Is Outside the Circle	417
We Can't Leave God Out of the Story	418
The Three Faces of God Which Are First Principles and First Values	419
The Third-Person Perspective of Reality	420
The First-Person Perspective of Reality	421

The Third-Person and First-Person Perspectives of Cosmos Are Not Enough	423
The Second-Person Perspective of Reality	424
Enacting The New Story Through Lived, Direct Experience: the Practice of Prayer	426
The Field of Eros Has a Personal Quality	429
Atheism: There's Heresy Which Is Faith	430
Prayer Is the Experience of the Personhood of Cosmos That Knows My Name	431

INDEX   **434**

EDITORIAL NOTE ABOUT AUTHORSHIP, EDITING, AND THE RADICAL CONTEXT FOR THIS SERIES

ORAL ESSAYS FROM THE ONE MOUNTAIN, MANY PATHS WEEKLY BROADCAST

This volume is part of the Oral library, a series of lightly edited, compiled transcripts of oral teachings given by Dr. Marc Gafni and the late Barbara Marx Hubbard in their weekly online broadcast, *One Mountain, Many Paths*, which they co-founded in 2017. Originally called an "Evolutionary Love Church," *One Mountain, Many Paths* became a key venue for the articulation of an inspired and deeply grounded new Story of Value in response to the meta-crisis. Marc and Barbara—together with Zak Stein,[1] Kristina Kincaid, Ken Wilber, Sally Kempton, Lori Galperin, Aubrey Marcus, and dozens of other thought-leaders over the years—began to articulate what they call a World Philosophy and World Religion[2] as a context for our diversity.

---

1 Zak, together with Ken Wilber, has been Marc's primary intellectual partner and an initiate lineage holder in CosmoErotic Humanism.

2 This project is grounded in four core organizational frameworks: 1) The Center for World Philosophy and Religion, co-founded by Marc Gafni, Zachary Stein, Sally Kempton, and Ken Wilber, and chaired over the years by John P. Mackey, Barbara Marx Hubbard, Aubrey Marcus, Gabrielle Anwar and Shareef Malnik, Carrie Kish and Adam Bellow, and Kathleen J. Brownback. 2) The Office for the Future, chaired by Stephanie Valcke and Ivan Bossyut. 3) The World Philosophy and Religion Press, founded and chaired by Aubrey Marcus, together with Marc Gafni and Zachary Stein. 4) The Foundation for Conscious Evolution, founded by Barbara Marx Hubbard and currently chaired by Peter Fiekowsky. For a complete list of key leadership, see the Office for the Future website, www.officeforthefuture.com.

EDITORIAL NOTE

Until Barbara's passing in 2019, she and Marc transmitted teachings together as evolutionary partners and "whole mates," weaving together insights and transmissions from their decades of practice, study, teaching, and activism into a synergy of wisdom, a grounded vision for future policy across all sectors of society.

Much of the Dharma material below comes directly from Marc, so it was originally all in quotation marks—but that looked a little odd. So per his suggestion we removed them, and the reader should consider the paragraphs on the next several pages as one extended quote from him. We are joyfully grateful to Marc for the clarity of his Dharma, the elegance and "second simplicity" of this language, and the mad, Outrageous Love with which he transmits his teachings.

Barbara and Marc called the mission of *One Mountain* "a Planetary Awakening in Evolutionary Love Through Unique Self Symphonies." We are an evolutionary community with a deeply grounded, radically alive, and "post-tragic" revolutionary spirit. We are activating a new humanity and awakening as a new species: *Homo amor*, the fulfillment of *Homo sapiens*.

One Mountain is committed to articulating a Story of Value that can become the ground for the new society that must be birthed in response to the meta-crisis. We recognize that we are living at a pivotal moment in history. In this "time between stories," the great moral imperative is to tell the new Story of Value. It is ours to do, personally and collectively, with great trembling and ecstatic joy.

FROM DOGMA TO DHARMA: ETERNAL AND EVOLVING FIRST PRINCIPLES AND FIRST VALUES

The teachings are grounded in decades of deep study across many wisdom traditions. Over the years, week by week, these teachings were incrementally developed within the framework of the *One Mountain, Many Paths* broadcast. We often refer to these teachings as *Dharma*.

This word was originally used in lineage traditions to refer to something like universal law. This is a crucial realization: just as there is universal law in mathematical value, there is also a sense of universal law in ethics and value.

Historically, Dharma often devolved into unchanging dogma. Evolution was ignored, and the natural process of Dharma evolution became disconnected from its deep, eternal context. The weakness of the word Dharma is that too often it did not include the evolving insights of the sciences, it confused local cultural truths with universal truths, and it used words like "eternal," as in "eternal Tao," as opposed to words like "evolution."

Eternal came to mean unchanging, and that kind of thinking often led to overly ethnocentric readings of Dharma. Local systems would claim their religious and cultural insights as immutable, which stood in the way of the emergence of a genuine world Story of Value that is real, inherent to Cosmos, and backed by the Universe—even as it is also always evolving.

Or, as we often say, "eternal value is evolving value. The eternal Tao is the evolving Tao."

We have shown that, emergent from profound insights in the "interior sciences," eternal does not mean unchanging in time; it means what we call the deeper Field of ErosValue that is beneath culture, geography, and history, which lives beneath all individual and collective values, and beneath time and space itself.

As such, we have gradually transitioned from the term Dharma to the term *Value*, in the sense of the Field of Value that lives beneath all values. This Field of Value discloses as First Principles and First Values embedded in a Story of Value.

Indeed, as the interior sciences knew and the exterior sciences imply, Reality arises in a Field of ErosValue in which an entire set of mathematical, musical, molecular, moral, and mystical values are the very ground of all being. That Field of Value is eternal—the true ground of the Good, True, and Beautiful—even as it is evolving.

But of course, it is equally critical not just to talk about evolving value, but to ground the evolving value in its true nature, the eternal Field of First Principles and First Values, always reaching for ever more life, ever more love, ever more care, ever more depth, ever more uniqueness, ever more intimate communion, and ever more transformation.

As such, when we refer to the word Dharma, which still appears in these texts together with the word value, we refer to an evolving Dharma grounded in an *eternal and evolving* Field of Value. Indeed, eternity and evolution are two faces of the whole, opposites joined at the hip, that characterize the nature of our Cosmos in virtually all of its expressions.

It's in these terms that we ground a robust world philosophy that integrates the validated, leading-edge insights of premodern traditional wisdom, modern wisdom, and more recent postmodern insights, weaving them together into a new whole greater than the sum of its parts.

This new whole is a shared Story of Value rooted in First Principles and First Values that are both eternal and evolving.

These First Principles and First Values of Cosmos are woven together into a new Story of Value as a context for our diversity, a new Universe Story. This new Story gives us the best possible responses we have to the mystery, and to the great questions:

- Who am I? Who are we?
- Where am I? Where are we?
- What should I do? What should we do?

It is only through such a shared Universe Story—a narrative of identity and ethos as a context for our blessed diversity—that we can realize how what unites us is so much greater than what divides us.

Only a new Story of Value will allow us to both respond to the meta-crisis and participate together in birthing the most true, good, and beautiful world that we already know is possible.

ORAL ESSAYS AS AN ENTRYWAY TO THE GREAT LIBRARY OF COSMOEROTIC HUMANISM

This Oral Essays series is part of the overarching project of the Great Library at the Center for World Philosophy and Religion, led by Dr. Marc Gafni, together with Dr. Zak Stein. The aim of the Great Library project is to articulate a robust and comprehensive new Story of Value, CosmoErotic Humanism, in the form of dozens of well-researched and extensively footnoted academic works.

Our vision is to provide the philosophical framework that will be vital for navigating humanity through this time of immense crisis and transformation.

To begin your journey into CosmoErotic Humanism, we tenderly refer you to the book *First Principles and First Values*, co-authored by Marc Gafni, Zak Stein, and Ken Wilber, under the name David J. Temple. David J. Temple is a pseudonym created for enabling ongoing collaborative authorship at the Center for World Philosophy and Religion. The two primary authors behind David J. Temple are Marc Gafni and Zak Stein, and for different projects, specific writers will be named as part of the collaboration, such as Ken Wilber and others.

Three other volumes complete this introduction: *A Return to Eros*, by Marc Gafni and Kristina Kincaid; *Your Unique Self*, by Marc Gafni; and *Education in a Time between Worlds*, by Zak Stein.

We hope that the Oral Essays in the present volume will serve as an allurement and entryway for you into the more formal books of the Great Library that provide the robust intellectual underpinnings of the new Story of Value.

EDITORIAL NOTE

A NOTE ABOUT THE EDITORS

This Oral Essays collection has been edited by students of the new Story of CosmoErotic Humanism. Each of us has actively participated in *One Mountain, Many Paths*, and most of us have been in deep "Holy of Holies" study with Dr. Marc Gafni for many years.

We have been privileged to find ourselves well-versed in the teachings, and even emerging as lineage-holders of CosmoErotic Humanism.[3]

We view this editing project as a privilege and a deep practice of study and clarification. We experience ourselves as a *mystical editing society*, frequently meeting and conversing together about the content—the depth of knowledge and wisdom offered here—as well as the technical intricacies involved with publishing a beautiful and coherent series of books. In so

---

3 CosmoErotic Humanism is a world philosophical movement aimed at reconstructing the collapse of value at the core of global culture. Much like Romanticism or Existentialism, CosmoErotic Humanism is not merely a theory but a movement that changes the very mood of Reality. It is an invitation to participate in evolving the source code of consciousness and culture towards a cosmocentric *ethos* for a planetary civilization.

The term CosmoErotic Humanism, initially coined by Dr. Gafni and colleagues, points to a complex, multi-faceted, layered, and nuanced evolutionary set of insights that has evolved over decades of intensive research, teaching, and spiritual practice from deep within a wide range of wisdom traditions (including the Wisdom of Solomon lineage tradition, Bodhisattva Buddhism, and Kashmir Shaivism), as well as multiple disciplines including complexity theory, chaos theory, emergence theory, molecular biology, and the more classical disciplines of the humanities.

The seeds of CosmoErotic Humanism were planted with Dr. Marc Gafni's work on a two-volume, 1,000-page opus called *Radical Kabbalah* (Integral Publishers, 2012). This scholarly work, sourced from deep study within the esoteric lineage texts of the Wisdom of Solomon, points to a non-dual, or acosmic, realization which—unlike the prevailing conceptualization of non-duality—does not efface the human being; rather, it is highly humanistic in its nature. The next step in the evolution of CosmoErotic Humanism was the insight that all of Reality is evolving Eros, which lives in, as, and through the human being.

A failure of Eros leads inexorably to the creation of narratives of "pseudo-eros." CosmoErotic Humanism is a response to the modern mental and social breakdown sourced in the proliferation of multiple forms of pseudo-eros and its broken narratives, such as rivalrous conflict governed by win/lose metrics and the dogmatic denial of intrinsic value in Cosmos, which together generate our current "global intimacy disorder."

doing, we function as a "Unique Self Symphony," which itself is a Dharmic term that connotes an omni-considerate collaboration between realized Unique Selves synergizing our unique gifts into a new emergence greater than the sum of the parts. Even as we worked diligently to standardize our editing styles, meeting on a weekly basis to debate the nuances of phrasing, we also operated from within a deep appreciation of the unique style that each editor brought to his or her work. As such, the reader might notice some variation in editing style among the books.

Please note that Dr. Marc Gafni has not reviewed these edited episodes, as he is deeply engaged in writing the formal books of the Great Library. But he has been generous in responding to questions and providing overall guidance in the project. Overall, as Marc's students and students of the Dharma, we have made it a key project at the Center to publish these pieces of work relatively independently.

OUR UNIQUE ORAL-ESSAY EDITING STYLE PRESERVES THE ENERGY OF THE ORIGINAL TRANSMISSION

Dr. Marc Gafni is a uniquely gifted teacher whose oral transmission is imbued with a quality that has proven transformative for his students. Many of us feel mystically transformed by both the content and the underlying energy of the transmission style. Therefore, as we like to say, *trust the magic ways the Dharma comes through your unique understanding!*

As Marc's empowered students, colleagues, and beloved friends, we have a deep knowing that these teachings are vital for the survival and thriving of humanity as we know it, and we recognize the importance of publishing his teachings in a written format that will be accessible by future generations. At the same time, we sought to preserve the Eros of the original oral transmission with all of its nuance, power, and depth. Our intention in the editing process, to the greatest extent possible, has been to keep these spoken artifacts intact in order to maintain the flow of the original transmission. We have therefore chosen not to engage in intensive formal editing, as we found that doing so resulted in the loss of the energetic transmission that is so key to fully receiving the Dharma.

After experimenting with many ways to present these texts, we developed a specific way of laying out the text on the page. Marc, in collaboration with Zak Stein and Russian intellectual/artist Elena Maslova-Levin—and ultimately all of the editors, through many conversations—developed a unique, artistic presentation of the text, using bolding, italics, bullet points, and other stylistic features which together serve to accentuate the immediacy of the oral transmission.

As part of this editing style, intended to preserve the integrity of the original transmission, we have refrained from removing the frequent recapitulations of key themes. We found that each recapitulation contributes something vital to the rhythm and music beneath the words, like the beating drum of our hearts. These recapitulations not only review previous material but also add important new emphases, perspectives, and elements of the new Story of Value. We ask for your patience as a reader to trust the rhythm of these texts, and we trust you as a reader to have the depth and steadiness to find your way through.

KEY COMPONENTS: LINK TO THE ORIGINAL BROADCAST, EVOLUTIONARY LOVE CODES AND PRAYER

To supplement the written word, each episode includes a QR code linking to the original broadcast on YouTube, as well as occasional links to featured songs and video clips.

Each episode also centers around an "Evolutionary Love Code," formulated by Marc. These codes are part of the ongoing articulation and distillation of the Dharma as it unfolds and emerges, week by week, over the course of many years, through the mystical process we call Outrageous Love or Evolutionary Love.

WORLD RELIGION AS A CONTEXT FOR OUR DIVERSITY

Another core component of the *One Mountain, Many Paths* episodes is what Marc and Barbara called "Evolutionary Prayer." Prayer is experienced in *One Mountain* not in the old fundamentalist sense of a "cosmic vending-machine god" who is alienated from Cosmos. Marc refers to this as the "god you do not and should not believe in"—and he often adds, "the god you don't believe in does not exist."

GOD IS THE INFINITE INTIMATE

In fact, in the Dharma of CosmoErotic Humanism, a new name for God has emerged: the "Infinite Intimate," who appears in first-, second-, and third-person expressions. Marc first shared this name as he heard it whispered in 2023, although earlier intimations and formulations of the name appeared as early as 2010.

In first person, God is infinitely alive and as intimate as our own first-person experience.

In second person, God is the infinitely intimate Personhood of Cosmos that knows our name and holds us—the God about whom we say, *whenever we fall, we fall into Her hands*. This is the God who is our Beloved, Father, Mother, Lover, and Evolutionary Partner.

Finally, in third person, God inheres in all of the First Principles and First Values of Cosmos, and in the laws of science (both interior and exterior) that govern manifest Reality.

Therefore, we have a realization of God as not only the Infinity of Power but also the Infinity of Intimacy.

In *One Mountain, Many Paths*, we are reclaiming prayer at a higher level of consciousness. And we are reclaiming prayer as deep, alive, loving, and intimate conversations with God as the Infinite Intimate who knows our name.

EDITORIAL NOTE

THE INVITATION

We invite you to find your way into this revolution. Each one of our Unique Selves and unique gifts are desperately needed as we co-create this new Story of Value together, as part of the covenant between generations, for the sake of the whole.

Let's *play a larger game* and evolve the very source code of consciousness and culture together.

With mad love,

The Editors

LOVE OR DIE

LOCATING OURSELVES: ARTICULATING THE ESSENTIAL CONTEXT FOR THE ONE MOUNTAIN, MANY PATHS ORAL ESSAYS

SETTING OUR INTENTION

Intention setting is everything.

We're here—as da Vinci was with his cohort in the Renaissance—**to play a larger game, to participate in the evolution of love, which is to tell the new Story of Value rooted in First Principles and First Values.**

- Our intention is to recognize the critical historical juncture in which we find ourselves.
- Our intention is to take our seat at the table of history and to say, *we take responsibility for this.*
- Our intention is to participate as revolutionaries for the sake of the whole.

What we're here to do is revolution; revolution for the sake of the evolution of love.

It's a revolution for the sake of the trillions of unborn lives that will not manifest:

- The unborn loves
- The unborn creativity
- The unborn goodness
- The unborn truth
- The unborn beauty

All of it looks to us.

Not because we're engaged in grandiosity. Not at all!

- We're trembling before She.
- We're trembling with joy at the privilege.
- We're trembling with joy at the responsibility.
- We're trembling with joy at the Possibility of Possibility.
- We have to enact a new Story in this moment of time. Because it is only a new Story that can change the vector of history.

The most revolutionary act that we can do—the greatest moral imperative of this time—**is to articulate a new Story at this time between worlds and this time between stories.**

Story is not made up, as postmodernity suggests. **We all live in inescapable frameworks; our framework is the story we live in.** Right now, Reality lives according to win/lose metrics, a story that is generating existential risk. **We need to change that story.**

When we change that story, when we tell a new Story—not a made-up story, but a new Story of Value, rooted in First Principles and First Values—**then it all changes.**

We need to participate in the evolution of the source code of consciousness and culture, which is the evolution of love.

It's the most important, exciting, evolutionary, revolutionary act that we can do to alleviate suffering: to be lovers.

Like Rumi, the great poet of Sufism, we have to be "mad lovers," because it's the only sanity.

To be mad lovers is to see around the corner, to not be so obsessed with the details of the contractions of my life.

Let me see bigger.

Let me take complete care of myself in every possible way, let me completely attend to those in my circle of intimacy and influence, and then—*let me expand my circle.*

That's what we're here for.

- Our intention is to participate in the *LoveForce*, the *LoveIntelligence*, the *LoveBeauty*, the *LoveDesire* that literally animates Cosmos all the way up and all the way down.
- Our intention is to participate in the evolution of love.

[*In the next few pages we will cover some key concepts which are essential to locating ourselves and setting the context for the One Mountain, Many Paths Oral Essays. —Eds.*]

OVERVIEW: EROS IS NO LONGER A LUXURY—IT'S LOVE OR DIE

Eros is life.

The failure of Eros destroys life.

Our lack of Eros is poised to destroy the world.

All civilizations have fallen because the stories that they lived in were, in some sense, stories based on rivalrous conflict governed by win/lose metrics. Every civilization was weakened by interior polarization caused by the lack of a shared Story of Value.

We now have a global civilization, but we haven't created a shared Story of Value.

We haven't solved the generator functions that caused all civilizations to fall. Our global civilization has exponential technologies and extraction models depleting the Earth of resources that took billions of years to create, which is going to lead to a civilizational collapse.

Existential risk is risk to our very existence.

The choice is clear: love or die.

It's that simple.

Eros is no longer a luxury. It is an absolute necessity for the survival of the individual and the planet.

In the last half a century, modern psychology has documented an age-old truth: a fully nourished baby who is not held in loving arms will die.

So too, our world, both personal and global—even with all the resources of intelligence and technology at our disposal—will die without being held in love, in the embrace of Eros.

We must embrace a personal path of love and a global politics of love.

Not ordinary love. Not love which is "mere human sentiment," but Eros, or what we sometimes call Outrageous Love, which is the heart of existence itself.

We live in a world of outrageous pain.

The only response is Outrageous Love.

WHAT IS EROS?

Eros is the experience of radical aliveness, moving towards, seeking, desiring ever deeper contact and ever greater wholeness.[4] Eros is the core fabric of Reality's being and the motivational architecture of Reality's becoming.

Eros is what animates the evolutionary impulse itself, from the very inception of Cosmos all the way to our very selves, who awaken to the realization that the evolutionary impulse throbs uniquely in each of us.

The realization of human awakening and transformation that lies at the core of the interior sciences is the invitation—or even the urgent and desperate demand—of a madly loving Cosmos animated by infinities of power and infinities of intimacy.

The demand—the desperate invitation, the plea, the tender and fierce command of Cosmos that lives inside every human being—is to awaken: to awaken to our true nature as unique incarnations of Eros and Ethos that are needed and desperately desired by All-That-Is. Said slightly differently: Reality is Eros. Or: God is Eros.

The failure of Eros destroys life. The collapse of Eros is always the hidden (or not so hidden) root cause for the collapse of ethics.

This is true both personally and collectively. We live in a moment of a worldwide and personal collapse of Eros. Our lack of Eros is poised to destroy

---

4 We define Eros through what we refer to as the Eros equation (one of a series of what we call interior science equations):

Eros = Radical Aliveness x *Desiring (Growing + Seeking)* x *Deeper Contact* x *Greater Wholeness* x *Self Actualization/Self Transcendence (Creation [Destruction])*

There are good reasons for the formal language of the interior science equations in these writings, and the reader is invited to explore them on their own, in particular, in our work, David J. Temple, *First Principles and First Values: Forty-Two Propositions on CosmoErotic Humanism, the Meta-Crisis, and the World to Come* (World Philosophy and Religion, 2024).

the world. Humanity is currently experiencing what has come to be known as existential risk, a risk to our very existence, or what I will refer to as the Second Shock of Existence.

EXISTENTIAL RISK: THE SECOND SHOCK OF EXISTENCE

The first shock of existence is the death of the human being—the realization that we will die, which dawns in human consciousness at the beginning of history. We are not talking about the biological fact of death but the *existential* realization of death. Although the interior sciences disclose that death is a portal between two days (there is vast empirical,[5] philosophical,[6] and anthro-ontological evidence[7] for the continuity of consciousness[8]), death is also, in our own direct surface experience, a stark end. And that is obviously not a bug but a feature in the system.

---

5   We refer to evidence gathered by the most serious of researchers, beginning with Henry and Edith Sedgwick at Cambridge University and William James at Harvard University, and continuing in highly rigorous form for the last 150 years, as recapitulated by Whiteheadian scholar David Ray Griffin in multiple volumes. See also, for example, Dean Radin, *Real Magic: Unlocking Your Natural Psychic Abilities to Create Everyday Miracles* (Potter/TenSpeed/Harmony, 2018), *The Conscious Universe: The Scientific Truth of Psychic Phenomena* (HarperCollins, 2010), and other books. Or see the earlier classic by Frederic William Henry Myers, *Human Personality and Its Survival of Bodily Death* (Longmans, Green, 1907).

6   This requires a cogent analysis of materialism and dualism, and the introduction of the far more cogent third possibility which we have called "pan-interiority."

7   We discuss Anthro-Ontology in some depth in *First Principles and First Values*, and see also the fuller conversation in David J. Temple, *First Principles and First Values: Towards an Evolving Perennialism: Introducing the Anthro-Ontological Method*—both published by World Philosophy and Religion Press, in Conjunction with Integral Publishers. For now, we will simply define it as an "innate and clear interior gnosis directly available to the human being."

8   See Dr. Marc Gafni and Dr. Zachary Stein's essay in preparation, "Beyond Death: Anthro-Ontology, Philosophy, and Empiricism." This essay is slated to appear in the book *Towards a World Religion: Homo Amor Essays*. The essay is also the ground for a larger book by the same authors, *Twelve Portals to Life Beyond Death: Responding to the Second Shock of Existence,* in which we discuss three forms of material: the empirical, the philosophical, and the anthro-ontological, and show how each form discredits the notion of death as the end.

Our first-person experience is that death ends this life. It is not the *totality* of our experience if we go deeper inside, but it is obviously intended to be the central, potent, and painful dimension of every human life. Indeed, as Ernest Becker potently reminded us, the denial of death is at our peril.

All the stories and all the plotlines and all the threads of living end at that moment. Whatever happens beyond, we have an actual experience of ending. **Paradoxically, that ending, the experience of the finality of mortality, is what presses us into life.** From the implicit demand of the first shock of existence, human beings were activated and pressed into creative emergence, and what emerged was all of human culture, both interior and exterior.

The second shock of existence is the realization of the potential death of all humanity. After all the stages of human history—matter, life, and mind in all of their stages of evolutionary unfolding—we have come to this place in the evolution of humanity, in which the gap between our exponentially expanding exterior technologies and our stalled (or even regressing) interior technologies of value has created dire catastrophic and existential risks.

This gap generates extraction models and exponential growth curves, rivalrous conflicts based on win/lose metrics, tragedies of the commons, and multipolar traps, in which everyone has to keep producing to the *n*th degree, including weaponized exponential threats to our very existence because we are afraid that the other parties are going to do it and not be transparent—hide it from us and then dominate us.

GENERATOR FUNCTIONS FOR EXISTENTIAL RISK

Let's outline clearly the main *generator functions for existential risk*.

Rivalrous conflicts governed by zero-sum, win/lose metrics. Rivalrous conflicts generate extraction models at the core of the economic system and exponential growth curves. Both of these drive and are driven by a contrived system of artificially manufactured desires and needs, delivered into culture by ever more precise forms of micro-targeting to individuals and groups through the ever more immersive environment of the internet.

Next, rivalrous conflicts and exponential growth curves animated by win/lose metrics generate **complicated, fragile world systems** highly vulnerable to myriad forms of collapse. Fragile local systems are made exponentially more fragile on a global level by our inability to meet global challenges with social, legal, political, economic, and ethical infrastructures that remain largely local.

All of this is a direct result of the failure to develop more adequate interior technologies that would be sufficiently compelling to displace "rivalrous conflict governed by win/lose metrics" as the motivational architecture for the human life world.

This failure has led to the conditions that will cause the implosion of systems that are already and quite literally on the brink of collapsing themselves. That's what we mean by the *second shock of existence*.

To recapitulate: the second shock of existence is not the death of the human being, but the potential death of humanity.

It is the *Death Star* moment of our species.

THE DECONSTRUCTION OF INTRINSIC VALUE

We stand in this moment poised between utopia and dystopia, at a time between worlds and a time between stories. We need a new Story of Value, eternal yet evolving, rooted in First Principles and First Values, which would become a universal grammar of value and a context for our diversity.

This is exactly what the Renaissance was. It was a time between worlds and a time between stories. In the Renaissance, we had been recently challenged by the Black Death, a pandemic that swept across Europe. The Black Death destroyed between a third to half of Europe and a huge part of

Asia. People died horrifically, brutally, in the streets. They had no idea how to meet this challenge, and so, in response to the Black Death, da Vinci and Ficino and their cohorts understood that they had to tell a new Story of Value.

That story was the story of modernity. Did they get it right?

- They got part of it right, which birthed, to use Jürgen Habermas' phrase, "the dignities of modernity," such as new ways of gathering information and universal human rights.
- But they also deconstructed the source of Value. They lost the basis for the Good, the True, and the Beautiful.

The basis used to be divine revelation: *God told us*. But this claim was owned by religion, and every religion began to overreach and over-claim. The revelation was thus often mediated through cultural categories and wasn't fully accurate.

Modernity threw out revelation, but was unable to establish a new basis for value.

Value was just assumed to be real. As it says in the founding document of the American Revolution: *We hold these truths to be self-evident*—that is, we don't really have a basis for value; we just take it as a given.

In other words, modernity took out a loan of social capital from the traditional world. The source of value was never worked out.

And then, gradually, value began to collapse.

- The Universe Story began to collapse.
- The belief that the Good, the True, and the Beautiful are real began to collapse.
- The belief that Love is real began to collapse.

As Bertrand Russell is reported to have said, "I cannot see how to refute the arguments for the subjectivity of ethical values, but I find myself incapable of believing that all that is wrong with wanton cruelty is that I do not like it."

What do you do if you grew up in a world in which value is not real? A world without a source of value, without a Universe Story, without a story of human identity, without a story of desire, without a narrative of power?

In the words of W.B. Yeats, *the center does not hold.*

- You have a collapse at the very center of society, because you no longer have Eros.
- You no longer have a Reality in which value is real, and so you have this lingering sense of emptiness.
- You have a complete collapse at the very center.
- We become *the hollow men and the stuffed men*, gesture without form.

And that's the source of our current existential risk.

THE DEEPER ROOT CAUSE OF THE META-CRISIS: A GLOBAL INTIMACY DISORDER

Above, I have outlined the major generator functions of existential risk. But there is a deeper cause for the existential risk that lurks underneath the rivalrous conflict governed by win/lose metrics and the fragile systems they engender.

And we cannot take the Death Star down without discerning and addressing this. We have already alluded to this root cause above, but at this point we need to make it more explicit so that, from this context, the adequate root response will become clear.

Modernity threw out revelation, but was unable to establish a new basis for value.

This ostensibly surprising statement can be understood in a few simple steps:

1. All of the catastrophic and existential risk challenges we face are global: from climate change to artificial intelligence, pandemics, systems collapse, and exponential arms races.
2. Every global challenge self-evidently requires a global solution.
3. Global solutions can only be implemented with global co-ordination.
4. Global co-ordination is impossible without global coherence.
5. Global coherence is only possible if there is a global resonance between the parts.
6. Global resonance is only possible if we have global intimacy.

ONLY A SHARED STORY OF VALUE CAN GENERATE GLOBAL INTIMACY

Global intimacy—just like intimacy in a couple—is only possible when there is a shared story.

Not just a shared history, but a shared Story of Value.

- It is only a shared global story that can generate a new emergent quality of intimacy: global intimacy.
- A shared Story of Value must be rooted in shared ordinating values, or what we have called evolving First Values and First Principles.
- Intimacy requires a shared grammar of value as a matrix for a shared Story of Value.

The global intimacy disorder is the root cause for existential risk. The global intimacy disorder underlies the core generator functions for existential risk.

The global intimacy disorder is rooted in the failure to experience ourselves in a field of shared intrinsic value. This failure derives from the deconstruction of value.

Indeed, it is wholly accurate to say that **the root cause of the two generator functions of existential risk is the failed story of intrinsic value, or what we might also call the breakdown of Eros.**

1. The first generator function is **the success story**. Our modern success story is rivalrous conflict governed by win/lose metrics, which violates all the terms of the Intimacy Equation: there is no shared identity and no mutuality of recognition, feeling, value or purpose, and instead of *relative* otherness, there is *alienated* otherness. Such a story generates complicated fragile systems with no allurement or intimacy between the parts, systems which optimize for efficiency (as an expression of win/lose metrics) and not for resiliency and life.

2. The second generator function is **the deconstruction of intrinsic value** itself. The deconstruction of value is the sense that human value does not participate in the intrinsic value of the Real, for the Real is dogmatically declared to have no intrinsic value. Thus, there is no shared identity between the interior of the human being and Reality. There is no common participation in a field of shared intrinsic value. Instead of being intimate with value, we are alienated from value. And only intrinsic value can arouse will: political, moral, and social will.

To sum up, without a shared grammar of value there is no global intimacy, and therefore no global coherence, and no global coordination in response to catastrophic and existential risk, which means, put simply, there will be, quite literally, no future.

WORLD RELIGION AS A CONTEXT FOR OUR DIVERSITY

HEALING THE GLOBAL INTIMACY DISORDER REQUIRES THE EVOLUTION OF INTIMACY

But we are not hopeless. On the contrary, we are filled with great hope. Hope is a memory of the future. That memory of the future *is* the direct hit that takes down the Death Star, the culture of death. **The direct hit must be**—as it has always been in history—**the emergence of a new stage of evolution.**

Crisis is an evolutionary driver, and every crisis is, at its core, a crisis of intimacy: from the oxygen crisis of the single cells dying which generated multicellular life at the dawn of existence, to the existential risk in this very moment.[9]

The direct hit is therefore structurally self-evident: the evolution of intimacy itself.

What is intimacy, as a structure of Cosmos all the way down and all the way up the evolutionary chain? We engage this inquiry in depth in other writings, but for now we will simply adduce what we have called the "Intimacy Equation":

> *Intimacy* = *shared identity in the context of [relative] otherness* × *mutuality of recognition* × *mutuality of pathos* × *mutuality of value* × *mutuality of purpose*

Intimacy is about the capacity of parts to generate a *shared identity* while retaining their otherness, or distinct identity. This requires multiple mutualities, including recognition, pathos (or feeling), value, and purpose. The parts must recognize and feel each other, even as they share value and purpose. But all of this must lead to intimate union—and not pathological

---

9 We demonstrate this principle in some depth in the multi-volume series, *The Universe: A Love Story* (forthcoming) (https://worldphilosophyandreligion.org/early-ontologies), *The Intimate Universe: Global Intimacy Disorder as Cause for Global Action Paralysis* (forthcoming), and in other writings of CosmoErotic Humanism.

fusion, where the distinct identity of the parts disappears—like subatomic particles that successfully become an atom, or two people who successfully become a couple.

THE DECONSTRUCTION OF VALUE IS THE DECONSTRUCTION OF INTIMACY

We have identified the global intimacy disorder as the root cause of existential risk. But the underlying ultimate failure of intimacy is the deconstruction of value itself.

The deconstruction of value means that human value does not participate in any sense of intrinsic value of the Real. This is not about individual *values,* but about *the Field of Value* that underlies all of them. **When the human being**—moved, often sincerely or even nobly, by myriad cultural, historical, and psychological confusions—**claims to have stepped out of the Field of Value, then intimacy itself is deconstructed.**

The deconstruction of value is the deconstruction of intimacy.

In the absence of a shared Story of Value, a story that is an authentic expression of Reality's Eros, a story rooted in *pseudo-Eros* takes center stage and becomes the generator function for existential risk. Our modern pseudo-Eros story is *rivalrous conflict governed by win/lose metrics*. Such a story catalyzes in its wake the second generator function of existential risk: *complicated fragile systems with no allurement or intimacy between the parts*. It is in that sense that we have argued that the first generator function for existential risk is the success story.

- The failure of intimacy is precisely the impotent experience that there is no shared identity between the interior of the human being and Reality. **There is no shared identity in the sense of any kind of common participation in a field of shared intrinsic value.**
- **But only a shared Story of Value can arouse the global will**

required to engage catastrophic and existential risk. For it is only global political, moral, and social will—and we can even say *erotic* will—that can generate the most Good, True and Beautiful world that we have always known is possible.

THE EVOLUTION OF LOVE IS THE TELLING OF A NEW STORY

Coupled with the Intimacy Equation is the scientifically grounded realization, in both the exterior and interior sciences, that Reality is a progressive deepening of intimacies, or, said slightly differently:

Reality is Evolution. Evolution is the evolution of intimacy.

- The evolution of intimacy requires—both personally and collectively—a deeper, more accurate discernment of the nature of our universe, ourselves, and our beloveds.
- This new discernment generates a new global Story of Value.
- The new global Story of Value generates an emergent, heretofore unseen global intimacy and heals the global intimacy disorder.

The new Story of Value is the direct hit that takes down the Death Star and replaces it with the hope that invokes the memory of our best future.

Global intimacy facilitates global coherence, which facilitates global coordination, which activates the possibility of our creative and effectively coordinated global responses to the global meta-crisis in its entirety and its specific expressions.

To solve Bertrand Russell's challenge—the apparent argument for the subjectivity of ethical values—**we have to reground value theory in eternal yet evolving First Principles and First Values, and articulate a new Story of Value.**

This is what we call CosmoErotic Humanism.

CosmoErotic Humanism—together with other emergent strands—**needs to become the ground of a world religion as a context for our diversity**. We need religion, even as we need science, to articulate a shared global grammar of value.

As we said at the beginning, our choice is simple: love or die.

- To love means to participate in the evolution of love, which is the evolution of the human Story of Value.
- To love means to evolve and activate a new cultural enlightenment—rooted in a new narrative of identity, a new narrative of value, a new narrative of intimate communion, a new narrative of desire, a new narrative of power—all of which will birth new narratives of economics and politics.
- The evolution of love is the telling of a new Story.

The new Story that must be told is a love story, for in fact that is the deepest truth of Reality, rooted in the best exterior and interior sciences, that we have at this moment in time:

- Reality is not merely a fact. Reality is a story.
- Reality is not an ordinary story. Reality is a love story.
- Reality is not an ordinary love story. Reality is an Outrageous Love Story.

Story doesn't mean it's *made-up*.

It means doing the hard work of integrating the validated insights of the traditional world, the modern world, and the postmodern world.

This is the intention at the heart of telling the new Story of CosmoErotic Humanism.

ABOUT THIS VOLUME

In *World Religion as the Context for Our Diversity*, Dr. Marc Gafni articulates a new "Story of Value" in response to the collapse of a shared global ethos. At the heart of this work lies the realization of Outrageous Love, a force that transcends ordinary romantic love. Outrageous Love is the animating Eros of the evolutionary impulse that drives the Cosmos. Outrageous Love incarnates Eros and Intimacy as the heart of Reality's Field of Value in which all of the manifest world unfolds.

Outrageous Love is not mere human sentiment but the heart of existence itself. It is the force of Eros and Value that live in us, locating our personal and collective lives within the larger context of the cosmic will and purpose.

At the core of world religion is a universal grammar of value. This grammar of value writes the chapters of a new Story of Value, not as mere conjecture or a constructed narrative, but as a story deeply rooted in the value structure of Reality itself.

We are not just participants in the story; we participate directly as the story. We are the personal face the evolutionary impulse of Cosmos, each of us an irreducibly unique incarnation of the Divine, as we contribute a desperately needed verse to the cosmic scroll. The cosmic scroll holds the record of the past and the memory of our future.

This volume attempts to reclaim the language of value, suggesting that the shared qualia of beauty, truth, and goodness as the inherent character of cosmic yearning—frozen in modernity, rejected by postmodernity—must be reawakened in this new global religion. For the new world religion must be one that weaves together the not only the validated insights of the exterior sciences but also the validated gnosis of the interior sciences.

Central to this new articulation is the "Unique Self Symphony," where each individual's Unique Self is an irreducible expression of the Field of Divine

ABOUT THIS VOLUME

Value, contributing a verse to the cosmic scroll, becoming a crucially unique part of the whole.

The demand of a lifetime is more than just one's individual spiritual growth; it is the imperative to participate in the co-creation of a world religion that holds a shared vision of value—a common musical melody of mystery—as the context for our diversity.

The vision described in this volume serves as the strange attractor which intends to draw us beyond the old success story animated by the deadly paradigm of rivalrous conflict governed by win/lose metrics. This is an outdated narrative of pseudo-value, birthed by the alienation from Eros itself. Our vision instead is of the emergence of a new human and new humanity—it is time for *Homo sapiens* to be fulfilled as *Homo amor*.

Ultimately, this volume speaks to the urgent need for us to rediscover our inherent dignity, grounded in First Principles and First Values, as the only truly valid (and valiant) response to the meta-crisis of our time.

In this new Story of Value, we realize our authentic identity as *Homo amor*, animated by Outrageous Love, committing Outrageous Acts of Love, and as such playing our Unique Self instruments in the Unique Self Symphony. Our personal transformation becomes the transformation of the whole, and so the split between the personal and the cosmic disappears.

We are invited in this time between worlds and time between stories to tell a new Story of Value, which demands—with Outrageous Love—that we transform not only ourselves but also the world. It is time to evolve together into a future where ever-deepening Eros, ethos, and intimacy are the north star for Reality's evolution.

Volume 17

These oral essays are lightly edited talks delivered by Marc Gafni between December 2019 and January 2024.

CHAPTER ONE

"I AM GLORIA"

Episode 168 — December 28, 2019

OH MY GOD! A DIRECT APPREHENSION OF SPIRIT

"Oh my God!" Those are the words we use when language can't hold the full extent of Reality. We're saying, "Oh my God! It's awesome!"

The word God, when used wrongly, can be a curse—you're not allowed to use it in vain; it can be used terribly. But it also can be the most awesome, gorgeous intensifier of experience. When we stopped using the word God, when God fell out of language, we borrowed other words. **We now need to reclaim the Eros of God. We need to reclaim that which says that words can't quite capture the full dimension of what experience is.**

- If you want to know God, if you want to know Spirit, you need to have a direct experience.
- You have to allow yourself to be ripped open.
- Your eyes open, your body opens, your heart opens—and then it's so clear.

The love that shimmers, that magnifies into existence, that delights, that moves up and down the evolutionary chain is so obvious, so certain. There's no question about it.

Have you ever been madly in love in such a deep and beautiful way with the exact right person, and then someone tells you, "Well, that's not real! Love's not real." No! It's the most real thing in the world. It's a direct experience that can't be held in words.

So this week, we're saying, "Oh my God! Here we are!" We are privileged to be in this Church of Evolutionary Love—and Barbara, this is the first time between Christmas and New Year, that you haven't been here.

This was our deepest intention, to have an evolutionary Church—which was God's dream.

REALITY IS MADE MANIFEST IN LOVE

We're going to be talking about dreaming, what it means to be a dreamer, and what the great dream is, the great dream of God—as God/Goddess, as Infinity Itself sat, lived, and existed in its own internal bliss, which was everything. Infinity made a decision: the decision of manifestation.

Infinity said, "I am madly in love, and because I'm madly in love, I want to manifest Reality. I want Reality to emerge, and that emergence of Reality will be an expression of Me. **I'm going to love Reality so much that I'm going to pour Myself into Reality.**"

In other words, Infinity *loved* finitude. That's the great mystical realization—but it's not a dogmatic realization, it's not a faith-based realization that somebody made up. When you experience the inside of Cosmos, you can actually *feel* that quality of love. We call that non-ordinary love.

We call it Outrageous Love.

We sometimes call it Evolutionary Love.

If you want to feel that, if you want evidence for that quality, or if you think this is a way-off idea because you've never experienced it—I can just give you an experience of it now. Just check out any love song ever written on the planet.

All throughout Reality, 99.9 percent of music is love songs. Why? Why does love move you so much? Why is being in love and being loved so wildly, madly important in your life? Why does attachment theory say that if a child is not well-loved it affects and destroys the entire trajectory of their life, even if they have all the material success in the world?

We're not making this up.

> *Love is the fabric of Reality itself. It's the intention of Reality.*

REALITY'S INTENTION IS THE EVOLUTION OF LOVE

Reality's intention is the Evolution of Love. The Evolution of Love is the most glorious thing you can possibly imagine. We want to create together a religion beyond religion—a synagogue beyond synagogues, a secular humanist center beyond secular humanist centers, a Church beyond churches. We don't want to make this a narrow, liberal, New Age movement where we're just talking to each other. We don't want to do that.

This is kind of shocking:

> *Seventy percent of the entire world lives in a great tradition, in connection to a religion.*

So if we want to heal the fractured planet, if we want to heal a fragmented world, we can't just talk to our own internet bubble.

We can't talk to our own narrow Facebook group, where we only get our own sense of the world reflected back to us.

We need to embrace all of Reality. We've got to "have the whole world in our hands." Seventy percent of the whole world lives in deep connection to a religion, so we don't get rid of it. We have to up-level religion; we have to evolve religion. Just like medicine evolved—you won't go to a fifteenth-century doctor, so we don't want to be doing fifteenth-century religion.

We have to participate in the evolution of religion and of Spirit, because **Spirit is actually evolving; it's becoming. There's more God to come.**

- Democracies are an evolution of Spirit.
- Human rights are an evolution of Spirit—for every human being is an evolution of Spirit.
- The emergence of the feminine is an evolution of Spirit.
- Technologies, with their new intimate interconnections, are evolutions of Spirit.

We want to reclaim Love as religion. We want to realize that all the great traditions share a core set of truths, and we want to articulate those truths. Then we want to participate in bringing all the sciences to bear, to realize that those truths are evolving. Finally, we want to realize that we *participate* in their evolution.

RECLAIMING THE GLORY OF GOD

I want to do a new pointing-out instruction to catch what we mean by "the glory of God." When we say this, we don't mean what traditional religion said: *God out there, who demands our obedience down here and says, I'm owned by one religion, and your body is the enemy of Spirit and science.*

No, not that God—the god you don't believe in doesn't exist.

We mean: God as the inherent ceaseless creativity of Cosmos—animated by love, seeking ever greater and ever deeper expressions of creativity, mutuality, union, and embrace, unfolding and intending your uniqueness as an expression of "more God to come"—we mean *that* God.

That's the glory of God. We want to find that. We want to reclaim those words in that sense. The glory of God is the glory of the Evolutionary Impulse.

The glory of God is the glory of the unbearable creativity, the unbearable dazzling complexity that lives in you now, which all the supercomputers in the world couldn't manifest.

Again, our intention here is to reclaim Love as religion. We're going to reclaim these words, "Glory of God," and make them mean something that is accurate in terms of the inner nature of Reality today.

Let's listen to Andrea Bocelli sing "Gloria in Excelsis Deo." Gloria!

That Gloria doesn't live *out there*.

That Gloria is not separate from Reality.

That Gloria is not here demanding obedience to some abstract god on high who's a cosmic vending machine.

Gloria is the nature of Reality.

I want to see if we can find, in this pointing-out instruction, in this meditation together, the nature of Reality.

THE GLORY OF THE PHYSIOSPHERE

Imagine the world of matter on a chessboard. And on this chessboard there are, say, fifty black pieces. But unlike chess, in which the job is to win—it's based on win/lose metrics in which we're always trying to take the other's pieces, and there is always one winner and one loser—this is a chess game for the glory of God. We want to evolve the chess game into one in which there are no winners and losers; we want a chess game in which there is more uniqueness, creativity, Eros, delight, and love...

This is the chess game for more Uniqueness and more Creativity and more Eros and more delight and more love than there ever was before.

In the world of matter, the great Flaring Forth, every chess piece—every rock and elementary particle and quark and muon and lepton—actually loves each other. They're allured to each other. They come together, these subatomic particles. Then they love each other madly and are wildly in love.

How do we know? We know because those quarks and leptons and muons all live in us, and we participate in them. They are our very own being. *We can feel into them because they are us, and we are them.*

They're part of our own identity.

Their story is our story.

Subatomic particles love each other, and then they form atoms. Atoms are the result of charged particles madly allured to each other creating greater wholes, moving towards ever deeper mutuality, recognition, union, and embrace in the entire world—you can feel it.

I was driving home from the grocery store three days ago, and I'm pulling the car around. It's about two minutes from where I was staying and the traffic slows. I start looking out and—Oh my God!—I'm seeing all the rocks and feeling all the elementary particles, and the entire material world. That's called the "physiosphere," the whole world of matter.

Every one of those black chess pieces is a unique configuration of intimacy—all the chemical elements, based on all the laws of physics—and each one of them is a unique dance of internal connection and intimacy. All of those fifty chess pieces are interacting, in intimate relationship with each other. There's this cacophony of intimacy which is the world of matter.

And then that world of matter—including both the intimacy among all the black chess pieces and the intimacy within each unique configured piece—that world explodes again.

THE GLORY OF THE BIOSPHERE

All of a sudden you've got a second chessboard, and this board has red rather than black pieces. It's not the world of matter—it's the world of life. It's the biosphere. All of a sudden, in this great Flaring Forth—this asymmetrical break, this punctuated equilibria, this momentous leap—complex molecules awaken as life! Metabolism and reproduction and sexuality awaken in an entirely new way in this biosphere teeming with diversity, color, life, delight beyond imagination.

All fifty of those new red pieces *are unique configurations of intimacy*: the entire chain of life with all its magnificence. And all fifty of those red pieces are interacting with each other: the plants, the animals, the gases. **The entire story of life is one of mad, wild, erotic interaction and constant allurement.**

Each unique configuration of intimacy—each unique expression of life—is its own interaction of ever-increasing complexity. Complexity simply means more nodes of connection, more nodes of intimacy.

All of those red pieces are now interacting with each other, and each one is a unique configuration of intimacy. But that's not all: the black pieces and the red pieces compound into new wholes. These two systems, the biosphere and the entire physiosphere, the world of matter and the world of life, are constantly interacting with each other. There are actually black/red chess pieces that form a larger whole.

As I'm driving back from the grocery store I see the grass, and I can literally *feel* the soil. I see a deer cross my path. *I realize life is running through me.* We're breathing into each other. The plants breathe into me, and I breathe into the plants. The plankton in the bottom of the ocean actually give me life. Without them I would die. All the chemical elements, all the configurations of matter, pour into biology, and all the systems of life interact with the laws of physics—it's one large whole.

And then the entire thing explodes again.

THE GLORY OF THE NOOSPHERE

Now we have a third chessboard. This chessboard awakens, wildly, from life to self-reflective consciousness, to mind, to culture: hominids walking on the savanna awakened 70,000 years ago. There's a breath of life which is breathed directly from Eternity into this evolutionary process—and *something happens which is unimaginable.*

We're no longer just animals in the gorgeous world of life. We become part of the world of culture. We begin to be able to speak to each other, as languages emerge. We tell stories, we create art.

- Nothing in the lifeworld anticipated poetry.
- Nothing in the lifeworld anticipated my heart being wounded.
- Nothing in the first chessboard—all the black pieces—anticipated life. Nothing!

Life is a radical emergence, a new Big Bang, but nothing in the lifeworld anticipates *a self-reflective human being who can not only reproduce but represent and then evolve Love—who can become conscious of Love.*

This whole new chessboard is a set of blue pieces. The blue pieces are every distinct culture and every distinct human being who is a unique configuration of intimacy. Each human being has billions of cells dying every second and billions of cells being born every second. We are composed of thirty-seven trillion cells which are utterly, radically, and irreducibly unique. Every single cell in your body—in this moment, now—knows what every other cell is doing in this ultimate expression of non-local Love.

The Reality of Cosmos is Love itself: the movement towards ever greater order and freedom and consciousness and connection and intimacy.

Love is actually self-organizing, moving Reality towards greater wholes. You're born because your cells differentiated. Then each set of cells emerged to form your kidney and your liver. How? Who did it? Who organized it? Love organized into newer, higher, and more gorgeous patterns.

An atom itself is not a thing. An atom is a probability of relationship. Atoms live in the biosphere. The world of matter lives in life. And all of that life—all of the atoms and all of the cells—lives in you, and lives in you *uniquely*. Every single person reading now understands that *you are a unique configuration of thirty-seven point two trillion cells intended by reality, chosen by reality, irreducibly unique.*

The evolution of intimacy moves towards the expression of utter and radical uniqueness. And this Big Bang, all of these blue chess pieces, are actually compound pieces. They're blue/red/black. The level-one chess board, the level-two chess board, the level-three chess boards are actually all operating together: three systems in radical intimacy forming a whole larger than the sum of the parts.

And then it explodes again!

THE GLORY OF HOMO AMOR

This is the fourth and final explosion—and it's wild beyond imagination. The fourth explosion is what we just began to describe. This is Unique Self becoming aware of him/herself. It's when David becomes aware that *Reality is having a David experience*, when Kristina becomes aware *that Reality is having a Kristina experience*. And there is "more God to come"—this is the Gloria! Gloria! The more God to come.

Hold on to your seat because this is not whimsy, this is not a faith construct, this is not some New Age declaration. **This is the actual ontological truth of reality in this moment. The *more God to come* is literally you! You are the leading edge of evolution.**

Imagine—because we are *Homo imaginus*, and we can only find this through the imagination—imagine this truth because this is the actual truth.

The leading edge of evolution—the leading edge of evolution's arrow, the leading edge of evolution's Love—lives here! We are the ones we've been waiting for, your Unique Self.

But you're not just any Unique Self in the world—you're not living in Somalia trying to just make it through the month—you have the privilege, we have the privilege of having the ability to be here together at the leading edge of evolution, to think these thoughts together. We are in this One Mountain, Many Paths, reclaiming Love as religion, formulating a pragmatic politics of Love.

- We are the leading edge of evolution.
- We are self-reflecting in a way that humans have never done before.
- We're telling the new Story, but literally—it's a true story.

Reality in this moment is being you, reading this sentence right now. Reality in this very moment is moving through you. All of the black chess pieces—matter—all of the red chess pieces—life—all of the blue chess pieces—the world of culture, mind, consciousness—are awake and interacting in you.

And then you're the Fourth Big Bang. You're the fourth explosion.

You are the tipping point of evolution itself.

> *When you work out a problem in your life and you find a way to love more—when you find a new way to be intimate, a new way to give your unique gift, you awaken to your Unique Self.*

Evolution becomes conscious of itself through you claiming your unique expression of God. Unconscious uniqueness becomes conscious uniqueness.

Unconscious loving becomes God awake as Love in you, as you, and through you—literally.

Gloria! Gloria! You are the *more God to come*. Wow. Oh my God! You can't even imagine. It bursts through you, literally.

As I'm driving up the hill everything stops—the car stops, and the grass and the rocks and the worms and the plankton stops too.

I'm feeling the technology and the car—the product of level three, all those blue chess pieces—and I'm thinking and feeling into it. I'm feeling into Church, I'm thinking about Church and I'm realizing:

> Oh my God! We are the dreamers. We are God's dream. We are God's next dream. We are the future. We are articulating the memory of the future. We are God's Office for the Future. Oh my God! That is the actual truth.

Let's play Gloria from Andrea Bocelli one more time, but this time as we play the song, we understand: *She's awake in me. She's living in me.*

We know: I am Gloria!

WORLD RELIGION AS A CONTEXT FOR OUR DIVERSITY

TRIBUTE TO RAM DASS

Ram Dass passed away this week. I loved Ram Dass. We became friends in 2005. He was a gorgeous man. He used to say: "You can't be late. It's happening now." He lived this gorgeous, tragic, beautiful life. He opened up the world of psychedelics. He was a Jewish boy, Richard Alpert, raised in a wealthy Jewish family in Boston who didn't find his way to the inner lineage of Judaism. It wasn't available to him. He went East, met Neem Karoli Baba, became Ram Dass and brought something deep from the East into the West in a gorgeous moment.

What he said to me was—we have a recording of this, we spent a bunch of time together—he had the sense that *we're part of the seamless Oneness with All-That-Is*—which was beautiful. That was what animated his famous book, *Be Here Now*. But he couldn't quite find the sense of radical Unique Self. The way he was taught, he identified Unique Self with ego. He couldn't make that distinction.

We sat together and had a long conversation, and I shared with him the Dharma, as it was emerging in 2005. He just got so excited. Even after his stroke, he had this quality of a child who was in this moment egoless, that he just got wildly excited about the Dharma, about the new Story, and he said, "If I had known this, it would have changed everything!"

What he meant is:

- We could have brought East and West together and articulated a new shared Story that directly creates a politics of Love.
- We could have reclaimed urgency—not the urgency of the ego, but the urgency and the ecstasy of the Evolutionary Impulse.

He got wildly excited. Then we talked together in Maui, at his home, and we just had a wildly beautiful ride. He was so honest in our private talks, so beautiful and so vulnerable, and he brought such gifts to the world.

Sir Richard Alpert, Ram Dass, thank you for your wild gifts. Go in peace. There is a continuity of consciousness. Be here with us, and we'll be here with you as we pour your love into this Church.

THE SECOND-PERSON FACE OF GLORIA

All of Gloria—all of *God in the first person*, all of *I Am Gloria*—then turns to the wider, larger field of existence: the infinite beauty of All-That-Is, the infinite complexity of All-That-Is, which also has a quality of personhood.

We are both *of* It, even as It holds us.

Hafiz, Rumi, the great Sufis knew this so well. The great mystics of Hebrew wisdom knew it so well. The great Christian mystics knew it well. On the one hand, God becomes Christ, God becomes Rumi, God becomes David, there's *more God to come*. On the other hand, there's this wide, infinite Personhood of God that's holding us at the same time.

We are of It, and Infinity holds us in the very same moment. We participate in Infinity—and in fact, we can say that shame is when our sense of Self stops short of Infinity—and yet, at the same time, Infinity holds us. The Infinity of Intimacy that knows our name lives in us and also holds us is more personal than your most personal love moment ever was.

Gloria is the first person of God but Gloria is also the second person of God that holds us and knows our name.

So we bring before God all of our brokenness, all of our pain, all of our yearning, and all of our unfulfilled dreams.

We bring before God all of our glory, all of our beauty, all of our gorgeousness—the holy and the broken *Hallelujah*!

CHAPTER TWO

GLORIA: RECLAIMING RELIGION AT A HIGHER LEVEL OF CONSCIOUSNESS

Episode 174 — February 9, 2020

GLORIA: THE GRAVITAS OF REALITY, LINED WITH LOVE

We're about to hear this word, which is glory. *Gloria, In Excelsis Deo*. It's so beautiful, so gorgeous—Gloria in Hebrew is *kavod*, which means the gravitas of Reality that is lined with love. And we forget this wild, intense Gloria, the glory of God, which is the glory of Cosmos.

Just consider your own creation. What is true in us? Right now—literally right this very second—there are about 300 million cells that die every minute in the human body. Half of your red blood cells are replaced every seven days. There are actually about fifty to seventy billion cells born every day in a human body—and a cell is the most stunningly elegant creation. All the supercomputers in the world, with all of the immense neocortex brain power in the world, can't produce a cell. **A cell is one of the most elegant, stunning mechanisms of Eros in Reality.**

Your tongue has 3,000 taste buds on it, which give you a sense of taste. We shed about 600,000 particles of skin—we're literally redressed by Reality—every second. If all the blood vessels in your body were laid out, they'd be about approximately 96,000 kilometers long—that is to say, extending almost twice around the Earth. You can begin to understand what I'm talking about. Your heart beats 103,000 times a day, pumping 10,000 liters of blood, performing such complex operations you can barely even imagine.

Just think about your brain. You have more neurons in your brain than there are stars in the galaxy, about 100 billion neurons. Each neuron has this elegant structure, and the neurons are all connected to each other. All neurons are passing signals to about 10,000 other neurons all the time via trillions of synaptic connections—and a synaptic connection is a way of talking, it's really a configuration of intimacy.

That's Gloria. It's in you right now.

You're a unique configuration of tens of trillions of cells that are stunningly, wildly alive in you, performing the most intensely, beautifully, dazzlingly complex, gorgeous functions—in this very second.

So take us inside to *Gloria*, all the way, *in excelsis Deo*. And let's reclaim Gloria, not as the old religion, not as premodernity—let's reclaim Gloria in this new moment as the divinely inspired Evolutionary Impulse, awake in us, as us, and through us. *Gloria*.

TOWARDS A COSMOCENTRIC WORLD RELIGION

It's not about the ethnocentric Christ. It's not about the ethnocentric Buddha. It's not about the ethnocentric Jewish Messiah. Each one of these, at their best, was the impulse of religion. The core religious impulse is this human understanding—which is the Divinity that lives inside of us—which understands and feels Gloria.

- We understand that there's the Good, the True, and the Beautiful.
- We understand that life matters.
- We understand that life is meaningful.
- We understand our curiosity, our search for truth.
- We understand the goodness of Beauty.
- We understand that it matters which choices we make.

This understanding—that life matters, that I am wildly significant, that my drive to survive is but an expression of self-love, that ultimately my life matters so immensely, I'm needed by All-That-Is, that the love that moves through me is the most real thing in the world and I'm willing to stake my life on it—is the religious impulse. And what we need to do is to correct the mistakes that the religious impulse historically made.

The religious impulse ran into dogma, just as science, as it took power, has adopted the dogma which we call dogmatic materialism, which has nothing to do with science.

Religion ran into dogma. Religion sought to draw down the voice of Divinity and make it widely available—and yet such consciousness from the past couple thousand years was profoundly ethnocentric. We thought that God spoke only to us. We weren't connected to other parts of the world. We thought that in order to be inside the circle, to feel genuine Eros, we had to be the chosen one and other people were outside the circle.

That was the tragedy not just of religion. It was also the tragedy of communism, which split into factions. It's the tragedy of us/them: we're inside, and you're outside. We're breaking through that tragedy. We're breaking through the ethnocentric religion in which we're chosen. We're removing the boundary.

RECLAIMING RELIGION AT A HIGHER LEVEL OF CONSCIOUSNESS

> *We're entering into no boundary religion, into no boundary consciousness.*

We first have to recognize that Love is real. But then we have to understand there's no "in-group" and "out-group"—*we have to move the boundary.*

Today, if we want to heal and transform the world, we can't do it by saying: "I live in Iceland, or I live in Tucson. I'm with my few human potential people. I'm post-organized religion. I'm doing my thing." No, that's not going to work.

We have to be committed—and to be committed means we have to speak to the whole world. **We're trying to evolve the source code of consciousness and culture, so we have to re-engage the religious impulse.**

This new Story that we're telling—we have to be able to feel this story and realize that it resonates with our own traditions. And if you're post-traditional, you have to feel that this is a new Story of human progress. You've got to feel that this is the new identity of *Homo sapiens*, who are fulfilled as *Homo amor*.

This realization of *Homo amor* is the realization of all the great traditions. It's post-traditional, and it raises all the traditions.

You can be a Jew, you can be a Protestant, you can be a Catholic, you can be an indigenous person, you can be an Aboriginal, you can be an atheist, you can be a secular humanist. We're feeling together the truth of *Homo amor*, and we're creating a new Story in which *that what unites us is so much greater than that which divides us.*

Barbara Marx Hubbard wrote a beautiful book called *The Evolutionary Testament*, which talks about how we actually evolved the Christian story. I wrote two volumes called *Radical Kabbalah*, which talks about how we evolved the Jewish story. Those are source code books in our Church, One Mountain, Many Paths. You can also read *Your Unique Self*, which I had the privilege of authoring. Or you can read Barbara's *Conscious Evolution*. These are other source code texts.

PRAYING TO THE DIVINE IN THE SECOND PERSON: THE INFINITY OF INTIMACY

Let's now dive into prayer. Are you ready? So when we pray, we're not praying to the god you don't believe in, because the god you don't believe in doesn't exist. We're turning to the Divine that is the animating impulse of all of Reality. We're turning to the Evolutionary Impulse, but in its personal face.

The evolutionary impulse is God in the third person, driving evolution for billions of light years, since the moment of the First Big Bang, when the space-time continuum was created—we're looking at infinite complexity, dazzling elements, biochemistry, stars, supernovas. It is a dazzling display of intelligence, beyond what all the exponentialized supercomputers in Reality couldn't even begin to manifest. That is the Evolutionary Impulse unfolding. This is God in the third person.

Realizing that God lives in me is God in the first person. That is the classical understanding of the interior sciences of enlightenment. Thou art That, it is me. The Divine lives in me, which is why I'm so committed to my own life. I *should* be committed to my own life, to the integrity of my own life, because I'm a unique expression of Divinity. My unique configuration of intimacy is a unique expression of Divinity—not metaphorically but literally, truly.

But now we turn to God in the second person, which is the Personhood of God. It's that intense moment where we look at each other face-to-face and say: *I can feel you. I hear you. I love you. I care about you. I care about you desperately. I care about you beyond the fact that you help me in some pragmatic way. I can feel your pain, and I can feel your joy, I'm madly in love with you.*

That's intimacy.

We create shared identity between us—because intimacy is shared identity—in the context of otherness, plus mutuality of pathos. We can feel each other. Intimacy means: *You feel me and I feel you. I feel you feeling me, and you feel me feeling you.* Those are the loops of intimacy.

> *God in the second person is the Infinity of Intimacy.*

It's the most intimate moment you've ever known. And just like you're with your beloved, your friend, your son, your daughter—we're all beloveds, whoever your beloveds are, you're with your circle of intimacy, you're with your closest beloved—and you're pouring your heart out, and your beloved holds every word. So God, who's not just the Infinity of Power, but who's the Infinity of Intimacy, lives in our lives, speaks to us, hears everything. And how do you know? How do you know that God hears everything?

How do you hear me talking? Not through the technical structure of your ears: there's an entire process of intelligent consciousness that allows you to hear me.

Is your intelligent consciousness singular, cut off from the entire field of intelligent consciousness in the world? Obviously not. You are *participating* in the field of Intelligent Consciousness. So if you can hear me talking, this is how the Field of Intelligent Consciousness, God, can hear me talking. That's it. We just threw out 2,000 years of bad theology. God hears every word.

We're going to go inside now. We're going to offer our holy and our broken *Hallelujah* before the Divine, right now.

We're going to pray, and we're going to ask for everything. the Holy and the Broken "Hallelujah," by Leonard Cohen.

EVOLUTIONARY LOVE CODE: REALITY NEEDS YOUR SERVICE

We're here to tell the new Story, so what's our vision? Our vision, our intention, is a Planetary Awakening in Love through Unique Self Symphonies. Unique Self Symphony means, *I'm a Unique Self. I'm a unique configuration of intimacy. I'm a unique configuration of Evolutionary Love.* That means Outrageous Love moves through me. **Who am I for real? I'm an Outrageous Lover, an Evolutionary Lover. That's the actual nature of my identity.**

I'm a unique configuration of the LoveIntelligence and LoveBeauty— that is the initiating and animating Eros and energy of All-That-Is— that lives in me, as me, and through me, that never was, is, or will be ever again, other than through me.

That's who I am at my core. As such, I have unique, Outrageous Acts of Love to commit that no one who ever was, is, or will be, can commit other than through me.

Imagine a self-organizing universe—it's not a corporate program, it's not a government. Rather:

- We become a cascading wave of Outrageous Love.
- We *are* the Evolutionary Impulse.
- The inside of the Evolutionary Impulse is Love.
- The interior of consciousness is Love uniquely configured in us.

It's one of the things that the great religions understood. I've got to become a member. I've got to give some of my resources. I've got to do things and give some of my time. I have to step up and actually pour in my enacted energy. Another way to say it: **Reality needs my service.**

CHAPTER THREE

THE GOOD NEWS: HOMO AMOR, WE ARE ALL NEEDED

Episode 233 — March 28, 2021

THE DANGERS OF A PARTIAL STORY

We are here in this moment in history, in this time between worlds, in this time between stories, to tell the new Story, to stand for the Story of the Intimate Universe—not as just another story, not as a fanciful conjecture, but as the deepest nature of Reality as we know it today, based on the highest integration available to us of the interior sciences, the exterior sciences, the validated insights from premodern, modern, and postmodern thought, woven together in a larger whole greater than the sum of the parts.

That is the new Story.

This new Story is the only genuine human response to the potential of catastrophic risk—which we've realized briefly, early on in the pandemic, when we sensed "it wasn't too big to fail"—and to the more profound threat of existential risk, which wipes out all of the future.

The most important response to existential and catastrophic risk is the telling of a new Story because one of the generator functions, or root causes of this existential and catastrophic risk, is a failure of Story. So we need a new Story about the human being, about

human identity. It's a story about the "we," about human community.

It's a story about power. And it's a story about desire.

Our current stories are inadequate stories. They're incomplete stories. They're stories that claim to be whole when, at best, they're only partial. **To the precise extent that a story about Reality—our universe story, our narrative of identity, our narrative of community, our narrative of power, our narrative of desire—is inaccurate, or overclaims, or leaves important things out of the picture, or ignores externalities, it undermines the structure of society.**

The generator function of existential risk is this failure of Story. For example, the story of modernity gives us a great gift in that it importantly sees the centrality of the individual in a way that premodernity never could. Yet its pathology is that it sees the individual as being only a separate self who's ultimately alienated from the larger whole, and that it disqualifies the Universe. It takes the Universe out of the Tao, out of intrinsic Value, out of its intrinsic Wholeness, out of its intrinsic, awe-inspiring, reverent nature. **We step out of the Tao and begin to tell partial stories.**

Evolutionary psychology says: "We take bits of the sciences, all sorts of astrophysics and astronomical information, we take those partial bits and we weave it into a false whole"—which is a reductionist materialist view of Reality in which the human being is but a separate self.

The human being gains value and status through their individual participation in the dominant success story of society. This success story is only about production and commodification, and it's governed by win/lose metrics.

This story of modernity, which apotheosizes the individual, brought great dignity to the world:

- It brought universal human rights.
- It brought third-person science.
- It brought modern medicine.

- It brought an explosion of life on the planet.

But it also brought great pathology—not just the dignities of modernity but modernity's disasters—that have marched us right up to the precipice itself, to the potential eleventh hour of human history, to the potential death of the future, the potential death of our humanity, which is what we call "existential risk" and "catastrophic risk."

RECLAIMING THE EVANGELICAL SPARK

Here's perhaps an odd but important question: What does it mean to be an evangelical?

When I was around thirty, I spent three years outside of the teaching world, where I worked in a high-tech, entrepreneurial setting. I worked for a company that bought start-ups, and I was very involved in the world of Apple computer for a few years. I wanted to know what the world looked like not from the perspective of the teacher, so I entered the business world just to feel the real world. I would go to Infinity Loop and to Cupertino a lot, and I had all sorts of meetings with people. Their cards always said, "evangelist"—"Apple evangelist," "Macintosh evangelist"—because evangelist means that we're sharing the good news, and we're excited about the good news.

That's a big deal. We get to be excited about the good news.

Because the good news is simple: **we realize that there's a choice in the world and that choice is simple.**

Either we're in the Tao or not—and being in the Tao means we're within meaning, within Value. We know that the world has a plentitude of meaning and a plentitude of Value.

All the stories we tell about it are important and sacred because, ultimately, there's an irreducible Value underneath everything—there's an irreducible Goodness, an irreducible Truth, an irreducible Beauty.

> *Either everything's meaningful or nothing's meaningful. Either I live in the Tao or I have the illusion that I'm outside of the Tao, and that difference is everything. That's the whole story.*

The word "evangelical" has been hijacked. We can't allow its hijacking to turn us into tepid, disinterested, semi-intellectual posturers who are talking about things from this third-person distance as if it was just an intellectual conversation. No.

The very One Heart, the very One Breath of Reality is at stake. The future's at stake. Do we live in the Tao in which every human being has irreducible uniqueness and irreducible value, in which *life itself is part of the overriding and overarching wholeness that inspires us to awe, and to reverence, and to service, and to delight, and to joy?*

Or did Shakespeare get it right in that last section of *Macbeth* that Faulkner quotes in his book title: "Tomorrow, and tomorrow, and tomorrow creeps in this petty pace, day after day, to the last syllable of recorded time. Life is nothing but a tale told by an idiot full of sound and fury, signifying nothing." **Those are the choices.**

A tale told by an idiot, full of sound and fury, signifying nothing? Well, we know that's not true because "anthro-ontologically"—in our own first-person experience—we feel Goodness, and we feel Truth, and we feel Beauty, and we know that it matters.

And if anything matters, then everything matters.

I'm either in the Tao or outside the Tao.

So that's good news, and we're excited about that good news, and we are not embarrassed to be excited about that good news. We're not ashamed of being evangelists.

Steve Jobs at Apple was not ashamed to be an evangelist, and all he was showing was an elegant operating system. We have to wrest the hijackers' grip from the term "evangelical."

Of course, the term "evangelical" can be hijacked, and when it's hijacked, we have to say no to the hijacking. The term evangelical can be hijacked by people who say, "We're going to induce a state experience of a kind of euphoria that we're going to use to transmit fear: fear of hell, fear of your own body, fear of all that stands against you. Your body stands against you, your fallenness stands against you, your lack of grace stands against you. We're going to whip you up to a state of fervor and we're going to download fear into your body. We're going to use that state for all manner of abuse: intellectual abuse, moral abuse, spiritual abuse."

That's not the "evangelical" we're talking about. **That's a total hijacking of the good news.**

In the frame of "evangelical" that we often associate it with—whether it's a New Age evangelical or a fundamentalist evangelical in one of the religions—we say, "We've got radical certitude, and we're the only people with access to the truth. We're going to whip you up to a frenzy until you step into our version of the truth, and if you don't, you're somehow damned, you're shunned" —whether it's a New Age shunning, or an Integral shunning, or a Catholic shunning, or a Jewish shunning, or an Islamic shunning, or a Confucian shunning, or a Tibetan Buddhist shunning, all of which have their own versions of shunning the outsider who doesn't step into their version of the good news.

No, that's not being an evangelical.

To be an evangelist is to be an Outrageous Lover.

TO BE AN EVANGELIST IS TO BE AN OUTRAGEOUS LOVER

Being an evangelical means that we enter into ecstatic states. Higher states of consciousness are utterly essential, and ecstatic technologies are critical. **All genuine human *gnosis* is based on ecstatic technologies of various forms: contemplative, pharmacological, intellectual, mystical, ethical, and embodied technologies.**

Ecstatic technologies are critical not just because they open us up to higher states of consciousness—and ecstatic technology is a state of expansion—but to higher *structure* stages of consciousness:

We can develop from egocentric to ethnocentric to worldcentric to cosmocentric consciousness, meaning we have a felt sense of love, care, and concern:

- Not just for myself and my survival, my people, which is the general state of most of the liberal community in the world.
- Not just for myself and my country, my survival, people in my country and my religion, which is the state of most of the conservative community in the world.
- Not even for all human beings, for all life, and for all things.

So from egocentric (felt sense of love, care, and concern for me and my people) to ethnocentric (for my country, my religion) to worldcentric (for every human being) to cosmocentric, meaning *I'm madly in love with Reality itself.*

I'm madly in love with love itself.

I'm lived as love. I feel the dolphins. I speak to the pandas. I dance with wolves, and I open up to extra-terrestrials and extra-dimensionals and other frames of being and anomalous experiences—because I'm madly in love with all of Reality.

HOMO AMOR, WE ARE ALL NEEDED

I move from being "Homo armor," the armored evangelical who's not sharing the good news at all, or pretending to share the good news but actually sharing the bad news: *I'm armored. I'm constricted. My body's somehow of the devil. I'm the only one with the truth. No one else has it. I think I'm telling you the good news, but I'm giving you the worst news in the world.*

No. We've got to move from "Homo armor" to *Homo amor*. This means that:

> ## *We're all irreducibly unique expressions of the LoveIntelligence. We're all desperately needed by All-That-Is. We're all intended, desired, chosen, needed, loved, and adored.*

That's the intrinsic nature of being an Evolutionary Unique Self. That's the good news. We are wildly excited about that, we are passionate about that, and we will not apologize for one second for our passion because *it's only that passion that will address suffering*. Only that passion will address two billion people on the planet who don't have sanitation or drinking water because we've somehow cut those people out of our lives as we're so busy and self-involved.

We have to be madly passionate.

We have to be Outrageous Lovers.

I remember back in 2012 and 2013, when Kristina Kincaid and I were deep in the early Dharma of Outrageous Love, and we wanted to build the OutrageousLove.com website. Kristina mocked up that first site and created this gorgeous, aesthetic holy place.

We looked online to see if anyone else had used Outrageous Love, and we realized that the only other people who had used the term were evangelical Christian communities. We looked at those communities—and mad blessings to those communities—but they weren't saying what we were saying. They got the sense of Outrageous Love, but it meant *Outrageous Love if you understand, like we do, our particular understanding of the exclusivity of Jesus's message and your need to have a particular kind of faith in Jesus*. This excluded anyone who didn't belong to that particular brand of Pentecostal evangelical Christianity.

No, that's not okay. That's not what Outrageous Love means. That's not Outrageous Love at all. That's ordinary, that's egoic, that's constricted, that's ethnocentric consciousness. We need to actually make Outrageous Love genuinely outrageous.

It's not just unlimited love—it's *outrageous*.

OUTRAGEOUS LOVE: WE'RE OUTRAGED

Outrageous contains the word rage in it. I'm *outraged* at anything that's small and contracted. I'm *outraged* that two billion people don't have access to drinking water. I'm *outraged* that there are child soldiers in the Congo. I'm *outraged* about the fire that just took place in Bangladesh that could have been stopped and is not being dealt with. I'm *outraged* that there are AK-47 and AR-15 guns all available across much of the Western world, particularly the United States, when there's no reason those guns should be available, and it's got nothing to do with politics.

We're outraged—and we're filled with the outrageous joy of knowing who we are.

We don't have all the details worked out. All models are limited. The Tao is underneath the 10,000 things. **The Tao means we're *inside* of Outrageous Love.**

We fall on our faces in rapture and reverence, and we stand tall, proud, audacious, dignified as irreducibly Unique Selves joining hands, expressions of the Tao. A Unique Self is the Tao in person, as you. Wow! That's our intention. Our intention is that we're a band of Outrageous Lovers: excited, passionate, outraged, standing at this moment in this time between worlds, in this time between stories, in this eleventh hour and saying: "We're going to give everything to tell this new Story in which everyone has a place, and to articulate a universal grammar of value that can become the matrix of the new Story, which is the plotline of a global ethos for a global civilization."

Wow. That's our intention. We're evangelicals all the way. We're excited. We're sharing the good news, and there's lots of ways we can share it. We need podcasts, we need festivals, we need Dharma labs, and we need study groups. We need all sorts of forums.

We're not embarrassed about it.

We're not ashamed by it.

We are privileged by our passion. We are just boldly, amazingly, radically humbled by our own ability to share this news. We share it every day, every hour with ourselves. Passion waxes and wanes. We re-choose again.

We choose joy, we choose the new Story, and we choose to respond to history, which desperately needs all of us together.

EVOLUTIONARY LOVE CODE: FOR TRUE EVANGELISM WE NEED BOTH ECSTATIC STATES AND DEVELOPMENTAL STAGES

We need to be evangelicals.

Evangelicals are bearers of the good news.

For true evangelicals, however, the good news includes everyone and everything. No one is left out of this circle of Eros.

For true evangelism, we need ecstatic states and developmental stages mediated through Dharma, or what we call First Principles and First Values.

The paradox of evangelicals today, and most of the great religions or movements, whether it's New Age evangelicals or political evangelicals, is that evangelism has become associated with polarity—the sense that "we're in, and you're out"—but that's the opposite of Eros.

You only have to place someone outside the circle when you don't experience the good news, when you don't actually experience yourself inside the circle, when you don't have the knowing, the awareness, when the Tao is not awake in you. You feel small and contracted. You desperately—I desperately, we desperately—want to be inside the circle, so we place everybody else outside the circle *to give ourselves the illusion that we're on the inside.*

That's not Eros. True evangelism is erotic.

Back to the code: "For true evangelicals, the good news includes everyone and everything."

No one's left out of the circle of Eros. Again, for true evangelism we need ecstatic states *and* developmental stages—both wake up and grow up, as John Welwood wrote so beautifully. We've got to be not just egocentric, not just ethnocentric, and not just worldcentric, but cosmocentric—and it's got to be mediated through a dharma, through First Principles and First Values.

I'm reading a book that a colleague of mine wrote about ecstatic technologies. He writes proudly about how Silicon Valley, Navy SEALs, and maverick scientists are hacking the great traditions, stripping away the spiritual content, and accessing ecstatic technologies and states. The entire book is about how wonderful that is.

However, **you don't want ecstatic states without developmental stages, without Dharma, without spiritual content because then it actually does become dangerous, just like the evangelicals of the old**

churches became dangerous. They were telling a story which defaced the human dignity of everyone outside of their circle. This is also true of contemporary tech evangelicals, who are hacking ecstatic states, "stealing fire" in order to perpetrate on society the control of a tech elite, a kind of "TechnoFeudalism"—that's equally dangerous. It's not true, erotic evangelism.

So Apple evangelicals and Google evangelicals and Facebook evangelicals are, in their own way, as profoundly dangerous because they're driven by a very small elite with a hidden profit motive, with a hidden lining of intense greed, just like the churches often tragically had. They're foisting upon society *upgraded algorithms and downgraded human beings.*

We've got to be wary of misguided evangelicals. At the same time, we can't give up our passion.

We have to reclaim the evangelical mantle, not only for ourselves, but for anyone and everyone who wants to get involved in telling the new Story— in a way in which everyone's inside the circle, in a way which integrates the most validated and important insights from all the streams of wisdom— from premodern, modern, and postmodern—into a genuine new whole greater than the sum of the parts.

We need a new Story that stands against suffering, stands against contraction, and stands against those limiting beliefs that keep us small, trapped by the win/lose metrics that is the generator function for existential and catastrophic risk.

IN EVERY GREAT TRADITION THERE'S AN INTIMATE INCARNATION OF THE DIVINE

We need to bring the best of evolutionary science, the best of superstring theory, the best of molecular biology, the best of horizontal gene transfer, the best of "symbiogenesis"—we need to bring all of the proven, leading-edge physical sciences, and the best sociology, psychology, and anthropology—

the best of everything together with the most critical validated insights of all the great traditions.

We're used to thinking that what's important about the great religions is their shared universal truths—and that's absolutely true. For example, what perennial philosophy is about, at its best, is bringing together the underlying shared truths of the great traditions, *extrapolating the general principles of shared truth from the particular settings*. That's often termed by perennial philosophers, including my friend, Ken, as *extrapolating the depth structures from the surface structures*.

There's great truth in that, but we need to go a step further. You see, the traditions of the great religions are not just surface structures. There are some surface social constructions of Reality that are structures, but often that's not the case.

> *Just like there's a unique love language between beloveds, so at the height, in the depth, in the authentic essence of every great tradition, there's an intimate language of the finite in the Infinite. There's an intimate incarnation of the Tao. There's an intimate incarnation of Eros.*

So, for example, Catholicism has many sins, as does Islam, as does Judaism, as does Tibetan Buddhism—but they also all have greatness. It's not just that the religions were disasters. The religions were expressions of a premodern world, and in the premodern world, governance was a disaster. **The flaws of the religions are not particular religious flaws; they're flaws of the structure of consciousness that dominated at the time, and those flaws, for the most part, existed in every part of society, not just religion.**

It's not like you had these beautiful, gorgeous, beneficent monarchies with ugly religions. No. You had ugly expressions of power, both in religion and governance. However, at their best, in their esoteric cores and in their most pure and beautiful teachings, **each of the great traditions contains an intimate language**.

Each religion has a Unique Self.

That Unique Self is not just a surface structure, it is a depth structure, *a uniquely, irreducibly intimate language of Spirit.*

PASSOVER: FOR THE FIRST TIME, I'M GOING TO FIND THAT HIDDEN DREAM

In the Hebrew wisdom tradition, yesterday evening and this evening are two, what are called *Seders*, and in the *Seders* there are three matzahs. I just want to share with you one dimension of this practice: you take the matzah in the middle, and put the other two down. You break the middle matzah in two, then take one broken piece of matzah and hide it. You wrap it in a cloth, and you hide it. Then this middle matzah is then searched for by the children in the home. When it's found, the children often negotiate with the parents or the caretakers for some prize for finding it.

What's at the core of this tradition, which lies at the very heart of the *Seder*? You see, all of us, at some point, were broken. Something broke inside of us. What happened is we split off; we broke off a part of ourselves. **That emergent adult in us went and hid that broken part, and we hid it so well that we ourselves couldn't even find it. We broke off a piece of our story and couldn't access it anymore.**

Pesach, "Passover" in Hebrew, in the language of mysticism is *Peh Sach*, or "the mouth that speaks." In the lineage, the practice of the day is to tell the story of leaving Egypt. But Egypt is not just a historical place. In the interior tradition, "Egypt" in Hebrew is *Mitzrayim*, which means "the narrow place." Egypt is the narrow place, or the throat in the body—because mystically, every nation mentioned in the sacred text represents a different part of the body. **Egypt is the narrow place, the throat.** It's the place where *I couldn't tell my story, I couldn't be my all, so I contracted. I made myself smaller, so I split off a piece of myself.*

I am the matzah—which is where the Christian tradition came from—I am the communion wafer. I am the body of the Divine. I am an irreducible Unique Self, and I've split off a part of myself and hidden it. I've split off a part of my dreams because I don't believe those dreams belong in an adult world. I don't believe those dreams belong in a mature and settled human being, so I split off that part of me.

And it's so hidden that I can't even find it myself. It's so hidden that I've forgotten about it, but not only have I forgotten—I've forgotten that I forgot.

> *Not only is this split-off part of myself hidden, but it's hidden so well that even its hiddenness it's hidden.*

It's an incredible sacred text: *Haster astir panai*, "I will hide, I will hide my face"—and *panai* means my interiority, my dreams, my deepest inner dream and longing and yearning. So the mystics ask: *Why does the text say, "I will hide" twice?* **Because it's a double hiding. The hiddenness itself is hidden.**

The Hebrew word for "world" is *olam*, and *olam* means hidden. The world is a place of hiding. It's a place of broken hearts and broken vessels. Hemingway reminds us *the world breaks all of us*. **We're all broken in some way, but, in the end, that breaking is not a bug in the system. It's a feature. There's nothing more whole than a broken heart.**

On this day of Passover (and the Christian version of Passover was the Last Supper), in this lineage tradition, in this particular intimate language, which you can learn, though you don't need to be part of the tradition, we say: *For the first time I'm going to find that hidden dream. I'm going to reclaim that broken part. I'm going to know that I can be a powerful, developed, mature adult and dream my dream and speak my passion and feel the potency and power of my passion, that my passion is good and that my dream is my evangelical message; it is my good news that I have to share with the world.*

So who's ready, my friends, in this moment, to find the broken piece of matzah? *I am the matzah.*

Who's ready to reclaim the dream?

That's what it means to be an Outrageous Lover.

An Outrageous Lover means *I outrageously love Reality; I commit Outrageous Acts of Love.* The very heart of it, it's got to always begin with *I outrageously love myself and outrageously love my dreams.* So then *I can outrageously love you, and I can outrageously love we, and I can outrageously love Reality, and we can dream together.* We can make those dreams real. Wow!

It's ours. We're a band of Outrageous Lovers. We're dreaming the dream.

What happens to a dream deferred? wrote Langston Hughes. *Does it dry up like a raisin in the sun?* When we defer the dream, we become corrupt. We dry up like a raisin in the sun.

Let's dare to dream the dream.

Let's dare to be evangelicals.

Let's dare to stand on the brink, to stand in this abyss at this time between worlds and time between stories, and be Outrageous Lovers.

Let's dare to speak into the darkness and say, *Let there be light*, and we are the light, for with you is the source of light.

In your light, we see light are the words of the Prophet.

CHAPTER FOUR

RELIGION NEEDS TO BE PART OF THE REVOLUTION: EVOLVING THE UNIQUE SELF OF THE GREAT TRADITIONS

Episode 237 — April 25, 2021

NO MORE "BUSINESS AS USUAL"

On the one hand, our hearts are broken open with joy at the privilege and power and potency to be here together as revolutionaries—literally, not figuratively. We are *literally* revolutionaries, with the capacity to step into the breach in this moment in time—in this Renaissance-needing-to-happen moment, in this time between worlds, in this time between stories—in which we experience ourselves quite literally as poised between utopia and dystopia.

This moment is filled with an unimaginably gorgeous, possible future: more stunning, more sublime, more filled with joy and goodness than any other time in history—it's possible. It's within our grasp.

And yet an equally unimaginable dystopia dawns. The abyss is right beneath our feet. If we follow the current trajectory, the vector of all civilizations, we will fall into dystopia, we will fall into existential risk. **In about 500-800 years, according to the best calculations, there's a**

very good chance we won't exist. We will have entered into the sixth mass extinction. We will have extinguished the future.

In order to take the other path, which today is quite literally the road less traveled by, we have to rise up.

We have to play a larger game.

We have to actually participate directly in the Evolution of Love.

We have to be ontological activists.

We have to be directly involved in evolving the source code of consciousness and culture, which is the source code of love.

We've got to stop business as usual. Tragically today, even at the places that should be the flashpoints—that should be the nodes of the future activist engagement—they're almost all involved in *business as usual*: egos engaged in rivalrous conflict, all the same old stuff. Even at the leading edge, all the same old ego-games are being played. It's almost like we've commodified the act of responding to existential risk or creating the new Story, and now there's competition even there. Really? Is that where we are?

BECOMING HOMO AMOR

We actually have to *be* the new Story. We can't be selling the new Story as a product. We have to be radically committed.

We have to place our lives and our hearts and our bodies on the line.

We have to rip our hearts open—truly, for real—and step out of the brokenness and step out of the trauma.

We have to *experience* the intensities of Outrageous Love and what it does to us. **We have to let Outrageous Love purify us, and change the rules of the game.**

We have to change where we invest our time.

We have to change where we invest our financial resources.

We have to stop playing by the old rules and start crossing over to the other side.

Let's come together and do something different.

I want to say something from my heart, with a little bit of sadness. I sometimes look at the underbelly of the world, and it seems like we're ostensibly trying to deal with some of these issues—just like the Catholic Church in the sixteenth century was filled with corruption, while it piously proclaimed redemption. So much of the world that should be standing for tomorrow is commodifying itself, prostituting itself, selling itself out, and just playing the same old games. It's business as usual with their product being a response to existential risk.

No, no, no!

> ## *The way we respond to existential risk is by becoming the New human and the new humanity.*

We're actually going to *become* the solution.

We're going to become the new narrative of identity and the new narrative of power.

We're going to become the new intimate communion.

We're going to become *Homo amor*.

Homo sapiens are going to evolve and become *Homo amor*. We've got to take this to the next level; we can't do business as usual. Let's actually *be* it.

It's what Mahatma Gandhi meant when he said we have to *be* the change.

We have to *be* the revolution. We have to *be* Outrageous Love.

We have to lay it all on the line—with so much joy and so much delight.

So, I want to ask you a question: Who are we? We are the revolution. That's who we are. And there's only one question we ask: **What does the revolution need in this moment?**

This is not a casual revolution. This is not, "Let's just declare things." We're spending day and night in the source code, trying to work out the best, deepest, interior vision of what a new world needs to look like. That's the da Vinci move. We're formulating this vision of Unique Self.

THE SOURCE CODE MOVE

Every failure in the world is based on the failures of frameworks at the source-code level of *story*. **The story dominating culture today is ruining everything.**

> *Our question is: Where are we? Our narrative of identity question is: Who am I? How we answer those two questions creates a new Universe Story and changes everything.*

I'm reading across disciplines and platforms to integrate pieces of the new Story, and I would say that what's missing in every book I'm reading is the deep source-code structure, the source-code move, and the actual depths of a new Story.

Someone sent me a new book a couple of weeks ago called: *The Global Revolt*. Bill Clinton wrote a nice little introduction to it. My friend Daniel Schmachtenberger wrote a limited introduction. I'm not necessarily recommending the book, but in the last chapter he's getting the idea of a new story. It's actually the title of the chapter: "A new Story." That chapter is about different ideas, structures, currency, governance, economic issues—which are all interesting and important—but none of them have anything to do with the depths of what we are calling the new Story.

Adam Smith's *The Wealth of Nations*, is, let's say, the economic story of modernity in the West. He also wrote another book about morals, called *The Theory of Moral Sentiments*, about the nature of the human being as a being who incarnates love. Adam Smith was deeply influenced by Islamic mysticism at its leading edge. His notion of the wealth of nations and the invisible hand of the market was based on an entire series of ideas rooted in a particular Universe Story and a particular narrative of identity. Without that you can't move.

If we don't articulate this new Universe Story and the new narrative of identity, friends, it's *Game Over*.

We're not going to go there.

We believe in the future radically and completely.

So let's do this all the way.

HONORING ISLAM: *ALLAHU AKBAR*

As mentioned, Adam Smith, in his *Wealth of Nations*, was profoundly influenced by Islamic mysticism. So let's honor Islamic mysticism. Let's honor Islam. Let's honor *Allahu Akbar*, which means "God is great." I want to talk a little bit about religion and why it matters.

RELIGION NEEDS TO BE PART OF THE REVOLUTION

- Why don't we just do the new Story?
- Why don't we just do evolution?
- Why don't we just do science?
- Why does Ramadan matter?
- Why does *Allahu Akbar* matter so much?
- Why does religion matter so much?

It's big and really important.

Let's feel the intimate feeling of *Allahu Akbar*. *God is great* is the translation, but we have to actually feel it. We have to feel the resonant beauty and gorgeousness.

Allahu Akbar, God is great. So, what does that actually mean? That's what we're going to talk about. Let's invite our Islamic brothers and sisters. For me, this is not meta-theoretical. I lived in Israel, in Jaffa. I shared a house with an Arab family. When I was there, Jews and Arabs lived together in Jaffa, in the midst of the mosques.

Why do Muslims fast during Ramadan? Why do we fast? **We fast because we step away from the physical for a short period of time in order to dis-identify with the body and realize that our true nature is *heart*. Our true nature is Spirit. We're in a body, but underneath the body,** *I am.*

I am not my body. *I am.*

Who am I? I am the expression of "Allah's" will. (For the purpose of this section on Islam we are using Allah as the name of God, but God goes by many names. The new name of God in CosmoErotic Humanism is the Infinite Intimate. We will get to that later.)

So Allah's will lives in me. I bow to Allah, in service to Allah. Wow.

We have to understand what that means. Where's the light? Where are the potential shadows? **How do we engage a unique religion, and what's its place today?** It's so deep.

This is one of the things that, for example, the Integral community got completely wrong in some fundamental ways. We need to up-level the way we understand development, the way we understand religion in a profound and big and beautiful way.

Allahu Akbar. With Allah's will.

EVOLUTIONARY LOVE CODE: EVERY RELIGION HAS A UNIQUE SELF

> Every religion has a Unique Self.
>
> The Unique Self of a religion is the intimate quality of meaning and meeting between the finite and the Infinite that is particular to that religion.
>
> That unique quality of intimacy is irreducible and utterly needed in the great Unique Self Symphony of Spirit.
>
> The rituals of every religion are not the surface structures of religion.
>
> The rituals of a religion are the unique, intimate expressions of that religion's erotic embrace of Divinity.

In one of the key teachings of Islam, at its deepest understanding, Islam talks about "Constant Creation." That is to say, there's not a one-time creative act, but an incessant creation happening. This, of course, is validated today in the evolutionary world. It's what Stuart Kauffman would call "the incessant ceaseless creativity of Cosmos."

But why did Islam, in the eleventh and twelve centuries, insist on the concept of Constant Creation? And why did they actually treat as heretics anyone who said there was a one-time creation? Who cares? Isn't that some detail of theological sophistry?

Imagine that we created our relationship seven years ago, ten years ago, twenty years ago, thirty years ago. So, the energy of creation was thirty years ago.

The energy of intimacy, the intimate moments—

- when we came together
- when we fostered this new reality
- when we generated this gorgeous explosion of love

—were initiated thirty years ago. And now we're in repeat mode. We're in Groundhog Day. We're doing it again and again.

So, Islam said, in its deepest mystical courts, we have a direct realization that Reality is generated anew every second. This was before we understood about the quantum vacuum or the zero-point field, where virtual particles are popping in and out at every second, quite literally. We can actually get an instantiation in the world of physics. **The world is created anew every second.**

The raw intimacy of that first meeting between the Infinite and the finite is literally happening right now.

If you open your heart, you can actually *feel* it.

> *The first explosion,*
> *the first kiss,*
> *the first look,*
> *the first blush of love,*
> *the first creative, ecstatic emergence,*
> *for the very first time, is happening anew in every second...*

Wow! Oh my God.

The human being is this unique node, caused by everything that came before, by all the gorgeous unfolding of atoms and molecules. The light of all of Reality shines within the heart of the human being.

The poet Rumi writes: I wish that I could tell you, when you are lonely or in darkness, the astonishing light of your own being.

This is the revolution. We are the revolution. Part of the revolution is: We can't ignore that seventy percent of the world lives in an organized religion. You can imagine someone saying: "Let's ignore it. Let's hang out in Berkeley and in Portland, some great communities near Glastonbury and in London. We're going to do the real work, people. We are at the leading edge. The rest of those people, they're primitive."

That's nonsense.

We have to bring the whole story together. Everyone has a place at the table. We can't do this without Ramadan. We can't do this without *Allahu Akbar*.

We can't do this without understanding the offering of the Unique Self of every religion.

EYE OF THE SENSES, EYE OF THE MIND, EYE OF THE HEART

God is Great. With God's love, let's see if we can do this. Now just notice: we're doing good, but some of us are a little uncomfortable.

What's all this?

What's religion doing here?

Why are we talking about Ramadan?

Let's go slow for a second, and see if we can go step-by-step.

Why does religion matter? Why does religion need to be part of the revolution? This is a very big deal. We can start to answer this by saying we have three eyes:

- One eye is the **Eye of the Senses.** Think of our eyes and ears, fragrance, touch—all the ways which we access sensory reality—that's one way of knowing things. An fMRI or the Hubble telescope is an expansion of the Eye of the Senses.

- The second eye is what we might call the **Eye of the Mind**. The Eye of the Mind is mathematics, logic, reason, and moral reasoning, from Ramanujan's mathematics to Kant's moral reasoning. All of that is the Eye of the Mind.
- But there's a third eye. The Islamic mystics called this third eye the **Eye of the Heart**. The great interior scientists, in every one of the great traditions, had a different name for it. The third eye, the **Eye of the Spirit**, is the hidden eye. But let's call it the Eye of the Heart.

The Eye of the Heart is what gives us information about the truth of Reality that is not accessible in any other way. The Eye of the Heart gives us information about all the truths that make life worth living: loyalty, love, joy, delight, Eros, virtue, kindness, creativity.

In other words, *every virtue without which we literally wouldn't want to be alive*. We would be automatized in a vast data machine, which is where dimensions of society are trying to push us, and which we have to actively rebel against.

With the Eye of the Heart, we know that all of those values are real. Love is real, Spirit is real, Choice is real. We have a living felt sense that choice and freedom are real.

All of this lives in the Eye of the Heart, in our first-person experience, and they're accessible through the faculty of perception. The Eye of the Heart allows me to know what I can't know in any other way.

In the last 200 years, we have developed—virtually exponentially—the technologies of the Eye of the Senses, such as the Hubble telescope. We have also developed the Eye of the Mind: advanced mathematics done through supercomputers, as well as complexity theory and chaos theory.

But we've utterly abandoned the field in terms of the Eye of the Heart, we've abandoned the inner, infinite subjectivity, the subjectivity of the Infinite that lives in me, as me, and through me, the Eye of the Heart.

My first-person knowing and the inner subjective space and the second-person knowing that lives between us have both been left to pop psychology and reduced by a Freudian reductionism. **We've actually denuded the human being of her grandeur and called it grandiosity.** We've stopped practicing in the Eye of the Heart.

THE INTERPRETATION OF REVELATION THROUGH THE PRISM OF CONSCIOUSNESS

We've lost access to that which was generated by the great traditions. We can look at the great traditions and say that religions were terrible in the premodern period. They were ethnocentric, and they were homophobic and… Those bad religions.

Now, is that true?

Do religions have enormous shadow? Were they ethnocentric and homophobic? Yes, of course they were. But so were governments. And so was all of Reality. It wasn't a religion problem. It was a Reality problem. It was a structure-of-consciousness problem, in governments and armies and farmers and technicians. Everybody was ethnocentric and homophobic. Reality was. That was the structure of consciousness, so naturally religion expressed that.

Modernity's response to religion came in a number of forms. We're not going to go with David Hume and all the thinkers who followed him, who essentially rejected and mocked religion. We're not going to go with those people, although that's a whole major school of modernity which dominated modernity.

There were people in modernity, like the perennial philosophers, who said: "Religions were important, but not the rituals, not all of their local cultural baggage—what a lot of Integral thinkers call 'surface' structures—that's not what matters in religion. What matters are the depth structures."

They're saying that there are hidden depth structures in every great tradition, which are about realizing that you're one with consciousness, realizing that you're awareness or the awareness of awareness.

I want to say a couple of things about that.

One, that's wrong. It's one of the great flaws in that kind of thinking. You see, the rituals of a religion are not just surface structures. The rituals of a religion are the Unique Self of that religion.

> *The Unique Self of that religion is the unique quality of intimacy. It is the unique quality of the meeting between the Infinite and the finite that is incarnate in that erotic embrace of the Divine, which expresses itself in those intimate caresses and whispers that we call ritual, what we call text.*

The Unique Self of a religion expresses itself:

- In the folds of language.
- In the ravishment and rapture of ritual.
- In gorgeous ceremony.

In its uniquely intimate quality, which is in some sense culturally untranslatable.

You can't translate it into universal principles—because it's not about universal principles. Yes, there are underlying principles of religions that are universal, that are shared by the religions—that's important, but that's not what a religion is. That's only one dimension of a religion.

A religion acts as a unique, intimate, erotic embrace of the Divine.

We can't actually have a conversation with the religions as long as we're looking at them as if they're the benighted natives and *we are the perenniallists, the integralists, the sophisticated post-postmodernists.*

We have to be able to enter into the intimate space of a unique religion.

If we can really open ourselves up, then perhaps for the first time in history we can actually receive or taste something: *the fragrance of their intimacy.*

Do we reject the ethnocentric dimensions of any religion? Of course we do. Because we understand that the word of God, as it appeared in that religion, was refracted through an ethnocentric prism of consciousness. That's a big deal.

I can have a deep experience of God, but then that experience of God is refracted through a prism.

That prism is my psychological maturity.

That prism is my structure of consciousness.

As an example, there's a great master in the Hebrew tradition named Isaiah. Another great master is named Ezekiel. Both Isaiah and Ezekiel do practices called The *Merkavah Adonai*, the Chariot of God. They describe the chariot differently. They are both great masters of mysticism, but they describe the chariot completely differently.

Then in the third century, the Aramaic masters say: What does that mean? "Ezekiel and Isaiah, these two great masters, these two prophetic masters, are seeing the chariot of the Divine, but they're describing it in substantively different ways. How could that be?"

So the Aramaic masters say: "*Ha ben-kfar, ha ben-krach*: This one was a farm boy and this one was a city boy."

What does that mean? That means that the master who was a city boy sees the divine chariot, but sees it through his cultural prism, which is of a city boy. And the farm boy prophet sees it through his farm boy vision.

So they both see the chariot differently. They're both seeing the chariot. But actually, their prism, their interior prism, shows them something different.

The same thing is true about our structural stage of moral consciousness. If my structural stage of moral consciousness is ethnocentric—meaning that the border of my love, care, and concern is for me and my people—then I'll have, for example, what Islam calls: *dar al-harb, dar al-islam*, the nation of Islam and the nation of the sword, and the two are pitted against each other. Or I'll have the Christian idea: *There's only redemption inside of the Church* (Augustine). Or certain strains in Judaism that talk about a chosen people and a convert can never become as full status as a Jew.

You'll have those strains because the word of the Divine is refracted through an ethnocentric structure of consciousness.

LIBERATING THE EXPERIENCE OF REVELATION

We need to liberate the experience of revelation. You can't talk about Reality without talking about revelation.

We have this narcissistic idea that we are the only actors in the Universe: *The human being acts. The human being initiates. The human being invokes.* This is true. We do initiate. We do invoke. But actually **there's a two-sided conversation in Reality.**

Reality is a history of revelations. And if you read the history of planet Earth, **Reality is a history of divine revelations.** They're not mythic. They're not made up. They're the actual lived experience of the deepest, most subtle and speculative minds across every period of history, across every cultural space, across every geographical space.

There's a cascading series of revelations.

> *Prophecy (or revelation) is when the Divine initiates, when the Divine invokes. But it is in the marriage—the hieros gamos—in the meeting between the human being and the Divine, where we fully and mutually co-participate in each other.*

We have to listen. We have to hear. We have to receive the revelation. The revelation is received through our structure of consciousness.

To recap:

- There are narratives of identity: the Universe stories. There's the One Love. There's the One Heart. There's the one unified Field of Meaning. There are the universals that bind us all.
- There are intimate cascading waves of relationship that emerge out of Infinity that personally address Reality—revelation is real. Revelation is not made up.
- Revelation is interpreted through your particular structure of consciousness.

*I need to receive the revelation. But then I've got to evolve the way I hear it. I've got to listen—**my listening co-creates the revelation.***

If my listening comes from an ethnocentric stage of consciousness, then there's going to be an ethnocentric hermeneutic interpretation of the word of the Divine that experiences it, as in the example of Islam of *dar al-harb and dar al-islam*, the nation of Islam and the nation of the sword.

The same goes for any religion.

RELIGION NEEDS TO BE PART OF THE REVOLUTION

If I evolve my consciousness, if I evolve my God-ness, then I'm going to hear revelation much more clearly.

I'm going to feel and realize that:

- I am Islam
- I am Judaism
- I am Christianity
- I am Taoism
- I am Buddhism
- I have an intimate language, and that language can't be reduced to "surface structures."
- I have an intimate ritual, and I have an intimate erotic dance with the Divine.

I'm loyal to that intimacy. I'm monogamous with that intimacy. But—God is also polyamorous.

- God's doing it with the Jews.
- God's doing it with the Christians.
- God's doing it with the *Sharia* in Islam, with the *Mu'tazila*.
- God's doing it with the Sufis.
- God's doing it with all the different sects of Buddhism, and all the different sects of Hinduism.
- God's doing it all over the place.

God is madly loving.

God is cascading streams of Intimate Infinity, incarnating in different structures and modes across time. Wow.

PARTICIPATING IN THE EVOLUTION OF GREAT TRADITIONS

So, let's talk about *Allahu Akbar*. Let's talk about Ramadan, this unique and gorgeous and stunning and beautiful frame of revelation which is Islam. We bow. That's what Islam—among many other beautiful things—is about. It's all in the bow. The utter submission.

We've got to be able to integrate these intimacies into a new Unique Self Symphony. The Unique Self Symphony is not a kind of benign imperialist reduction of the religions to their universal principles. That's the major developmental Integral mistake.

No. **The rituals of the religion are not their surface structures.**

The religious rituals of the religion are their intimate, culturally untranslatable, ecstatically urgent embraces and incarnations of their erotic dance with the Divine.

We have this very strange idea in modern identity politics, that if we take something from a different religion, we're somehow appropriating it, that we're somehow doing some cultural appropriation. Somehow, if we use something, we're stealing it from another tradition.

Of course that's not true. In fact, the greatest, most beautiful, most wondrous developments of every tradition are when other people received the tradition and developed something in it and honored something in it.

My gentle, humble suggestion to everyone is, if you can, **find a great tradition to practice in and participate in the evolution of that great tradition. And at the same time be a dual citizen of** *Homo amor*, of

CosmoErotic Humanism, of world spirituality, of this great new Story that we're telling. We need both.

We need the great traditions *and* we need a new Story, with new languages and new rituals and new practices. We need a new world spirituality—the underlying vision of the New human and the new humanity, what we call *Homo amor*, rooted in this vision of the Amorous Cosmos—with an enormous set of distinctions.

We're actually, in some sense, creating a new universal great tradition. It's not one that obliterates or undoes the great traditions as they are. **The great traditions do have to be updated and evolved.** Just as governments from the fourteenth century have evolved, so too must religion evolve.

But religion must evolve within its own internal core, not by becoming a liberal Protestant, liberal Jewish, liberal Islamic: *No rituals. It all looks the same. No one really believes it anymore.*

We need to stay passionately committed to the Unique Self, the unique structures and the unique intimacy of every great tradition, *and* we need to evolve the tradition from within its own sources.

Each tradition has to go to its own esoteric depth, and to its own ethical depth. Within the framework and mechanisms and structures of the tradition, it evolves.

Eternity evolves—always.

Of course it does. **The eternal Tao is the evolving Tao.**

The responsibility that each great religion has is to *participate in its own evolution of consciousness*. Not by becoming a vapid, secularized, tepid version of itself, but by staying in all of its ritual power.

We need to have a world conference of religions in which each religion shares its unique intimate instrument and offers it to the Unique Self Symphony.

- Each religion takes responsibility for the dimensions of their tradition that are not evolved.
- Each tradition takes responsibility for the voices in that tradition that are still ethnocentric and still homophobic.
- Each religion brings the texts that it's madly proud of and the texts that it's ashamed of, the texts that it has to leave behind.
- Each religion takes responsibility for its own evolution of consciousness.

This cannot happen by someone imposing it upon the religion, but rather, by the deepest thinkers, figures, prophets, mystics, practitioners from *within* that intimate tradition—they must evolve it internally.

Can you feel that? Wow. *Allahu akbar.*

I can't take responsibility for the internal evolution of Islam.

It's not my job. I can't do it, and it would be offensive.

For those of us that are not Muslim or at least not Muslim-born:

- We can honor Islam.
- We can bow with reverence.
- We can use the language.
- We can access something of the fragrance of the revelation of *Allahu Akbar.*
- We can begin to invite Islam into the Unique Self Symphony.
- We can let go of the colonialist dominance, which demands the reduction of Islam to abstract universals.

We're going to create this incredible, unbelievable, great new world tradition. Part of this great *Homo amor* tradition is going to be holding "dual citizenship":

- I'm going to be a dual citizen.
- I can be fully *Allahu akbar* and fully *Homo amor.*
- I can be fully *Adonai Elohim* and fully *Homo amor.*

RELIGION NEEDS TO BE PART OF THE REVOLUTION

- I can be fully optimal as Brahman and fully *Homo amor*.
- I can be fully the Father, the Son, and the Holy Ghost—and *Homo amor*.

The leading-edge prophets of each religion, at their core, are early adopters of *Homo amor*.

We've got to bring the religions to the table in order to evolve the source code. We do that by realizing that we need rituals which express the intimate erotic embrace of the Divine—before which we bow—rituals found in each and every unique religion.

CHAPTER FIVE

REWEAVING CHRISTMAS: FROM BIOLOGICAL FAMILY TO HOMO AMOR FAMILY

Episode 272 — December 26, 2021

WEAVING A NEW CLOTH OF OUTRAGEOUS LOVE INTO NEW VISIONS OF VALUE

There's a beautiful tradition of the Rebbe of Belz, the Hasidic master from a town called Belz in Eastern Europe in the 1920s. These were the Roaring Twenties in the United States and in Europe. The time between the wars was a time in which nothing was resolved, but there was the sense that somehow *it would be okay*. It was a false sense; we hadn't gone to the root causes of things. But there was this explosive party happening throughout America, and all through Paris and Berlin.

But it was pseudo-eros; it wasn't Eros.

In the Dharma of CosmoErotic Humanism, we have this distinction between Eros and pseudo-eros: **Pseudo-eros covers over the emptiness, while Eros swells from the fullness.**

The master from Belz said, translated loosely: "Satan knows how to make a party; we've got to make a better party." You can skip the word Satan if you wish—he was translating from a kind of Hebrew, Yiddish, Aramaic

tradition—but what he meant was *there are too many pseudo-eros parties, so let's have an Eros party.*

Remember, pseudo-eros approximates Eros, and an Eros party comes from this realization of the utter fullness of being.

So, are we ready for a party? We're going to have a *feastalla*, which in Yiddish means a great party. But it's an Eros party, where we're celebrating Reality. We're not going to be able to respond to existential risk and catastrophic risk without telling the new Story of Value rooted in First Principles and First Values, which realizes that the collapse of Value is the root cause of every existential risk. But we've allowed Value to be hijacked by premodern regressive fundamentalist claims, while liberal modernity and postmodernity have deconstructed all Value.

We need new visions of value. It's one of the things we're working on very hard together.

But from within that vision of value, we need to understand there's a story. In that story, each one of us is a star, quite literally. We're in a Unique Self Symphony together. We're telling this new Story of Value, weaving together. We are tailors of Eros; that's who we are together. We're not prophets of Eros, that's too audacious.

We're tailors of Eros, weaving together the strands from premodern, modern, and postmodern validated insights into a new cloth of Outrageous Love—grounded with policy implications, with vaccine implications, with healthcare implications, all throughout the map.

Let's weave, we're going to play today. Let's just step in, as we've set this intention. Let's step into this night. Christmas Eve was a couple of nights ago, and Christmas ended yesterday, but we're in the Christmas weekend. Let's start, and let's find it in "Silent Night."

We're going to study together. We're going to look at these texts, and we're going to unpack them, and we're going to play wild.

SILENT NIGHT: SON OF GOD, LOVE'S PURE LIGHT

I want to start with you with "Silent Night." Let's find it deep inside on the second day of Christmas, on this Sunday of Christmas. This "Silent Night" is from Sinéad O'Connor. We're going to read texts of culture together, so listen to the words and watch the action. Let's look at that text.

So first, "Silent Night"—where's that from? This is the first of four texts of culture we're going to look at. *Stille Nacht, Heilige Nacht: Silent night, Holy night*. It's the same words in both German and Yiddish.

All is calm, all is bright
Round yon Virgin, Mother and Child
Holy infant so tender and mild
Shepherds quake at the sight
Glories stream from Heaven afar
Christ the Savior is born
Hallelujah
Silent night, holy night!
Son of God
Love's pure light

First, we've got to take this out of its uniquely Christian context. We're going to read texts of culture and do something wildly important. When we started the Center for Integral Wisdom, we called it originally the Center for World Spirituality. **World spirituality means that every tradition is holding something—in what we call the Unique Self Symphony of Spirit—that matters.**

This is very different from the way the great traditions were read by modernity, which dismissed them, but was ignored even by Integral thought, which said: *when you go to the traditions, get rid of all the rituals and the surface structures and find the depth structures, with their emphasis on meditation and the realization of interior consciousness, which is the essence of being they all share.*

That's precisely half right. **There are certain surface structures that you've got to let go in the religions, and then there are a lot of mutually exclusive competing truths you've got to let go for sure. But every religion is a unique intimacy; it's a unique quality of being.**

ON THE OTHER SIDE OF GUILT IS OUR SECOND INNOCENCE

"Silent Night" is this uniquely gorgeous Christian moment. At the source of the Christian moment—which got completely lost in Christianity itself over 2,000 years ago, and which Christianity now has to reclaim—is this notion of *Son of God, Love's pure light*.

Love's pure light is not ordinary love. *Love's pure light* is purely innocent. It's the virgin, but it's the virgin of "second innocence," not a "first innocence." Second innocence means that the innocence is never lost; it never goes away. *I never lose my virginity; I claim it again.*

In this Christmas weekend, we revirginate; we find the innocence in ourselves that hasn't gotten lost. We find the virgin, and we find the child: the Infinite. "The great master," write the interior scientists in the third century, "is always a virgin and always a child." That's a passage from the Talmud, written in Aramaic in the third century. Meaning:

- Each one of us, we've always got to be a virgin, and we've always got to be an infant.
- We've always got to be purely innocent, even as we navigate the complexity of the world.
- Even as I map strategies and understand complexity, on the other side of complexity is a second simplicity.
- Even after I realize: Oh my God, my feet are so guilty, and guilty feet have got no rhythm (to quote George Michael), on the other side of guilt is my second innocence. So we've got to find each other.

If you watch the clip from Sinéad O'Connor singing "Silent Night," who do you have in the clip? You have the lovers of the Song of Solomon. If you've ever read the great Song of Solomon—the great Song of Songs, one of the greatest love songs ever written—it's a story of two lovers searching for each other in the dark streets, which is exactly what Sinéad intuitively recapitulates in her version of the song. They're looking for each other and can't quite find each other, but they never stop looking.

Then at the end you see pages flying around—those are all Outrageous Love Letters. All of those are a book of Outrageous Love Letters scattered in the wind, but never lost.

> *Oh my God, Love's pure light is Outrageous Love.*

That's what it is. It's not ordinary love. It's the innocent, gorgeous, virginal, stunning love, which is our true nature.

Our true nature is to be lived as Love. Now, that doesn't mean that Love is natural. **We're not naturally lovers; we're *inherently* lovers.** *We've got to train love, and we're training in love all the time. We're always training our innocence.* Second innocence is real, while first innocence is not.

The baby is not good, but the wise woman who is still an infant and a child at the same time, she's good. **We train our innocence; we train our goodness.** How paradoxical! *We're always training our innocence. We're always cultivating our innocence.*

But this is not the innocence of the victim. The victim is a false innocence. It's a pseudo-innocence, where the price of innocence is impotence. A genuine innocence is filled with power.

Do you ever notice that when a baby enters the room, everything stops? If the baby is fully alive, all the energy goes to the baby. There's enormous power in that. **Imagine that each one of us is an ambassador of**

Outrageous Love, and we're innocent. But it's not a first innocence, it's a second innocence, and it's filled with power. This sweet Solstice Joy child, that's us; that's an Outrageous Lover.

Love's pure light. Radiant beaming from Thy holy face.

Beloved, thine holy face. Literally, your holy face—this is second innocence filled with power.

We're now going to read some texts of culture, and we're going to articulate this next stage in this great story of *Homo amor*: the fulfillment of *Homo sapiens*; the New human and the new humanity, who is innocent—second innocence—*and* who also is training in goodness.

Love's pure light—this is Outrageous Love.

OUTRAGEOUS LOVE KNOWS NO BOUNDARIES

Outrageous Love knows no boundaries. It doesn't stop at the boundary of Catholicism. It doesn't stop at the boundary of the Jesuits. It doesn't stop at the boundary of any particular branch of Christianity—Christianity got hijacked and commodified. Crosby, Stills, Nash & Young in the 1960s were right when they said: "How many people died in the name of Christ, I can't believe at all!" How many false crusades? **We've got to liberate the spark of** *Love's pure light* **from deep in the Christ moment and reweave it.**

Why? Because we absolutely need that unique instrument of the Christ moment.

Just like we need Ramadan. Just like we need Confucianism—not the kind of Confucianism being sold by the Chinese Communist Party to cover up genocide, but the genuine spirit of Confucius that China is so rightly proud of. We need the genuine spirit of Islam, the genuine spirit of the Sufi masters, and the genuine spirit of Kabbalists. **We've got to weave that all together into a new world spirituality, in which the Unique Self of every**

great religion plays its unique instrument of intimacy and plucks the heart chords of Reality on the Inside of the Inside.

LEVEL ONE OF LOVE: BIOLOGICAL FAMILY

There are three classical levels of love that we have to go through before we get to *Love's pure light*, Outrageous Love.

The first place that culture has placed love in the world is in this institution which we call the biological family. The biological family is an enormously important institution. It's strong; we need family. *Familia*, those we're intimate with, those we're close to, who we can touch and taste and feel their fragrance, and we've got this radical loyalty to each other. That's what biological family was intended to be, was for a couple thousand years, and in many ways still needs to be.

Biological family is enormously important. But it's far from the end of the story; biological family is the beginning of the story. You can take any value, and you can turn it into an idolatry. **When biological family is my whole story, it becomes idolatrous.** It becomes my Value when I spend ninety-nine percent of my time, ninety-nine percent of my money, and ninety-nine percent of my sense of being wounded and hurt in the family—and I'm continually reviewing scenes from my biological family.

Then I'm cut off from the Mother—not the biological mother, but Mother as the field of *Love's pure light*: the field of Outrageous Love.

So I've got to be able to transcend and include it and move beyond it. For about 100 years in culture, we began to do that. Biological family remained, but then something else emerged.

LEVEL TWO OF LOVE: ROMANTIC LOVE

That which emerged had existed in different forms for several thousand years of course, but then *it emerged at the very center of culture*. It became not a fringe, but the center of gravity of culture. The second level is romantic love. Romantic love is when you realize that *biological family alone is not doing it*. Biological family used to tell me who to marry, who to love—in order *to serve the biological family*; sons and daughters married to serve the family.

That was true whether you were of nobility, kings and queens, or whether you were a commoner: *you married in order to survive and to help your family survive*, and *you were utterly loyal to biological family*, which is beautiful. But then we went to romantic love and said: *There's a second way to experience love, and this is romantic love, the love between two people.*

It doesn't matter whether you're a Montague or a Capulet, in Shakespeare's *Romeo and Juliet*. *It doesn't matter whether you're a Hatfield or a McCoy*, in that great story of the feud. Romantic love is the beginning of the understanding that Love is deeper than even biology; that Love *animates* biology. Love is not just an *expression* of biology, which cloaks the need to survive. **Love is driving this whole thing, and Love matters all the way.** That's romantic love.

It's a key wild step. And there's such glory in romantic love. Romantic love is between me and my beloved: my man, my woman. By romantic, I don't mean sexual; I mean this kind of couplehood. You can have a kind of romantic love between a sister and a brother. You can have a kind of romantic love where you're like, *Oh my God, I'm madly in love with my dog.* Now, I'm not sleeping with my dog. **But we're connected, and we've got this romance together; we've got this deep bond between us that lights me up in this wild and insane way.**

I want to feel into that quality of romantic love. By romantic love, I don't mean only classical romance, but all those *dyads of love* with those who are immediate and close to me: my family, my uncle, my dog, my brother, my sister, my wife, my son, my daughter. They're a little bit beyond biological family, and they're beautiful. You've got this sense of: *Wow, I found you!* It's very unique, very specific, and very particular.

Now let's take it home, let's go the next step from romantic love. By romantic love, again, *my bromance*, and *my circle*, and *my close friends*. It's not quite my biological family, it's the next level. It's *my circle*, and *I'm going to hold those friendships*.

Those are beautiful and necessary, but they're not enough.

We're not going to be able to stare in the face of existential risk and catastrophic risk, we're not going to be able to be in this moment poised between utopia and dystopia with only these two types of love.

We've got to take the best of biological family and leave the other stuff behind. It's complicated. Someone sent me a video this weekend. She was playing guitar for her immediate family, and you could see in the clip that nobody got it; no one in the family got who she was and what she was about. You know the feeling? You can be talking to someone close, you can be talking to a brother, you can be talking to a daughter—and they don't quite get it. Your brother cannot even understand the whole course of your life, and you can feel completely anonymous and completely unseen in this terrible and painful way.

Biological family. Yes, there's a reason we were born there, and there's a fixing to do in biological family. But we have this idolatrous sense that "we've got to have the perfect picture of the biological family, and that's what takes us home."

Yes, engage with your biological family in the most beautiful way, but don't use it as either an excuse to be in the victimhood of what wasn't, or the end-all and the be-all. Because it's neither. It's an important piece, but it's just the beginning.

LEVEL THREE OF LOVE: EVOLUTIONARY FAMILY AND OUTRAGEOUS LOVE

Let's differentiate between biological family and Evolutionary Family. Evolutionary Family is the realization and the understanding that I'm walking with a band of brothers and sisters. They see me and I see them. We look in each other's eyes and we've got each other's backs all the way. We're not building a war room; we're building a peace room. We're finding the inside of Reality and creating a new society.

We're telling the new Story together.

Often when guys remember their best days—even if they're completely beautiful, peaceful guys—they remember the utter gorgeousness of those times when they were at war, which was also a horror, which they hated.

Yet they knew that the six people around them had their back. Not because it was romantic love but because they were Evolutionary Lovers. They had a mission and a vision; they were willing to lay down their lives for the vision, each other, and the person next to them.

Imagine doing that—not in some contrived war, as part of the rivalrous conflict governed by win/lose metrics success story, a tragedy—but imagine we're not in a great war, we're in a great peace.

In American history, in a very famous battle in the Revolutionary War, as John Paul Jones is losing and the British ask him to surrender—he turns in and says: *I have not yet begun to fight.*

What the Evolutionary Lover says is: *I have not yet begun to love!* We have not yet begun to love. At One Mountain, Many Paths, we're just getting started to love each other; we're at the beginning. **Our love is going to change the world.**

That's an Evolutionary Lover.

That's an Evolutionary Family.

It means we're committed to each other because we understand that we're living in a field of Outrageous Love, and that Love is the most real force in the world.

ARTICULATING THE INTERIOR AND EXTERIOR SCIENCES OF LOVE: OUTRAGEOUS LOVE DRIVES COSMOS

Part of our dedication is to articulate the sciences of Love: both the interior science and the exterior science. In our culture we dismiss Love, but Love lives freely at every level of Reality.

Last night I was looking at pictures of these gorgeous, bioluminescent fish in the ocean that light up in these wild ways. The lights meet all the criteria of language, so there's language actually happening between these deep-sea creatures. However, according to scientific explanation, *bioluminescence is a result of several chemical reactions.*

Friends, what's a chemical? A chemical is a configuration of intimacy. Its different elements woven together in a particular dance of love, and that chemical comes alive in a human being. Reaction means we react to each other because we're madly in love. Reaction means *I feel you and you feel me.* **A chemical reaction at a cellular level is an expression of the force of choice and love and freedom.**

Stuart Kauffman's book called *The Origins of Order* is all about the notion that mathematics does not define the lifeworld. Biology is not an expression of physics. You can't do math on the lifeworld; theorems don't work in the lifeworld. Pythagoras and Isaac Newton got it right to a point, and then they got it wrong.

The attempt to reduce everything to mathematics, which is measurement, is wrong. The lifeworld is immeasurable. There's a freedom even at the level of cells, and chemical reactions are cells coming together with an interior awareness, fully alive, and creative.

That's *Love's pure light.*

That's Outrageous Love.

We're reading the sciences and clearly demonstrating that **the force that drives Cosmos, that animates all the four forces, is Eros itself. It's Outrageous Love.**

WE ARE EVOLUTIONARY LOVERS LOOKING DEEPLY INTO EACH OTHER'S EYES AND TOGETHER AT A SHARED HORIZON, READY TO LAY IT ALL DOWN FOR THE SAKE OF THE WHOLE

Evolutionary Lovers know that each one of us is a unique configuration of *Homo amor*. Each one of us is a unique configuration of intimacy and desire and Eros. Each one of us is a unique configuration of the *LoveIntelligence* and *LoveForce* and *LoveBeauty* and *LoveDesire* that's the initiating and animating Eros of All-That-Is. It's living uniquely in me.

Love is a Unique-Self perception that I see when I fall madly in love. But I fall madly in love not just at the romantic level, not just because I'm looking deeply into your eyes. **We're looking deeply into each other's eyes *and* looking together at a shared horizon.** We're whole mates. We're joining genius to co-create for the sake of the whole. We're omni-considerate for the sake of the whole. We're willing to lay it down, to sacrifice, and to pour our energy into this moment between utopia and dystopia, which is for real.

Friends, this is for real! We're poised between utopia and dystopia, for freaking real, and evolving the source code and telling the new Story is the single most important thing we can do.

Even in our gang, and I love our gang madly, everyone gets involved; we've got to do this, and we've got to do that. And we should get involved. We need to get involved in our families. Biological family matters of course, and everyone should handle biological family in the best way we can. Of course, we're in our circle, and we should be. Those first two levels of love matter greatly. But friends:

This is ours to do! We're the band of Outrageous Lovers.

We've got to feel *Gloria*; the Glory lives in us, *in Excelsis Deo. Gloria* is the realization that we're in a Field of Glory, that Glory lives uniquely in each of us, and that the inside of that Glory is Love.

The movement of Love in this moment in time is to tell the new Story— and to integrate that new Story, to work hard at telling that new Story, to footnote every page of that new Story, to create a Great Library, and deliver it into the world.

So if you're spending most of your time and money on your biological family and inner circle, you're lost. You have the capacity to step up and be part of this response. **Oh my God, we've got to create this world together, and we've got to have the same passion for this that I have for *Gloria*—** for the field of the Divine that lives uniquely in me, which is the Field of Outrageous Love. It's the same passion that I have for romantic love. Romantic love has to be at a very deep level, at level three, with each other. When I say romantic love, I don't mean we sleep with each other. I mean, *we've got to fall madly in love with each other; we're madly committed to each other, we've got each other's back in a deep way.*

Let's say we get together and have a romantic moment, and it doesn't work. We don't fall out and disappear. *Oh, we're a little hurt, and we're gone?* No, we don't allow ourselves to be hijacked. We're looking together at a horizon. We're going to articulate the source code, and we're going to throw it into culture. Oh my God, can you feel that? This is it. This is the moment.

Here's the litmus test for Evolutionary Family:

- In an Evolutionary Family, you can actually show up and live large.
- When you're with your Evolutionary Lovers, you don't have

to play small.
- When you're with your Evolutionary Family, you get to live large—*you get to confess your vulnerability, and at the same time, confess your greatness.*
- When you're with your Evolutionary Family, you can speak and be and live your deepest heart's desire, and you know that your deepest heart's desire is the desire of evolution and the Evolutionary Impulse moving through you utterly, uniquely, and gorgeously.

Let's now look at the code for this week.

EVOLUTIONARY LOVE CODE: EVOLUTIONARY AND SOUL ROOT FAMILY

Biological family is wondrous, and we are committed to it.

Evolutionary Family or Soul Root Family is not less—and sometimes even more—significant.

We need to be, at the very least, as committed to our Evolutionary Family as we are to our biological family, and often much more so.

It is before your Evolutionary Family that you can confess your greatness, take your unique risk, speak and live your deepest heart's desire, and be seen in the depth of your true glory.

We will not be able to respond to existential risk without making the momentous leap from only biological family to Evolutionary and Soul Root Family.

We have to find the energy of romantic love—biological family and romantic love in its broadest sense, and in its close-friend sense—then **pour that into being an Evolutionary Lover.**

We're going to do a practice: we're going to access two qualities of *Gloria*. We're going to start with a song by a fantastic woman, Laura Branigan, who did a song in the 1980s called "Gloria." I want you to feel the energy. Laura was married, and in 1993, her husband got very sick. She took off two years to nurse him, and he died after an intense and agonizing two years. She didn't perform for years afterwards. Then she started performing again in the 2000s and passed away tragically in her sleep from an aneurysm.

IN EXCELSIS DEO: LIBERATING THE EXILED ENERGY OF GLORIA

But I want you to get this: Laura is alive, and she's real. I want you to get the energy of "Gloria," but we're going to now liberate it from exile. It's not just you and that one special person. We're going to take that energy, and we're going to mix it with the glory of *In Excelsis Deo*, from that great Christmas hymn, because this is our Christmas Day.

It doesn't matter whether you're Jewish (I'm an Orthodox rabbi Jewish dude).

It doesn't matter whether you're Muslim.

It doesn't matter whether you're a secular humanist.

We're weaving together the Unique Self Symphony.

We're going to take in the glory of In Excelsis Deo, which is the glory of the Field of Outrageous Love.

- We're going to liberate it from its unique fundamentalist Christian grasp.
- We're going to realize that this is the field of Outrageous Love in which we all participate, and which lives uniquely in us.
- We're a band of Outrageous Lovers, and we're going to love each other with that wild energy of *Gloria*.

- We're going to take the energy of romantic love and blow it open at level three.

That's how we feel for each other.

We pour our effort, our resources, our time.

We pour it in because we're looking at this vision.

We've got a vision together.

We're holding something so precious, beyond imagination.

We're holding the best version I know of the new Story.

We're in the middle of it, and we need all of us in the game.

We need all of us to come to the table.

All of us are a search engine of the Cosmos looking to articulate the next story. We are da Vinci. We're at this time between worlds, this time between stories. But we can't do it unless we realize *we're a band of Outrageous Lovers*. It's not the movie *Don't Look Up*. No, we're looking up, and we're looking up *together*. We're looking at a shared horizon.

THE PRACTICE: BIRTHING A NEW STRUCTURE OF INTIMACY

Let's get the energy of this in our bodies. We're going to take the romantic love energy and the biological family energy, and we're going to blow it open and lift it to the next level.

We're going to do this practice to weave something in the source code, to change something in Reality, and to become Evolutionary Lovers. We have each other's back, and we're going all the way in this lifetime.

This is not minor, this is not clever, this is not cute—what we're actually doing is:

We're birthing a new structure of intimacy.

If you get that Reality is not just the movement from simplicity to complexity, but that **Reality is the progressive deepening of intimacies**, then you get that what we're doing now is **we're birthing a new level of intimacy**. That's what Evolutionary Family is, that's what Evolutionary Family does.

Evolutionary Family has the same energy, the same charge, the same Eros as romantic love, but it's even more dramatic and more gorgeous. So take us into "Gloria," Laura Branigan. Let's go back to the 1980s for a second, because she got this right. Just feel it, meditate on it, and let it kind of ripple through you.

GLORIA: FEEL YOUR INNOCENCE SLIPPING AWAY

What's happening here? You've got this energy, but it doesn't quite happen. In other words, it's a story about the *Gloria* that doesn't happen. *Feel your innocence slipping away.* You can't hold the innocence. When you make the whole thing about that one romantic relationship—it doesn't matter whether it's your dog, or your friend, or your brother, or your sister, or your romantic lover—those are gorgeous, that's level two. It's gorgeous, and we've got to keep that. But it's not enough. *Feel your innocence slipping away. Are the voices in your head calling, Gloria?*

But we don't know what's going on. Listen to the words. Where are you going to find the guy?

> *Will you meet him on the main line, or will you catch him on the rebound?*
> *Will you marry for the money, take a lover in the afternoon?*
> *Feel your innocence slipping away, don't believe it's comin' back soon.*

Gloria, you're always on the run now
Running after somebody, you gotta get him somehow.
I think you've got to slow down before you start to blow it
I think you're headed for a breakdown, so be careful not to show it
You really don't remember, was it something that he said?
Are the voices in your head calling, Gloria?

Meaning: there's no way back to second innocence.

We've studied a text together about Leah, who marries Jacob in the darkness, in Chapter 29 of the book of Genesis: "*Running after somebody, you've got to get them somehow.*"

I want you to get this, and it's gorgeous. This is a song about: Oh my God, you can't really find it. You can't really hear the person who's calling your name, Gloria. It's just voices in your head, and you can't hear your name being called.

Just like we turned biological family into an idol, we've turned this romantic moment into an idol, and we put all of our energy right into that moment—and we never actually hear our name being called.

GLORIA: IN EXCELSIS DEO IN THE FIELD OF LOVE'S PURE LIGHT

With my Evolutionary Family, I can be myself—but not my lowest-common-denominator self.

- I confess my greatness.
- I take my unique risk.
- I play large.
- I live out loud.
- I give my gifts.
- I sing in the shower.
- I understand that I have superpowers, and they're needed by All-That-Is.

Then I step into the field of glory, and *Gloria* becomes Glory—not just Christian Glory, but the Glory of the band of Outrageous Lovers. That's the story. That's the *In Excelsis Deo*.

We invest the energy of "Gloria," of Laura Branigan, into the glory of *In Excelsis Deo* of the Field of *Love's pure light*. Then we liberate it from the grips of a particular Christian context—though, of course we love the Christian context—and we realize: *This is who we are*. We are *Homo amor*.

This is the emergence of the New Human. We tell the new Story. But friends, none of this is fanciful, clever, or cute. This is actually how history works. It's the capacity to tell a new Story, a Story of the New human and the new humanity. That's the only way true transformation ever happens. It's the only way it ever blows up. So we're here to be *Homo amor*.

I invite you to confess your greatness: "I am wonder. I am beauty. I'm giving my gift. I'm showing up. I'm ready to show up. I'm here to go all the way in this lifetime. I am delight." However you confess your greatness, confess your greatness and say: I'm here for you. I've got your back. Let's do this together. **I don't want to be written in the Book of Life without you.**

This last clip is also *Gloria*, but now it's the *Gloria* of *In Excelsis Deo*. It's the field of the Divine in which Jesus is born. But now we realize that *your birth is the birth of Jesus*. Your birthday is the day you realize that Goddess says: *I can't do it without you*. You realize: *I am Jesus being born. I am the elect. I am the chosen one. We are each the chosen one*.

You are the Messiah; we're all part of the stature of the Messiah, and we're doing it together—none of us is acting individually. We're a band of Outrageous Lovers. We're a Unique Self Symphony.

We're weaving these songs and reweaving the source code of culture literally, right now.

Take us inside, last song, text of culture, "In Excelsis Deo," sung by Andrea Bocelli.

CHAPTER SIX

RECLAIMING THE EVOLUTIONARY TECHNOLOGY OF CHANT FOUND UNIQUELY IN EACH RELIGION

Episode 278 — February 8, 2022

SETTING OUR INTENTION IN THIS TIME BETWEEN WORLDS, THIS TIME BETWEEN STORIES

Welcome. Let's be in the silence, and let's be in the words. We're doing a special week. It's a kind of "inner" week, if you will. We wanted to spend some time going deeply inside of ourselves and accessing the field out of which we live and the field out of which we work.

What's our intention? Who are we?

We're a band of Evolutionary Lovers, Outrageous Lovers; we're standing for the evolution of Love. We're in this moment, this time between worlds, this time between stories, like da Vinci in the Renaissance. We're faced with an enormous potential utopia of unimaginable beauty; we can create a world more beautiful than we could possibly imagine. Yet, looming on the horizon is this sense of catastrophic risk and existential risk, which is not utopian but dystopian in the extreme.

I've spent the last ten years looking at these possibilities with great intensity. This is not the threat of one person doing something crazy. **These are structural problems**

in the very structure of things, which will inevitably lead to a level of collapse and suffering which will either be catastrophic—in seven or eight different scenarios that we've outlined before in great depth—**or existential, meaning *there's no future; it's the end of the future.***

We've said here at One Mountain that we have to take responsibility for the unborn—that we are the voice of the future, that the future speaks through us—and that we can articulate a new Story of Value, a new vision. We can articulate the dream which carries us forward.

"A man's reach should exceed his grasp, or what's a heaven for," wrote the poet Robert Browning. That is to say, we need always to be reaching for a dream; we need to be reaching for a vision, to articulate that vision—that new Story of Value which is a new Universe Story:

- A new narrative of human identity.
- A new narrative of purpose.
- A narrative of passion.
- A narrative of power.

To tell that new Story is the single most important thing we can do.

In fact, this is what da Vinci, Marsilio Ficino, and all the rest did in the Renaissance. They came together to tell that new Story, and it's that new Story that created modernity. It's that new Story that created the hopes of modernity and the dignities of modernity, but the failures in the plotline of that new Story also created the disasters of modernity. It created the breakdowns, which have brought us to this moment of potential catastrophic and existential risk.

So that's who we are. Our intention is to play a larger game. Our intention is to participate in the evolution of Love. Our intention is to tell this new Story. But today we're going to stop for a moment; we're going to pause. We're going to go inside in a way that we touch on every week, and it may not seem like the center of what we're doing. But really, it's the center of everything in our hearts and our minds, which is: *We have to be able to know—where does the new Story come from?* How do we know anything?

We've talked a lot about First Principles and First Values. How do we know anything at all about First Principles and First Values? Where do we know from?

HOW DO WE KNOW ANYTHING? ACCESSING THE FIELD OF VALUE

How do we access the Field of Value and listen deeply into that Field?

That's a big question. We don't do that exactly with the Eye of the Senses. The Eye of the Senses is for accessing empirical information, which is really important. You want to know if it's raining outside, step outside and see. If you want to get a little more empirical information at other levels, get a Hubble telescope, get an fMRI machine. Those are amplifications of the Eye of the Senses, and those are wildly important; those are critical.

Then there are other kinds of information that I can get from the Eye of the Mind: mathematics, moral reasoning, rational discourse—from which the Western world created its law. The Eye of the Mind is obviously wildly important, so we need the Eye of the Mind.

But with this new Story of Value that we're telling based on First Principles and First Values, the Eye of the Senses is insufficient to take us there, and the Eye of the Mind is insufficient to take us there. We need something more.

I want to call this third eye the Eye of Value. The Eye of Value has gone under many names. The Sufis called it the Eye of the Heart. The mystical Christians called it the Eye of the Spirit. The Hebrews called it *ayin nistar*: the Hidden Eye. Sometimes it's been called the Third Eye. But actually, I'm going to call it the Eye of Value. I'm excited about that word. **The Eye of Value allows us to sense and to know the Good, the True, the Beautiful.**

It tells us that Love is real, that Eros is a true Value of Cosmos, and that intimacy matters ultimately.

So how do we access the Eye of Value?

ACCESSING THE EYE OF VALUE BY BECOMING THE MUSIC

There are about ten different doors into the Eye of Value. Of course, you use your mind and your body. But you do more than that. We actually want to find our way to the Inside of the Inside, to what we might call the *interior face of Cosmos*.

Value lives on the inside. Value is an interior. It's an interior that's Real.

When I lose touch with Value, I let my values be hijacked. Sometimes people will say, "Fundamentalists stand for values." No, that's a premodern hijacking of Value, saying: "Value is given to me by my God and no one else; this is what it is, and here's the list, pay attention, be obedient, or burn—and not in a good way—in hell." That's not what we're talking about. We're talking about an Eye of Value, where we can all access Value.

One of the most stunning ways we understand Value is through chant, through music.

- Music opens something up.
- Music is a key that opens up the interior face of the Cosmos.
- All true music opens up new Value.

Pythagoras, the great pre-Socratic Greek mathematician, talks about two things: mathematics and music. He talks about the value in mathematics and the value in music, and how music and mathematics are intimately bound up with each other. **Music is the mathematics of Value in the Cosmos. Music is the mathematics of intimacy.**

A chant can open me, or it can close me. It can open a door and allow me to see. And I want to be really clear: I'm talking about the *practice* of music;

I'm not talking about just listening to music. I'm talking about the actual practice of *becoming* the music. *I'm not just listening, I'm not passive—I AM the music.*

We're going to go into the practice together.

There was this gentleman about a thousand years before Jesus, and his name was David. David had a son named Solomon, who was a beautiful figure. David had a harp—and Leonard Cohen likes to write songs about David's harp. When David wanted to feel and enter the Field of One Love and One Heart, he would take out his harp, and he would make music, and he would sing.

In David's lineage, there's this master named Elisha, who's a student of Elijah. Elisha, when he wants to feel the Field of Value—when he wants to know the Good, the True, and the Beautiful—in the original text, he says to his associate, *ve-atah kekhu li menagen, vehayah kenagen ha-menagen, ve-ativ alay ruakh Adonai*: "take for me a music-maker (*menagenn*: a minstrel), and when the music-maker becomes the music, then I've entered into the Field of the Divine, the Field of Value."

It's a very big deal.

So we need to always up-level our consciousness, from egocentric (I just love me and my family), to ethnocentric (I love myself and my tribe), to worldcentric (I love every human being), to cosmocentric: I love every human being and every animal—I love the whole thing.

We always have to be in the evolution of love. **But at the highest levels of worldcentric and cosmocentric, I've got to be able to step into the Field of Value.** I can do that through a rock song, or an opera, or a rock opera. I do it through chanting. I do it through becoming the music.

I can't just listen to the rock opera; I've got to become the rock opera. I've got to become the music.

ENTERING THE PRACTICE OF CHANT: LET THE CHANT ENTER YOU

The practice of chanting is the practice of becoming the music. Let yourself enter the chant. If you can, sit up in your chair or in your bed, uncross your legs, uncross your arms. Let your back become the *axis mundi*, the pole of the world itself. Your spinal cord reaches deep into the earth, then goes up, and then reaches heaven. You become the *axis mundi*, the connection point and the pole, connecting the inner and outer worlds: Heaven and Earth, interiors and exteriors.

Just let the chant enter you.

Now, what's going to happen is, your attention is going to wander—not because you're a bad person, not because you're not gorgeous and beautiful and stunning—but because attention *always* wanders. **The act of meditation is to non-judgmentally bring your attention—with delight—back to the chant until you gradually begin to fall in.** I promise you: you won't have your attention wander once, it's going to wander every few seconds. So just keep bringing it back to center.

- Let's go all the way together in this lifetime.
- Let's stand for the evolution of love.
- Let's dream the dream that's impossible, and let's make it real.

But to do that, we can't do it in our skin-encapsulated ego. We need to open the Eye of Value. We need to access the Field, and let the Field pour into us even as we pour into the Field.

That's the practice of the Avatar throughout the generations. But we can't rely anymore on one avatar; we have to be that avatar together. Remember, when we looked at the movie *Dune*? It's not just one Messiah. That was the mistake of the Fremen in *Dune*; they're waiting for the one Messiah.

No, we are all the Messiah together. We are the movement together. We are the movement of evolutionary energy, the Eros, the *Shakti*, moving awake and alive in us.

We have to always be able to access that Field, and let it move in us and activate us. When it activates us, it doesn't just give us this intense feeling of aliveness. It actually gives us access to Value—to the Good, the True, and the Beautiful. It gives access to Love itself, to Eros itself. So let's close our eyes, hear the code, and then let's engage with and become several different chants, from different spiritual traditions.

EVOLUTIONARY LOVE CODE: THE PATH OF CHANT—EACH GREAT RELIGION IS A DIFFERENT QUALITY OF INTIMACY AND EACH OPENS A DIFFERENT DOOR

> Undoubtedly one of the most crucial paths toward gnosis, true knowledge, is the path of chant.
>
> The path of chant opens the gates to the interior face of the Cosmos.
>
> It's not accidental that every great tradition of knowing in the classical era—from the mysteries in ancient Greece, to the tribal traditions, to the warrior traditions, to the speculative and subtle schools of science and tantra—all of them deployed the core technology of music and chant.
>
> The path of chant reveals true knowledge.
>
> All knowledge emerges from the Field of Eros.

KASHMIR SHAIVISM: DEVI PRAYER

This first chant is from the tradition of Kashmir Shaivism, whose practitioners are wild, passionate lovers of She, and which has produced the gorgeousness of Hinduism in its most clarified and beautiful forms.

All great traditions are in some ways imperfect, and filled with tragedy. But we need to take their essence and integrate it into the new vision. Seventy percent of the world lives in a great tradition, and we need to up-level and liberate the spark from each broken vessel. It's the spark of chant, of accessing the Field of She.

Chant 1: Kashmir Shaivites — Devi Prayer

> *Ma Amba Lalitha Devi*
> *Parashakti Sundari*
> *Namastasyai Namastasyai Namastasyai Namo Namah*
>
> *Ma Amba Lalitha Devi*
> *Mahamaye Mangale*
> *Namastasyai Namastasyai Namastasyai Namo Namah*
>
> *Ma Amba Lalitha Dev*
> *Mahakali Bhairavi*
> *Namastasyai Namastasyai Namastasyai Namo Namah*
>
> *Ma Amba Lalitha Devi*
> *Mahalakshmi Vaishnavi*
> *Namastasyai Namastasyai Namastasyai Namo Namah*

That's the chant to the Goddess, to She, to the Eros that moves through all of us.

CATHARS – LO BOIÈR

Here's another taste. This next chant comes from the Cathars, a mystical Christian sect that was wiped out by the Church, that stood for the One Love and the One Heart. We go to the Cathars, in the thirteenth century, and hear the **pure, explosive access to the Field of the Christ**.

It doesn't matter whether the Christ is your tradition or not. It happens not to be the tradition I was raised in, and my mother's turning over right

RECLAIMING THE EVOLUTIONARY TECHNOLOGY OF CHANT

now in her grave, saying: "Why is my son talking about the Christ, *Gevalt*? What's happened to me? What did I do wrong?"

But actually, it's all One Field.

It's all One Love.

It's all One Heart.

Rama and Sita, Radha and Krishna, Christ and Mary Magdalene, it's One Love, One Heart. But there are different qualities of intimacy which all matter in the symphony.

So now let's just let it in. And inside of you, let it weave with the first chant as a different quality.

Chant 2: Cathars – Lo Boièr

Quand lo boièr ven de laurar,
Planta son agulhada...
A, e, i, ò, u!
Planta son agulhada...
Tròba sa femna al pè del fuòc,
Tota desconsolada...
A, e, i, ò, u!
Tota desconsolada...

Se'n sès malauta, digas-o,
Te farai un potatge!
A, e, i, ò, u!
Te farai un potatge!

Amb una raba, amb un caulet
E una lauseta magra...
A, e, i, ò, u

GYUTO MONKS – MANDALA OFFERING

The Gyoto monks are chanting and accessing the inner quality—the Goodness, the Truth, the Beauty—of Reality in its Tao, in its Dharma, in its inner form, in its First Values and Principles. **It's a different sound, and a different quality of intimacy.**

It's not that all the religions are the same. They're not. It's not that religions are not often mediated through an ethnocentric context and broken in so many ways. They are.

In order to create the new Story of Value, we can't have just Dharma.

We need yoga, and yoga means practice, and practice means we can access the field of She.

To access the field of She, we want to get a sense of the unique quality of each instrument.

We're just going to taste the qualities for a second, then we're going to practice together. No instrument is extra; they are all unique qualities of intimacy.

The Gyuto order was originally based in Tibet. In 1950, the Chinese invaded Tibet, and they massacred thousands of monks. Fifty-nine of the Gyuto Monks managed to escape across the Himalayas with His Holiness, the Dalai Lama, into India, and they founded the Gyuto Monastery in Dharamsala.

One of the people on that trip was a man named Achok Rinpoche, a beautiful man who became a dear friend of mine.

When I met the Dalai Lama, we had a little bit of an argument that I've told you about once, and so he invited me to Dharamsala to resolve our arguments. Achok Rinpoche was my dear beautiful friend and guest. Achok was on that pilgrimage, and he ran the Tibetan library for forty or fifty years. So Achok Rinpoche, this is for you, brother!

RECLAIMING THE EVOLUTIONARY TECHNOLOGY OF CHANT

Chant 3: Gyuto Monks – Mandala Offering

Each great tradition is chanting, but each great tradition is a unique quality of intimacy, and it accesses and opens a different door.

Our hearts are open. Our minds wander, and we bring our minds back to center.

NATIVE AMERICAN – SACRED SPIRIT

Let's now go to the world of the native Americans, and let's feel the sense of the dance of sacred spirit and its chant.

Chant 4: Native American —Sacred Spirit

Here's another beautiful example from the indigenous world. Let's have a listen now.

Now we've got a sense of becoming the music using chants from spiritual traditions from around the world. Chant opens the door to this deep understanding and knowing.

WISDOM OF SOLOMON CHANTS

This is a chant that comes from David and Solomon. So if you'll allow me, as a spiritual friend, I want to give you just a transmission of the chant, of the energy of Solomon, of the energy of the lineage and the knowing of Solomon.

I've translated, or "trans-luminated," a sense of the words into English. You can actually follow the words in Hebrew, or you can just close your eyes and receive it. Again, this is a special week.

First, I want to tell you just a brief story. There's a dear friend of mine, who's on our board at the Center for Integral Wisdom, a wonderful human being, who was a lead teacher and headmaster at one of the most important educational institutions in America, for the elite of America. It produced people like Mark Zuckerberg, and it formed a generation of American business, with all of its dignity and all of its tragedy.

She once said to me: "When I came to this institution, everybody thought that the job of the teacher was to evoke the Values of the Good, the True, and the Beautiful. But everyone assumed that those were Values, that those were Real. Now, forty years later, when I'm leaving, no one even knows whether those Values are Real." That's what happened in postmodernity: it collapsed the Field of Value.

We've got so much music but few songs that truly take us inside into the interior face of the Cosmos. Music is not entertainment. Music is the most ecstatic, urgent, pleasurable yoga practice. So let's go inside together with mad audacity and mad love—because **the only way to be sane is through mad love.**

The reason we're doing it this week is because, in a certain sense, not to do it is deceptive. It would be deceptive because we're hiding something essential. How do we get to First Principles and First Values? Yes, we study, we integrate, we read, we engage visionary imagination. **But in order to get to First Principles and First Values,** *we must enter the Field that lives in us.*

I chant all the time, and I couldn't live without chanting, without accessing that Field. To chant, you don't need a good voice—I'm evidence of that. It's got nothing to do with a good voice. It just has to be done with an open heart, a yearning for She, a yearning for Value, madly in Love. So let's be madly in Love.

MIZMOR SHIR LE'YOM HA'SHABBAT

Mizmor shir le'yom ha'Shabbat
Tov lehodot Ladonai
Lehagid baboker chasdecha
ve-emunatcha baleylot

> *To sing a song of the Sabbath*
> *It's good to sing with God.*
> *To speak of your love in the morning*
> *and trust you through the night.*

Really, when we chant all day and all night, why would you ever want to stop?

Kant said, you can't get to the ultimate nature of Reality—the *noumena*—you can't get inside. Kant was partially right; your mind can't get inside all the way. But there are bypass roads which take you directly to noumena itself, to the numinous, to the Inside of the Inside. That's what chant is. When all the gates are closed, the gates of chant are open.

KI ATAH HU BA'AL HA-YESHUOT: FOR YOU ARE THE MASTER OF LIBERATION, FOR YOU ARE THE MASTER OF TRANSFORMATION

The second chant is: "For You are the Master of Liberation, For You are the Master of Transformation"—a translation from the original:

> *Ki Atah Hu Ba'al Ha-Yeshuot,*
> *V' Atah Hu Ba'al Ha-Nechamot*

> *For You are the Master of liberation*
> *And You are the Master of transformation*
> *For You are, Beloved, the Master of Transformation,*
> *And You are the Master of Liberation.*

The words come from the silence. So notice that the chanter also chants with their body, with their hands, because you can feel the subtle currents of Shakti—access them, reorganize them, clarify them, purify them, and open up worlds in a chant.

Here's the third chant, written by a master of mine at a place of great tragedy. **He went to this place of tragedy, and he went *inside* the tragedy**

to turn fate into destiny, to turn the tragic into the post-tragic, to turn suffering into transformation and joy.

So we'll begin slowly, and we're going to try to actually enter the Inside of the Inside and open up new gates, to reorder something, clarify, set direction, and weave the sacred power of the chant.

I want to gently invite anyone and everyone to chant wherever you are, and to find a way to the practice of chant, to access to field. Let's access the field together.

HINACH YAFAH

This next chant is a love chant from the Song of Solomon. He chants to she, and she chants to he, but not just the romantic beloved. We're madly in love. Our love lists are too short. We're Outrageous Lovers together. No person's a stranger in the world, everyone's already my beloved. Not my romantic beloved. No, it's Outrageous Love. We're friends. We're walking together. We're partners in this revolution, and we're committed together.

> *Hinach Yafah Rayati*
> *Hinach Yafah*
>
> *Behold You Are Beautiful, Beloved*
> *Behold Behold*

You feel the different quality, holy brothers and sisters, here we go. You can be wildly intellectual and wildly secular and be fully of the world and yet access the field. Because without the field… oh my God, oh my Goddess.

Sing it to someone. Look in the mirror and sing it to yourself. Feel Reality singing to you.

Behold we are beautiful together beloveds, behold, behold.

Behold means, Oh my God, wow! I'm blown away by your beauty. Behold, You are beautiful, Beloved!

RECLAIMING THE EVOLUTIONARY TECHNOLOGY OF CHANT

We're going to end with one last chant. We wanted to drop into chant this week before going deep into the Dharma.

> *We're not operating just within an analytic mind. We're operating in deep practice. In order to create a new Grammar of Value, we need to access the Eye of Value.*

We're not bypassing the mind. I sit for seventeen or eighteen hours a day and read, research, write, and teach. I'm doing everything I can with all of my power—and we're all da Vinci together—to enact and tell this new Story and to write it down in key volumes, with hundreds of pages of primary-source footnotes across the sciences.

But underneath that, where do we live? We live in the Field of Value—the interior sciences and the exterior sciences—we live in the Field of Value. **We've got to access that Field every day, again and again.** I could not live if I didn't chant, and I'd be lying to you, I'd be utterly deceptive if I told you anything else. So this is my confession.

Let's confess who we are. We are participants in the Field. She lives in us, and we live in Her. We call that Anthro-Ontology. It's a fancy name we gave it. Anthro: meaning, "within me." Ontology: meaning, the realness of Value. **The mysteries are within us; we've got to open the gate.**

So here's the last chant with your permission. It's so good to be with everyone. This is our prayer, Leonard Cohen's "Hallelujah." When Leonard Cohen is singing about the holy and the broken Hallelujah, he's actually chanting. That's why there's more covers of that song than anything else. He's not singing, he's chanting. People ask *What's Leonard Cohen doing, he's not quite singing?* No, he's chanting.

WORLD RELIGION AS A CONTEXT FOR OUR DIVERSITY

We don't need to sing it in a particular way, but *find your song*; we live our song.

We're opening all the gates. Here's the truth, and this I swear to you on my life. The chant is always there. Mozart didn't create it, he heard it.

MY UNIQUE SELF IS MY UNIQUE CHANT

There's a beautiful African tale, that when a person's born, the mothers of the tribe go to the rocks and they go to the earth—from the rocks and the earth and the sky and the ancestors—they weave together the unique melody, the unique song of that new person being born.

Because that new person being born is a new quality of intimacy.

If God is the Infinity of Intimacy, then the human being is a unique intimacy, meaning a unique God.

They weave it together.

And then when the person is born, they greet the person into the world, the boy or the girl, with their song. At every stage of the person's life, the tribe gathers and they sing their unique chant. **And if the person goes wrong, if they made a mistake or a violation, they don't punish them in this horrific way. They bring the tribe together and they sing the person their song, to call them back to their Unique Self.**

My Unique Self is my unique chant.

SAMEACH TE'SAMACH

The whole world, as they say in Aramaic, is *kol ha'olam kullo hilulah damyah*: it's all a great wedding, and we're all each other's bride and groom. We don't mean this in the romantic sense—that's a particularly gorgeous and stunning journey, if that's my journey in this lifetime, and for some of us, it is, and for some of us, it's not. That's beautiful both ways, but at some deeper level, none of us are strangers.

So I'm going to finish with this last chant that a friend heard coming down in Safed in the Sea of Galilee and then shared it with me. It's when I turn to every person in the world and say: *Oh my God, we're not strangers. We know each other. We love each other madly already. And your hurt is my hurt, and your pain is my pain, and your joy is my joy. There's no one outside the circle.*

That's *Homo amor*; that's when *Homo sapiens* becomes *Homo amor*. That's the New human and the new humanity. It means: *Oh my God, beloved. Like we were in the Garden of Eden, we love each other madly today.*

Sameach Te'Samach Reim Ahuvim,
K'Samecha'cha Ye'tzir'cha B'Gan Eden Mi'Kedem

It's true: She'll never let you down.

She'll always be there if you call Her.

CHAPTER SEVEN

THE NEW WORLD CALLS FOR A NEW WORLD RELIGION AS A CONTEXT FOR OUR GLOBAL DIVERSITY

Episode 289 — April 25, 2022

WHAT WOULD IT MEAN TO ARTICULATE A VISION OF A NEW WORLD RELIGION?

At this moment between utopia and dystopia, our intention is to come together—with such a radical joy, such a radical positivity, such a radical *knowing* that the Evolutionary Impulse quite literally beats in us, as us, and through us, which is the new knowing of our identity: *I am a personal face of the Evolutionary Impulse.*

Our intention is to step into the space in between, this time between worlds and this time between stories. In the Renaissance, the structures of the premodern traditional world were breaking down, and the most potent response was to articulate, enact, envision, and tell a new Story.

But we're very careful, and every word matters here. It's not a new Story of conjecture, not a new contrived story, not a new fairytale—a fairytale is a story that's not about

Reality, which is why it's called a fairytale—but to actually tell something far more compelling than a fairytale. We need to tell a **new Story of *Value*.**

- A new Story of God, and man and woman, and the relationship between all three.
- A new Story of gnosis—of knowing, and how we know.
- A new Story of human beauty.

In the great interior science lineage traditions of Kabbalah, and, for example, in someone like Alfred North Whitehead, beauty always means the inclusion of everything on the inside.

I'm not a big reader of Whitehead, but occasionally I'll be thinking about something or feeling into something, or deepening some version of a lineage, and I'll be perusing through Whitehead and notice that he's actually getting a sense of the same ideas. It happened to me recently, as I was preparing a talk on beauty. Just as I was falling asleep, not even reading, but kind of perusing a bunch of unlinked paragraphs in Whitehead's *Process and Reality* and *Adventures of Ideas,* I realized he gets this:

Beauty means nothing is split off. Beauty means that *it's whole*. Beauty means there's no part of us we're not intimate with, and there's no part of Reality that we're not intimate with.

Beauty is a form of intimacy in which there's the widest sense of shared identity that's possible.

If you just got those two lines, that's huge!

Beauty means the deepest intimacy. Intimacy means the widest sense of shared identity.

I'm identified with all. Nothing is split off—there's nothing split off in me, there's nothing split off between us. There are no words that can't be spoken. All words are spoken in the right way, in the right tone, at the right time, and are integrated into a larger whole. That's what beauty is.

That's what the Renaissance was all about. They wanted to generate a new possible vision of human beauty, a new vision of human truth, and a new vision of human goodness. To the extent that they were able to express that—that da Vinci was able to paint, that Marsilio Ficino was able to write, and that these thousand thinkers involved at the core of the Renaissance were able to formulate this vision of Beauty accurately, beautifully, with nothing left out—to that extent, this vision of beauty generated *the great dignities of modernity* (which Habermas speaks so beautifully about).

> *To the extent that things were left out, to the extent that things were overlooked, to the extent that there were dimensions of Reality that were split off from the larger beauty and larger vision, it turned ugly.*

That's actually what happened. What happened is that we exploded with new interior technologies at the beginning of the Renaissance:

- A new Story of God
- A new vision of the human being
- A new vision of the feminine
- A new vision of universal human rights
- A new vision of third-person scientific method

They articulated and unfolded the story of modernity—it was huge. But then we stopped. The interior technologies froze there, while the exterior technologies kept developing. We froze at this moment in modernity, in which we had this loose, ill-defined sense of what the human being was. We said: *the human being is no longer a vassal, a serf, or a slave—the human being has dignity as a separate self.* That was a huge and important revolution: *all human beings have dignity.* That's part of the third-person view: all human beings are part of the same, larger, great set. But we didn't work out the deeper structures of Value.

- Why does the human being have dignity?
- Where does that dignity derive from?
- Is Value real, or is it not real?

What modernity did is it *borrowed from the spiritual and social capital of premodernity* to assume Value, to assume that Goodness, Truth, and Beauty were real. But actually, to blur the conversation, modernity did not really look at what the *root* was, or talk about the importance of the first-person voice of the human being—to root the idea of personhood and essentially *feel* the Value.

> *Modernity borrowed from the assumptions of the spiritual and social capital of premodernity, but it didn't do its own work, so the development of interior technology stopped.*

We assumed that life, liberty, and the pursuit of happiness—as, for example, in the American founding documents—are *self-evident truths.* But by saying these truths were self-evident, we were actually ducking around something.

- Why are they self-evident?
- How do we know them?
- Where are they from?
- What's our new Story of Value?

We skipped all that. We thought that wasn't necessary. We thought we could just assume it.

We talk about this in our new vision of CosmoErotic Humanism[1] when we're talking about modernity **articulating a list of what I call "Common Sense Sacred Axioms."** We merely assume: "Wow, we have free will. Yeah, we choose. Goodness matters. Yeah, our choices matter." In other words, we made all these assumptions about virtue and what it means to be a good person, but they were really drawn from premodernity. We then universalized them in modernity, but we didn't actually root them in real thinking, real heart, real knowing, or real value.

In the deep writings of modernity, for example, David Hume says something like: "Value is not really real, we're really making it up. We don't really have a ground for it. But that's okay, we'll just put that in the space. Everyone just kind of assumes that's true, so it's okay." If you think I'm exaggerating, I'm not. In other words, we avoided all the real issues about God, about Divinity, about human beings, about whether love or value is real. We said, "You know what? We're going to bypass all that stuff."

But it didn't work. Along came postmodernity, and postmodernity said: "Actually, if you read the last 200 years of the best thought, Value is *not* actually real. It's actually made up. The Good, the True, and the Beautiful are not actually real. All we really have is everyone's individual perspective and nothing else." **So Value collapsed, and we found ourselves in a world in which there was no longer a shared Story of Value.** The assumed story, which bypassed the real conversations and the real hard work, that dominated modernity fell apart. Postmodernity pointed out all the flaws of that story, and at the very center of society, there was a collapse of Value.

We are on day seventy-two of the war in Ukraine. This war should not be happening. The reason the war in the Ukraine is happening is because, since modernity didn't establish a shared ground of Value, what you have is all these attempts to create visions of pseudo-value. Ethnocentric pride in Mother Russia and the intrinsic rights of Mother Russia are a grab at value,

---

1 David J. Temple, *First Principles and First Values: Forty-Two Propositions on CosmoErotic Humanism, the Meta-Crisis and the World to Come* (World Philosophy and Religion Press, 2024).

a claim for a certain kind of ethnocentric value. *We've got to have some value, so our value is going to be Mother Russia.*

But there's no objective standard of Value by which we can actually hold Putin responsible in any way, because there's no universal ground of Value that exists between the nations.

We're going to look at what it would actually mean to create a *new vision of Value* in the world, articulated for the first time in world history—not just pseudo-value, amorphic, flaccid, wimpy, lacking potency, and full of New Age sweetness. That's not going to get us home.

What would it mean to truly articulate a vision of a new world religion? That's the question we're asking here.

A COLLAPSE OF VALUE IS A COLLAPSE OF EROS

So what do we have to do? We're at a moment in which there's a collapse of Value at the very center of society. Whenever you have a collapse of Value, you've got a collapse of Eros, because Eros and Value are intrinsically related.

> *What's Eros? Eros is the aliveness of Cosmos that's filled with Value.*

When you don't live in Eros—when you don't live in the fullness of Eros, when you're not part of the movement of Eros, when you don't feel the Eros of Cosmos alive in you—then it breaks down. You're lost in the emptiness. You're not filled with Value. We are not filled with Value. When we don't have Eros, we don't have Value, so what replaces it? What replaces it always is pseudo-eros. When we don't have Eros, we always have pseudo-eros. When we don't have Value, we have pseudo-value. That's step one.

IN THE ABSENCE OF A GENUINE STORY OF VALUE, HUMANS CREATE PSEUDO-STORIES OF VALUE

Now let's take the next step. What is pseudo-value? What is pseudo-eros? Pseudo-value and pseudo-eros are attempts to cover up the emptiness when there's no real Value and there's no real Eros. So what would be an expression of pseudo-eros and pseudo-value?

First, real Eros and Value means there's a real Story of Value. It means Cosmos has a real Story of Value, and that *I'm part of that Story; I participate in the Story of Value of Cosmos.* Cosmos actually has direction. It has purpose, intrinsic meaning.

If we don't have that—purpose, Eros, intrinsic meaning, real Value—we get pseudo-eros, we get pseudo-value, and we get pseudo-meaning.

What is the primary example of pseudo-eros, pseudo-value, pseudo-meaning—or said differently, a pseudo-story of value—that dominates Reality at this moment in time, all over the world? It drives Putin. In different ways, it drives the United States. It drives Europe. It drives Asia. What is it? It's another story, what we're going to call the *success story*. The success story is: "The world is dominated by rivalrous conflict, governed by win/lose metrics. Power means winning in rivalrous conflict that's governed by win/lose metrics; there's a winner and a loser. The winner is successful, and the loser is not."

This pervasive, pseudo-erotic idea of rivalrous conflict—whether it's in the basic structures of economics, whether it's in politics, whether it's between sports teams, whether it's between divisions in companies, whether it's between people in a family system—that idea drives the story, drives society.

A couple years ago, I was talking with my friend, Dick Schwartz, who created something called Internal Family Systems, who's been on our Board for the last bunch of years. We were talking about the fact that in a family system, the real hidden structure is rivalrous conflict. There's rivalrous conflict between the people in the family, and unless you can introduce Eros into the family system—something deeper than rivalrous conflict, a deeper story of Value—the family collapses.

All systems collapse if they're driven by rivalrous conflict.

Now what have we done?

> ## *We've removed the Eros from Reality, meaning we've removed the Value from Reality.*

We've stepped out of the Field of Value—although you can never *really* step out of the Field of Value. Rather, we *experience* ourselves as having stepped out of the Field of Value. In the Field of Value, there's purpose, and there's meaning, and there's direction. But we've stepped out of that Field of Value. We've stepped out of it for some really good reasons, but let's bracket that for a second.

We can't remain in a place where "we've stepped out"—we simply can't live that way for long. Human beings can't live without a story. It's one of the ways we know Story is real, that Story is part of the ontology of Reality. You can't live without being part of a Story of Value.

So if I'm not in a real Story of Value, if I can't find a real Story of Value, what am I going to do? I'm going to make up a story about it; I'm going to create a pseudo-story of value.

That's what Foucault meant when he said it's all a drive for power. Without a real sense of value, we're making up stories of value that are not real because all we really have left is rivalrous conflict based on win/lose metrics.

EXISTENTIAL RISK IS A DIRECT RESULT OF PSEUDO-STORIES OF VALUE

I want to put one last thing on the table. There are eleven forms of existential risk—we've been using that word for a decade here. Existential risk means we're rapidly getting to a point where there's not actually going to *be* a future.

It's not just *catastrophic* risk—it's *existential* risk, meaning there won't be a future; we're going to actually self-terminate. Because of the growth curves, driven by exponential technology, which are governed by a race to the bottom by the tragedy of the commons and multipolar traps—meaning, there's highly dangerous weaponized technologies of multiple forms, but no one can afford *not* to develop them because you're afraid that the other guy will.

These exponentially proliferating technologies are being developed right now at breakneck speed, particularly in the realms of artificial intelligence—I think the biggest dangers are in those realms—which have the capacity to terminate human existence on the planet. Yet the technologies are being developed anyway because of the multipolar trap, that fear that somebody else might develop it. The reason someone else will develop it is because the only story we have is a pseudo-eros story: "The success story: rivalrous conflict governed by win/lose metrics."

As long as that's my identity, I'm going to fulfill my identity. In the success story, my identity is: *I've got to be more powerful, I've got to be more successful, I've got to accumulate more wealth, I've got to accumulate more status.*

There's no other identity that I live in. As long as that's my only identity, as an individual or as a collective, I won't be able to ignore the invitation to develop exponential weaponized technology. Since I think you certainly will, and then I'm going to have to. The entire system is governed by this pseudo-story of value, rivalrous conflict governed by win/lose metrics. That's the entire system.

So if we don't replace this with a new Story of Value, we're gone. End game!

TRIALECTICS OF RELIGION: WE NEED TO TRANSCEND AND INCLUDE THE PREMODERN AND MODERN

The truth is that every society has always had some version of a Story of Value that challenged power. Even when that story was corrupt, it still held society somewhat in check. That countervailing force was often called Spirit and was formalized in something called religion. Now, I'm obviously completely aware that religion was hijacked in a thousand ways. **But in its ideal form, religion was meant to be a system of Value that guides power.**

Religion is meant to be an interior technology that guides the deployment of the artifacts of politics, the artifacts of public power, and the artifacts of external power. Clearly, religion got hijacked by power. Clearly, religion got degraded and corrupted in a thousand different ways.

But the idea was that it functioned as a balancing force. And it functioned this way, to some extent, in premodernity.

Religion formed a system of Value that was beyond rivalrous conflict governed by win/lose metrics.

Religion was in the public space, and in some sense it did create a balancing force, although insufficiently so. Religion became *ethnocentric*. It was hijacked by particular kingdoms, by particular ethnocentric groups; it was co-opted and bound by local power structures. Yes, that's all true. But the idea, which was always half-fulfilled, was that religion would be a structure within the state, within the local domain, that would guide us in the right direction.

Then religion collapses, for all the reasons of corruption:

- It collapses because it overreaches.

- It collapses because it claimed to know things that it didn't know.
- It collapses because it tries to control the sciences, and tries to stop the flow of knowledge and creativity.
- It collapses because it became drunk with power.

That's all true. Premodern religion collapses, and then we head into modernity. Let's take a look at it—it always comes in three levels. Step one, premodernity: religion. Step two, modernity: no religion. Now when I say *no religion*, it doesn't mean religion disappeared. It doesn't mean religion doesn't exist, but rather that religion moves from the center of culture to the sidelines.

God is no longer at the center of culture.

The priest is no longer at the center of culture.

Religious doctrine is no longer at the center of culture.

In modernity, the notion of science—the human being, third-person information, knowledge—moves to the center. It's a fantastic progression! So again, step one: religion. Step two: no religion.

But in this no-religion space, exterior technology started exploding exponentially. **Now, in the absence of a guiding Story of Value—of devotion, worship of God, self-transformation, the cultivation of virtue, the development of the ethical, spiritual self—in the absence of this Story, we created a new pseudo-story of value: the success story.** And that success story now drives all exterior technologies.

Interior technologies freeze at the beginning of modernity, and exterior technologies go wild. In that gap, existential risk is created.

Level two is: no religion, an absence of stories of intrinsic value. Here's level three—because *She comes in threes*, it's always threes, it's always a tripartite structure. In this new Story of Value we call CosmoErotic Humanism—it's always trialectics, which means *She comes in threes*. Religion, no religion, religion. Level three has to be religion again.

But level three can't be level-one religion—it can't be dogmatic religion, it can't be religion hijacked for power, it can't be ethnocentric. It can't be any of the things that the old religion was, *and* it's got to be something new. It has to transcend and include the best insights of premodernity (the old religion) and of the modernity that rejected religion. Those two sets of insights need to be integrated. We negate—as Hegel said—all the bad stuff, while we preserve all the good stuff, as we create something new.

That's the new religion.

THE NEW WORLD RELIGION CAN'T BE LOCAL, AND COMPASSION AND KINDNESS ARE NOT ENOUGH

The new religion can't be local. It has got to be a religion of universal compassion and kindness, but that's not enough. The premodern religions also said they were religions of compassion and kindness, and modernity said they were all about compassion and kindness—so we need to do more than that. We need to establish Value. How do we establish Value? Compassion and kindness are values. How do I establish compassion and kindness as values, and what do those mean?

This is a story I know personally: Putin comes to Israel and finds his third-grade teacher, and he has total compassion that she has no money, and he wants to be kind to her, so he buys her an apartment. That's compassion and kindness, but it's insufficient. Rather: **We need a set of First Principles and First Values that establish what compassion fundamentally is, what kindness fundamentally is, and how we unfold them.**

We've got to move from ethnocentric compassion to a larger universal vision of compassion. We've got to know what that means, though. Let's call it Eros. Let's call it Love. What does kindness mean, and who's in the circle of kindness? We need to articulate a new religion which is not a local religion but a world religion.

A SHARED WORLD NEEDS A WORLD RELIGION

What we're working on here together is, how do we articulate a set of First Principles and First Values that are binding, that will be recognized by everybody in the world, that will be actually self-evidently true? But we can't just *say* they're self-evidently true. We've got to say *why* they're self-evidently true.

> *It's only a world religion that's going to stand against win/lose metrics.*

It's only a world religion that's going to say *no* to win/lose metrics, *no* to pseudo-eros, *no* to no Story of Value, *no* to rivalrous conflict based on win/lose metrics. There's a bigger and wider story, and it's only that wider story that's going to stand against a global technocracy, which upgrades algorithms and downgrades human beings—which is where we're going.

I was talking to a young friend of mine who's working in blockchain. He's a beautiful young man, and it's fantastic that we're talking. All of his peers of the same age are getting absorbed into blockchain.

So what's all their energy about? How to succeed in blockchain to please Mom and Dad, to be successful, to make a salary, to get kudos for making a salary, and to be rewarded in the system of success story. If you're not talking about a wider frame of Value, and you're stuck in that success story, then all you want to do is succeed in that success story, and you spend virtually all of your time and energy succeeding. You spend all of your energy, let's say, in perpetuating a blockchain—which the way it's going now is going to become another tool for rivalrous conflict, leading to more disaster. You get completely caught up in that system because that's your system, the story you're living in.

BUILDING A FOUNDATIONAL FRAMEWORK OF FIRST PRINCIPLES AND FIRST VALUES

We've got to create a *better* Story of Value, and that better Story of Value has to be rooted in First Principles and First Values. But we can't just *declare* them—we've got to show *how* you get there and *how* you actually establish them.

I know this deep dive in First Principles and First Values is not easy. It takes thinking. This is not easy to follow. If we say, *let's talk about loneliness, let's talk about sexuality, let's talk about gender*, these are great and important topics. I've spent my life talking about them and trying to innovate on them. But now we're doing something harder. We're saying: can we go for the framework itself? Can we access the source code? Can we go to the *foundations*?

We want to do foundations together. I want to talk about the *method* to articulate a set of First Principles and First Values.

I want to begin with: why have First Values and First Principles been attacked? Because we can't be naive. We can't get lost in our bubble and say, let's just declare First Principles and First Values.

There are good reasons why the notion of universal First Principles and First Values was decimated. I want to understand that with you together. Let's understand why they were rejected. Let's respond to the reasons they were rejected, and then steelman those reasons. Let's show why there are powerful reasons to reject them, and then show why, in the end, they're not valid.

I think we can respond to the critiques—definitively and powerfully—in a way that hasn't happened yet in the universities, which are twenty-five years behind on this.

WORLD RELIGION AS A CONTEXT FOR OUR DIVERSITY

We can show that it is completely possible to articulate universal sets of First Principles and First Values that are real.

We're not only going to talk about it; we're going to actually *do* it. We're making the revolution, and we're going to do it here together. That's our frame.

SPIRITUALITY WITHOUT RELIGION IS NOT ENOUGH

A world religion requires prayer. **You can't have a real religion without prayer.** However, prayer is not going to mean what it meant at level-one religion. Let's say level one is premodernity, the traditional period up to the Renaissance.

Then level two is no religion—modernity. Now there's a lot of ways to say no religion. For example, in the United States in the last thirty years, the most common self-identification for the younger generation is "spiritual but not religious." That's a version of no religion. We're going to talk about why that's insufficient. It's too wishy-washy. It's non-binding. There's no sense of obligation. There's no sense of intrinsic value. It doesn't take you home. That's level two: no religion, spiritual but not religious. "I do yoga, I do therapy, and I live my life—and I keep doing yoga and therapy as the Ukraine war is happening. I live my life. I'm in a very egocentric bubble. It's about me, it's about my transformation." It's a form of spiritual materialism.

I may pray for my own businesses to be successful. But I'm living in a global world where I'm affected by everything. I'm actually parasitizing off the world in my little spiritual-but-not-religious bubble—I'm not actually a citizen of the world.

- I don't feel evolution moving through me.
- I don't feel like I'm participating in Cosmos.

- I'm not omni-considerate for the whole.
- I'm not taking the whole into account.

I'm in this very narrow bubble, living my own spiritual life, reading some sacred texts if I'm really sophisticated, doing my yoga, going to retreats, healing my wounds, working on my trauma, etc.

We live in a world in which the entire world is interconnected today, but I'm actually not part of that interconnection in any real way. I'm not part of the Unique Self Symphony that's part of the healing of Reality. I'm in this very limited, separate self, spiritual identity that's spiritual but not religious—and there are lots of versions of that in modernity. So there's this "no religion" moment.

Then, level three, now we've got to claim religion again—*She comes in threes.* "Trialectics." So level three is: *Whoa, this is not working! When we removed the Eros of a world Story of Value, we were left with pseudo-eros. Pseudo-eros became a rivalrous-conflict success story, governed by win/lose metrics. That leads us directly off the freakin' cliff! Exponential growth curves driven by exponential technologies, race to the bottom, tragedy of the commons, multipolar traps.*

That's the meta-crisis. The meta-crisis means that we don't have interior technologies to govern our exterior technologies, and our exterior technologies are going to destroy us imminently.

NEW LIFE CONDITIONS DEMAND A NEW LANGUAGE OF VALUE

Said simply, *we don't have a Story equal to our power.* **When we don't have a Story equal to our power, our power literally destroys us, at this moment in history where our power is exponential.**

Those sentences are critical. We don't have a story equal to our power. Our power is exponential. It drives us off the cliff of exponential growth curves, which are driven by this race to the bottom based on win/lose metrics.

In other words, there are new life conditions. New life conditions means, thirty years ago, we could afford to go spiritual but not religious. Thirty years ago, our friend Jerry created Shalom Mountain and said, "Let's work with our trauma." That was a great idea at the time. We could have these principles of love that were basically about how we relate to each other as individuals working with our trauma, and we can do these circles of healing. That's fantastic, and those should continue—they're wonderful and important and critical and gorgeous.

But thirty years later, there are new life conditions:

- We're part of a whole that's inescapable, and we're living in the unbearable intimacy of that wholeness. There's no place to hide. There's no place to go.
- We're collapsing Value and colliding into each other.
- Small groups of people can destroy the planet using exponential technologies.

There's a list of crises—from climate change, to AI, to the gap between haves and have-nots, a long list that we've talked about many times before—all of which places us in this very unbearably intimate, small planet. If we don't create a new common language between us, we're destroyed. Those are the new life conditions. Wow!

> *These new life conditions demand a new shared language of Value. That's what we mean by a world religion—it's not just a world spirituality.*

When I started working with my friend Ken Wilber in 2010, we started the Center for World Spirituality to address the issue we're talking about right now. We called it world spirituality, not world religion because the word religion was just too threatening. By world spirituality, though, we meant not spiritual but not religious, but rather a trans-lineage vision, in which we took the best elements of all the great lineages, and we integrated them into a new whole. However, we hadn't yet articulated the notion that we can't do that unless we have shared First Principles and First Values.

We need to take all the lineages of knowing—the lineages of premodernity (of the great traditions), the lineages of modernity (of science and psychology), the lineages of postmodernity (of history and how history develops, and how social constructions happen). **If we link the true gnosis and validated insights from all the lineages of knowing together into a larger whole, we will give rise to a new Story of Value rooted in First Principles and First Values.**

We can't do that by making New Age declarations, and we can't do it by writing academic papers—yes, we need great academic writing, *and* we need great writing and thinking that is not in a narrow academic form but which is also not pop. In essence: **We need to articulate the core propositions of Value in a way that they become so self-evident and so true that they become widely adopted.**

"UNTIL PHILOSOPHERS ARE KINGS... CITIES WILL NEVER HAVE REST FROM THEIR EVILS" —PLATO

In order to do that, we *need institutional power*, meaning, we need *funding*, we need *resources*, we need *research*. We need to be able to deliver these memes. We can't just stand in a little corner and say, "We're going to mystically do this."

Yes, there's great value to having a mystical society, and we're a mystical society together. The Center for World Philosophy and Religion, One Mountain, Many Paths—we're a mystical society. We're a group of people in this new Renaissance that we're trying to articulate, and we're connected to each other. We're a band of Outrageous Lovers, and we're functioning as a mystical society. That's true, and that's beautiful.

But then we have to translate the mystical society. As Plato said, we have to become not only philosophers but also philosopher kings.[2]

> *We have to generate the resources to deliver this into the source code of society, and then we step aside and give up power.*

In other words, we don't hold on to power. **We create the codes, we create the documents, we create the structures that can hold and deliver this into society, and then we step back.** We do that because the principles and values that we're articulating *require* us to step back. Then leadership moves from generation to generation, and we're held together by this *evolving* vision of Value. It can't be fixed or frozen—it's an evolving vision of Value.

POWERFULLY ADDRESSING THE RIGOROUS CRITIQUES OF VALUE

We're going to show how to articulate a universal grammar of value. We're going to go into the laboratory together, not just talk about it.

- We're literally going to enact together the beginnings of a universal grammar of value, and we're going to *show* how we do it. What's the secret sauce? How is it done methodologically?
- We're going to see what are the challenges to Value, and we're going to go *do* it together.

This world religion topic is explosive. It's a slippery slope—and we have to get it right. But again, why do we need to do this? Because there are new life conditions, we can't afford *not* to do it. We need a world religion, and the code below is an example of a new world religion text:

---

[2] "Until philosophers are kings, or the kings and princes of this world have the spirit and power of philosophy, and political greatness and wisdom meet in one, and those commoner natures who pursue either to the exclusion of the other are compelled to stand aside, cities will never have rest from their evils." – Plato, *The Republic*

The God you don't believe in does not exist.

God is not only as She has been described by the great traditions, the Infinity of Power, but more profoundly: the Infinity of Intimacy.

God is the Infinity of Intimacy desiring finitude.

Prayer is intimate communion between the Divine and human.

It is true that human beings participate in Divinity. This is the first person of the Divine that lives as us.

It is no less true that we are held by Divinity in every moment. Every time we fall, we fall into She. This is the second person of the Divine.

Prayer is intimate communion between the Infinity of Intimacy and the intimacy of finitude.

Finally, Divinity is the force of Eros always seeking deeper coherence and wider intimacies, from quarks to culture and beyond. This is the third person of Divinity.

Of course there have been people before who have said, "Let's affirm universal value. Let's learn from the Universalists who came before us."

The weakness is that these universal claims were deeply criticized by very rigorous philosophy, and ninety-nine percent of the time, they didn't respond to those criticisms, so they were dismissed.

They became the province of folk intuition, folk religion, New Age, or whatever it is, but they weren't taken seriously, so they can't be the ground of a shared grammar of value. **We have to take seriously the rigorous critiques of Value *and* the idea of creating a universal grammar of value.**

I think we can do that very powerfully. We have to do that, and from there, we articulate the source of this universal grammar of value.

Ten years ago, when we started the Center for World Spirituality, I coined this term *dual citizen*. That's what I meant when I said that a *world religion is a context for our diversity*, so that all the religions continue to exist, they continue to make their contribution, but **there's also a recognition that there's a shared grammar of Value, that we can articulate what it is, and we can express why it's binding.**

For example, this means that the Russian Orthodox Church in Russia, the Catholic Church in America, and the Sunni Muslim church in Syria all have to relate to this world religion. We can't use religion as a fig leaf for power, or as a fig leaf for evil, which is what we're seeing tragically. It's tragic beyond imagination to see how Islam, in its beauty, has been radicalized for power, to see how the Russian Orthodox Church has been radicalized for power, to see how over 400 years of European history Christianity was radicalized for power, serving motives that violate Eros and violate Love, that violate Goodness, Truth, and Beauty.

We need to come to this new place, level three, where we articulate that *something new is happening.*

Now, is this possible or impossible to do? It's completely possible, and it hasn't been done! So you ask: how could it even be possible? Well, we're going to do it here. I know that there's this big part of you that says: I don't believe you, this is just Marc grandstanding. No, this is actually how it happens. It's not going to happen in the classical universities. I did my doctorate at Oxford.

Universities are run by success stories, driven by rivalrous conflict, governed by win/lose metrics.

Science today is driven by success stories, governed by rivalrous conflict, governed by win/lose metrics. Today, science and the academies of learning have been completely hijacked by the success story on multiple levels.

We can't rely on the old Church or on the new university to do this for us.

It's going to happen on the fringes where groups of people come together, people who are fiercely committed, who are holding a *purity* in their hearts, a kind of *second innocence,* people who are going to take everything they have—their minds, their hearts, their bodies—and take a *stand* for this possibility, and articulate it in the *deepest*, most *beautiful*, and most *profound* way it can be articulated, using all the best methods. That's us, and of course, we have partners around the world.

However, beware of knee-jerk humility. It's very easy to look away and say: No, this couldn't be on us to do.

Could this be on us to do? Could that be possible? We don't want it to be on us. We don't want it to be on us because it's too much responsibility. But this is on us to do! And we're not going to do it ourselves. Once we articulate this and put it into the world, I think it's going to catch like wildfire. But this next step is on us now. It's on us to get this right. **And remember: joy and responsibility go together.**

I was just going to write an email to a young friend of mine in England, about the necessity of having a beautiful paper comparing CosmoErotic Humanism to Schelling, for example. I was just thinking in my mind how that paper is going to ricochet to that article, which is going to ricochet to that, which is going to ricochet to that, and then the whole system is going to come together, and it's going to explode. But everyone has their unique piece to do, their unique gift to offer.

So here's our practice, and we're going to just conclude with this. I want to ask everyone, *what's yours to do?*

What's yours specifically to do that requires *heart* and *resources* and *time?*

What's something that's *hard*, that *challenges your comfort zone?*

Something that doesn't fit into, *this is part of my personal therapy, my journey, my trauma.* No, what's yours to do that's a *gift*? It's not self-help, which says, "What can I get out of it?"

It's *transformation*, which asks, "What can I pour into it?" **What's yours to do as an Evolutionary Unique Self?**

That's the invitation! So I just want to ask you that question gently: What's yours to do, and what's the unique risk you need to take to do it? What's yours to do that gives up ego for a moment and just says: "Oh my God, I am *lived as*, and *I am Outrageous Love*, and I'm going to blow this open outrageously."

What's yours to do? So let's hold hands, and let's do this together.

With joy.

CHAPTER EIGHT

TAKING THE NEXT STEP IN THE URGENT NEED FOR A NEW WORLD RELIGION: CELEBRATING BARBARA MARX HUBBARD

Episode 290 — May 1, 2022

A SHARED GRAMMAR OF VALUE FOR A GLOBAL CONVERSATION

Where are we? We're in One Mountain, Many Paths. What is this place? It's a place of realization. It's a place of rapture. It's a place of revolution. That is to say, we're interested in the biggest possible picture of the widest possible vision of who we are, where we are, and what needs to be done. We locate ourselves in the stream of time. We're omni-considerate for the sake of the whole. **We feel the whole moving in us, as it moves through time. We survey all of the past in an encompassing glance, the sweep of history, and understand how we got here. Then we can access a memory of possible futures.**

When we access that memory of possible futures, we realize that we are literally poised between utopia and dystopia. We realize that we're literally—in Hebrew we would say *mamash*—at a time between worlds; we're at a time between stories. One very potent and real possibility is that there actually won't be a future as we know it.

The choice space we're in requires such depth and such wisdom, while our exterior technologies are exponentially growing—and they're clearly not governed by a shared grammar or language of Value.

Those exterior technologies are being weaponized. They're all being developed, even when they're wildly dangerous, because there's what we call a multipolar trap or a tragedy of the commons or a race to the bottom. That is to say, *I'm afraid someone else is going to develop it so I have to*. Rogue, non-state actors developing exponential weaponized technologies across a series of platforms are but one expression, though a main one, of about ten different existential and catastrophic risks that can eliminate the future as we know it, in a relatively short period of time.

Now, when I say that everyone just keeps listening. *Oh right, what are we going to talk about today?* Meaning, it's very hard to take that in. **It's the move from the pre-tragic to the tragic. But we don't remain in the tragic, we go to the post-tragic. But we can't go to the post-tragic until we actually get the tragic.**

Often when I talk to people there's this sense that, *this is something that we do*—but we don't fully get it. It literally depends on us. This is ours to do.

You've got to take the tragic deep into your heart, and from there, step into the post-tragic. The post-tragic comes from the realization that we're not just poised or looming above an abyss of dystopia, which lurks right behind the facade of the ordinary and the everyday. We're also invited by the great ocean of utopia.

There's a possibility, and God is nothing if not the Possibility of Possibility.

The same energy that animated the Big Bang, the same energy that generated the first nanoseconds in which Reality moves from the unmanifest to the manifest—that same energy lives in us. We are the possibility of possibility, and we can create a new future. We can actually access a memory of the future that's more Beautiful, more Good, and more True than we ever imagined possible. Yes, we can!

We get to be excited about it—and not because we're dreamers. It's because Reality dreams, because Reality dreams the Possibility of Possibility. Of course we can.

But this sense of *yes we can* does not come from the pre-tragic. It means that *we've actually taken the tragic in*, and then from that place of seeing the tragic, we then move to the post-tragic.

Throughout history, what consistently changes the vector of history is a new Story of Value based on First Principles and First Values. That's what we're about. That is actually another name for the possibility of a world religion.

But again, watch how the word "religion" sits hard in our bodies. *Ugh, world religion!* Well, you're right: it should sit hard. Religion got hijacked. Religion got corrupted. Religion got degraded. The answer is not to reject it. Instead:

- We need to evolve religion.
- Religion is not monological. It doesn't just speak to us; we participate in creating it.
- It's not one religion in the sense that "everyone's doing the same thing"—it's one context. It's a shared grammar of value. It's a world religion that's a context for our diversity, which is for a hundred religions, but there has to be a shared context.

This is a First Principle and First Value of Reality: we're both the same, and we're unique. We share an enormous amount, so we're the same—ninety-nine percent of our bodies are the same, but then there's this one percent which is radically unique. We need to create the context for our diversity, the shared grammar of Value.

It's only a shared grammar of Value that allows us to have a global conversation.

When there's no shared grammar of Value, then there's no conversation between Russia and China and Bulgaria, between the United States and Canada and Asia. So we're all in this unbearable intimacy, colliding into each other on a planet with rapidly developing exponential technologies, with no possibility of engaging in the most fundamental human act, which is conversation.

WE LIVE IN A CONVERSATIONAL COSMOS

Conversation is the essential mode of Reality. Reality is made up of conversations. The fundamental monad of Reality is conversation. Or said differently, we live in a conversational Cosmos.

The conversation begins in the first nanoseconds of the Big Bang. There's a conversation that takes place between quarks. Three quarks come together. The reason that remains and doesn't disappear in the first nanoseconds of the Big Bang is because there are protocols for conversation between quarks—there's a shared Value structure between quarks that allows for quarks to exist.

Then when subatomic particles come together to create a new whole, which is an atom, which is a new intimacy and a new shared identity, it's because those subatomic particles are talking to each other. Literally, by any definition of conversation, they're exchanging information. They have a shared syntax of meaning.

Of course, conversation evolves. It's not that our conversations are the same as the conversations between subatomic particles; they're not—but there's continuity and discontinuity. It's a conversational Cosmos. So we need to evolve the conversation. In other words, just like subatomic particles need a shared syntax, shared nouns, and shared dangling modifiers, as well as shared verbs and pronouns, we need a shared grammar of value as the syntax for our conversation.

Paradoxically, just like the world could not exist if atoms couldn't come together and create the possibility of a shared conversation, we've now again come to that moment where the micro and the macro meet, in which we're colliding into each other, like in the first moments of the Big Bang. In this unbearable intimacy, we are unpacking or allowing this unconsciously; it's just happening. There's this massive gap from our exterior technologies, which are exponentially self-replicating, following the dictate of win/lose metrics: create, create, create—but create because "we're funded by people and systems who are driven by win/lose metrics."

We create, create, create. We exponentialize and weaponize. Then there's this huge gap between these exterior technologies and our interior technologies. Our interior technologies means the Value structure and the syntaxes of our conversation.

Currently, we can't have a conversation. We don't even know what peace means. We don't know what wholeness means. We can't just use words—we have to know what they mean and why they're rooted in the structure of Value. We've got to create a shared grammar of Value.

That's what we mean by a world religion.

A world religion is the new emergence.
It's the possibility of possibility.

When we started One Mountain, Many Paths, we realized that we need to start it not with a "war room," but with a "peace room." A peace room needs all of the energy of a war room, all of the energy of radical presence, full on focus, complete willingness to lay my life down for this, to create this possibility and create this future. Knowing that it depends on us that we need to do it. That was the energy which began One Mountain, Many Paths.

We have to clearly articulate together the tenets of what it means to create a new religion. What does and doesn't it include? What are the safeguards?

We're going to be unpacking together the pieces of what might a world religion look like in this revolutionary moment, and why it's such an essential and radical necessity. I want to share with you the fragrance of these early conversations that Barbara and I had about all of this.

EVOLUTIONARY LOVE CODE: NEW NEED GENERATES NEW EMERGENCE

God is the Possibility of Possibility.

God is the Real. Reality itself is the Possibility of Possibility.

Religion means *religare*: to reconnect with Reality.

The new world religion we are articulating is a new emergent in Reality, an expression of the Possibility of Possibility.

New life conditions generate new emergence. New need generates new emergence.

World religion as a context for our diversity is a new divine emergent, a new quality of the Real and an urgent joy, a necessary response to the new life conditions of global catastrophic and existential risk.

God is the Possibility of Possibility—that's the Real. The Real is not just *being*. It's not just that *I'm being*, or just awareness. I'm not just consciousness. I am that, of course. **I am consciousness. I am being. But I'm** *evolving* **being. I am moving. I'm dynamic.** We can't ignore this.

> *The greatest slave driver in the world is the belief that yesterday determines today.*

Evolution is the structure of Reality itself. It's Reality's dangerous idea. Religion is *religare*: to reconnect with the Real. A world religion needs to be an evolutionary religion, a new emerging Reality, an expression of the Possibility of Possibility. The possibility of a world religion until recently—

say, 200 or 300 years ago—meant that *one nation conquers everyone else and imposes their religion in a totalitarian way on everyone else.* That was the only possibility of a world religion 500 years ago. We couldn't imagine anything different.

Today, we have this new possibility of a world religion that can include everyone. It can include the future Putin so that they won't become future Putins. It can include Biden. **World religion can include those people who would have become terrible expressions of humanity. The reason they could become terrible expressions of humanity is because they feel the world is nihilistic; they feel there's no fundamental structure of Value, that there's nothing intrinsic.** They feel it's all a realpolitik play of power—because no one has presented them with a theory of Value that says that *Value is real.*

Someone wrote me this week, essentially challenging this, saying: "Hey, dude. Why are you talking about Value? Value is completely made up. Value is not a molecule, it's not an atom, you can't measure it. You can't test it in the laboratory. You're just making it up." I love that challenge. It's important, and it's exactly wrong—because we're not just making it up.

How do we know Value? How do we determine Value? Where does Value come from? Why is Value not imposed but emerges from us? How does it allow for such huge diversity? It is a context for our diversity, without which Reality stops being meaningful in its very essence—we stop being motivated, and our aliveness dissipates and disappears. That's what we mean by a world religion, we mean a shared conversation in the world. This is a new possibility; this is a conversation that wasn't possible before.

A couple who has been in a relationship for some time are having new conversations, because they've been in relationship for X amount of time. There were conversations they couldn't have had two or three months ago, and now there's new conversations they can have because there's a new emergence, a new possibility. Love evolves, that's the wonder of love. The wonder of intimacy is you don't ever exhaust intimacy.

Krishna and Radha, or the great God Rama and Sita, never say something like, "We're as intimate as we could possibly ever be." No, not even close. **Intimacy is infinite, and we can always go deeper and deeper; we are constantly evolving intimacy.**

We evolve love by deepening the conversations that take place between us. New life conditions generate new emergence, which means that we can have new conversations. How is this possible?

We have new conversations when there's a new need—need generates new emergence.

World religion is a new conversation; we're in a new conversation. We've got to be open to the conversation. We've got to define the conversation together. **World religion as a context for our diversity** is a new divine emergent, a new quality of the Real—an urgent joy, a necessity, and a response to the new life conditions of global catastrophic and existential risks, which require this new conversation in order to respond to them.

A PLANETARY AWAKENING IN UNIQUE SELF SYMPHONIES

One of the key ideas that Barbara and I talked about all the time is what we called together a Planetary Awakening in Unique Self Symphonies. If we use the old language, it's a kind of planetary Pentecost. I called Barbara in the middle of a very hard moment in 2016. I said, let's start a church, a synagogue, a mosque. She said, "No, we're past religion." We spent like half the night talking, and we realized **we need to reclaim church, and we need to reclaim synagogue, and we need to reclaim mosque, but in a new form.**

We've been moving in that direction in fits and starts since then. We called it originally The Church of Evolutionary Love, and then we renamed it One Mountain, Many Paths.

It's the emergence of a Unique Self Symphony, where we each are voices of prophecy, speaking from a shared syntax and a shared conversation. It's a shared conversation as a context for our diversity, for our irreducible, gorgeous uniqueness. That shared conversation is going to allow us to heal the sick and to end disease, and to establish freedom, and to create a new life and a better tomorrow.

Yes, it's messianic. But messianic means the possibility of a New Human and a New Humanity. It counterposes and countervails Armageddon, which is existential risk and catastrophic risk.

The urgent life conditions of this moment demand this emergence. The promise will be kept!

CHAPTER NINE

SEDUCING HOMO SAPIENS INTO HOMO AMOR: THE MORAL OBLIGATION OF A NEW WORLD RELIGION

Episode 292 — May 15, 2022

THE ROOT CAUSE OF EXISTENTIAL RISK IS A GLOBAL INTIMACY DISORDER

Imagine that you have a world religion—you don't lose all the other religions. A world religion means you have a basic shared score; you've got some basic core ideas which are First Principles and First Values. Then each religion weaves them together in a particular way, but there's a shared universal grammar of value. That is the only response we have today to existential risk, which means no future.

That's a very, very big deal. Existential risk means there's no future.

We've diagnosed this carefully here in One Mountain, at the Center for Integral Wisdom, the Office for the Future, and the Foundation for Conscious Evolution, which is the set of institutions that are all interlinked, that we're all part of.

What we've very clearly understood is that there are two generator functions of existential risk. Win/lose metrics, which is the failed story that everybody lives in, which has caused an extraction model, multipolar traps, a race to the bottom, and the tragedy of the commons. It has caused people to develop exponential weaponized technologies that are owned and directed by rogue players and non-state actors, that causes the inability to monitor in any way and control the gap between the haves and the have-nots, the inability to actually direct AI where it needs to go, etc., which then generates fragile systems.

Those are the two generator functions of existential risk: rivalrous conflict based on win/lose metrics, and fragile systems that are dissociated from each other that fall apart.

But underneath those two generator functions, there's something deeper. The root cause is a global intimacy disorder.

Now why is that the root cause? Global intimacy disorder means we can't come together and act with global coherence; we can't act with global coordination. All our challenges are global, but we have no global coordination.

Why do we have no global coordination? Because there's no global coherence. Why is there no global coherence? Because there's no global resonance; we don't resonate with each other, we're not resonating to the same music. Why is there no global resonance? Because we don't have a shared story.

A shared story generates intimacy. A shared story in a couple, and a shared story globally, and a shared story in an organization, and a shared story in a company all generate resonance, which then generates coherence, which then generates the possibility for co-ordination.

So to co-ordinate, we need shared ordinating values; we need a shared grammar of value and a shared grammar of practice. That is the desperate need. It's not cute. It's not casual. It's the only response to existential risk is to actually articulate a new shared story of value, which generates a new human being; a new human being is a new way of being human.

THE MODERN WORD FOR ARMAGEDDON IS EXISTENTIAL RISK, THE MODERN WORD FOR MESSIAH IS *HOMO AMOR*, THE NEW HUMAN

So we're at this moment in history that all the great traditions saw, but they didn't have the same language for it as we do. One word is Armageddon, which means it all falls apart.

The great traditions all interpreted Armageddon in terms of their own ethnocentric tradition, and they said, *If you don't keep our law*—if you're not doing Ramadan well, if you're not doing Jewish law well, or Christian law—*Armageddon comes, and the Christians will win, or the Jews will win, or the Muslims will win.*

So the idea of Armageddon was hijacked. Armageddon means the end of days, it means it all falls apart. It was hijacked by ethnocentric religions, that's true.

But they had this intuition, they understood that it's not going to go on forever. They understood that we're going to come to a place in which two paths diverge in the woods, and the question is, will we be able to take the one less traveled by?

The modern word for Armageddon is existential risk. Existential risk is Armageddon. Now, what's the response to existential risk? In the traditions, what did they call it? They called it Messiah.

In the traditions, they called the response to existential risk Messiah, or the Messianic days.

But what does that mean? Messiah means a new vision, a New Human and a New Humanity. What do we call Messiah here? We've actually reformulated it, and we call it *Homo amor*; *Homo amor* is the New human and the new humanity.

FIRST VALUES AND FIRST PRINCIPLES ARE AT THE CENTER OF IT ALL

At the center of this community is not Barbara Marx Hubbard. At the center of this community is not Marc Gafni. At the center of the community is Evolving First Principles and First Values, and the new Story of Value. So Barbara passed, but she's totally with us. If I pass—and I very much hope to be here for another few decades, because we're just getting started—it doesn't matter, we stay in. This community is not based on a charismatic leader, neither Barbara or Marc or Zak Stein, or anybody. It's based on the Dharma.

We're a Unique Self Symphony. We're in together.

We need decades to do this, so let's do this together. Oh my God, what a crazy mad delight! Every book is going to get out with the help of She. We're creating a Great Library, and the Great Library is not just books. It's going to be books, movies, videos, and even TikTok videos. But first, we've got to get down and write the Great Library.

I had a wonderful time doing a podcast with a dear friend of mine. In his introduction to the podcast, he said this is the most paradigm-shifting podcast I've actually ever recorded. Not because of Gafni, but because of the First Principles and First Values. **The First Principles and First Values that are at the center.**

Yes, it's great to have teachers, otherwise I wouldn't have a job. It's great to have a powerful community. So we need teachers, and we need a powerful community, for sure. Of course we all have different places and different roles. Each one of us who's doing a book is going to be the master of that book, and anyone who's doing a project is going to be the master of that project. Anyone who comes to One Mountain and participates, it's your One Mountain, it's our One Mountain; we're doing this together, we're holding this together. But at the center of everything is the Dharma. It is, if you will, the Torah. It is the First Principles and First Values.

EVOLUTIONARY LOVE CODE: HOLY AND UNHOLY SEDUCTION

This is a provocative code because it's deep. This code is actually clarifying First Principles and First Values, so that we can really understand the nature of Reality as it continues to evolve. Seduction is the key word here.

> There's no love without seduction.
>
> Seduction is a First Principle and First Value of Cosmos.
>
> And we need wisdom to distinguish between "holy" seduction and "unholy" seduction.
>
> Holy seduction seduces upwards; unholy seduction seduces downwards.
>
> Unholy seduction: I seduce you to violate your appropriate boundary for the sake of my greed.
>
> Holy seduction: I seduce you to transcend the boundary of your limitation—of your contraction—for the sake of yours and Reality's deepest need.
>
> Everyone is seduced; the question is, to trust the right person to seduce you. Or people, or art, or music, or Dharma.

Here we go, let's dive in. This is wildly exciting. Are we ready to play a larger game? Are we ready to participate in the evolution of love? Seduction is a very big deal. This is a provocative code, an unbelievably important code.

We need to engage in self-seduction; we have to actually seduce ourselves.

PRACTICE: CLARIFYING YOUR DEEPEST HEART'S DESIRE

Here we go, let's step into seduction.

What does seduction mean? Let's start as follows. Let me ask a gentle inquiry, we're going to invite a practice. I can't become *Homo amor* without evoking the New human and the new humanity, and I can't evoke the New human and the new humanity in me unless I practice and train.

So here's the practice: This week, write your deepest heart's desire for the next ten years, and then go backwards from ten to seven, five, three, two, one years. Envision your deepest heart's desire. Now, desire is very connected to will; desire and will are deeply connected.

My deepest heart's desire is my deepest will, and my deepest will is the will of evolution. So desire is actually very important, we place desire here at the absolute center. Desire is not something to avoid—we have to embrace desire, but we have to clarify desire. The clarification of desire is called *berur* in the interior sciences of the sixteenth century.

So I want to **clarify my desire to identify my deepest heart's desire.** My deepest heart's desire is the yearning of evolution—because evolution desires.

Alfred North Whitehead, the mathematician who writes *Principia Mathematica* with Bertrand Russell at Cambridge, says evolution, or Reality, has appetite. Whitehead was a Cambridge Englishman in the 1920s, so he couldn't say more than that. But by appetite, he means desire. Evolution is hungry, it has desire, and desire is the call of the future. Desire means I have a will in me that wants to manifest a future that's different from the present.

In other words, the eternal Now is important, but insufficient. The Power of Now is important, but insufficient. I need to identify what is the future that calls me: what's the memory of the future that calls me? I'm called by a memory of the future, both a personal memory of the future and a collective memory of the future. As we say, *hope is a memory of the future.*

So what I need to do, as a practice, is **activate my will and my desire and envision the future.** But when I envision the future, I want to access, I want to eavesdrop, as it were, on the evolutionary conversation, on the divine conversation. I want my will to be identical with the will of Cosmos, or what's called often *Ratzon HaShem* in the interior sciences, which means the will of God.

Now, how do I do that? I need to identify my own deepest will. I need to embrace my desire, but my deepest heart's desire, which is my will. And there's an ontic (meaning, for realsies, true) identity of wills between my will and God's will. **It's not that I have to submit to God's will. No, my deepest will *is* the Divine Will.** That's a shocking idea.

These are core tenets of what needs to emerge as a shared grammar of value.

So I want to try and find that idea with you, that my own deepest heart's desire, which is my own deepest will, is ontically/ontologically identified with the Divine Will.

Let's take a look at a word in the original Hebrew. As Wittgenstein reminded us—and this is one of the great contributions of logical positivism—language tells us about the nature of Reality. The Hebrew word for will is *ratzon*. Then *Ratzon HaShem* means the will of God. The will of God is actually what the word means, but what the real word means is the will of the name. *HaShem* means God, but it means "the name." So it's the will of the name.

Now, whose name are we talking about?

SCREAMING THE NAME OF GOD: THE SACRED MYSTERY OF EROTIC EXPLOSION

This is very important and deep. So, for example, at a moment of sexual explosion, we know that cross-culturally, people cry out: "Oh God." They also cry out the name of the beloved. Why? Because at that moment—which is a Holy of Holies moment, in the context of beautiful commitment and respect and honor and mutuality and Eros and joy—**in that moment, you realize the truth that the name of the beloved and the name of God are one; there's no distinction between those names.**

You recognize the truth that the name of Goddess and the name of the Beloved are one.

That's what we call the ontic identity of wills: my will is God's will. My deepest will, my deepest heart's desire, is the divine desire. That's a shocking idea!

Let's seduce ourselves toward our conversation on seduction and go the next step.

SEDUCE ME, AND I WILL RUN AFTER YOU

The word *ratzon* is a Hebrew word that's the same as another word, and the second word is called *ratz*, which means to run, but particularly it means to run towards in Eros.

There's a verse in the most important document in Western civilization on Eros, written by the ancient King Solomon. Think wisdom of Solomon. It's sometimes referred to as the Canticle of Canticles, or the Song of Solomon, or the Song of Songs.

In the Song of Songs, at the very beginning of Chapter 1, there is a text which reads *mashkheni aharaka be-na rutzah*: draw me after you. So the Lover says to the Beloved, draw me after you! The word *mashkheni* is a three-letter root in Hebrew, which means seduce me. *Mashkheni*: draw me after you, seduce me. That's what the word means. *Aharaka*: draw me after you. You seduce me, and then when you seduce me, then *na-rutzah*: I will run after you.

Now, the wider context here is Eros: personal Eros, emotional Eros, and also sexual Eros. But it's not about sex at all. In our *Phenomenology of Eros*, which is a twelve-volume work that we've completed and are now working on the last stages of edits, one of the major principles is that the sexual models the erotic. Eros is the experience of separate parts becoming greater wholes, seeking deeper contact.

Our Eros equation: Eros equals the experience of radical aliveness, seeking, desiring ever deeper contact and ever-larger wholes.

So there's twelve billion years of Eros before sex. The emergence of sexuality, when you have a differentiated cell, is the next stage of Eros. Eros seeks more newness, more novelty, more wholeness. So there's twelve billion years of Eros before sex, and once there's sex, sex doesn't exhaust Eros. **Sex is just an expression, it's a model of Eros; we live erotically in every facet of our lives. So the sexual models the erotic.**

The Song of Songs is the master document in Western civilization. It's a love song, a song of Eros. In every text of the Song of Songs, we say the sexual models Eros. There's a poetic, often explicit description, using agricultural metaphors of ancient Israel, describing sexuality, the lover and the beloved, and their play. But the book is not about sex, but about Eros. Because we have to live erotically in every dimension of life. So this text is about a sexual seduction story. But it's not about sex, it's about Eros. It's about how do I need to be seduced in all dimensions of life?

So now let's go back. Let's look at that text again, *mashkheni aharaka be-na rutzah*: draw me after you, seduce me, and I will run towards you. Now, is that consent? Is this a story of consent? No, this is so much more than consent! Literally, the only distinction we have around sexuality today is consent, which is tragic.

We've lost all distinctions around sexuality. The most powerful force in Reality, we have no distinctions around it other than was there consent? Of course we need consent, it's insane to think you wouldn't need consent. We quibble about what consent is, but that's not the issue.

We need a sexual narrative. But this story is not a consent story. It's not I consent to have you seduce me. No, this is: ***I invite you to seduce me, I demand that you seduce me.*** You get how much bigger, how much wider, and how much deeper that is than consent? No, it's not like I'm consenting. No, please seduce me. *Mashkheni aharaka be-na rutzah*, the Lover says to the Beloved. Seduce me, please! Draw me after you. *Be-na rutzah*: and I will run towards you.

So what does that mean?

Why are we so afraid of seduction in the Western world?

We are, and we should be, because there are so many forms of seduction that are actually degraded. Let's see if we can now go in really deeply and really understand this set of distinctions. So we react in two ways in our bodies to the word seduction: one, we're allured, and two, we say, *no, that's terrible*. They're both right because **there's actually two forms of seduction, and we need to distinguish between these two forms of seduction.**

Now, in the Western world, the reason seduction is considered so dangerous and so violating is because—and by the way, virtually the entire world is some version of the West today, whether it's China or the United States—individuals understand themselves as a separate self with boundaries; the dignity of the individual is based on the boundaries of the separate self. So if someone comes along to violate the boundaries of my separate self, they're violating my humanity. Because who am I? I'm a separate self.

So if you violate my separate-self boundaries, if you seduce me and you get me to violate the boundaries of my separate self without invitation, or at least consent, well then, that's a disaster; that's a violation of my essential humanity.

If that's what seduction means—if seduction means to seduce a person without consent and without invitation, to violate the boundaries of their separate self—well, then our understanding of seduction is going to be massively negative and massively pejorative. Seduction will be understood as a downward causation; seduction will be understood as moving a person downward. So if I seduce you, I'm appealing to your animal; I'm taking from your human, and I'm seducing you into your animal. So it's downward on the phylogenetic chain. It's a regressive move, and hence massively negative.

SEDUCTION, UNIQUE SELF & UNIQUE SELF SYMPHONY

But what if we actually have a deeper understanding of the human being? The distinctions that we've articulated here in CosmoErotic Humanism, one set of these distinctions is articulated in a full book called *Your Unique Self*, and there's an entire Unique Self Institute initiated by Claire Molinard that's dedicated to this distinction. Tom, you and I have a book coming out on a process to actually activate that distinction.

So what if I'm actually not just a separate self? But number one, I'm a True Self, meaning I'm part of the seamless coat of the universe. What if my true identity is that I'm actually not separate from the Field of Consciousness and desire? I'm not just awareness. That's a Ramana Maharshi mistake, with all due respect to Ramana Maharshi. No, I'm one with the Field of Consciousness and Desire.

Then what if I'm not only True Self, one with the Field of Consciousness and desire? But I'm actually a unique individuation of that field, which is Unique Self. Unique Self is higher individuation beyond separation. Now, am I excited about this? I know some people get annoyed when I get excited. I'm excited about this! This is a new understanding of human identity. This is the new human; this is *Homo amor*. This is exciting.

So I individuate beyond separate self, meaning I've now realized I'm part of the one Field of True Self *and* I'm a unique expression of that field—that's Unique Self. Then I locate myself in an evolutionary context. **I'm part of the Field of Evolution. I realize the Evolutionary Impulse is awake and alive in me, and I realize that my deepest heart's desire is the desire of evolution.**

All of a sudden, I'm Evolutionary Unique Self. Then Evolutionary Unique Selves come together, and each one begins to play their own instrument and their own jazz movement in the Unique Self Symphony. Wow, that's a whole world.

Now, how do I get from separate self, to True Self, to Unique Self, to Evolutionary Unique Self, to Unique Self Symphony? That's to be seduced upwards. To be seduced upwards means I'm not seduced as downward causation; seduction is not a regressive move. Rather, **I'm seduced to be my highest self. I'm seduced to be my most wondrous. I'm seduced to be my most beautiful.** I'm seduced from separate self, upwards to True Self. I'm seduced into greater depth. I'm seduced into my uniqueness and into my Unique Self. I'm seduced into my Evolutionary Unique Self. I'm seduced into picking up my instrument and playing in the Unique Self Symphony.

So when we say the practice is to articulate a vision of your deepest heart's desire, to articulate a vision of your will, what we're saying is: seduce yourself into your deepest heart's desire. Your will is the will of the Divine, so when you seduce yourself, you seduce God. You seduce God, who experiences Her own shocking self-recognition in you, the highest version of Reality being you. But that requires seduction.

It's not simple. It's not easy, it requires training. But that training is not just a hard, rigorous training. It's also gorgeous and beautiful. It's seduction.

THE DISTINCTION BETWEEN HOLY AND UNHOLY SEDUCTION

So there's two kinds of seduction, let's see this distinction again. There's an unholy seduction, where I'm seducing you downwards. Unholy seduction means that I seduce you to violate your appropriate boundary for the sake of my greed.

But in sacred seduction, I move to seduce you and you move to seduce me. I move to seduce you to transcend the boundary of your limitation, to transcend the boundary of your contraction. I transcend the boundary that says I'm just a separate self, transcend the boundary that says I'm an isolated monad in the world, transcend the boundary that says I'm ultimately alone.

I transcend the boundary that says I can never transcend loneliness because I'm separate from everything.

To transcend the boundary of my coiled contraction, in order to emerge and to transcend (trance-end: to end the trance) of being merely a separate self. That's sacred seduction. So sacred seduction is, *I seduce you and you seduce me to go beyond the boundary of your contraction, not for the sake of my greed, but for the sake of your own deepest need.*

ARTICULATING A WORLD RELIGION THAT CAN SEDUCE REALITY TOWARDS THE HIGHEST VERSION OF ITSELF

So we need to articulate a world religion which can seduce Reality towards the highest version of itself. In this moment in which we're poised between utopia and dystopia, in this time between worlds and time between stories, as a Unique Self Symphony, we need to articulate a new Story of Value. **That story has got to be a seductive story.**

But seductive is beautiful. Seductive means the allurement, the Eros of Cosmos, calls me to break the boundary of contraction, to break the boundary of yesterday's patterns. It calls me to trance-end (to end the trance) of the contraction, to end the loops of fixation, to end the loops of trauma, and to step into and be called forth by the memory of my future.

The great master, Nachman of Breslov, one of the favorites of Franz Kafka, writes gorgeously in Aramaic in the early nineteenth century. He says, *When you wake up in the morning, the first thing you have to do is Zichron Alma De'Ati: to remember your future world. Seduce yourself!*

PRAYER: DRAW ME AFTER YOU

So we're now going to step into prayer. In prayer, we turn to the Infinity of Intimacy that knows our name; the personal force of Cosmos. Not Santa Claus, although I like Santa Claus.

But actually the Infinity of Intimacy, the personhood of Cosmos that knows our name. We say, seduce me! *Mashkheni aharaka*: draw me after you, *na-rutzah*: so that I run towards you. That's what prayer is.

Prayer is the turning towards the Divine and our plea to the Divine. "Seduce me please, I beg you. I'm on my knees, seduce me." *Mashkheni aharaka bena rutzah*: draw me after you so that I may run towards you.

It's one Field of Eros. The divine human field, and within the manifest world all the way down and all the way up the evolutionary chain (matter, life, and mind), and then before the evolutionary chain (the world of pure Divinity), it's all one Field of Eros.

So just like in human Eros, we know that when we step over that line and when we've stepped inside, there's that moment in sexing where you've stepped over the line. You're not will I, won't I, am I in, am I not in? You're in! You're over the line. You've stepped over the line. Often, you're so far in, you're near the explosion of sexuality, and you enter into a kind of erotic consciousness—an orgasm consciousness, if you will. You look at each other, and you're madly in love, and you say, "I love you." You can ask each other for anything because you want to say *Yes*. It's all *Yes*.

So what prayer actually is, is we're making love with the All, with the Infinity of Intimacy. We're on a journey to God. We're on a journey in God.

We say, Infinity of Intimacy that knows my name—God is the infinite personhood of Cosmos that knows my name, that holds me in every second—and we're making love, we've crossed that line. I begin by saying: God, seduce me, take me.

- Then I step inside.
- I'm in prayer.
- I'm in dance.
- I'm in psychedelic journey.
- I'm in meditation.

- I'm in ecstatic chant.

And then I ask for everything.

When you think God, think of the most precious moment of tenderness and fierce Eros you've ever experienced in your entire life, and then times it by a billion. The deepest desire you've ever felt, the most tenderness you've ever felt, times it by a billion. The personhood that lives between you and me, that sense of personal doesn't exhaust itself in you and me. We're part of the Field of Personhood.

God is not only the Infinity of Power; God is the Infinity of Intimacy.

If you can hear me talk, what in you hears me talk? Your intelligence hears me talk. Not just your ears, it's your intelligence. So if you can hear me talk because your quality of intelligence hears me talk, are you separate from the Field of Intelligence? Of course not, you're not separate from the Field of Intelligence. That Infinite Field of Intelligence—that's God, the Infinity of Intimacy. So if you can hear me talk, is it possible that the Divine Field of Infinite Intelligence can't hear me talk?

So prayer is this radical Eros; prayer is making love with the Divine, quite literally. So we start with: God seduce me after you, I will run towards you. Then when we're all the way on the inside, we ask for everything.

So here's a simple prayer. I just turn and say: *Goddess, Reality*—or whatever word you want to use—*seduce me! Seduce me to my Unique Self. Seduce me to my highest.* **Oh Goddess, seduce me to myself that you need so desperately.** That's my prayer.

I can't do it myself. I need the force, the current of Eros of Reality itself that knows me personally. Seduce me! Take me.

Mashkheni aharaka be-na rutzah: draw me after you so that I may run towards you.

CHAPTER TEN

RESPONDING TO THE THREE GREAT QUESTIONS OF COSMOEROTIC HUMANISM

Episode 310 — September 18, 2022

TWO KINDS OF EXISTENTIAL RISK

Our intention is to step into the fullness of this moment in time, to refuse to look away, to actually acknowledge, recognize, and face full on the particular quality of meta-crisis, which characterizes the deepest truth of this moment for humanity. *Meta-crisis* means:

- The possibility of *catastrophic risk*, which is suffering for billions of human beings
- The possibility of *existential risk*, which is the end of human beings, the death of humanity

However, meta-crisis is not only the death of humanity, it's the death of *our* humanity. There are two kinds of existential risk:

- **The death of humanity:** there simply won't be human beings. There's a genuine possibility that we will generate—through widely distributed exponential technology, weaponized in multiple forms, coupled with a list of other very serious existential risks—the end of humanity.

- The second possible existential risk is this: in order to respond to existential risk, through various modes of surveillance and various modes of top-down, command-and-control closed societies, we will generate **the death of *our* humanity. The human being as a free, creative, unique expression of personhood—the human being we currently recognize simply won't exist anymore.** Humanism will have died, and it will be replaced by a top-down totalitarianism, mediated through the nervous system of the planet, that is, the structures of the planetary stack, particularly the Internet—and the structures of that Internet will become totalitarian.

Already today in China, there is widespread monitoring and surveillance of where you are, who you are near, what your social credit score is, and what the social credit score is of the people that you are in proximity to. All of that information is constantly fed into machine intelligence that then evaluates whether you should be able to buy food and how much food, whether you'll be admitted to a university, whether you can get a job—that's where it's going.

So how you *respond* in China to various issues—how you respond politically, how you respond socially—all affects your social credit score. It is also affected by the people you associate and affiliate with. All this is used to evaluate who you are and then decide whether you deserve a job, forms of insurance, or certain kinds of medical help. That's nascent in China, but it's being up-leveled all the time now and used for utter brutality.

Paradoxically, in the United States and Western Europe, a similar form of the social credit system is developing, not organized by the top-down closed society, but as **a self-organizing division of society into polarized groups.**

This is creating a shocking, horrific downward pull towards the most vicious, most negative, and most polarizing.

It's not yet organized into a formal social credit system, although there are multiple vectors that are moving in this direction, as outlined in a recent book by Brett Frischmann called *Re-Engineering Humanity*.

These are potential visions of the death of our humanity.

EVOLVING THE SOURCE CODE OF CONSCIOUSNESS AND CULTURE

Now, we have to realize that **it doesn't need to go this way.** That we *can* face the meta-crisis—and by facing it, by internalizing it, by knowing it, by understanding it, by deconstructing it, **we can actually understand its root causes.**

We can see *beneath* the headlines, we can see *through* the enormous confusion in the daily news, and we can understand that **there are certain fundamental, structural, essential things happening that are cause for the breakdown.** Once we can see what causes the breakdown, once we can see what causes the meta-crisis:

- We can re-vision Reality.
- We can actually *heal* those causes.
- We can actually *rewire the very planetary stack* by evolving the very source code of consciousness and culture, which enables us to then enact a planetary ethos for a planetary civilization, a global ethos for a global civilization.

Yesterday, we had a meeting of the inner board of the Center for Integral Wisdom, Office for the Future, and the Foundation for Conscious Evolution, the cluster of think tanks that are working together and host One Mountain, Many Paths.

One of the things we talked about was **the absolute need to evolve the source code of consciousness and culture**—because the source code determines what's happening everywhere.

So we've got to be able to get into the source code, to see the source code, and to evolve the source code. Evolving the source code is what we call *the da Vinci move*, referring of course to Leonardo da Vinci. We are also referring to Marsilio Ficino and about twenty other people in the Renaissance who lived at that time, much like our time—**this time between worlds, this time between stories, where the planetary systems are breaking down.**

You can't get—I've said this a thousand times—you cannot get to every village and heal the Black Death. **You need to do something to address the breakdown.** Da Vinci, Ficino, and the rest of the Renaissance gang addressed the breakdown at the time between worlds and the time between stories by *telling a new story of value*.

That new story of value became modernity.

And so, what we've said is that we're going to commit, here in One Mountain, Many Paths:

- To telling this new Story of Value, and articulating what value is.
- To articulating a new set of equations and values that we can download into the very source code of consciousness and culture.
- To actually healing and evolving the source code.

To our best understanding, this is the best shot—and maybe the *only* shot—we have, of avoiding existential and catastrophic risk.

It's not a pipe dream, though. It's completely possible.

The only thing that is unchanging in the world is that it *always* changes. It never remains the same. And so we want to be able to ride that great course of change, and find our way, and set a course by entering the very source code of Reality itself, rewriting that source code, re-authoring the human story—which is of course what human beings have always done. But this time:

THE THREE GREAT QUESTIONS OF COSMOEROTIC HUMANISM

- We need to do it consciously.
- We need to understand that we are in the *Anthropocene*.
- We need to realize we're in the world in which human beings determine the future of evolution.
- We need to move from unconscious evolution to *conscious evolution*.

Conscious evolution is the realization that **the entire evolutionary process is awake and alive** *in us*, and that we can move to this place in which we can actually assume the gravitas of our power.

Our power is to create a future—or to not have a future.

We have the powers of ancient gods, but we need a new story *equal* to our power. And that new Story of Value, that new Story of conscious evolution, is what we're calling CosmoErotic Humanism.

CosmoErotic Humanism is the new Story of Value, rooted in First Principles and First Values.

I repeat some version of this every week not to give you new information **but for invocation**. We are *invoking* the conversation. This is a unique and important conversation.

It's the Renaissance conversation—we are in Florence. But we are in a much more dangerous time, exponentially more dangerous because of exponential technologies, and because of a world in which infotech unites and interdigitates the entire planet. Exponential technologies and an interdigitated planet of infotech, nanotech, and biotech—when you put all those together, you have the capacity both for a utopia that's unimaginable and the potential end of humanity.

It is an incredible time we're in…

- And we're filled with hope.
- And we're filled with passion.
- And we're filled with possibility.

- And we're filled with a radical commitment to actually write this Great Library of CosmoErotic Humanism, to *re-soul* the very matrix of consciousness and culture itself.

That's what we're up to—and we're up to it day and night. It's not a hobby. It's not a side gig. It's the ultimate gig. It's the ultimate moral imperative. It's the ultimate erotic imperative of humanity, of being a human at this moment in time.

The greatest single act to alleviate suffering that a human being could do, at this moment in time, is to say:

- What is my role to play in the Unique Self Symphony?
- What is my role in evolving the very source code of consciousness and culture?
- What is the art that's mine to create?

Because it's all art. **All of Reality is art**. There is no God, and there is no art. It's all God, and it's all art—everywhere and every place.

By God, I mean that which is holding the whole thing, the LoveIntelligence and LoveBeauty that inheres in everything and that holds everything. That is pure art, pure color, pure symmetry, pure pattern, pure depth, pure value: *evolving* value, goodness, truth, and beauty, all of that. We are here to do that.

It's shocking. It's ecstatic.

And it's urgent beyond imagination.

WHAT ARE EVOLUTIONARY LOVE CODES?

Every week, we offer an Evolutionary Love Code. *Evolutionary Love* refers to a specific quality of Cosmos.

- Sometimes we call it *Evolutionary Love*.
- Sometimes we call it *Outrageous Love*.

- Sometimes we call it *Eros*—but we're referring to the same central First Value of Cosmos that lives all the way down and all the way up the evolutionary chain, and that appears, in a unique and evolved form, in the human world.

These codes are the intrinsic codes of meaning and information that live in Reality, and that continuously evolve—through matter, through life, through cosmological evolution, through biological evolution, and ultimately to the depth of the self-reflective human mind. **And it is knowing those patterns, identifying them, validating them, and then articulating them—articulating a universal grammar of value that is a context for our diversity—***that's* **what is going to change the very source code of consciousness and culture itself.**

Are we ready to actually step up and actually play an instrument in the Unique Self Symphony?

It is a huge shift. And if I can, with permission, I always say *We*, and I mean *We*. But I want to say the *We* in a way that all of our *You*'s, each of us individually, feel personally addressed. I want to address myself, and if I can, I want to address our larger *We*. And if I can, with your permission, gently, tenderly, I want to address *you*.

- Are *you* ready to play a larger game?
- Are *you* ready to participate in the evolution of consciousness and culture, that is, to evolve the source code, to articulate a planetary ethos, a global ethos for a global civilization?
- Are *you* ready to actually say that you have a seat at the table? That you're at the inner cabinet meeting, which is actually responsible for the destiny of humanity?

Here is where it gets almost unimaginable.

The old elites have crashed. The old structures of authority have broken down—and the new authority is going to come from those who are willing to take responsibility for *authoring* the new Story. Not to *make it up*—but to do the deepest research, the deepest study, the deepest contemplation, the deepest practice, to integrate from the leading-edge wisdom streams across space and time, and to articulate this vision, this new source code, the shared grammar of value.

So are *you* ready to step up and to contribute the best of you, the most beautiful of you, the deepest truth of you? Time, resource, energy (it is all about energy, *where's my energy going?*) Are you ready to actually say, I have a seat at the table and I actually *can* be part of the Unique Self Symphony in this lifetime—affecting, activating, actualizing, and articulating the change that changes *everything*?

And if you're a student of history—if we don't know anything about the past, we can't know anything about the future—it's only these *groups of people* who establish Unique Self Symphony, though they never had a name for it. Because unlike the old world, where there was no real vision of Unique Self, it's actually about *each* of our Unique Selves and *each* of our unique gifts, coming together and forming an evolutionary *We*-space that has the capacity to generate these new source code structures.

That's our move. Our move is going to be this Great Library—and out of this Great Library of books, we're going to go to movies, we're going to go to media, we're going to go to popular books, we're going to go to children's books. But first, the next years are about getting down deeply the source code structures of the Great Library. Wow!

EVOLUTIONARY LOVE CODE: THE THREE GREAT QUESTIONS

There are three great questions in life.

The first question is, "Where am I?"

The second question is, "Who am I, and who are you?"

The third question is, "What is there to do?"

THE THREE GREAT QUESTIONS OF COSMOEROTIC HUMANISM

The response to these three great questions is the source of all joy, all power, all Eros, all creativity, all Goodness, all Truth, and all Beauty.

The response to these three great questions is the set of First Principles and First Values that are the North Star of a life well lived.

We call these questions the Three Great Questions of CosmoErotic Humanism. CosmoErotic Humanism is the story of the New human and the new humanity.

CosmoErotic Humanism is the expression of what may be the most potent and powerful self-understanding that humanity has ever been able to articulate.

What we want to do today is *address* those three questions in a huge, *meta* way. And then we get very specific, so we get a sense of what that actually means.

First, I want to give just a glimpse of **a set of evolutionary source code principles, which respond directly to these great questions of CosmoErotic Humanism.**

PRINCIPLE ONE: OUTRAGEOUS LOVE IS OUR RESPONSE BOTH TO PAIN AND TO BEAUTY

First, a simple phenomenological observation (*phenomenological* means what's actually happening in front of us):

- We live in a world of outrageous pain.

That's just true. We live in a world filled with outrageous pain, and **the only response to outrageous pain is Outrageous Love.**

- Second sentence: we live in a world of outrageous beauty, and the only response to outrageous beauty is Outrageous Love.

Now, *both of those* are true. We can't look away from the pain, and we can't look away from the beauty—and our response to both the pain and the beauty is Outrageous Love.

> *Outrageous Love is an experience that moves through our body, through our heart, and through our mind, which enables us, which activates us, and allows us to not answer the question of why is there beauty and why is there pain—but to respond to the beauty.*

We respond to the beauty through Outrageous Love, and we respond to the pain through Outrageous Love. *Only* Outrageous Love can hold the pain, and *only* Outrageous Love can hold the beauty.

PRINCIPLE TWO: OUTRAGEOUS LOVE IS THE HEART OF EXISTENCE ITSELF

Our response to both the pain and the beauty is Outrageous Love—what does that mean? It means that the human being at its core is animated by a quality that we're calling Outrageous Love.

And what do we mean by Outrageous Love? By Outrageous Love, we don't mean ordinary love. This is why **we cannot root Value solely in the world of human social constructions.** By Outrageous Love, we mean, as Dante said, "The love that moves the Sun and other stars."

Or as Tagore, the Bengali mystic said it, "Love is not mere human sentiment, it's the heart of existence itself."

This means **it is not enough to root Eros or love in a *human construction*,** which is arbitrary. This human construction, which is emerging in the human being, which is flowing through the human being, is *the current* *of Cosmos*, the interior face of Cosmos, and the interior face of the human being who participates in Cosmos.

Bertrand Russell has misunderstood it as articulating a position of value which is intrinsic only at the level of human beings. What Russell actually says is: *The only problem with my atheism is that I can't quite believe that the only problem with mass murder is that I don't like it.* That's a big deal!

The problem with materialism is that it assumes that our objection to un-love (for example, to mass murder) is simply a collective human preference, a particular social structure—and that collective human preference is unreliable. Ask Mao. Ask Stalin. Ask Hitler. Ask the 100 million people, non-combatants, killed in the twentieth century if that collective human preference is sufficient to generate the most beautiful world that we know could, and should, and must exist. Outrageous Love, as Tagore said, is *not* mere human sentiment. It's literally the heart of existence itself.

Outrageous Love is the very heart of existence itself.

PRINCIPLE THREE: I AM A UNIQUE CONFIGURATION OF OUTRAGEOUS LOVE

Who am I, in the most profound interior that animates my body?

My body is generating three million cells every second, billions of cells a day—and *each cell is a configuration of allurement and desire. That is to say, Eros. That is to say, love.* That is to say, **my very physical constitution is the movement of Eros in my body. Eros** *embodied.* **I am a unique configuration of Outrageous Love.** That's who I am. That's my nature. That's my essential nature. My nature is that I'm a lover.

- I've got to *train* in the art of love.
- I have to *cultivate* love, like we cultivate great art.
- I have to participate in the evolution of love *in me, as me*, and *through me.*

- I have to train my *goodness*, which is an expression of my love.

But **my goodness, my love, my Eros is *inherent*.** It's not automatic. It's not *natural* in the sense that it doesn't need to be trained. It's *inherent*.

Human beings are not naturally or automatically good. They are not good or loving by "default." They are *inherently* loving. They are *inherently* good. **But that intrinsic good, that intrinsic love, that intrinsic Eros, needs to be cultivated.** It needs to be trained. But that is actually who we are in our very core as a human being. It's why the world is filled with music, and why music is mostly love songs—trans-culturally, trans-temporally, across space and across time.

So who am I? I am a unique configuration of Outrageous Love. That's who I am.

Outrageous Love is the Eros of Cosmos that moves towards ever deeper contact. It's a love story. Whitehead, who wrote *Principia Mathematica* with Russell, says correctly that *the appetites of Reality live in us*. But *appetite* simply means *desire*. **So we can say: the desire of Reality lives in us, and the fundamental desire of Reality is the erotic.**

And the erotic motive of the Cosmos is to generate wider and deeper fields of love, of Eros, of separate parts coming together to form larger wholes with deeper intimacy, with shared identity between them, with deeper feelings.

Eros moves towards separate parts becoming larger wholes.

Eros is Outrageous Love.

Eros moves towards deeper intimacies.

And intimacy is, in our **intimacy formula:**

- **Shared identity** in the context of otherness
- Plus **mutuality of recognition**: we recognize each other
- Plus **mutuality of pathos**: we feel each other
- Plus **mutuality of value**: there's a shared field of value
- Plus **mutuality of purpose**: we have a shared purpose, shared direction, shared *telos*

This begins at the subatomic level, and it moves all the way through the cellular level, all the way through the level of the organism, and all the way up the evolutionary chain.

There's an *evolution* of love, but there's also a *continuity*. At each level, love becomes more conscious, love becomes more inclusive, love becomes more refined. **Love evolves. But at the core, there is this quality of Outrageous Love.** Not ordinary love. Not love as a mere human construction. But an ethos, rooted in Eros.

There is no split between the erotic and the ethical: **the erotic and the ethical are one**. Eros and ethos are one thing because Eros is the movement of separate parts, governed by love to form larger wholes and wider intimacies, with mutualities of pathos, recognition, value, and purpose.

So who am I? I am an Outrageous Lover. That's actually who I am.

I am actually constitutionally—not conjecturally (if I can make up a word), not made up, not contrived—**I am *constitutionally* an Outrageous Lover.** That's who I am. I am constitutionally an Outrageous Lover. Wow!

- I am not an ordinary lover.
- I don't love according to the particular sentiment of my time.
- I am called to something which is deeper than my time, which is the shared quality of Eros that's lived through all time and that lives in me. It expresses itself through social prisms, but it's also *beyond* social prisms.

This is why even at times of tragic levels of human development, there were already people who saw beyond that, who were already reaching for the next levels, who already embodied them in their center of gravity, a center of gravity that was beyond where culture was at that time.

PRINCIPLE FOUR: OUTRAGEOUS LOVERS COMMIT OUTRAGEOUS ACTS OF LOVE

Who am I? I'm an Outrageous Lover. That's who I am. Outrageous Love lives in me, as me, and through me. David Bohm, a student of Einstein, wasn't wrong when he said: *The human being is a clue to the universe.* Meaning: **when I access that quality of Outrageous Love, I access the interior face of Cosmos.** Outrageous Love is constituent to Cosmos, is the essential force, the Eros—

- That animates the four fundamental forces of Cosmos
- That animates each of the 37.2 trillion cells that move in us at every second
- That animates the hundreds of trillions of atoms and atomic structures, all of which are configurations of allurement

Outrageous Love is the interior face of Cosmos, and my interior *participates* in this love.

Number four: **what does an Outrageous Lover do?** Well, it's simple: **An Outrageous Lover commits Outrageous Acts of Love.**

That's what an Outrageous Lover does. So the question is, **where am I?**

I'm in a Cosmos animated by Eros. That's where I am. **I'm in a love story.** I'm a character in a love story. My being-ness and my becoming-ness (meaning, my very ground of being and my changing, evolving self) are rooted in a matrix of Eros. I'm living in a love story.

That's what we mean when we say **the universe is not merely a fact, the universe is actually a story.** We're going to talk a lot about story, about what that means that the universe is story. Even **the principle of** *story* **doesn't begin with the human being.**

If you really understand the principle of story, you realize that **story is a property of Cosmos, from matter to life to mind. Story** *evolves*, **but story is a property of Cosmos at all levels.** Reality is not merely a fact; Reality is a story. It has direction, it's going somewhere. There are plotlines that *animate* a story. Those plotlines animate the story of Reality, all the way down and all the way up the evolutionary chain. It's a big deal.

So I am in a story. Reality is not merely *a fact*. I'm not living in a dead mechanistic universe of reductive materialism, where I am *making up* stories, which are mere social conjectures—to which Bertrand Russell's response was: *That doesn't work for me in the end. It breaks down. I cannot construct an ethos; I can't raise children based on that.*

Because in this dead mechanistic universe, the only thing wrong with mass murder is that I don't like it—and that's not enough. No, **mass murder is a problem because it violates the structure of Eros which is the intrinsic ethos of Cosmos.**

And that structure of Eros *evolves*, and at the human level, we come to understand and articulate clearly this realization that *you don't get to mass murder people*. You don't get to do that—it's not okay. It is not just a violation of a social norm; it's a violation of the intrinsic structure of Reality itself. As such:

- I need to care for every man, woman, and child.
- I need to feel the intrinsic dignity of every man, woman, and child.
- I need to support the emergence of the unique story of every man, woman, and child, who has their own poem to write, and their own song to sing, and their own way of laughing, loving, living, and being in the world.

Those are the principles of Eros which are intrinsic to Cosmos. They *emerge*—they are ever-emergent, and they evolve at every level of evolutionary development.

At the human level, I become *conscious*. Evolution becomes conscious of itself uniquely in me, in a way that it never has before.

- So who am I? **I am an Outrageous Lover.**
- What do I do? **I commit Outrageous Acts of Love.** Not because it's a pretty costume that I am putting on my otherwise beastly old self—but because it's in my inherent nature to do so.

My inherent nature is to love, and to love *madly*—which is why **in every society, people love madly.** They made a mistake: they often placed the boundary of their love at the tribal level, or at the ethnocentric level, and their love ended at the border of their tribe, which is tragic. We need to move the borders that circumscribe and limit and contract love to a particular geographical place, or to a racial place, or to a religious place, or a national place—*of course* we do, that's the evolution of love. But everybody *loved*. Everybody loved! Everyone felt some sense of: *I need to care, I need to be concerned with, I need to feel.* And then, as evolution moved, what that feeling meant, and the boundaries of who was included in that feeling, expanded.

So who am I? I'm an Outrageous Lover. What does an Outrageous Lover do? An Outrageous Lover commits Outrageous Acts of Love.

PRINCIPLE FIVE: OUTRAGEOUS ACTS OF LOVE THAT ARE MINE TO COMMIT ARE A FUNCTION OF MY UNIQUE SELF

So which Outrageous Acts of Love are mine to commit, what's mine to do? There is so much that needs to be done in the world, but what are the

Outrageous Acts of Love that are *mine* to commit, that *I* need to do? That's number five.

- The Outrageous Acts of Love that are mine to do are the those acts that are a function of my Unique Self.

We have asked three great questions of CosmoErotic Humanism:

- **Where am I?** I am living not merely in a world of facts—**I am living in a story.** A story has plotlines, and the nature of the story is it's a love story. That's what we mean when we say: Reality is not merely a fact. Reality is a story. Reality is not an ordinary story, animated by ordinary, socially constructed realities. **Reality is a love story.** But Reality is not an ordinary love story, where love is a social construction. **Reality is an Outrageous Love Story.** Reality is an Evolutionary Love Story. Meaning: love is a core principle of Reality itself. That's what Outrageous Love means. Outrageous Love, Eros, and Evolutionary Love are all ways of saying the same thing.
- **Who am I?** I am an Outrageous Lover (Principle three).
- **What is there to do?** Acts of Outrageous Love (Principle four).

Let us see if we can get this together, because this is absolutely core.

Reality is not merely a fact, Reality is a story. And the story *matters*. Science says Reality is just a fact. That's true. Reality is a series of facts, and science is doing an incredibly gorgeous job at unpacking those facts. But science is doing more. **Science is also sensing—if it admits its own enterprise to itself—patterns in Cosmos, patterns written on the walls of nothingness.**

Reality is not merely a fact. Reality is a story. And this story is not just a story about getting to the next world, which is what religion historically said in response to the old sciences. No. In CosmoErotic Humanism, **we are articulating a New Universe Story that integrates the best of the exterior sciences (biology, physics, etc.), and also the best of the interior** sciences. There is *telos*, Reality is going somewhere. Reality is not merely a fact, Reality is an Outrageous Love Story. It's an erotic love story. **Reality is an Evolutionary Love Story.**

And *my story* **is unique.** My story is not "extra"; the very definition of it being my story is, my story is unique. My story is not merely my victim story, which is the common story we all share (although we're all victims in unique ways as well). **But my story is: I am a player. I am actually an actor, and I have a unique set of lines.**

That's what Whitman meant when he said, "You contribute a verse to the world." There is a verse that you need to contribute. There is a letter in the cosmic scroll that's *yours* to write, and yours alone.

That's what it means to be **an irreducible Unique Self**.

- You are an irreducibly Unique Self.
- You are an irreducibly unique Outrageous Lover.
- You are an irreducibly unique configuration of Outrageous Love.
- You are a unique set of allurements.

You are not an extra on the set; **there are no *extras* on the set**.

I am *intended* by Reality itself. Uniqueness implies intention. Uniqueness implies choosing.

I am *intended*, I am *chosen*, I am *recognized* by Reality.

And therefore, I am *needed* by Reality.

I am needed to commit my Outrageous Acts of Love. And which Outrageous Acts of Love are those? Those that are a *function* of my Unique Self.

And what *is* my Unique Self? This is principle five. My Unique Self is the unique configuration of allurement, and my unique configuration of capacity for gifting, that's mine and mine alone.

It's my unique way of being.

It's my unique way of presencing in the world.

It's my unique way of contributing my gifts—gifts that address unique needs in my unique circle of intimacy and influence, needs that can only be addressed in a unique way that I can. Needs that could be contributed through the verse that's mine to write, in a way that no one that ever was, is, or will be can do, other than me. That's number five.

- Three: I'm an Outrageous Lover.
- Four: I've got Outrageous Acts of Love to commit.
- Five: which Outrageous Acts of Love are mine to commit? Those that are a function of my irreducibly unique and gorgeous quality of being.

Because of my unique place in the spacetime continuum, my unique perspective is mine and mine alone. **I'm the puzzle piece that fits uniquely into this particular place in the spacetime continuum.** And when I fit uniquely, I actually complete the puzzle.

- I fit in *perfectly*.
- I am *exactly* where I need to be.
- I was born at the right place, at the right time, to the right people—because there's something for me to do at this moment, at this place in time.

And I've got to do that, I've got to contribute that, I've got to be that. It's unimaginably beautiful.

PRINCIPLE SIX: FIND THE OTHERS TO PLAY IN THE UNIQUE SELF SYMPHONY

Then I realize it's not just about me.

- It's not about me.
- It's about you.
- It's about you and me together.

Find the others. Find the other imaginal cells that come together to turn a caterpillar into a butterfly. When enough imaginal cells find each other, they rewire, they evolve the source code, the cellular structure of the caterpillar, and the caterpillar becomes a butterfly. Find the others. **Enact, in your local world, Unique Self Symphonies that come together to participate in the evolution of love.**

And then as Reality proliferates with Unique Self Symphonies, as Unique Self Symphonies multiply exponentially—we actually experience not a closed society, not a totalitarian, top-down, command-and-control society, mediated through a totalitarian internet, but **a bottom-up, self-organizing, self-actualizing Reality of Unique Self Symphonies.** I was delighted to call it—together with my beloved Whole Mate partner, Barbara Marx Hubbard—**a Planetary Awakening in Love through Unique Self Symphonies. Wow.**

So who am I? I'm someone who has a unique instrument to play in the Unique Self Symphony. It's not just a symphony that's playing an old score. It's a symphony that's playing an old score *uniquely*, and then adding to the score. *It's jazz.* We each have this instrument to play in the Unique Self Symphony. We don't play it by ourselves. **We actually listen into the Symphony and we ask, at this moment in time, what is it that Reality needs from me?**

It's not just about my artistic expression, or what I want to create. We listen to *Zohar*. We listen to what's the unique need. **Unique Self is not just my creativity.**

People always post on the internet about one thing: themselves. **We would change the world if everyone would spend two months, eight weeks, posting on the internet *not* about themsleves.** Two months, and your life will change. If you're posting on social media, spend two months posting not about yourself. This is a two-month challenge. You know what, I'll make it easier. One-week challenge, seven days, **don't post anything about** *yourself.* **Just post about the beauty that you see. Your entire life will change.** It's not just about me—it's about what the need of the moment is.

> *It's when my deepest quality meets the most urgent need of the moment that I am able to access knowing what my unique instrument is in the Unique Self Symphony.*

It's not exactly what makes me feel good superficially, although playing my unique instrument makes me feel better than anything else.

It's about being part of the Unique Self Symphony, playing my instrument in resonance with the Unique Self Symphony, and then at moments playing my jazz piece that's never been played before, as everyone steps back and listens to my music. That's Unique Self Symphony.

You notice we've answered all three questions of CosmoErotic Humanism:

- The question of *where? Where am I?* **I am in a love story**.
- *Who? Who am I?* **I am a unique Outrageous Lover**, and my love story is chapter and verse in the Universe: A Love Story.
- *What? What's there to do?* To commit my Outrageous Acts of Love.

BE OUTRAGEOUS

I want to, if I can, share something: *You've got to be outrageous.* Life is way too short to be superfically polite. Be civil, be respectful, have integrity, be loving—but **be outrageously loving**.

- Don't be just *a little bit* loving.
- Don't be just appropriate.
- Don't just do what is the "right" thing to do so that your

psychologist, therapist, counselor, or coach says: *Oh, this makes sense.*

Be outrageous! Of course, listen to your psychologist or coach, and be sensible. Of course you should—but you absolutely must be outrageous.

Because Outrageous Love is the love that animates all of Reality—quite literally, it's the love that moves in *we*, moves in *thee*, moves in *me*, moves in *you*. And it's only when you step up outrageously that you realize:

- You are larger than life.
- You are a superhero.
- Your superpower is that unique quality of Outrageous Love that moves in you, that wants to commit Outrageous Acts of Love that are unique, unlike anything else.

Don't be afraid of being grandiose: you are not being grandiose—you're grand, you're gorgeous. You are larger than life. You are wondrous beyond imagination. You are beautiful beyond anything that words could possibly hold.

So commit Outrageous Acts of Love! Step up to the plate, and hit a home run, bases loaded (I apologize for the American metaphor). Out of the park, blow the lights out in the park! **Because *that* is what's yours to do—and you cannot truly be filled with joy, or filled with integrity, until you do that.**

And remember that there's no person in the world who can tell you exactly what your Outrageous Act of Love is to commit it.

- You can be *guided*.
- You can get *input*.
- You can access voices of those who *see* you.
- You can get *reflections* of who you are from other people.

But in the end, you've got to listen not to the surface voice, but to a voice that's beneath the surface, that lives on the Inside of the Inside of you, that voice that actually participates in the Field of Outrageous Love.

- You can hear it sometimes in the middle of the night.
- You can hear it when you are deep in nature.
- You can hear it when you are deep in the creation of art of any form.
- You can hear it when you allow the quieting of the vagaries of the ego, seeking to soothe itself from the slings and arrows of outrageous misfortune.

Outrageous misfortune is responded to through Outrageous Love. Wow.

PRAYER: HALLELUJAH

When we pray, we turn to the Infinity of Intimacy and we say:

> *Oh my God, blow me open.*
> *Let me be Outrageous Love.*
> *Let me be your verb.*
> *Let me be your dangling modifier.*
> *Let me be your noun.*
> *Let me be your sentence structure.*
> *Let me be your art.*
> *Let me be your painting.*
> *I know that you are Outrageous Love through me.*
> *Guide me. Open me. Love me. Caress me. Kiss me. Demand from me.*
> *Demand from me that I be, and help me be, and stand me up to be, and hold me as I'm being a unique, gorgeous Outrageous Act of Love, which is the verb of Infinite Intimacy, the verb of the Infinite Intimate alive in me.*

That's what prayer is.

We are going to prayer, to Leonard Cohen, to the holy and broken *Hallelujah*. And we don't use the word *God*—because the God you don't believe in doesn't exist. We use the word *Infinite Intimacy*. When we say God, we think and we feel *Infinite Intimacy*. We turn to God, to the *Infinite Intimacy*, and we say:

Hold us, love us, make us, allow us to make ourselves into the Outrageous Mad Lovers that we already are.

Let's go into prayer—let's listen to Leonard Cohen, "Hallelujah." Let's come together and just offer our prayers: *I pray to be an Outrageous Lover, to commit my Outrageous Acts of Love.*

CHAPTER ELEVEN

FROM PERENNIAL PHILOSOPHY TO WORLD RELIGION AS A CONTEXT FOR OUR DIVERSITY: IN RESPONSE TO THE META-CRISIS

Episode 311 — September 27, 2022

OUTRAGEOUS LOVE IS REALITY

When we say *Outrageous Love*, it's not a casual slogan. It's an understanding about the phenomenological nature of Reality—that is, the actual, *real* nature of Reality—which is a Reality animated by Eros. Eros is the experience of Radical Aliveness that desires and seeks ever deeper contact and moves towards ever greater wholes, towards ever deeper wholeness.

- It is Eros that animates the four forces of physical Reality.
- It is Eros that moves separate parts into becoming larger wholes.
- It is Eros that animates your body, and my body, in this very moment—as 37.2 trillion cells are in constant communication with each other, in a non-local awareness of each other's depths, purpose, and vision. All of those cells can actually feel each other, and in some profound biological sense, they *recognize* each other. That's happening.

Eros holds and moves *everything.*

When undifferentiated cells differentiate in the process of embryogenesis, they each move towards a particular *telos* (a particular vector) and form a particular organ, transforming as they go, in ways that are unimaginably beautiful, unimaginably complex, unimaginably wise, which all of our exponentialized supercomputers couldn't even *begin* to replicate.

Eros is the LoveIntelligence, LoveBeauty, and LoveDesire of Reality:

- That lives in every muon, and every hadron, and every lepton
- That lives in protons, neutrons, and electrons
- That lives in atoms
- That lives in molecules and macromolecules
- That lives in cells and multicellular and tissue structures, up until organelles and organisms

That's the nature of Reality.

And *that* Eros is not the ordinary love between human beings (who all too often reduce love to an egocentric strategy)—but the love that moves the Sun and other stars, as Dante described it. **It's the love that's the heart of existence itself; the love that is the motivational architecture of each and every one of us, and the motivational architecture of Cosmos itself.**

So when we say *Outrageous Love*, it's not a byword, it's not a slogan.

It's not some unreal fantasy.

In fact, the illusion that we live as skin-encapsulated egos in rivalrous conflict governed by win/lose metrics, trying to somehow soothe our unresolved trauma in aggressive forms of all kinds, which actually prevent us coming together as a global community and engaging existential risk—*that's* an illusion!

It's based on a fantasy—a traumatized fantasy—of what it means to be a human being, which is both unscientific in terms of the exterior sciences, and unscientific in terms of the interior sciences.

Outrageous Love is not a fantasy—Outrageous Love is Reality. It's more real than anything we could possibly know.

We come together here in One Mountain, and we set our intention: as a band of Outrageous Lovers, in intimate communion with each other and with all of Reality. We are here to become *Homo amor*, the fulfillment of *Homo sapiens*.

We're here to become the New Human:

- The New Human who is alive and *omni-considerate* for the sake of the whole.
- The New Human who is radically *feeling*, who can feel unimaginably, and who can think gorgeously and clearly, and who can do sensemaking, and who can create, and who can create uniquely and in dazzling ways.
- The New Human who knows that she has a song to sing, and a poem to write, and a way of laughing, living, and being and becoming in Reality that's desired and needed by *All-That-Is*. And that knowing, that gnosis, is the birthright of every human being.

We come together in Unique Self Symphony to address the unique invitation of Reality in this moment, to address the unique needs in our unique circles of intimacy and influence, and **we move towards a Planetary Awakening in Love**.

We foster *a culture of Eros*—a Planetary Awakening in Love through Unique Self Symphonies, in which each of us is playing our own gorgeous, unique instrument, and **each people, each religion, each form of knowing, each discipline in the Academy, each one plays their Unique Self instrument in the Symphony**. It's not a form of contrived identity—which then darkens, obfuscates, ignores all the other instruments—but an identity in *deep resonance* with all of the instruments.

What emerges is the sound of music, the gorgeous music which is the mathematics of intimacy that governs Cosmos, all the way down and all the way up the evolutionary chain.

That's why we're here, for this revolution.

- We understand we are not just poised before *dystopia*—but we are also poised before *utopia*.
- We have the capacity to create heaven on earth.
- We have the capacity to create a world of unimaginable beauty, the world that we all know is possible—and we are here to stand for that.

We are here to do it together. We are here to *activate* that possibility.

This is our Renaissance moment—but it's far more intense than the Renaissance, because this is a moment in which we have exponential capacities for self-annihilation.

And so, let us come together. Let us come together—not in fear, not in a kind of doomer sense of resignation. But with the hope that's born of a memory of the future, that lives in us, as us, and through us.

We know that we're not alone. **We are not alone, but welcome in the Cosmos.** We are personal expressions of the LoveIntelligence of the entire Field. And that LoveIntelligence is not a person sitting someplace—it's personhood exponentialized.

EVERY RELIGION HAS A UNIQUE SELF

There is a God, and God is the Infinite Intimate.

And as we move towards the construction not just of a ***world spirituality***, but of a ***world religion***:

FROM PERENNIAL PHILOSOPHY TO WORLD RELIGION

- A world religion which is *not* **dominating**,
- A world religion in which **there is room for** *everyone*,
- A world religion which is committed to manifesting **a world that works for everyone**,
- A world religion that is **a context for our diversity**.

There will be Christianity, and there will be Islam, and there will be all forms of Buddhism, and there will be Judaism, and there will be Confucianism, and there will be indigenous Aboriginal paths—all of the instruments of the Symphony remain.

But we also realize that **we are all part of something that's greater than the sum of the individuated parts.** And that new whole is a world religion that's rooted in a universal grammar of value rooted in First Principles and First Values that are embedded in a Story of Value, which is the story of us going *somewhere*. There are *plotlines* to the Universe Story.

And when we say the Universe is a story, we're not engaging in a fanciful conjecture. The nature of Reality is narrative. **There's a narrative arc to Reality—it's going somewhere.**

- We move from mud to Mozart.
- We move from bacteria to Bach.
- We move from quarks to culture.

Not accidentally, but filled with contingency, filled with surprise, filled with spontaneity—within an overarching arc of non-randomness. **That non-randomness is the Eros itself that drives Reality, and manifests as the Good, the True, and the Beautiful; it manifests as value—seeking, desiring ever more value.**

That's who we are. **We are unique incarnations of cosmic value**—not as a fantasy, but as the most fantastic Reality that you can possibly imagine. What a delight to be here! And to be weaving and participating together in evolving the very source code of Reality itself.

EVOLUTIONARY LOVE CODE: EVERY RELIGION HAS A UNIQUE SELF

Here is our Evolutionary Love Code for today—and it's a very critical code.

> The Unique Self of a religion is the intimate quality of meaning and meeting between the Infinite and the finite that is particular to that religion.
>
> That unique quality of intimacy is irreducible and utterly needed in the great Unique Self Symphony of Spirit.
>
> The rituals of a religion are not merely the surface structures of a religion but rather the unique, intimate expressions of that religion's erotic embrace of Divinity.

This is a very big deal because we cannot respond to the meta-crisis without an actual *sense* of a universal grammar of value—a world religion. And a world religion needs to bring together two components:

- It needs to bring together a *shared Dharma*, meaning **a shared Story of Value**.
- It has to be rooted in a shared set of **First Principles and First Values**.

But in that Dharma, every religion is going to have its unique contribution, its unique voice.

This is very, very important. It's one of the things that the perennial philosophy got wrong, and it was a critical mistake, and it is one of the reasons it didn't work.

THE PERENNIAL PHILOSOPHY

The perennial philosophy was—and *is*—a very important dimension of Reality (*philosophia perennis*, as Leibniz called it). It's the shared truths of the great traditions. That's important. And that's real. **There are shared**

truths of the great traditions that are absolutely critical. Does everyone get that? They're *absolutely critical.*

The *philosophia perennis* was this moment in the Renaissance where we did this uniquely modern move. Modernity starts around the Renaissance, and the modern move was to look back at premodernity, which was filled with *localized*, particularized moves. Every religion was, for example, *ethnocentric*: they all claimed, *we're the only ones with the truth, and only our truth is The Truth.*

Although there were other voices in the medieval period—voices of revelation and reason, voices seeking the identity between a revelation and reason, voices looking for a universal sense of reason—those voices were ultimately overridden by the sense of radical particularization, radical separateness, radical triumphalism, and a kind of rivalrous conflict governed by win/lose metrics between the religions themselves. **There was no sense of a genuine coherence, of world intimacy**—it wasn't a possibility. Every religion was located in its own triumphalist struggle, and each religion viewed the end of days—the future *eschaton*, the fulfillment of history, the end of history—as being *their* triumph over everyone else, when everyone else realizes: *Wow, we completely got it wrong*, and they bow to the particular God of this or that medieval religion.

Along came perennial philosophy and did something unbelievably important. Perennial philosophy said: **let us extrapolate shared *universals* from the *particulars.***

Each religion has its own, if you will, "separate self." If we can talk about religion as a person—ontogeny and phylogeny recapitulate each other, the communal and the personal recapitulate each other—each religion in the premodern period was a separate self, in a kind of nasty, Hobbesian state of war, quite literally, with all the other religions.

Perennial philosophy came along and said:

- No, *underneath* the separate selves of all the religions, there is

a shared truth, a shared consciousness.
- There is a deeper True Self, if you will, that's shared by all the religions.
- The perennial philosophy identified this shared True Self with the realization of emptiness, or *sunyata*, or consciousness, or whatever word each religion chose—*Ayin*, or Christ Consciousness, or *Atman is Brahman*, or the Great Spirit. There is a shared ground of being which is infinitely valuable, the infinite Field of Consciousness. That is the true nature of Reality. And **if you practice, you can get beyond your separate-self story and realize that ground, and the experience of that ground will create the better world that we all know is possible.**

That was what the perennial philosophy said.

Of course, perennial philosophy said that you can obviously continue practicing your religion, but the real thing is *not* your individualized or localized religion. The real story is this realization of your True Self, and **that personal realization—that you are not a separate self, but a True Self—*that* is actually the True Self of all the religions.** In other words, there's a shared set of universals.

That's powerful. And that's true.

So let's see if we can summarize the perennial philosophy. The perennial philosophy says that **we can extrapolate *shared universals* from the particularized localized visions of medieval life Spirit.**

Aldous Huxley was a famous popularizer of perennial philosophy who even wrote a book called *Perennial Philosophy*, and he did it quite grandly—without a computer, so he did an intense amount of research to put it together well. It's an excellent little book. Then in 1943, he published, in *The Vedanta* journal of the LA Vedanta society, a three-page article about what he calls *The Minimum Working Hypothesis* for perennial philosophy

FROM PERENNIAL PHILOSOPHY TO WORLD RELIGION

(and the Integral world has done its version of this). But basically, it comes out as follows. These are the basic grounds of the perennial philosophy (and perennial philosophy, again, means the shared truth of all the great religions):

1. Spirit is real. And I would reconfigure that and say not *Spirit is real*—we're now doing that work, redefining and rewriting and redrawing perennialism—but I'd say **value is real**. However you want to tell that story, Spirit is real, value is real, and **interiors are real**. Spirit is real, *not* a social contrivance.

2. To access the Reality of Spirit, **you go inside**. And the way you go inside is, *you practice*. You do something, an experiment. You do *an action*, an experiment that yields *a result*. That might be a whirling dervish, certain forms of ecstatic prayer, contemplative prayer, zazen meditation in Zen Buddhism, or indigenous practices. **You do a practice that takes you inside, and then you access the truth that Spirit is real.**

3. We *always* fall away from the lived realization that Spirit is real. **We forget; we always forget.** No one ever doesn't forget at times. There is *always* an exile from Eden, and the exile from Eden—both in your personal life, and mine, and in the collective life of culture. **The crisis is not an accident; it is part of the nature of Reality.**

4. After the *shattering*, after the vessels break, after we lose access to that realization, after we're exiled, after our hearts break and we cannot find our way back, after *Paradise is lost*—after that happens, there is a way back. **There *is* a way back. You can always find your way back.**

5. When you find your way back—which is, again, through practice; you find your way back through practice—you get to a level of realization that is deeper, more true, more beautiful, more good than *anything* you could have known before. You don't *just* find your way back and return to where

you were. You don't just find the place that you were lost from and recognize it for the first time. You actually find a dimension of that place that's deeper, that's more wise, that's more beautiful, that's more wondrous, that's more alive, that's more tumescent with the living God than *any* experience you've ever had. When you find your way back, you are *more*; you are wiser, you are deeper.

6. In that new state, **you actually wake up without all of the unnecessary suffering**. You release the anxiety. You are healed from the dimensions of *samsara*, the dimensions of the world of fragmentation, and you actually know your true identity. You can feel the larger whole, and the larger whole can feel you. And you have this experience of, for the first time, **being at home**.

7. But then, finally: you are motivated, you are awake and you are activated, you are aroused to move and act in the world for the sake of the healing of *all* sentient beings, for the sake of transforming Reality to higher and higher levels of the Good, the True, and the Beautiful. That experience actually awakens you and moves you to action; you become an activist. The ontology that moves in you, meaning the realization of the Real that moves in you, transforms you into an *ontological activist*. You move for the sake of the healing and transformation, what Lurianic Kabbalah called the *tikkun*: the fixing, the rectification, the evolution.

The word *tikkun*, if you look at it carefully, philologically, in the early Aramaic texts from the thirteenth century, *tikkun* means not quite *fixing*, but *evolution*.

- You participate in the evolution of the whole thing.
- You have a realization that **the Evolutionary Impulse is awake and alive in you,** by whatever name the Evolutionary

Impulse might have been called. The pulse of the Real—as evolutionary thought moved to front and center, we realized it expresses itself in *the pulse of the evolutionary process*, but let's call it *the pulse of the Real*—moves in *you*. **You participate in the Real, and therefore, you can transform the Real**. Wow.

Those seven dimensions were utterly essential to the perennial philosophy. And they said, *let's build the new world on this vision.*

And that's good. And that's true. And that's beautiful.

But it's insufficient.

And so, we go back to our code—one of our core Evolutionary Love Codes.

THE NAME OF GOD IS THE INFINITE INTIMATE

Let's look at the code again in full:

> Every religion has a Unique Self.
>
> And the Unique Self of a religion is **the intimate quality of meaning and meeting between the Infinite and the finite**, particular to that religion.
>
> And that unique quality of intimacy is irreducible and utterly needed in the great Unique Self Symphony of Spirit.
>
> **The rituals of a religion are not the surface structures of a religion, but rather the unique intimate expressions of that religion's Eros**, that religion's erotic intimate embrace of infinite Divinity.

That's a very big deal. Does everyone get how important this is? **The perennial philosophy didn't work because it didn't get this**. Right, friends? It didn't get this. The perennial philosophy said, *you don't need the religions anymore.* It said that you need perhaps *the esoteric core of each religion* that knows these seven principles that I just articulated.

I just articulated a particular summation of the perennial philosophy; I drew part of it from Huxley's *Minimum Working Hypothesis*, and one or two pieces from Integral thought. But really, it's much broader. It's neither Integral thought nor Huxley, but *a new synergy*, a new list of seven that I've never been privileged to share before—so I am delighted to share it.

When you integrate the best understandings of the great traditions, you get to those seven principles. So that's a contemporary recasting of perennial philosophy. And yet, it's still insufficient. There was a version of it in the sixteenth century and a version of it in the twentieth century, each slightly different. But basically, they're both insufficient.

It is insufficient because what perennial philosophy claimed—and this exists in the writings of almost every great perennialist, from Frithjof Schuon to Huxley, to many other writers—what they basically thought was that **the rituals of religion were *surface* structures.**

This is also a core feature, for example, of Integral philosophy. It's repeated again and again throughout that important and wonderful corpus of thought. But this is a mistake. It says that the rituals of a religion, for the most part, are almost entirely surface structures. You can let go of the rituals of the religion; you only need to embrace their esoteric core, which is this realization of emptiness. Meaning: *sunyata*, or the living ground of being, which is our True Self that lives underneath our stories. So the stories, the rituals, the rituals that emerge from the stories, the particular stories of the great religions—those are all nonsense. We call them *surface structures*, which is a nicer way to say *nonsense*.

But that's exactly not true.

Of course there are *some* dimensions of every religion that are purely historical, and there are some dimensions of every religion that are mediated through a broken historical prism which is the best that history has at that time.

For example, an *ethnocentric* prism, in which the realization of Spirit is mediated through ethnocentric consciousness, comes out with something like "We are the chosen people." And every religion had its version of *we're the chosen people*.

So clearly, there *are* broken mediating prisms that generate belief structures in a religion that are limiting and broken—and from a larger perspective, even corrupt. Yes, that's absolutely true, and we need to recognize that. It's true that there *are* some dimensions of a religion that are purely surface structure, that are nonsense, that are purely local, historical, sociocentric, rooted in a particular age and a particular moment in history.

But that's not the *core* of a religion.

- The core of a great religion is a **particular movement of music**.
- It is a particular *quality of intimacy*.
- It is a particular bridge between *the infinite* and *the intimate*.
- It is a particular instrument in **the Unique Self Symphony of Spirit**.

Just like an individual has not only a *separate self* (which is their nonsense story, their surface structure story), an individual also has a *True Self*—meaning, they're one with the Field of consciousness, one with the Field of desire and consciousness. That's True Self, and *that's* what perennial philosophy pointed to in each religion.

But an individual also has what we've called a thousand times together, a Unique Self, and a Unique Self is the unique expression of Infinity intimately configured in me.

It's *She*.

It's the Infinite Intimate.

That's the name I want to offer as part of this new world religion. **The name of God is *the Infinite Intimate*.** The names of God are very important. We need a new name of God that integrates the names of God from all the great traditions, and the new name of God is the Infinite Intimate.

Remember what we always say? The God you don't believe in doesn't exist.

> *God is either too infinite and becomes an infinity of indifference—or God is too concretized, too intimate, and becomes an intimacy of impotence.*

In history, we have moved between names of God that don't validate our inner knowing about the nature of Reality, names that don't validate the deepest realizations about Reality in an integrated synergistic form.

- We've got descriptions of the Divine that are non-personal, which don't actually reach or *feel* our lives, the depth of our humanity, or the depth of love and kindness and goodness. So it's an infinity, but it's an abstract infinity. It's **an infinity of indifference**.
- Or we have concretized expressions of the Divine that live in the mountain right next to us, our local tribal gods that are concerned with us but not potent. **They are not omnipotent; they are not omni-considerate for all of Reality**. They are close to us, but they cannot do the God work. They're not potent. And so there's an **intimacy of impotence**.

EVERY UNIQUE SELF PARTICIPATES IN THE NAME OF GOD

When I say *they*, I mean the God-Force, the Field of Divinity.

- The Field of Divinity is *infinite*, beyond any kind of personhood, as *we* understand personhood.

- And yet, the Field of Divinity is ***intimate***, more intimate than any personhood we've ever experienced.

Can you feel this? Any personhood we've ever experienced *participates* in that Field of Infinite Intimacy, which is the nature of the Divine. So we are here to proclaim and to declare, in this moment, a new name of God, for a world religion.

It's *only* through the articulation of a world religion, which is the generative ground of a shared grammar of value, that we can actually respond to the meta-crisis. **Every infrastructure move we make will break down, and every social structure move we make will break down, unless we actually address the *source code* itself, which is the Story of Value in which we live.** It's the name of God which we call out, which lives in us and holds us in the same moment.

So we are here, friends.

We are here to declare, to call out the name of God, and to call out the name of God as the Infinite Intimate.

This means that every human being—who is an irreducibly unique incarnation of the Infinite Intimate, an infinitely unique incarnation, a configuration of intimacy and desire that never was, is, or will be ever again—**every human being participates in the name of God.**

Actually, there is a reason why your name is your name. And sometimes we even take on a new name. I'm taking on a new name because I realize that my name participates in the Divine name. And **the Divine name is the sum total (past, present, and future) of every name of every human and every being, that ever was, is, or will be**—all of them together is the Divine name.

That Divine name then holds, transcends and includes, and synergizes in a larger whole, *all* of that humanity, and *all* of that being, and *all* of that becoming.

Every human being's Unique Self is the name of God.

This is why in moments of orgasm—*or'mugzam* in the original Hebrew, *the extreme light*, when I can see clearly—and I look at my beloved, and I say *Yes!*, and I call her name, or I call his name. And then I scream out, in every language: *Oh God!* Why? Because in that moment of *intensified light*—in that moment of intensified *illumination*, I realize that your name, your Unique Self, your name which is expressed, which incarnates as your Unique Self, actually personifies and participates in the name of God.

That's also true of the Unique Self of every religion. The Unique Self of every religion is an expression of the name of God.

- *Allahu Akbar*
- *Adonai Hu Ha'Elohim*
- Atman is Brahman
- *Ēl*
- Christ, our Lord
- *Ma'at*
- *Geist*
- The Implicate Order
- The Great Spirit

Each one of these names of God—all names of God—**each name of God is *true*.**

Each religion is *not* lost in some kind of demented, premodern, infantilized primitivity, as so many modern and postmodern scholars would have us believe. The core of every religion isn't *just* its realization of emptiness. **It's its intimate play. It's the intimate structure of ritual and practice.**

Unless we realize and honor that, we'll never be able to create a world religion that *recognizes* the intimate infinite beauty of the Unique Self of every religion. We won't be able to create a world religion that invites those religions, *as themselves*, in their uniquely configured pattern of the Infinite Intimate, to participate and play their instruments in the Unique Self Symphony.

If that doesn't happen, there is *no* world religion, there is no Unique Self Symphony, there is no moving beyond division.

There's no moving beyond the intense divisiveness.

THE SEAMLESS COAT OF THE UNIVERSE IS *SEAMLESS* BUT NOT *FEATURELESS*

The Secretary General of the UN just gave a fantastic speech in which he said that we've lost the capacity for collective action, both in our official bodies, and in our extra-official bodies like the G20. He said that *geopolitical divides*—what we call rivalrous conflict governed by win/lose metrics—**prevent collective action.**

We've been saying that here for a decade—that if we don't have global coordination, we cannot actually address global challenges.

- Since every existential risk is a *global* challenge, we need **global coordination.**
- But we have said that you can't have global coordination unless we have **global coherence.**
- And we can't have global coherence unless we have **global resonance.** And resonance is resonance between notes of *music*—unique, intimate notes in the Unique Self Symphony.
- And we can't have global resonance unless we have a **global intimacy.**
- And we can't have global intimacy unless we have a **shared Story of Value.**

But now we're going to add something to this.

A shared Story of Value is not one which *homogenizes* all differences.

It's *not* one which *only* realizes that what unites us is greater than that which divides us.

That's just the first part of the story. Yes, that's true: There is a shared Story of Value, a universal grammar of value.

But in that universal grammar of value, there are *individual* unique chapters and whole books that are the *unique* expression of the Infinite Intimate in a particular religion, and a particular way, and a particular path, each of which is holding a name of God. Each Unique Self of every religion is a name of God, like the Unique Self of every being is a name of God. **It's only when those names are spelled *together* that we create a true Story of Value, in which we are *all* part of the same seamless coat of the universe.**

But the seamless coat of the universe is *seamless*, not *featureless*. Its unique features are the irreducible, gorgeous, infinitely individuated expression of the fractal pattern of the Divine, uniquely expressed in the Infinite Intimate, configured *as* and *in* each particular religion.

Oh my God. **We've just evolved the source code.** Does everyone get that? We just evolved the source code right now, it just happened right here.

So it's not that the religions are just *surface structures*, and we need the *depth structures*. No. **Every religion has its *Dharma* which is unique, and it has its *yoga* which is unique.** Every religion has its Torah, its Dharma, and its *mitzvah*, its practice.

Every religion has its First Principles and First Values, and every religion has its First Practices.

There are First Principles and First Values on the one hand, and there are First Practices on the other hand.

This is the reason we made a decision to change the name of the Center. We have to evolve. Our name always has to get richer and deeper. We don't want to stay ossified in our original name.

- We began in 2009 as the Center for World Spirituality. Then we wanted to include *wisdom*, and spirituality seemed too narrow for us, and we wanted to include the great Integral map.
- So we called it the Center for Integral Wisdom, which I founded together with Sally Kempton and Ken Wilber.
- Now we're evolving it, transcending and including, including and transcending. We are renaming it the *Center for World Philosophy and Religion*, which includes all of Integral wisdom and all of world spirituality. But we need religion back on the table—we can't just say *spirituality*. **We need the *binding* character of religion.**

WE NEED SHARED UNIVERSAL RITUALS TO BIND US IN A GLOBAL INTIMACY

When I hear that people say, *wow, we're making up all these fantastic new rituals*—that's beautiful. Beautiful, but it doesn't quite get you there.

New ritual actually comes from the depth of a lineage, and that lineage has attainment. That lineage has realization. And that lineage has, as Rupert Sheldrake called it, a morphic resonance with everyone who has ever fulfilled that ritual and poured their unique realization into that ritual. These rituals were sourced in the most subtle mind-hearts. **A ritual needs the crucible of realization; a ritual needs the crucible of attainment.**

And so, whenever we create a new ritual, it can't just be this kind of modern, liberal, Jewish, Protestant, New Age, Buddhist—or whatever it is—practice. Ritual has to come out of the depths of *Her* attainment. **You**

have to hear *She* whispering in your heart-mind before you create a new ritual; we have to create new rituals carefully.

And a new ritual has to be that which *binds* us.

A new ritual cannot be: "Hey, I'm going to do it today. Ah, I don't really feel up to it, I guess I'm not going to do it for a few weeks." No, no, you must lay your life down for the ritual. It creates you, it molds you, it forms you—even as you help form it.

So we need a shared language, a shared grammar of value—and we *also* need shared rituals. **We need shared universal rituals that bind us in a global intimacy.**

- The root of existential and catastrophic risk is *not* simply **rivalrous conflict** governed by win/lose metrics, which then generates **complicated and fragile systems**. That's only part one.
- The underlying root, which generates *both* of those two generator functions of existential risk, **the underlying cause is the global intimacy disorder**—and the global intimacy disorder is rooted in the absence of a shared Story of Value.
- **A shared Story of Value needs to include both value *and* practice**, both Dharma *and* yoga, both realization *and* ritual, both Torah and mitzvah, both First Principles *and* First Practices.

That's what we're here to do. I can think of a no more noble task. And I can think of a no more daunting task. Wow!

So what I want to do is model this next week, with your permission. What we are going to do next week is we are going to come together—and we are going to do this several times during the year; this will be kind of a leitmotif this year, running through the year.

- We are going to do this around Christmas and Easter.

- We're going to do it at particular moments in the Hindu calendar.
- We're going to do it in moments in the Islamic unfolding.
- Next week, we're going to focus particularly on Hebrew wisdom because it's that time of the year—we live the calendar, and the calendar lives us—and we are going to focus on two lineage structures called Rosh Hashanah and Yom Kippur.

Now, it doesn't matter whether you are Jewish or not— it's not about that.

It is not going to matter whether you were born Christian for our Christmas conversation, or whether you were born Hindu for our Kashmir Shaivite conversation, or you were born in an Islamic country for our Sufi or classical Islam conversation. This is about:

- What's **the unique contribution** of a particular lineage?
- How do you actually **extrapolate** from it?
- How do you actually *feel into*, listen into, this unique teaching from the Unique Self instruments of a particular tradition, and place its instrument inside the Unique Self Symphony, and begin to play it as part of your life?

That's what we are going to do next week—we are going to model that. The particular topic for next week will be *tears*, the instrument of tears, of crying.

We are going to talk about four kinds of tears, and the path of tears, and the voice of tears, and the language of tears, which, as we will see, is a unique instrument in the ritual and Dharma of Hebrew practice that we want to place at the center of Unique Self Symphony.

Oh, my God. What a gorgeous code! What a gorgeous, gorgeous code. Wow.

PRAYER: WHEN I SPEAK, THE FIELD OF LOVEINTELLIGENCE LISTENS AND RESPONDS

I want to invite us to prayer—to invite *my* prayer, *your* prayer, and our prayer *together*.

Prayer means that we turn not to the caricatured God, not to the cosmic vending machine God, but **we turn to the Field of Infinity, which is the Infinity of Intimacy.** To the God/Goddess who knows our name, the *Shekhinah* who is the Infinite Intimate, that yearns for intimacy with you, with me. And who knows that through intimacy with me, with Thee, with all of us together, *She* becomes more; *She* becomes more through that intimacy.

We turn to that God—the God who knows our name, who knows that we are part of *Her* name—and we ask for *everything*. We say: **help us, hold us.** You live in us, *and* you also hold us. Because that is the nature of the personhood of Cosmos. Cosmos is not merely impersonal. **Cosmos is more personal than the most personal moment we've ever experienced.**

That's not a *dogma*—that's *realization*.

What allows me to hear you is my *intelligence*, not just my *ears*. My ears are a critical functional instrument, but my ears are animated by Eros, by LoveIntelligence. **It's the LoveIntelligence in me that hears you.**

Now, in this pointing-out instruction, is *my* LoveIntelligence separate from the Field of LoveIntelligence? All of science tells me that that's absurd.

If my individualized LoveIntelligence can hear you today, can it be that *only* I can hear you? Only my LoveIntelligence can hear you, but the Field of LoveIntelligence cannot?

Of course that's not possible.

When I speak, the entire Field of LoveIntelligence listens and responds. And just like in human intercourse—as below so above, the hermetic principle rooted in Kabbalah—the deeper I speak, and the more urgent and alive and authentic my plea, the more *deafening in gorgeousness*, the more *profound* the response.

When I turn to the Infinity of Intimacy, to the Infinite Intimate, and I share my holy and broken Hallelujah, with all my heart, and all my mind, and all my soul—*bekol levavecha, u'bekol nafshecha, u'bekol meodecha*, in the language of the original text—with everything I have, I ask for everything.

And I say: Hold me, and know my holy broken Hallelujah.

Then *She* says, Wow! There's a blaze of light in every word, it doesn't matter which I heard. But it's *all* the holy and the broken Hallelujah.

And I'm holding you right now, and I've never let you go.

CHAPTER TWELVE

RESPONDING TO THE META-CRISIS THROUGH THE EROTIC GNOSIS OF TEARS

Episode 312 — October 2, 2022

EVOLVING THE SOURCE CODE OF CONSCIOUSNESS

What we are here to do—our intention in One Mountain, Many Paths—is to respond to the meta-crisis in the only way that it can be responded to, through understanding:

- That crisis is an evolutionary driver
- That our crisis is a birth
- That every crisis is, at its core, a crisis of intimacy
- And that at the core of the meta-crisis, in this moment in time—which is driven by extraction models, exponential growth curves, multipolar traps, a race to the bottom, and tragedies of the commons, which themselves are rooted in rivalrous conflict governed by win/lose metrics, which generates fragile and complicated systems—underneath all of that, the source of it all is a *global intimacy disorder*.

A global intimacy disorder means:

- We are split off from value.
- We are split off from the Field of Value.
- We are split off from each other.

- We are split off from the deepest answers to the core questions of our lives: *Who am I? Where am I going? What's there to do?*

Of course, win/lose metrics is an intimacy disorder; rivalrous conflict is an intimacy disorder; fragile systems—in which the parts don't know what others are doing—is an intimacy disorder. But most deeply, **we are non-intimate with each other. We are not in a shared Story of Value.**

The Dharma is a shared Story of Value that allows us to respond to global challenges, because every global challenge requires global coordination.

- We cannot *coordinate* unless we have *ordinating values*, and we cannot coordinate unless we have *global coherence*.
- We cannot have global coherence unless we have *global resonance*; we have to *resonate* with each other.
- We don't resonate with each other unless we are *intimate* with each other, unless we have *global intimacy*.
- We cannot be intimate with each other unless we live together in *a shared Story of Value*.

So that's what we're here to do—**we are in this revolution**.

This revolution is about articulating the new Story of Value based on the deepest read of the leading-edge wisdom streams of the premodern world of gnosis (deep knowledge), the modern world of gnosis, and the postmodern world of gnosis. Every week, when we get together, we are here to move forward, to *turn the wheel*, and **to evolve the source code of consciousness and culture itself.**

And we do that.

Then Kristina Amelong goes in, listens carefully, reads the transcription, and she retells the story the following week. She *re-weaves* the story using the exact same words, the same sentences, but in a new order, mediated through the prism of her Unique Self, and that comes out as the *Dharma recapitulation*. That's a great service, a great devotion, a great art. I want to take the time this week to not take that for granted, to show up for the first time and be just absolutely delighted. We have actually, recently made a decision, Kristina and I, that we're going to be putting out a separate book of Dharma recaps, which is fantastic and gorgeous.

ROSH HASHANAH IS THE PORTAL TO TRANSFORMATION

This week, we are here to do something very, very specific. **We're going to talk about tears, and about *the language of tears*.**

Last week, we set up a context:

- Every great system of gnosis, including every religion, has a unique instrument to play in the Unique Self Symphony.
- We don't want to *merge* religions together, but we want each religion to be a *unique instrument* in the larger symphony of world spirituality, of world religion.
- "World religion" is really just another way of saying **a universal grammar of value, embedded in a Story of Value**, that generates intimacy, resonance, coordination—it generates goodness, truth, and beauty—which allows us to respond to the invitation of our lives *and* to all the global challenges.

This week, **we are going to model this using one particular tradition**.

We are going to do it later in the year with Islam, and we will do it with Christianity. We will *model* what it means to receive the deep, esoteric—not surface—teachings, **the profound inner teaching of a great tradition. We will *listen* to its voice and begin to integrate it in our lives.**

We are citizens of this new world religion, of this new global spirituality—and yet we are *also* often unique citizens of a particular dimension of a particular religion. We call that being *dual citizens*; we can actually be citizens of both together.

- I can be a citizen of Christianity, and I can be a citizen of world religion.
- I can be a citizen of Hebrew wisdom, often called Judaism, and I can be a citizen of world religion and world spirituality.
- I can be a citizen of Sunni or Shiite Islam, or Confucianism, or Russian Orthodoxy, or Buddhism, and I can be a citizen of world religion.

We also have to *evolve* those traditions. We cannot be in their old, exoteric, ethnocentric, premodern versions. We've got to evolve those traditions *from within*. We must let them speak their unique and gorgeous truths that then come together as part of **the great Unique Self Symphony, where we see both the universal grammar of value that they all share, and the unique quality of intimacy**—the unique insight, the unique heart, the unique ecstasy, the unique radical aliveness, the unique instrument, the unique music, the unique melody—that forms the score of this world religion, of this universal grammar of value.

We're going to model that this week with a particular tradition, a tradition that happens just to be up this week. Welcome, everyone. Welcome.

This week, we just finished a holy day called Rosh Hashanah, which literally means the beginning of the year. But it also means, in the original Hebrew, *the beginning of transformation*. *Rosh* means not just the beginning, but the entry point, the portal for transformation. **So *Rosh Hashanah* is better translated as *the portal to transformation*.**

And again, in a world religion, this is not for the Jews who are here. Just like the Christmas conversation or the Ramadan conversation, this is for everyone. We are going to weave a fabric that we can all participate in, and a fabric where we can all be inspired and transformed by each of the great traditions in their particular language.

WHEN GOD AND GODDESS ARE BROUGHT TOGETHER, BLESSINGS FLOW INTO THE WORLD

We are currently in between Rosh Hashanah and Yom Kippur (Yom Kippur is this coming Tuesday night and Wednesday). I just want to share something with you, which is actually a little bit shocking, and it literally just happened.

This Wednesday, I am going to be in Austin. There's a critical decision that has to be made about an important piece of work called *The Phenomenology of Eros*, which is one of the key source-code-changing projects we've been working on for many years. It's twelve volumes in the complete *Phenomenology*, and four volumes in the *Abridged Phenomenology*, and there will be a one-volume popular version. I am going to be meeting with someone in Austin to make a very, very essential decision on Wednesday about *The Phenomenology*. It's a critical moment.

I want just to get a *sense* of how the Intimate Universe works. This literally just happened, like, eleven minutes ago.

The Phenomenology opens with the story of the cherubs above the Ark in the Temple in Jerusalem, because that's core to Yom Kippur. This holy day that we're about to enter on Tuesday night, which includes a twenty-four-hour fast day, revolves around the high priest in Solomon's wisdom. Solomon, the great king in ancient Jerusalem, built the Temple. The Masons and the Templars all come from that world, and the Mary Magdalene tradition comes from that world, and all of the Great Western mystery traditions, and Eastern mystery traditions that are rooted in Solomon's wisdom. It actually helped form the Renaissance, and modern science, and shaped the fabric of Reality. All of this comes in large measure from the wisdom of Solomon.

The wisdom of Solomon is connected with the Temple, and at the center of the Temple, there is what's called the *Holy of Holies*. It's the place where the

Ark of the Covenant rests. Remember Indiana Jones in *Raiders of Lost Ark*? The Ark is the Ark of the Covenant.

The Ark rests in the inner sanctum of Solomon's Temple in ancient Jerusalem, and above the Ark of the Covenant are two cherubs, and they are described in the hidden esoteric mystery tradition as being *not* hallmark angels with childlike faces. The two cherubs are childlike in that they are innocent, but they're also locked in erotic embrace; they are sexually entwined. They are entwined erotically, one with the other.

On Yom Kippur, the High Priest enters the Temple and arouses the feminine waters of the *Shekhinah*, the feminine face of the Divine, the Goddess. When *Her* waters are aroused, **the High Priest**—that is to say, the perfected human being, the awakened human being—**brings the feminine Divine into erotic union with the masculine Divine.**

This is not two puppets. It's two qualities of Cosmos.

- It's attraction and repulsion.
- It's allurement and autonomy.
- It's the *line dimension* and the *circle dimension* of Cosmos.
- It's autonomy and communion.
- It's the two great forces of Cosmos, *God and Goddess*, who inhere in every moment, in every person.

When they are split from each other within ourselves—psychologically, spiritually, existentially, emotionally—Reality collapses, and our own personal Reality collapses. However, when we bring together these two qualities:

- The quality of my own fierce unique autonomy and power—together with communion, my desire to love, to participate with, to be part of.
- The desire to receive and be penetrated—and the desire to penetrate.
- Tenderness and fierceness.

When we bring those qualities together, the God and the Goddess, then blessing flows in the world.

That's what the High Priest does in the Holy of Holies. That's what Yom Kippur is. He enters the Holy of Holies and becomes a catalyst of divine tumescence. He becomes an arouser of the Divine—*that*'s what the human being is, *that*'s the essence of the lineage. **A human being arouses the Divine, and brings the world into erotic, intimate union.** Wow.

The Phenomenology of Eros opens with this set of texts. By pure divine intimacy in the Intimate Universe—we call it coincidence, but it's *not* coincidence—we've been waiting for about nine months for this, with lots of conversations about when to have this conversation. I just got a text from my friend who said let's have this conversation on Wednesday.

Now, my friend is a beautiful, beautiful man, and he doesn't know that Wednesday is Yom Kippur. He doesn't know that he picked the time and the moment in which the Priest is actually entering the Holy of Holies to catalyze and arouse the Divine—*that*'s the time we are going to sit and talk about this *Phenomenology of Eros* which opens with that text, which is about bringing that particular teaching of Eros into the world.

What a wondrous, gorgeous Intimate Universe moment!

TEARS ARE AN EXPRESSION OF THE EROS OF COSMOS

I want to add a couple of things just to frame this, and then we're going to create a model of **how a unique tradition contributes to this world religion in a stunningly exciting and important way.**

On Rosh Hashanah, we're engaged in the catalyzing of this divine union—this union that takes place all the way up and all the way down, everywhere, because this is a Divinity that's *inherent* in Cosmos and that *holds* Cosmos. This is the inherent, ceaseless creativity of Cosmos that lives in us, that lives in every quark, lepton, and hadron, and that lives in every dimension of Reality, that suffuses all of Reality.

When we bring together the masculine and feminine Divine into a new intimacy, a new shared identity, then a new whole is created that explodes blessing in the world.

- We do that politically.
- We do that socially.
- We do that economically.
- We do that in every dimension of Reality.

We are bringing together the masculine and the feminine, the line and the circle, and creating a new whole. In the tradition, that's called *arousing the feminine waters*.

The feminine waters is obviously a sexual allusion, but by *sexual* we don't mean, in this case, *human* sexual. Human sexual just *approximates*—it's an intimation of the Eros of Cosmos, of the Amorous Cosmos, in which lines and circles are seeking to come together all the time.

In the Amorous Cosmos—and here's the big sentence—there is *not only* the wetness, the tumescence, the feminine waters *below*. **There is also the feminine and masculine waters *above*.** There is what's called in the lineage, *a lower face* and *an upper face*. The lower face, in the feminine expression, has lips, and cries, becomes aroused with the tears of the lower lips. But the upper face also has lips, both in the masculine and the feminine. **Tears are considered the sacred waters of the upper face.**

Tears are understood in the lineage to be *erotic*; **tears are an expression of the Eros of Cosmos itself.** It's about:

- The *arousal of tears*
- The engagement with *the language of tears*
- The ability to hear *the voice of tears*
- Identifying the *revelation of tears*

- Letting *tears* be my teacher, my master

When I allow tears to be my teacher and master, I am gradually *in devotion* to tears, and ultimately, **I become a master of tears, and I participate in the process of the *evolution* of tears.**

The instrument of tears in the lineage is the instrument used on Rosh Hashanah, and which ends the service on Yom Kippur. It's called *shofar*, and that *shofar*, as we're going to see, is an instrument of tears itself. We're going all the way inside now—that *shofar*, in the lineage tradition, arouses the tumescence of Divinity, and arouses the feminine waters, to bring the masculine and feminine Divine together. The way the feminine waters are aroused is through *shofar*, and *shofar* is a crying instrument.

***Shofar* is tears, *human tears*.** It is our capacity to cry, to engage in the great crying game of Reality, to enter into the wail of tears.

- There's tears of *ecstasy*.
- There's tears of *union*.
- There's tears of *breakdown*.
- There's tears of *breakthrough*.
- There's tears of the shattering of the old paradigm.

There are many forms of tears, and **our capacity to *engage* tears and to cry authentically opens *all* the gates. It arouses the healing, the fixing, the evolutionary transformation of all waters.**

Every time I cry, those tears are original, those tears have a voice, and those tears speak.

This is our Evolutionary Love Code for this week:

> Tears have voice. The voice of tears speaks the language of the Divine.
>
> Tears are not one voice. There are many voices to tears, many dialects in the language of tears.
>
> Tears tell a story about the true nature of self or Reality.

Tears of pain, tears of ecstasy, tears of breakthrough, tears of breakdown, tears of gnosis, tears of revelation, tears of transformation, and more. Tears are the poetry and prayer of Eros desiring ever deeper contact and ever deeper wholeness.

The greatest tragedy is to die without having cried the tears that were yours to shed. Every time we cry, we cry for all the times we never cried before. There is no goodness, truth, or beauty without cultivating the gnosis of tears.

GOD IS THE INFINITY OF INTIMACY

This is the language, the instrument of the lineage, *speaking the language of tears*. We are going to enter tears. I am going to reverse the order today, and we will do our prayer at the end. Because *shofar*, as we will see, **these tears are actually a form of prayer itself.** So we'll climax, but in this new form of prayer. It's not fundamentalist prayer, and we're not praying to a cosmic vending machine. **We're reclaiming our capacity to turn to the Infinity of Intimacy, to the Infinite Intimate—and *that*'s the name.**

In order for a tradition to become real—to actually articulate in the world, to actually find its way to *transform* Reality, to *evolve* Reality—it needs to articulate its *name of God*.

What's the name of God in CosmoErotic Humanism, in this great new Story of Value which we are telling in this moment—in this Renaissance moment, in this time between worlds and time between stories, where we are integrating the insights of Reality into a new tapestry of intimacy?

What's the name of God? **The name of God is the *Infinite Intimate*.**

- God is not only the Infinity of *Power*.
- God is the Infinity of *Intimacy*, which is the quality of *personhood* that lives in Cosmos.

Personhood is a quality. **Our personhood participates in the quality of personhood in Cosmos, which is not a person.**

It is more than a person.

It is infinite *personhood* in which we participate, and that infinite personhood knows our name, just like we know each other's names. **The same quality that allows us to know each other's name participates in the Field of LoveIntelligence and the Field of personhood—and** *knows our name.*

In prayer, we turn to that Infinite Personhood, and we blow the *shofar*; the *shofar* of the holy and broken *Hallelujah*.

But let's take it step-by-step.

We said that the instrument of this lineage moment is the *shofar*. So let's now take a look at what *shofar* looks like, and what it sounds like, so we can feel that instrument in front of us. This lineage instrument is 3,000 years old, in an unbroken tradition core to the practice of Solomon's temple, and it's core to the practice of this lineage all over the world today. It's an unbroken lineage chain. Let's just hear it for a second, so we can feel it.

That's a *shofar*.

ROSH HASHANAH AND YOM KIPPUR ARE DAYS OF TEARS

We have a text in the canon of the lineage, which says: *this shall be for you a day of blasting.* The blasting of a horn.

What I'm now going to engage in is a kind of *mystical hermeneutics*: **the weaving of inner interior sciences.** It's what you *don't* hear about in the synagogue. This is the inner interior science, which actually *animates* the tradition. It is almost completely hidden until you see it—and then it becomes clear. *That's* **the way secrets are: until your consciousness is available and you can access them, the secret can be spoken right in**

front of you—and you still won't hear it. A secret is a secret because you don't have the consciousness to hold it. When the consciousness is there, then all of a sudden, you see it is everywhere.

So, the text reads: *this day,* Rosh Hashanah—which concludes with Yom Kippur (it's a two-part holiday, called the High Holy Days)—*should be for you a day of shofar blasting.* But the word for the *shofar* blast also means *intimacy, friendship.* So, it's also a day of deep friendship and intimacy.

But in the inner tradition, those who read most carefully, the Aramaic writers, said on this text—based on a set of reasons which I won't go into now, but they're accurate—they say, **this day is a day of tears.**

Now I'm going to weave hidden, esoteric texts from different places. In another Aramaic text in the third century that no one notices—and it's always hidden in the most obvious place—the Masters ask a question: **what is the reason that we blow shofar the way we do?**

What do they mean, *the way we do?*

If you just heard the *shofar* blowing,

- You heard: *buuuuup*—a straight blast.
- Then you heard: *Uh-uh-uh*—three or four wailing sounds.
- Then you heard *teruah,* and *teruah* is *tu-tu-tu-tu-tu-tu-tu-tu-tu.*

The word *teruah* generally means *shofar* blasting, but it's also a particular kind. So, there's basically a *buuuup,* the introductory note, but then **the essence of** *shofar* **is in** *uh-uh-uh, tu-tu-tu-tu-tu-tu-tu-tu, uh-uh-uh, tu-tu-tu-tu-tu-tu-tu-tu.*

In the original tradition, there wasn't someone who blew the *shofar* for the entire community. Everyone had a *shofar,* and they would blow it themselves. *Shofar* is an instrument, in this Aramaic hidden tradition, of tears. **It's a crying instrument.**

Now, I want to look now at just *one form* of crying. Remember, we need to hear the voice of tears. There are about twenty major movements in the symphony of tears. In the hidden lineage (you can go to lots of synagogues and never hear a single word about this), these two days, Rosh Hashanah and Yom Kippur—considered solemn days of judgment—**at their core, these days of accountability are actually days of *tears*.**

And the entire drama is a theatre of tears, expressed through the heart and the body, through ensoulment and personal myth, by different figures in the great drama of the text. **The different biblical dramas that are read in the community are actually about people who are *crying*.**

It's a symphony, a cacophony of tears. But it's *hidden*. You can participate in these services your whole life and not think about tears even for a second, which is what most people do. Because **the lineage always hides its essential teaching until you have the consciousness to *hear* it.**

THE LANGUAGE OF MOTHERS IS THE LANGUAGE OF THE SACRED

So in the third century, an Aramaic text asks, *why do we have this particular form of tears?*

- Why do we have *uh-uh-uh* and the *tu-tu-tu-tu-tu-tu-tu-tu-tu*?
- Why do we need *both* of those, and what are they about?

The word for tears comes from a particular story, in what's called the Book of Judges, where there is a woman whose name is Em Sisera, the Mother of Sisera. Her son, Sisera, is an evil figure, like a Saddam Hussein figure of the Book of Kings. She is Sisera's Mother. He's gone to battle against the Israelites. In this story, the Israelites are trying to establish peaceful relations. He doesn't want peaceful relations, so he attacks them and goes to battle. He has attacked this Israelite community. And his mother, Em

Sisera—her name in the text is Sisera's Mother—waits for him to come home, and he *doesn't* come home.

The text reads: *Sisera's Mother cries.* She is looking out the window, and her son's chariot is not coming, and she raises her voice in tears. If you remember, the hidden Aramaic text said that this day of *shofar*-blowing is a day of tears, and these tears are based on the tears of Sisera's mother. We are not sure *how* Sisera's mother cried.

- Did she cry *uh-uh-uh*? Or did she cry *tu-tu-tu-tu-tu-tu-tu-tu-tu*? There are these two different qualities of tears, and we're not sure which one she cried.
- Or did she cry both of them together, *uh-uh-uh, tu-tu-tu-tu-tu-tu*? We're not sure.
- Did she cry three wailing sounds?
- Did she cry nine or ten staccato sounds?
- Did she cry them together?

Since we're not sure, says the text, which way she cried, and because we model and pattern our *shofar*-blowing after Sisera's Mother, **we cry *all of them*.**

Now, if you're with me, what you're asking is, *what can that possibly mean?* Obviously, it's a code. Remember *The Da Vinci Code*? *The Da Vinci Code* is a popularization of the method of this lineage of the Solomon Temple. This is clearly a code; it's trying to say something. It's not just, *Oh, there was this historical woman named Sisera's Mother who cried in a certain way, so let's make sure to pattern our shofar-blowing after her.*

Why would you possibly pattern after her the blowing of the *shofar*, which is considered in the tradition, in the lineage, to be *the* most sacred ritual act?

In fact, it's the *only* ritual act in the tradition where you're considered as if you're in the Holy of Holies of the Temple, standing next to the Ark of the Covenant, with the High Priest. The *only* ritual act that gives you that ontological status, mystically—in the entire lineage—is the blowing of *shofar*. Wow! So the blowing of *shofar* is the highest of the high.

- It is the deepest of the deep.
- It is Holy of Holies.
- It is on the inside of the inside.

This ultimate interior act of ecstatic expression, in which we actually become intimate with Divinity, is patterned after the crying of Saddam Hussein's mother? Because remember, Sisera is a Saddam Hussein figure, a Hitleresque figure. **Could that be that we are patterning our crying on Yom Kippur after the crying of Saddam Hussein's mother?** We are not sure how Saddam Hussein's mother cried. Did she cry *uh-uh-uh*? Or did she cry *tu-tu-tu-tu-tu-tu*? Or did she put both of them together? So let's make sure that we repeat precisely the way she cried. Does that make any sense to you at all?

What could that possibly mean?

There's a mystical, esoteric, profound, powerful source-code-exploding discernment here.

What is the tradition saying?

What could it possibly mean?

On one level, **the language of mothers is the language of the sacred**. When a mother cries for her child, it doesn't matter who she is, and it doesn't matter whether she is the enemy or not the enemy.

- There is a language of authenticity.
- There is a language of integrity.
- There is a language of the sacred, which is the language of the mother crying for her child.

B.F. Skinner, the great twentieth-century psychologist who is, in many ways, one of the most influential theorists in the world still today, completely misunderstood this quality of Mother Love. I'm completing, with my friend Zak Stein, a book on how Skinner's thinking has actually formed the thought structures of modern Reality that are the source of the breakdown and the meta-crisis. Skinner wrote a novel called *Walden Two* (published in 1948, right after George Orwell's *1984*), about a fictional utopian community. Skinner says in *Walden Two*: we know that mother love is not real, we know that mother love is just a social construction of Reality. We know that it's just a social custom, not about anything that's essentially *real* in Cosmos. We have a custom that mothers are sad when they lose their kids, because that's an evolutionary motivation for mothers to take care of their children.

All of this, of course, is completely wrong.

The *shofar* is the language of the mothers. It's the language of the sacred. It's that which is the ultimate Eros of Cosmos. We therefore model the *shofar*-blowing specifically on the mother of an evil enemy because she's still a mother, and her tears are still holy.

That's beautiful, and there is some deep truth to that.

TEARS THAT SHATTER OUR FALSE IDENTITY

But it goes so much deeper even than that. Are you prepared, friends? Let's go inside all the way, to the deepest of the deep right now.

What is the *shofar*-blowing? The question of Rosh Hashanah, and the question of Yom Kippur, is the question of *judgment*. And judgment means, *I'm accountable*.

What am I accountable for? Not for some petty list of kind of imposed obligations that I couldn't quite meet perfectly, like I missed some ritual prayer or I forgot to do it, or I did it a minute too late or a minute longer. Or I got upset one day.

No, I am accountable for one thing:

- Am I *myself*?
- I am accountable for my *I*.

I am accountable for the ultimate question: Who am I?

I want to read you a stunning text from Abraham Kook, the great evolutionary mystic. He's quoting a verse from the Book of Isaiah, where Isaiah says, *I'm in the exile* (because Isaiah was in Babylon, he was in the exile). Kook rereads the text and says, not I but *my* I. Not *I'm in the exile*—historically, geographically—as Isaiah seemed to say it. Kook says, no, what Isaiah is really saying is *my I is in exile. I can't find my I. I don't know who I am.*

So that question of identity, that question of *who am I*, is the ultimate question.

When we identify ourselves by labels—I'm a mother. I'm a father. I'm a musician. I'm a cellist. I'm a plumber. I'm a friend. I'm a writer—that's legitimate, that's real, that's not wrong, and that's sacred.

- I am part of my community.
- I am part of my organization.
- I am part of my company.
- I am a brother.
- I am a daughter.
- I am a father.
- I am a mother.

These are all important, beautiful, and critical ways to identify who I am. And yet, **they don't exhaust the question. I am much more than all that. I am deeper than all that.** Am I willing to rip away all of those surface identifications, and stand naked before Infinity, and ask the great question of *who am I?*

THE EROTIC GNOSIS OF TEARS

Recall the name of the actor in our story. Sisera's Mother. But one second. Yes, she's *Sisera's mother*, but what's her *real* name?

The answer, my friends, is that *she doesn't have a name*. She is called Sisera's Mother. Now, imagine you're Sisera's Mother, and Sisera is going out to battle, and Sisera has not come home, so you're sitting at the window, and your identity, your name, is *Sisera's Mother*. You're looking out the window, waiting for him to come back, but his chariot is late.

How many of us have had the experience of someone being late?

- When someone is late, **first we're mad at them**. *You're late. I'm here, and why are you not here?* Like, I can't believe you're late. You get really mad.
- By the time you get to half an hour, then **you start getting worried**. What if they don't come? What if something happened to them?
- If it's someone close to you, somewhere about 45 minutes or an hour, you start having feelings. We can all recognize this: wow, **what if something *actually* happened to them? What if they had a car accident?** What would happen? Let's say it's a wife or a husband, a son or a daughter. **All sorts of thoughts go through your mind about them, but also about *you*. Who would I be if they were gone?**

When you're waiting like that, *everything* goes through your mind.

That's what this story is about—this is a waiting story. She is waiting. We don't know her name. She's identified as, *I am a mother*. And *I am a mother* is real and beautiful, but **it doesn't exhaust her identity.**

On Rosh Hashanah, she's there: I'm Sisera's Mother, and Sisera is not there, and she's waiting.

Now I'm going to tell you something, a little dark secret about myself (we've got to share our dark secrets somewhere). I come from a family without financial means, so one of the ways I got through school was by babysitting. In high school, sometimes part of college also, in the summers, whenever I could. Now just between us, I'm not sure I would hire me as a babysitter. I mean, I kept everybody safe and all that, but I was massively committed to reading, to understanding as much of Reality as I could. So I'd say hi to the kids, make sure they were safe, let them do what they were doing, and then I'd go to read.

Sometimes, I would babysit a family that had a little baby who was actually still in a crib. So there you've got to take a little more care. So I'd put the baby down to sleep, and then I'd go back and read. Every so often, you would hear the baby crying loudly, a shriek or a wail. I would drop whatever I was reading, leap up, and run upstairs to find the baby. **It's an unmistakable wail, and everything stops. It stops Reality.**

What would happen, almost every time when I got to the crib, is that the baby had lost a security blanket of some form, or a teddy bear or a doll—something that, for the baby, gave them their sense of security, their sense of belonging. Winnicott, one of the greatest psychologists of the twentieth century, called them *transitional objects*. **When the mother leaves, the baby forms their identity by holding onto what Winnicott called a transitional object**, which could be that blanket, a teddy bear, a pacifier, or a toy.

But when that *object* would drop from the crib, the baby would *scream*! The baby couldn't find herself, and for a moment didn't know who she was. And then I would get the object, or pick up the baby, and she'd feel safe again.

That's Rosh Hashanah. On Rosh Hashanah, in the lineage, we pattern the blowing of the *shofar* on the crying of Sisera's Mother.

This is because the mother of Sisera—in this moment in the lineage text which *shofar*-blowing is patterned on, which captures the inner phenomenology of this moment—**realizes, all of a sudden, that her son Sisera is not coming home.** She is the queen mother, and the king is clearly no more. So if the king is no more, if Sisera is no more, then in some fundamental sense, her position as the queen mother has disappeared. Her entire identity, her entire life, has been to give birth to Sisera, to protect him, to ascend him to the throne, and then to function as queen mother. **All of a sudden, she's not queen mother anymore, and she understands that in the depth of her being. Instead of turning away, she shrieks, she screams, she wails, she cries!**

And we want to cry *exactly* like she did. Whether it was *uh-uh-uh*, whether it was *tu-tu-tu-tu-tu-tu-tu-tu-tu*, or the two of them together, we want to cry like she did, because **we want to capture that capacity to shed those tears that shatter our false identity.**

These are tears of shattering.

These are tears of *Shevirat haKeilim*, the shattering of the vessels, when I shatter the identity that I am basing myself on. It might be: I'm spiritual, I'm perceptive, I'm writing books, I'm kind, I'm a lawyer, I'm a doctor, I'm a parent. Those are all beautiful, but however I form my identity, in this moment, in this New Year, Rosh Hashanah—as we translated at the beginning of our conversation, this *portal to transformation*—**I have to be willing to shed tears which wash away *all* of my old identity, and to literally stand naked before Infinity and to recreate myself from the very beginning.**

Can I let go of the tyranny of all the yesterdays, and actually find my unique voice? *Who am I?*

THE GATES OF TEARS ARE NEVER CLOSED

Let tears clarify the confusion.

Tears, in Hebrew, is from the same root as the word for *chaotic confusion*.

- **Tears clarify the confusion:** All of a sudden, I can see clearly now.

- Tears bypass all of the rationalizations.
- Tears bypass all of the stories we tell about what we need and who we are.

I remember I was in the Far East with an assistant of mine, some twenty-five years ago when I had taken a break from the world of teaching to understand what the world felt like from the perspective of business. For three years I was involved in entrepreneurship, in a company that was buying, selling, and taking high-tech companies public. We were in the middle of trying to close a particular deal with a company in the Far East, and I was there with my assistant, who's essential to the whole story. Her name is Mickey.

We were about to close the deal in the next couple of days, and we were being wined and dined. Mickey comes to me and says, *Something happened with my family and I feel like I need to go home.* She tells me what happened.

I said, Mickey, *You're awesome, but I think they can handle this. We need you here to close this deal. We need to take this company public, and we need this deal closed in order to do it. So I apologize. I love you madly, but I can't let you go.*

By all rational calculation, I was right. But then Mickey looked at me, and these tears start running down her cheeks. She is just crying, weeping. I said, *Whoa, Mickey!* You know what? I got this wrong, I think we can manage without you. Get a ticket, and fly home the next day. It'll be fine. Go home, take care of it. And off she went.

So what happened? What changed?

What changed was: **Her tears spoke something that entered my heart. They communicated a truth, a depth, a value that bypassed my reason and my words. Tears have a bypass mechanism; they take us directly into essence.**

Even when all the other gates are closed, the gates of tears are never closed.

So on Rosh Hashanah, we cry.

But **these are the tears of transformation**. It's the willingness to be naked before ourselves, and to literally recreate ourselves in the full depth and wonder of our unique expression.

I AM A *UNIQUE* DESIRE OF THE INFINITE

Now, who am I?

What is that unique expression that's *me*?

That's our topic for next week. But to take that step to know who I am, *who am I*, **I first have to be able to cry the tears that shatter denial, the tears that upend the old paradigm, the tears that liberate me from the tyranny of yesterday, the tears that free me from my imposter stance.**

Am I willing to actually be *me*?

The truth is, it's the only person you can be, because everyone else is taken. **But to be *you* is an outrageous act**. It's an outrageous commitment.

It means to move through the traumas, through the contractions, through the pettiness, through the smallness—and **actually feel a unique flame alive in you**. We're going to talk more about this next week, but that flame is a unique constellation, a unique quality of Outrageous Love, the love that's the heart of existence that moves through each of us.

That Outrageous Love, that Outrageous Love which is Eros, flames with desire.

The answer to the question of *who are you* is: *I am desire*.

I am desire.

In my deepest essence, in my clarified essence, in my *clarified* desire—what we call here my *deepest heart's desire*—**I am the desire of the Divine**.

I'm the desire of the Infinite.

But I am a *unique* desire of the Infinite.

The Infinite desires through me in a way in which *She* cannot desire through anyone else that ever was, is, or will be, other than me.

I am a unique configuration of desire, which means I'm a unique configuration of Outrageous Love—which means that I have Outrageous Acts of Love to commit in this world that are a function of my Unique Self. And **the committing of those Outrageous Acts of Love is my deepest heart's desire, which is the desire of Divinity awake and alive in me**.

But those aren't just words. To be a participant in Unique Self Symphony you actually have to *feel* this quality in which we have washed away through the tears. We've screamed and wailed because we realize we are not Sisera's Mother anymore. We are standing naked. We have dropped the pacifier.

And the pacifier takes many forms:

- *I'm a mother.*
- *I'm an entrepreneur.*
- *I'm a writer.*
- *I'm a lawyer.*
- *I'm a sister.*

Those are all beautiful, but **they can ultimately be a security blanket, a transitional object, or a form of idolatry that stands between me and my Essential Self**—the unique quality of desire that lives in me, as me, and through me.

TEARS TELL A STORY ABOUT THE TRUE NATURE OF SELF AND REALITY

Let's read the Evolutionary Love Code again:

> Tears have voice. The voice of tears speaks the language of the Divine.

Tears are not one voice. There are many voices to tears, many dialects in the language of tears.

Tears tell a story about the true nature of self or Reality.

Tears of pain, tears of ecstasy, tears of breakthrough, tears of breakdown, tears of gnosis, tears of revelation, tears of transformation, and more. Tears are the poetry and prayer of Eros desiring ever deeper contact and ever deeper wholeness.

The greatest tragedy is to die without having cried the tears that were yours to shed. Every time we cry, we cry for all the times we never cried before.

There is no goodness, truth, or beauty without cultivating the gnosis of tears.

We have just given voice to a particular form of tears. The voice of tears speaks the language of Divine. Tears are messengers of God. But tears are not of *one* voice. There are many voices to tears, many dialects in the language of tears.

We just told one story that's told by tears, using one dialect. Tears tell a story about the true nature of Self and Reality.

We began with one movement, one language of tears. And it's those tears that arouse the Divine. Those are tears we can only cry in this time of New Year, when we're willing to shatter our yesterdays, when we're willing to literally be born again. The notion of being born again that found its way into fundamentalist Christianity is actually rooted in Rosh Hashanah.

To be born again means that **I can actually reclaim my Essential Self that I've forgotten.** I've forgotten how to enter the question of *who are you?* I've given so many idolatrous and false answers. I'm willing to actually rip off that security blanket, to drop that pacifier, to drop all of the distressing disguises that stand between me and my essential identity.

I am desire. **I am an irreducibly unique divine desire.**

When I'm willing to shed those tears, when I'm willing to clarify my desire—and you only clarify your desire through the deepest of tears—**when I am willing to listen to the voice of tears, then I can pray.**

Tears are the ultimate form of prayer.

That's what tears are.

In the deepest teachings of the tradition, they tell of a boy who comes to the service on the High Holy Days, and everyone's there with their prayer shawls and they're speaking all of their words. The boy doesn't know the words. He doesn't know the prayers. So he takes out a whistle, and in the middle of the prayer service, he blows hard on that whistle. Everyone goes, *stop! What's the kid doing? He's interrupting the services.*

The Baal Shem Tov, the master of the Hasidic movement, turns and he says: *No, only that boy knows how to pray.*

He says, *That's what shofar-blowing is.*

Shofar-blowing is the pure tears. When we shatter the yesterdays and stand naked before ourselves, we can say *I am desire*. Because that's actually who I am.

- In my very core, I am desire, and I desire value.
- I desire goodness, I desire truth, and I desire beauty.
- But I desire it *uniquely*.
- I am the unique desire of the Divine, who discloses value that can be disclosed *only* through me. Through each one of us.

That's what it means to be Unique Self—and it's those tears that we pour into God when we pray. Wow!

So let's turn to prayer, to Leonard Cohen, who comes from this lineage tradition. The holy and broken *Hallelujah* are about the act of tears. It's about the act of coming before the Divine and offering my broken heart.

It doesn't matter which I heard, there's a blaze of light in every word, the holy and the broken Hallelujah. And the holy and the broken *Hallelujah* is always suffused with tears.

Remember, friends, **every time we cry, we cry for all the times we never cried before**.

We cannot respond to the meta-crisis without articulating a universal grammar of value embedded in a Story of Value—and **in that Story of Value, there has to be tears. We have to be willing to cry with each other.** But it's not just about crying with each other.

- We have to be willing to listen to the language of tears.
- We have to feel the gnosis of tears, the revelation of tears.
- We have to weave the tears into public policy.
- We have to weave the tears into economic policy.
- We have to weave our tears into cultivating a culture of Eros and a politics of Eros, into being Outrageous Lovers.

There is no response to the meta-crisis without tears. The holy and the broken *Hallelujah*. In prayer, we:

- Ask for everything.
- Ask for the capacity to cry.
- Ask for the ability to have those tears answered.
- Pray for your uncle, for your brother, for your sister.
- Pray for the whole world.
- Pray for all the tears that have been shed—so for the first time, we can dry up all the tears.

And then we can transform the tears of pain and yearning into tears of ecstasy, and tears of joy.

CHAPTER THIRTEEN

TEN PRINCIPLES OF OUTRAGEOUS LOVE: CLOSING THE GAP BETWEEN FEELING AND HEALING OUTRAGEOUS PAIN

Episode 313 — October 9, 2022

CROSSING TO THE OTHER SIDE

It's a mad delight to be with everyone, and to be here in this place, and to be here together, in One Mountain, Many Paths, and in this seat of the revolution. And when we say *the seat of the revolution*, we don't mean it metaphorically. We mean it literally.

Last week's *Evolutionary Sensemaking* resonated us into this place, this *resonance of tears*—and we are about the *evolution* of tears. Can you feel that with me? We are about the evolution of tears. The evolution of tears means that:

- I'm able to cry for *more* than I ever thought I could cry.
- I'm able to cry, I gain the capacity to cry, tears of ecstasy, for those I never thought I could cry for.
- I'm able to feel joy that's so much wider and so much bigger than any of the joys I thought I could feel.

Can you feel what it means to expand your field of the tears of joy?

I can actually feel joy. Who can feel that?

Normally—as a normal, separate-self human being—I'm able to cry a very narrow field of tears of joy:

- If I win the lottery.
- If something particularly good happens.
- If I start going out with a new person.
- If I get a present.
- Maybe, if I'm particularly sensitive, when I got some new insight.

We cry tears of joy for a very, very narrow field.

But when I *wake up* to my true identity, when I move from being merely a separate self—from being *Homo sapiens*, who's lost in the wisdom of separation—and I become *Homo amor*.

I cross to the other side.

I cross to the other side. I become the New human and the new humanity.

I begin to embody what it means to be the New human and the new humanity. I'm able to cry tears of ecstasy for much wider circles.

I cry tears of ecstasy for things I see on the news, for things I read in the newspaper, for a friend I've never met—because *no one* is a stranger to me.

I begin to cry tears of ecstasy for *Reality itself*. I feel.

I'm inspired by the chant of Reality itself.

I'm inspired by the pulse, the throb of a tumescent Reality awake in every second.

WORLD RELIGION AS A CONTEXT FOR OUR DIVERSITY

THE DHARMA IS THE PSYCHEDELIC OF REALITY

I'm always doing a kind of psychedelic journey. And in this psychedelic journey, it's *lions and tigers and bears, oh my*—and I see dazzling images coming at me.

Often, a person will do a journey—let's say a psychedelic journey—if it's done in a guided and appropriate way, if you take it with people who really understand the path deeply, you can actually see an incredible array of Reality.

But only if you really understand what's happening, and you don't *get lost*, which is why I generally don't suggest journeying—because both for the guides and the participants, it's quite easy to get lost. Because medicine doesn't work without Dharma.

Psychedelic medicine needs the Dharma, just like the Dharma needs the expanse of the medicine.

But if you actually find your way, and you see these dazzling cacophonies of Reality, you realize that those dazzling cacophonies are actually the true nature of the Reality that you inhabit.

That if you were able to visualize and to feel what actually lives between you and the next person—between you and the tree, between you and the atmosphere—you would see a dazzling cacophony of electromagnetic waves, of gravitational fluctuations, particles of every kind and form moving in the space of mirror neurons, weaving webs, invisible lines of connection and intimacy, every place and everywhere.

You would think, *oh my God! Oh my God!*

You'd be *blown away* by the rapture of the fullness around you and the unimaginable, subtle beauty of dazzling interpenetration.

That's actually the truth of Reality right in front of you, the ecstasy of Reality disclosed and naked in front of you. And you would realize that actually *this* is the journey, right now, right here.

This is the journey! And it's so fully awake, so fully alive. And you'd be able to cry tears of ecstasy, literally, for Reality itself.

The Dharma is the psychedelic of Reality.

The Dharma takes us into the inner quality of Reality itself, so that I can actually evolve my tears. *That's* the evolution of tears.

THE EVOLUTION OF TEARS ON THE SIDE OF JOY AND ON THE SIDE OF PAIN

The evolution of tears is my capacity to cry ecstatically by meeting the unimaginable fullness of the present, quite literally this very moment, right now:

- Where I'm actually experiencing myself as being *breathed* by Reality;
- I am aware of *everything* happening all around me.
- I experience myself as the very center of the whole thing—even as I know that *you* are the very center of the whole thing at the same time, so I have actually entered the Field.

If I can use a term from contemporary science, the Field has *multiple centers*. We are all multiple centers of the Field, and it's actually always happening right now, this very second.

So as we gather from around the world, and as you feel the cables of connection, both on the exterior and the interior, binding us and weaving us together, as our hearts begin to beat in a synchronous beat, and we actually open our hearts, we cry.

Because how could you not cry in response to that dazzling beauty?

> ## *We live in a world of outrageous beauty, and the only response to outrageous beauty is Outrageous Love.*

And Outrageous Love *always* cries tears of ecstasy. That's the evolution of tears: I'm actually able to cry in a much wider way. **I move beyond the narrow confines of my separate self, and I begin to cry from the place of my Unique Self.**

I am a unique expression of the Field. I am in the Unique Self Symphony, which means I am actually *listening* to the Field. I don't experience myself as a separate self sitting in my little box and asking, *did One Mountain entertain me today?*

No, I'm saying: *Oh my God, I'm part of this revolution.* I'm part of this planetary awakening in love through Unique Self Symphonies.

That is what my beloved Barbara Marx Hubbard and I talked about every week, one way or the other, for many years.

- I'm playing my instrument in the Symphony, and I can see the notes of music.
- I literally see everyone around me as a note of music.
- I see the Dharma as music—the music of the interior dance of Reality, which guides the exteriors.
- And then I say *Hallelujah*!

That's the evolution of tears on the side of joy, on the side of delight, on the side of ecstasy.

Then there's the evolution of tears **on the side of pain, of unbearable heartbreak**. And I'm able to evolve my tears—I don't only cry for my own, for my own loves, for which I should cry; for my loves won and my loves lost, and the shatterings of love.

Because any true love will experience a shattering. Sometimes there is a love that's true and deep and beautiful, and real—but it doesn't have a temple. Every love has its temple, every truth has its temple, but sometimes we cannot quite find the temple for that love—and so we cry. We cry not that the love has been broken, but that it didn't have—in this world, or at this time—a temple.

So we feel that pain, and we feel it personally. To be able to feel that pain personally is a great quality of an Outrageous Lover.

But then we expand.

We don't locate ourselves *only* in those tears.

We actually enter into *the depths of our personal tears*, and those personal tears become our chariot.

We literally ride those tears into the *wider* tears, the tears of those I don't know, or who I do know but barely pay attention to. **And I begin to actually feel the pathos of other people's pain.** Because *intimacy* means:

- Feel me feeling you
- Feel you feeling me
- Feel me feeling you feeling me
- Feel you feeling me feeling you feeling me

But not just between me and you, the particular localized Beloveds—I begin to feel beyond my immediate circle, and I begin to feel wider and wider circles of intimate resonance with the heartbreak, with the breakdown, with the collapse.

And then I feel into the whole thing.

And I feel into existential risk.

And I feel into the potential death of humanity.

And I feel into the potential death of *our* humanity.

And I stop doing business as usual.

DEEPENING OUR COMMITMENT TO REBUILD THE NEW WORLD WITH "MONOGAMOUS POLYAMORY"

I stop being busy in this New Age, Human Potential addiction to yet another program and to yet another modality. Can I get another program and another modality? It's the New Age opioid crisis of modalities and programs. I stop being so busy, and I *deepen*.

I deepen my monogamy, which means that I deepen my primary commitment to being in this revolution, the understanding that the only response that will shift the future, the only genuine response to the meta-crisis is:

- Not an *infrastructure* response, although that's necessary, and we absolutely need to rebuild certain critical infrastructures.
- Not just a *social structure* response, which is laws and social covenants—although some of that is completely critical.
- But it's a *superstructure* response, which means **we've got to tell a new Story of Value.**

And we lay down our lives—as da Vinci and Ficino did in the Renaissance—to actually *telling* that new Story, because we know only that is what's going to heal suffering. It's the one thing that's going to allow us not to collapse. And if we do collapse partially, that's what's going to rebuild us the next day.

> *We are building, we are enacting, we are activating the new Story—not only to avoid the collapse but also to rebuild when parts of the system do collapse.*

What are the codes through which we will rebuild the new world? We are writing those codes now, together, here. Can you feel that? **We are writing those codes now, together, here.**

The overwhelming moral imperative of this moment is to tell this new Story to avert all the dimensions of the collapse that we can legitimately avert. And we're going to spend the next ten years writing that story, and telling that story, and delivering that story into culture.

That new Story comes from here; it comes *from us*.

It comes from One Mountain.

It comes from our commitment.

It comes from our love.

It comes from our circle of intimacy and influence.

It comes from us showing up, week after week, *for* each other and *with* each other, in this profound and beautiful and stunning monogamy.

It's a monogamous polyamory. Meaning, *of course* we can dance at more than one wedding, and *of course* we should take different dimensions and pieces appropriately from different places, and have them be part of us, and give of ourselves.

But in the end, we understand that the *only* thing that takes down the culture of death, the Death Star—episode six, the third movie of *Star Wars*, one of the most watched movies ever—is a **direct hit**. And such a direct hit comes from one place and one place only: from enacting and activating a new Story of Value, from *living* that story—from articulating First Values and First Principles embedded in a Story of Value.

That's what we're here to do.

Oh my God, what a great honor, what an insane pleasure! Oh my God, yes.

And here's the thing. When I say polyamory, I don't particularly mean sexual polyamory—although it's true there as well. The weakness of polyamory, of always loving a new person, is that you are not really *loving*.

You are just engaged in:

- The pseudo-eros of a new modality
- The pseudo-eros of a new body
- The pseudo-eros of a new place
- The pseudo-eros of a new song
- The pseudo-eros of a new chant

Of course, newness is beautiful. And we *should* engage, we should love widely and broadly.

But polyamory also always has to be monogamous.

This is a paradox, not a contradiction. There is a monogamous polyamory, and that means I have to be *deeply at home*. We are here at home in One Mountain.

We say the Dharma every week. We say it in a different way, we approach it through a different door, we deepen the Dharma in all sorts of ways and all sorts of nuances, we add new chapters to the Dharma—but in the end, we are *here*, and we are here *every week*.

That's the strength of the great traditions, which the New Age World, and the West Coast Human Potential world, the San Francisco and Portland kind of world, hasn't yet been able to replicate, which is why it hasn't had power.

Everyone's *dilettanting*. Everyone is running from place to place in the opioid epidemic of new modalities and new experiences. And that's a kind of superficiality, when it becomes addictive, when it actually prevents me from dropping into depth.

The opposite of the holy is not the unholy.
The opposite of the holy is the superficial.
Depth is the holy.

And depth is singing the same thing again and again, but each time it's deeper.

It's not that I saw you naked once, or twice, or three times, or four times, or five times—and we're over. No, it's that I am blown away by your naked shoulder. I am blown away by your naked belly because **I always see with fresh eyes.**

That's how we chant.

It's what we do each week in One Mountain.

It's always with fresh eyes. Soft eyes, fresh eyes.

WHEN GOD IS DETHRONED, OUR SOLUTIONS BECOME THE GREAT TRAGEDY ITSELF

We are about to pray. We're about to play that song by Leonard Cohen, "Hallelujah." It's about the holy and broken *Hallelujah*.

And I'm going to invite myself if I can, with your permission, and invite *you*, to step into this prayer like we never have before—to actually *open up* the Field of Prayer, which is the Field of the Intimate Universe. **We turn to the Divine whose new name, the new name of God, is the *Infinite Intimate*.** God who is the Infinity of Intimacy, who knows our name, who holds us in the holy and broken *Hallelujah*.

WORLD RELIGION AS A CONTEXT FOR OUR DIVERSITY

Part of reweaving the source code of consciousness and culture and telling the new Story of Value is the realization we are not in this alone.

So we can't have TechnoFeudalist Thanos solutions, if I can borrow the image of the archvillain from the last *Avengers* movie. Thanos is a Singularity University technocrat who comes up with solutions to existential risks that kill half of humanity, solutions that downgrade the essential quality of humanity of those people who are left alive. But he's doing this because he thinks it's the only way to save humanity.

No, no, no. The Thanos solutions are without First Values and without First Principles, and most importantly, without *partnership with God*.

When God is dethroned, we step out of the Field of the Tao. God means the Tao, the Field of Value. When we step out of the Field of Value, out of the Tao, and seek solutions to existential risk, **then our solutions become the great tragedy itself**.

Our solutions themselves become the fulfillment of existential risk. We seek to *heal* existential risk, but our solutions for its healing *create* the destruction. That's the Thanos image in culture, which comes from the end of the *Avengers* movie. He wants to get the Infinity Stones in order to, in one instant, painlessly as it were, kill half of humanity to save the rest.

That only comes from human hubris, a Thanos hubris—

- That isn't *partner*ed with the Divine
- That's not *in search* of the Divine
- That doesn't *feel* the Divine in search of humanity

No, we are *partnering* with the Divine, which means we are partnering with First Values and we're partnering with First Principles. **We are partnering in a Story of Value.**

We are in the Song of Solomon which says, *Ani le Dodi, ve Dodi li:* I am from my Beloved, and my Beloved is from me.

Oh, my God! Oh my God, what a joy, what a delight!

We're going to resonate the code, then go into the holy and the broken *Hallelujah*, and then we'll pray together. We're going to invite the Partner to pray with us. And then we'll do some Evolutionary Sensemaking: we're going to go through the ten principles of Outrageous Love. That's what we've committed to today. We've done six of them already. We'll review those, and then we'll get to the last four.

We're going to see something just so dazzling, just so beautiful, which opens up so much possibility. Because *that*'s what we are.

- We are at *One Mountain*.
- We are living and breathing **the Divine Field**.
- We are the Evolutionary Impulse.
- We are the Possibility of Possibility.

PRAYER IS ONE OF THE MOST POWERFUL MEDICINES

I want to say just one sentence as we go into prayer.

We live in a world today where there's an enormous amount of *medicine journeys*. Have you noticed that?

For example, Steve Jobs wrote in his autobiography about doing medicine journeys, different forms of psychedelic journeys. In fact, Jobs wouldn't hire someone at Apple who hadn't done some dimension of journeying—so journeying went from the fringes to the center of culture.

The problem with journeying is that by itself, it can be neutral, or even dangerous. Meaning: when you go inside—depending on what kind of plant you're on, what kind of ride you're on—that ride inside doesn't *work*, and it doesn't get you home without Dharma.

So, again, Medicine needs Dharma. And Dharma needs medicine.

A better way to say this is: Dharma needs yoga.

- Yoga can be prayer.
- Yoga can be chant.
- Yoga can be meditation.
- Yoga can be writing, sacred writing (Aurobindo's great yoga, his great medicine).
- Yoga can also be an occasional journey with medicine.

But Dharma needs yoga; yoga needs Dharma.

Dharma needs medicine; medicine needs dharma.

You can't do psychedelics, or any other kind of yogic practice, without Dharma, because then it becomes only the *cultivation of a state experience*, and that state experience by itself is neutral.

There's a reason why there were practiced Zen monks serving as kamikaze pilots for Japan in World War Two; they cultivated their journeys, their deep state experiences. **But if those state experiences are not mediated through the Dharma**, through an understanding of the Amorous Cosmos, the Amorous Cosmos that lives in me—through First Principles and First Values—then **the medicine becomes poison.**

And at the same time, Dharma always needs yoga. It means **the Dharma always needs to be *alive*. I always need to feel it, in my spirit, in my soul, in my body.** Otherwise, the Dharma gradually ossifies; it gradually petrifies, and it can become scary. The Dharma becomes *dogma*. So the Dharma needs the medicine, and the medicine needs the Dharma.

One of the most powerful medicines is prayer.

Praying is a psychedelic journey—that's what it is.

I step inside, I feel. I train myself to feel, to arouse myself to feel the Field of the Infinity of Intimacy.

And then I can access the holy and broken *Hallelujah* that lives in me.

And I can feel Her holding me and touching me and gracing me, and kissing my holy and broken *Hallelujah*, and kissing my broken heart.

And I show up deeper and deeper to tell the new Story, to be the new Story, to articulate the new Story of Value.

And I ask Her: *help me!*

Help me be healthy.

A dear and close friend of mine, just called me and said she had Parkinson's. Like, wow, that's a big deal. Dear friend of mine, a personal friend of mine. So I'm praying for her. She's going to be good, she's going to be fine, she's going to walk through it. You can walk through Parkinson's these days. There's actually that real capacity if you really approach it with Divine grace, and there are new openings in that. And I have great hope for it.

So we pray. We pray for our friends that are sick, and the parts of ourselves that feel sick. And we pray for those who have a need for physical healing, and need of financial healing, and need of heart healing.

We pray for all of it, and we pray for the whole thing.

That's the evolution of tears: we cry for the whole thing.

And we feel our joy, and we feel the joy of the whole thing.

That's the holy and the broken *Hallelujah*.

Let's track this in our hearts, and let *it* track in our hearts.

And let's pray like we never have before.

Ask for everything you need.

Prayer is about dignity. Prayer affirms the dignity of personal need.

That's what evolution is. **Evolution is love in action responding to need.** *That's* what evolution is. And the dignity of personal need is what prayer is about.

- Prayer affirms dignity of personal need.
- Prayer tells me what I need.
- It reminds me of what I need.
- It forces me to clarify what I need.

So let's pray together.

Let's hold hands with *She*, and let's ask.

Ask for everything. Let's ask for everything.

Let's go in, the holy and the broken *Hallelujah*.

WE ARE THE INFLUENTIAL AND THE POWERFUL

Everyone saw in the chat box, someone called Randy showed up and just screamed "Hey Niggers"—and we don't know who the person was.

Whenever you go to enact a revolution, there's someone who's going to act out. And that's a tragedy. Because actually, all over the web, those voices are dominating the threads and the chatrooms—voices of polarization, voices of hatred. We have to actually *drown out* those voices. We have to be a revolution of Outrageous Love. And so, Randy, *that's not okay*.

Whoever you are, I am sorry for the tragedy of your life.

But I call you to know and to feel your goodness, and to feel the joy that lives in you.

And to feel the pain, and not let that pain become poison.

And I call you to your potency.

And I call you to your poignancy.

And I call you to your power.

Because when you come and throw a bomb that says *nigger* in a chat box of love, you're *not* powerful. You're *powerless*. You're *not* poignant, you're pathetic. You're *not* potent, you're impotent.

So let's stand for the voices of love.

And let's feel not the voices of polarization, but the voices of potency.

Oh, my God. Let's take a look at the chat box. Oh, my God. Let's just look at a couple of prayers. Let's feel a couple of the prayers.

I pray that tears, says Margie, kiss the cheeks of those most influential and powerful.

Yes, Margie! And, beloved Margie, you are awesome, and you are a rock star. And you know, **we *are* among the most influential and powerful**.

- All the places you think are influential are only peddling pseudo-eros.
- What's actually going to evolve the source code of consciousness and culture, and change the very superstructure of Reality, is *a story of value in which we live*—that's us.

It is hard to kind of take that seriously. We run away from our own power—when actually we *are* the influential and powerful.

Let me ask you a question. Imagine you are in Jerusalem, and it's the moment of the crucifixion. It's literally the moment of the crucifixion, that epic moment in Christianity. **At that moment of the crucifixion in Jerusalem, who is powerful?**

There were many influential and powerful people in Jerusalem at that moment. But how many of us have *any* idea who those people were? We haven't heard a word about them. We don't know who they are.

Their power was illusory.

It was impotent power.

It was the power of pseudo-eros, not the power of Eros.

And that little band of Outrageous Lovers that gathered around the cross at the moment of the crucifixion, when Eros itself was being murdered—we know who *they* are.

We know every one of them.

We know every move they made, every breath they took.

And we honor those breaths, because **those were the breaths of the powerful**.

We think we know who's influential and powerful today. But we're *deflecting*. Because actually the powerful—that's *us*, my friends. Do you get that? *We* are the influential and powerful.

And that's an incredible realization.

EVOLUTIONARY LOVE CODE: HEALING WHAT'S *UNIQUELY YOURS* TO HEAL

Why do we not act to *heal* outrageous pain?

It's not, as often suggested, because we do not *feel* the pain. Rather, it's because we feel the pain so intensely and don't *know* how to heal it.

In the gap between our ability to feel the pain and our ability to heal the pain, we close our hearts. Therefore, the only way to open our hearts is to close the gap.

We close the gap by restoring our capacity to heal the pain, thus allowing us to take the first step toward healing, to feel the pain. **The precise method of closing the gap is to realize that it's not ours to heal** *the whole thing*.

It's ours to heal the pain that is *uniquely ours* to address, in our unique circle of intimacy and influence.

To be a Unique Self is to be a unique healer, that's to say, the healer of the pain that is yours to heal.

We are all healers.

THE TEN PRINCIPLES OF OUTRAGEOUS LOVE

Why do we not heal outrageous pain?

Let's just go through ten steps, and let's see if we can get this really, really clear.

I'm recapitulating here, so I'm going to start from the beginning. I'm going to go through it just very simply, very gently. We can see all ten pieces in there, they are stunningly beautiful.

1 . WE LIVE IN A WORLD OF OUTRAGEOUS PAIN, AND THE ONLY RESPONSE TO OUTRAGEOUS PAIN IS OUTRAGEOUS LOVE

The first step is: We live in a world of outrageous pain; the only response to outrageous pain is Outrageous Love.

- We live in a world of outrageous pain.
- We don't deny the pain.
- We don't explain the pain away.
- We don't say the pain is an illusion.
- We don't say the pain is a result of some sin we've done for which we deserve punishment.
- We don't do the New Age version of that when we say we "attracted" the pain into our life.
- We actually stand before outrageous pain, but we don't try to give answers.

You cannot *answer* the pain—there are some questions that don't have an answer. Therefore, we say the only *response* to outrageous pain is Outrageous Love. It's not an answer; that *nullifies* the question. It's a *response*.

We respond to outrageous pain by protesting. **We protest because we know we live in a Field of Outrageous Love, so pain is a violation of Outrageous Love.**

And we respond with Outrageous Love by moving to heal the pain, by moving to transmute the pain, to transform the pain.

We are unique incarnations. We are *lived as love*.

We are Outrageous Love in action.

We are evolution, and evolution is *love in action*.

We are unique incarnations of evolution.

So we are unique incarnations of love in action, individually and together, as Unique Self Symphony.

2. OUTRAGEOUS LOVE IS THE HEART OF EXISTENCE ITSELF

What does *Outrageous Love* mean? What does that word mean?

By Outrageous Love, we mean not ordinary love but *love which is the heart of existence itself*.

Ordinary love is the sense that love is a mere human creation, a mere human contrivance, a social construction of Reality.

We are saying no, no, no…

Love is not mere human sentiment. Love is the heart of existence itself.

---

3. THE OUTRAGEOUS LOVER COMMITS OUTRAGEOUS ACTS OF LOVE

Who are we? We are unique incarnations of Outrageous Love. That's what it means to be a Unique Self. We started with:

- One, we live in a world of outrageous pain, the only response is Outrageous Love.
- Two, we made the distinction between ordinary love and Outrageous Love.
- Three, we ask *what does an Outrageous Lover do?* An Outrageous Lover is lived as love.

And what does it mean to be lived as love? It means **the Outrageous Lover commits Outrageous Acts of Love.**

That's our great crime: we are committing the crime of Outrageous Love. And I'm calling it a crime because it breaks the boundaries of the proprieties of ego, of not giving too much, of being closed, of giving of my heart, but *not* of my funds, because those are only for me. It's outrageous.

You know who a person really is:

- By who they are when they're scared,
- By who they are in sexing,
- And by who they are with their money.

Those are the three ways you can really know a person.

My money is not mine. I give my money. I pour my funds. I've done that my whole life. It's all we need. You've got to *pour funds* into your holy circle. The notion that there are actually just individual people, and everyone should *self-commodify*, and get a particular job in a particular way, and function in that self-commodified role is not exactly right.

We need to move in the world as bands of Outrageous Lovers, and in those bands, we all have different roles. We have to give *everything*. For some people, commodifying and monetizing works well—and for other people, it doesn't. So we have to move down the field and take care of each other in a thousand ways together.

So Outrageous Acts of Love are our *crimes* of Outrageous Love because they're *outrageous*. They break the boundary of the conventional, of what is conventionally acceptable in the myth of separation.

I become an Outrageous Lover, filled with that sense of outrage against contraction, an outrageous joy—and so we commit our Outrageous Acts of Love.

4. I COMMIT OUTRAGEOUS ACTS OF LOVE THAT ARE A FUNCTION OF MY UNIQUE SELF

Which Outrageous Acts of Love should we commit?

Those that are a function of our Unique Self.

Every person is a *unique* incarnation of Outrageous Love, and every person has *unique* Outrageous Acts of Love to commit.

5. OUTRAGEOUS ACTS OF LOVE ADDRESS A UNIQUE NEED IN MY UNIQUE CIRCLE OF INTIMACY AND INFLUENCE

So I commit the Outrageous Acts of Love that are a function of my Unique Self. And which ones are those?

Number five, those are the Outrageous Acts of Love that address a unique need that needs healing, in my unique circle of intimacy and influence.

I'm not here by mistake. The Intimate Universe allured me into this place where I am, with these people, in this life, and this situation, and this dynamic. I came here through the allurement of Reality that drew me here.

And speaking and addressing my unique circle of intimacy and influence—that's where I commit my Outrageous Acts of Love.

6. I PLAY MY INSTRUMENT IN THE UNIQUE SELF SYMPHONY

As such, number six, I begin to play my instrument because my Outrageous Acts of Love are my instrument. I begin to play my instrument in the Unique Self Symphony.

That's what it means to be truly alive.

7. WHY ISN'T EVERYONE MOVING TO HEAL THE OUTRAGEOUS PAIN?

Seven, why isn't everyone doing it, why isn't everyone moving to heal the outrageous pain?

It's not, as is often suggested by so many spiritual teachers, because we're locked in our ego, because we don't feel the pain. We are too busy with our lives. We don't feel the pain, so we don't actually respond. We actually turn away.

That's actually not true for so many of us. It's actually deeper.

8. THERE IS A GAP BETWEEN OUR ABILITY TO FEEL THE PAIN AND OUR ABILITY TO HEAL THE PAIN

Number eight, actually, we *do* feel the pain. We *allowed* ourselves at one moment to feel the pain, and we felt it so acutely, so painfully, so immensely, that we couldn't bear it. It became unbearable in some essential way. We turned away because we didn't know how to *heal* the pain.

> *In the gap between our ability to feel the pain and our ability to heal the pain, we turned away; we closed our hearts.*

We didn't close our hearts because we were lost in a kind of narcissistic ego. We closed our hearts because at one point we opened our hearts, we were fully open, and we felt it. But we felt impotent to heal it. The gap between our ability to feel the pain and our ability to heal the pain was unbearable. And so, in that gap, we closed our hearts.

9. WE OPEN OUR HEARTS BY CLOSING THE GAP

So what do we have to do to open our hearts, my friends? How do we *open hearts*?

We open our hearts—and this is our code—we open our hearts by closing the gap. **We close the gap between our ability to feel the pain and our ability to heal the pain.**

10. CLOSING THE GAP BY HEALING THE PAIN THAT'S MINE TO HEAL IN MY CIRCLE, MAKES ME POWERFUL AGAIN

Okay, now number ten: How do we close that gap? We close that gap by giving up the narcissistic delusion of the ego that I myself *can* or *must* heal *the whole thing*.

- It's not mine to *heal* the whole thing.
- It is mine to *feel* the whole thing.
- What's mine to heal is the unique need that can be personally addressed by my capacities and my gifts, in my unique circle of intimacy and influence.

We actually turn away from healing the unique need in my unique circle of influence and influence because we cannot heal the whole thing. It's a deceptive strategy.

No, I've got to *feel* the whole thing, and then I've got to turn to my neighborhood, to my circle, to my community. If I am privileged to have a community which is actually engaged in the revolution directly—wow, we get to be the privileged and the powerful!

Let's just feel that, friends. Let's just feel that. It is so beautiful, so beautiful:

I can actually heal the pain that's mine to heal in my circle, and that makes me powerful again.

Do you get that? *That makes me powerful again.* All of a sudden, I'm powerful again.

I'm powerful because I am actually *living* my Unique Self, addressing the unique pain in my unique circle of intimacy and influence—doing what's mine to do.

And when I do that, and I experience my power again, my heart opens again, and I can feel more than I ever did. And when I feel more than I ever did, **it fills me up with even more power and expands my potency, and I can heal wider and wider circles**. That's the Dharma, and that's the yoga.

First, I have to throw off that notion that it's *all* mine to heal. It's not all mine to heal. That's a narcissistic delusion of the ego.

It's mine to *feel* the whole thing—that's the evolution of tears. The evolution of tears is, I can not only feel *my* pain, I can actually feel the outrageous pain of *the world*.

And then I turn to my unique circle of intimacy and influence, and I act there heroically, outrageously, committing my crimes. My crimes—meaning, my great and gorgeous acts. They're crimes in the sense that:

- They are crimes against contraction,
- They are crimes against smallness,
- They are crimes against pseudo-conventions that keep us locked in our impotence.

We have to be outrageous!

I commit my Outrageous Acts of Love, addressing the unique need in my unique circle of intimacy and influence.

Oh, my God! Can you feel that, my friends? How gorgeous, right? How gorgeous! All the way! Can you feel that? Wow. Wow. How gorgeous indeed! How gorgeous indeed.

What an honor, my friends. It's a crazy honor to be with you.

It's a crazy honor to be part of our band of Outrageous Lovers.

It's a crazy honor to be articulating, together, these Evolutionary Love Codes, and downloading them into the source codes of culture.

It's a crazy honor to love each other.

It's a crazy honor to be monogamously polyamorous with you, to be in the depth monogamy.

It's a crazy honor to be the Dharma for the medicine. Wow.

Crazy, crazy delight and honor to be here together.

Oh my God. Thank you. Thank you. Thank you.

CHAPTER FOURTEEN

HOW BIG IS YOUR HEART? FROM THE AGONY CRUCIFIXION OF THE CROSS TO THE BLISS CRUCIFIXION OF THE CROSSING

Episode 320 — November 27, 2022

TO BE NON-INTIMATE WITH REALITY IS TO BE LOST IN THE DRAMA OF MY OWN LIFE

Every week, we are participating together—in this revolution, in this commitment to *the crossing*, in this commitment to *know* that we are literally at a unique moment in history. We are at a moment that we've never been in before. We are literally in a time between worlds and a time between stories.

The beginning of the crossing is the beginning of being willing—

- To wake up,
- To not turn away,
- To *not bury my head in the sand of my life*— my business, my relationship, my kids, which are all beautiful, of course—we absolutely love our kids.

I love my kids. One of my favorite things to do in the world is to be with my son, Zion, who is 12, and to

throw a ball with him. Just to throw a ball back and forth, what a crazy joy! Our relationships, our children, our friends, our places of work where we create, all that matters enormously.

But, friends, it's not enough. In the old world, the integrity of that was enough. But in the new world, in order to actually *have* a new world, in order to have *a tomorrow*, there needs to be a group of us who say:

- We are going to look *at the whole*.
- We're going to understand that we are challenged in a way that we've never been, that existential and catastrophic risks are real. And as the pandemic—which was just a dress rehearsal—reminded us, it's *not* too big to fail.

I want to *get this* with you for a second. Can you join my heart for a second? Can I join your heart? **Let's enter the depth of truth** for a moment, and just throw away the *public* ways we talk, and just enter the truth and enter the heart, *for real*, for real.

Last night, I was looking at what's happening in the oceans—and particularly in the waters between Turkey and Greece, and other places of crossing into Europe, where refugees from the Middle East have been crossing into Europe, whether it's finding your way to Greece, and then trying to get to Hungary or trying to get to Germany. I was reading story after story about boats lost at sea. Little dingy boats with women, children, men... and the coast guard was not stopping because it's *against policy*.

You've got a world in which there are **millions and millions of refugees**—and we have enough to feed the world *twenty times over*. And yet, we don't have a big enough heart. We *look away*—and they literally drown in the sea, week by week, desperate for freedom, desperate for new possibilities, desperate to live the beauty of an ordinary life—and to laugh and to eat and to sing and to pray. To eat, to pray, to love.

And we look away.

To be *non-intimate* with Reality is to be so lost in the drama of my own life that I cannot feel *beyond* my own life—to begin to *feel* those people in those little boats, in the middle of the night, the mother with her child clutched against her breast, and to say: **that baby is *me*, and that baby is *you*, and I can *feel* her.**

At a certain point in my life, in 2006, I wanted to join an organization which was working on exactly these issues. I was going to give up teaching, because I thought teaching was a waste of time, and I needed to just get directly hands-on involved in this day and night.

The reason I didn't go down that route is because I literally didn't have enough power. I didn't have enough power. There was so much infighting, and so much ego, and so much just utter nonsense—it was just tragic— within the organizations that were supposed to be helping, with all the infighting between them, and the egos of their leaders. I realized I didn't have enough family power, I didn't have enough funding power to make a difference. And I realized that what I needed to do was to put my attention to actually birthing—together with you, together with *we*, as our Unique Self Symphony—**to birthing a New Human, birthing a New Humanity, birthing a new Story of Value that we all live in.**

Because that's the only thing that's going to change the way we engage suffering in the world.

WE HAVE TO FACE THE PAIN—BUT WITH RADICAL JOY!

That was 2006. And then, as I studied more clearly, I realized, every day more and more, the increasing level of risk and the increasing level of breakdown. And I began to understand—around 2008, 2009, and 2010 and 2011—that we are facing genuine existential risk. Like wow, *genuine existential risk*!

Existential risk can express itself in one of three ways:

- In **extinction**—humanity actually goes all but extinct.
- In a **collapse**, in which we lose several billion people.
- Or there is **this split in a *caste system***, in which there's this very tiny elite that somehow manages to live in its own sterile internal environment, while ignoring the utter suffering as systems begin to collapse—whether ecosystems, or governmental systems, or nuclear waste systems, or dead zone in the ocean systems, or runaway artificial intelligence systems—systems begin to collapse, and billions of people die or suffer immeasurably.

To be intimate with Reality is: *Oh my God, we can feel that!*

Now, we are gorgeous and stunning and beautiful human beings.

We are not selfish and contracted; we feel everything.

But we often *turn away* from our feeling.

The universe *feels*, and the universe feels *love*. We are each a unique expression of that feeling of the universe, and so I understood, and we understood—many of us here today—that we have to come together, and **we have to write a new constitution.**

Because I'm *not* willing to live in a world in which a woman clutching her baby drowns at sea, and I turn away. We have to create a new world—and the world is filled with gorgeous people.

I am going to talk about *why* we turn away a little bit later.

- It's not because we're evil.
- It's not because we're selfish.
- It's not because we're narcissistic.
- It's not because we're contracted.
- It's for a much deeper reason. It's a reason that we can *transform*. It's a reason that we can *heal*. It's a reason that we can *solve*.

We *can* do this, friends! We can do this together. I think about this day in and day out, and I sleep in it every night. We cannot turn away from the pain. We have to *face* the pain, but **we've got to face the pain with radical joy.** You cannot face the pain by abandoning joy.

> *The only way to change the world is to be willing to live in a world that's already changed, right now.*

Meaning:

- We've got to live in the liberated world.
- We've got to live in the celebration
- We've got to live in joy.
- We've got to be in *radical* joy.
- We've got to experience our *second innocence*. We've got to experience play and joy, food and delight, dancing and music.

And we are going to be coming together, by the way, this summer, for a week in the second half of August, to do Mystery School, **to celebrate and to write the constitution of this new world**. We are going to be doing this fabulous week of radical dance, radical music, radical study, radical Dharma. All day, all night, for seven days. **We're going to have this wild party to change the world—a wild party to transform the world.**

We've got to do it.

WE HAVE TO ARTICULATE A NEW POLITICS OF OUTRAGEOUS LOVE

We have to step out of our ordinary lives.

We cannot let the trauma of our ordinary lives so *close us down* that we look away. We've got to take care—we've got to take care of our child, and we've got to take care of the inner child in us that's traumatized—*and* **we also have to step *beyond* in the very same time, and be omni-considerate for the sake of the whole.**

> *The universe feels and the universe feels love, and the universe feels through me.*

The personal is political, there's no split—and so **we have to articulate a new politics of Eros and a new politics of Outrageous Love.**

So we come together to look in each other's eyes. And we say to each other, *Revolution!*

We come together, we face each other—heart to heart, and mind to mind—and we say, *Evolution!*

We want to begin to chart the personal, collective, and cultural path, from a politics of *polarization* to a politics of *meaning*—which is a politics of Eros, which is a politics of Outrageous Love.

Now remember, the personal is political.

- If I don't *embody it*, if I can't feel it in my body, then I cannot do it.
- If I don't embody my own politics of meaning, if I can't feel it in my body, then I cannot join the great *polis*, the great community of meaning.
- If I don't feel, in my body and heart and mind, my own personal politics of Eros, then I can't join in the enactment of the great *polis*.

Polis means *community*, the great *polis* of Outrageous Love. And each of these words *means* something—and that's what we've been talking about here in One Mountain.

Value, *Eros*, *Outrageous Love*—each of those words has a very deep, profound meaning.

We are writing a Great Library, like da Vinci and his cohorts did in the Renaissance, at that time between worlds and that time between stories. We realize we are in a time between worlds, in a time between stories— so **we are writing a Great Library, like the great library of Alexandria, where we come together and we tell and retell a Story of Value**. We integrate the best of the sciences—the best of physics, and the best of biology, and the best of molecular chemistry, and the best of anthropology. And we're trying to fund this, we're trying to resource this, so we can hire enough researchers to work across all disciplines, and to write the great new Renaissance Story of Value.

Because, friends, we're facing a meta-crisis. It's a true meta-crisis.

And we can either look away—or we can say, no, we are actually going to be the New human and the new humanity, we are going to cross to the other side.

Homo amor doesn't look away.

Sometimes *Homo amor* has to step back.

Sometimes *Homo amor* steps forward.

But *Homo amor* never looks away.

WE LIVE IN AN INTIMATE UNIVERSE AND THE INTIMATE UNIVERSE LIVES IN US

We are facing a meta-crisis, and in facing this meta-crisis, we have two radical invitations—or, maybe better, two radical *demands*, made upon our heart, mind and body, soul and psyche.

- The first is a demand *to know*; an invitation to know.
- The second is a demand to incarnate, to be, to embody.

First, we need to *know* something of the nature of the Cosmos. And to know is carnal, to know is erotic: and Adam knew his wife Eve. It's carnal knowledge, and you've got to *know* it.

> *We can know something of the nature of Cosmos because Cosmos lives inside of us.*

We know because we participate in the Field of Eros.

We participate in the Field of Eros and Grace.

We participate in the field of meaning.

The politics of meaning, and the politics of Eros, and the politics of Outrageous Love literally lives *in us*, and we can *feel* it—in the same way that the mathematician *feels* the equations that span billions of light years.

How does mathematics work? The fact that a mathematician can *think* in mathematics, and that those mathematics *match* the Cosmos—the unbearable elegance, the unreasonable elegance of mathematics—is because it all lives in me, in each of us. **There is a mathematics of intimacy that lives in us**, the same way the mathematician feels the equation that spans billions of light years—because those equations, the elegance of mathematics, lives *inside* the mathematician.

You see, **it's not only that we live in an Intimate Universe, it's that the Intimate Universe lives in us**. That's actually the truth. **The mathematics of intimacy that governs Reality lives in us**—and it's not just the mathematics of the physical world, it's the mathematics of *interiors*—and these are the laws of Cosmos.

The laws of Cosmos literally live in us.

I want to be really clear: when I say *law*s, I'm not making a fundamentalist claim. Fundamentalism is the premodern view of the world that lives in a lot of the world today. There's lots of fundamentalism—and bless our friends who are fundamentalists, and they must have an important seat at the table. I want to welcome fundamentalism to the table because it also stands in this Field of Meaning.

But the weakness of fundamentalism is that fundamentalism almost always says, *my system has all the meaning and all the laws.* We understand it all, and **there's no more mystery**. We understand why people suffer, and we understand what we need to do to get to whatever heaven means, we know *exactly* what heaven looks like.

That's dangerous. We can never give up our humility. We can never give up the realization that we're always in devotion. **We are always kneeling to kiss the ground before the mystery.**

The laws don't obfuscate.

They don't blur the mystery—the mystery is *always* there.

The laws don't occlude the uncertainty. They don't birth in us a hubris, an arrogance that blinds us to our radical devotion, humility, amazement, and awe before the great mystery. That doesn't happen.

And yet—we *can* know. There *are* certainties that live in us.

Knowing the laws of Cosmos, my friends—as they live in us, as us, and through us—empowers us and emboldens us. It calls forth our sacred audacity to enact a politics of meaning, a politics of value, a politics of Eros, and a politics of Outrageous Love.

WE ARE COMING TOGETHER FROM AROUND THE WORLD TO WRITE A NEW CONSTITUTION

There are words that come *from words*—and there are words that are deeper, words that come from *silence*—when we get quiet enough, when we enter into the world of the depth of silence, we can hear the **words that come from the silence.**

When we enter into those words, when we enter into the field of play, when we enter into our second innocence, and we can feel the goodness of Eros moving through us—then we have direct access to the laws that govern Reality, and it's from these laws, my friends, that we must write a new bill of universal human value, and from that universal human value comes universal human rights—in other words, a new bill of universal human joy and responsibility.

There's no joy without responsibility, but responsibility won't work without joy. I cannot take responsibility for the suffering around me—whether it's in my family, whether it's in myself, whether it's in the world, whether it's the women and men clutching babies dying in the seas, trying to get over to Europe—we cannot do it unless we are *already* in joy.

> *We laugh out of one side of our mouths, and we cry out of the other side.*

We live in a world of outrageous pain, and the only response to outrageous pain is Outrageous Love—but we also live in a world of outrageous beauty, and the only response to outrageous beauty is Outrageous Love.

And when I go to do wild Tantra, wild Tantra is not *an escape* from Reality. It has to embolden me to pour the steadiness of my Eros, so that—

- I am holding, and I am opening, and I am playing my instrument in the Unique Self Symphony.
- I am realizing I am a leader, that I have the ability to bring things together—and I was born to bring this together in a way that no one else can.
- I was born to stand next to my friends in Unique Self Symphony—for you to stand next to me, and for me to stand next to you—so we can do this together.
- We *can* write this new constitution, and we can download it into culture.

- I can wrap my head around the whole thing, and I stay steady.

And that's what we are here to do.

> *We are here to begin to enact, from these laws, a new universal grammar of value as a context for our diversity.*

I want to say that sentence again because it's so shocking.

I want to enact—*we* want to enact—a new universal grammar of value, which is the source of a new grammar of human rights, a new bill of human rights, that's going to serve as a context for our diversity.

That's what we are here to do! Wow.

Wherever you are, whatever country you are in, wherever you are around the world—in your country, there was a moment when they came together to write the founding documents of your government.

It doesn't matter whether you're living in China, or Russia, or Holland, or Brazil, or the United States, or Belgium, or South Africa, or Antarctica, or New Zealand. It doesn't matter where you are. Wherever you are, there was a time when they wrote the founding documents. **We are now coming together to write the founding documents of the New World.**

That's what we are actually here to do. For real, not for pretend.

We are coming together here now to write the founding documents—together as a Unique Self Symphony—the founding documents of the New World.

> *We are coming together from around the world to write a new constitution.*

WORLD RELIGION AS A CONTEXT FOR OUR DIVERSITY

But that constitution is *already encrypted*, the code is already encrypted *in us, as us, and through us.*

That's what anthro-ontology means: *ontology*—the true Reality of Cosmos—lives i*n me.* What we said seven minutes ago: *We don't just live in an Intimate Universe, the Intimate Universe lives in us.* **It is already embedded, ever and always, in our deepest interior—waiting to be revealed, waiting to be disclosed, and waiting to be clarified.**

We do what only human beings have the capacity to do. We are recovering a memory of the future.

We recover a memory of the most beautiful world that we already know is possible.

We respond to the meta-crisis by invoking this most beautiful world, this most true world, this most good world that we already know is possible— and yearning to be born.

And we can do this together. Oh my God, we can do this together! Who can feel that?

Where are we? We are in this time between worlds. We are in the revolution.

And am I too excited about this? Am I too emotional about it?

Hell no! We are not looking away, and it's such a delight to be here with you.

FORGIVE YOURSELF! FORGIVE ALL THE PEOPLE WHO BETRAYED YOU!

I just want to add something personal because maybe it'll help. Last night, I received a file from Suzette and Krista, which was a file of a bunch of things I did twenty years ago.

I was in the Middle East, and I was doing a national television show in Israel. We were participating in these gorgeous festivals; we had 40,000 to 50,000 people, and we created a series of study programs in Israel and America. I watched it, and I looked at it, and it just blew my heart out. It just blew my mind how beautiful it was.

And I'm just going to share something deep with you.

I went through a personal tragedy then, a great personal tragedy. There were two or three people who quite deliberately went to take it down. They wanted to take it down for political egoic reasons, and they did it by making a couple of false complaints against me—and were able to. Afterwards, I went into complete silence for two years. It took us two years to recover the information to show that it was completely false. But for two years, I went completely offline. It kind of froze. It never unfroze—because that's what happens in the internet world.

I was watching it last night. Again, I haven't looked at this for twenty years. And I watched it from midnight till three in the morning—and I was shocked, just shocked again at the brutality. The way we can be so brutal to each other, and the way we can get lost in our own win/lose metrics, and the way we can make these very short-term moves to give ourselves a sense of being alright, and to deal with our own trauma. Of course, the people who organized this hit were traumatized, and they were dealing with whatever their own sense of their pain was.

And I said, wow, **how do we do that to each other?** It just blew my mind. And for about an hour, I just cried. I just cried at how cruel we can be—and how incredibly *stupid*.

The world is burning, friends—and I just said to myself, *wow, all is forgiven, who cares?*

I was watching a particular program, and there was someone in it who I was very close to at the time, who was involved in that betrayal. And I just said, *wow, I forgive you*. Done, it's over. We've got to turn to the men, to the women, to the babies, to the next generation, to catastrophic risk, to existential risk. **We don't have the luxury of staying in the trauma.**

So I want to turn to everyone here, and I want to say, whatever you've experienced, you're my closest friends. We are close friends. This is our inner community, this is our inner space. And we've *all* gotten hurt, and we *all* get stuck in the hurt. And we all get stuck in our little family systems, however beautiful they are—and they are so beautiful, so important—but it's not enough. If you are here, then you are one of the people that's in the Unique Self Symphony.

And I want to just invite everyone:

Forgive yourself! Forgive all the people who betrayed you!

Forgive—and get out of the story of retelling the story of the trauma again and again. Do what you can today to heal it—and turn your vision to the world. Liberate yourself! Let's liberate ourselves—so we can actually join hands and be at this moment of the crossing. We've got to do all the inner work, yes. But that's just the beginning, and that will never end.

This is the moment right now to say, *I forgive you.* I forgive you. I'm sorry, I forgive you. It's over. And now, for the rest of my life, I'm putting my attention on the world, and I'm going to hear the cry of the world, and I'm going to respond in the most gorgeous and beautiful and stunning way that I can. That's the only thing there is to do. Oh my God, wow!

FROM THE CROSS TO THE CROSSING

Our Evolutionary Love Code for this week:

> We are at the time of the crossing. The time of the crossing is a time between worlds and a time between stories.
>
> Unlike any time we have ever been in before, the crossing is a pivoting point in history. Unlike any time we have ever been in before.

The Crossing takes place as we are poised between utopia and dystopia. It's the moment that Abraham stood in, when he heard the call to cross to the other side. It's the moment that the slaves stood in, when they needed to decide whether to return to Egypt or to cross the Red Sea to the other side.

This is the great moment of The Crossing. All the wisdom traditions in the world—premodern, modern, postmodern—knew that this moment would come.

We are at a phase transition which will either mean the collapse of human history or the birth of the most beautiful world we can imagine. We will either birth a New Human and a New Humanity, *Homo sapiens* will fulfill itself and become *Homo amor*, or we will experience collapse, stagnation, or extinction.

This is the moment where every human being and humanity as a whole is asked the following questions:

Am I ready, am I willing to play a larger game, to participate in the evolution of love?

Am I willing to become the New human and the new humanity?

Am I willing to stand for all of the past and all of the present and all of the unborn in the future, and cross over from *Homo sapiens* to *Homo amor*, and birth the most good, true, and beautiful world that we all know is possible?

Are we ready? Who's ready to cross to the other side? Are you ready? We go from the cross of our lives, the crucifixion of our life—because we *all* get crucified—to the crossing.

We go from the pain crucifixion of the cross to the bliss crucifixion of the crossing.

Can you feel that?

We go from the *pain* crucifixion of the cross, when our lives are nailed to the cross and we are betrayed—and there's *always* betrayal, there's *always* a Judas. And **we are *always* betrayed by people who could never *possibly* betray us.**

Say I'm doing business with a close friend, and all of a sudden, that close friend is thinking about something else. And all of a sudden, they can't feel who we were, and they betray me. And the only reason it's a betrayal is because they could never betray me. It's somebody who would *never* betray me. So we are only betrayed by the people who could never betray us. And, friends, **sometimes we betray ourselves**. Wow, we sometimes betray ourselves.

When I look back at 2006—and the claims were completely false, I was literally completely innocent of anything claimed in the attack, a political attack that was disguised as something else—and yet, I look and I say, *what an idiot I was!*

I was just *blind*. I didn't understand the danger. I protected our organization against every possible threat from the outside, and I was completely naive about what the other dangers were; they didn't even occur to me. And so I have to forgive *myself* for that.

How could I *not* have known? I don't know, it didn't even occur to me that people could betray each other—it wasn't even a possibility in my mind. I was quite naive and an idiot, a blithering idiot! And I've got to forgive myself for being a blithering idiot.

We absolutely have to forgive ourselves.

We must forgive ourselves for the crosses of our lives, for the agony of crucifixion. **We must go from the cross to the crossing, to the *bliss* crucifixion of Reality's Eros—shimmering, awake, and alive in us, calling us to play our instruments in the Unique Self Symphony.**

That's what it means to be alive!

We're going to cross to the other side.

We are going to go all the way in this lifetime.

So who's willing, my friends? Who's willing to go all the way in this lifetime? From the cross to the crossing, from the agony crucifixion to the bliss crucifixion?

WE DESPERATELY NEED EACH OTHER

We don't have to do it alone.

I can't do it alone. Honestly, friends, I can't do it without you. You are my family, and we're a family together. We are a Unique Self Symphony. **We are here to arouse a Planetary Awakening in Outrageous Love through Unique Self Symphonies.**

The old world of just one leader is not going to take us home. We need leaders; leadership is important. We need teaching—sure, that's important. But we need to give rise to a new possibility.

That new possibility is that we are all in the crossing. We are *all* on the cross in our own lives, and we are *all* moving from the cross to the crossing.

We need to move from the enlightenment of the elite to the democratization of enlightenment, to the democratization of greatness, to the realization:

- That every man, woman, and child has an instrument to play in the Unique Self Symphony.
- That every man, woman, and child has a song to sing.
- That every man, woman, and child has a poem that needs to be written, a story that needs to be lived.
- That the command of your life is, **live your story. Live your story as chapter and verse in The Universe: A Love Story.** Live your story as chapter and verse in the music, the opera, the emergence, of the new Story of Value.

Oh my God, friends! Friends, **we need each other**. And we think that we can love and *not* need.

This is a very funny thing. This is a completely vulnerable, honest day. So I'm going to tell you something else: **We think we can love without needing.**

Sometimes, in my close circle of friends, some of the people in my close circle of friends—they are all fabulous human beings, and some fund or resource the organization with their time, others with their creativity, others with financial funding—I noticed that sometimes people have this sense, *does he really love me, does she really love me*, whoever it is? Because, after all, he *needs* something from me.

So that's bullshit, let's get clear. *Of course* we need things from each other. **To say *I love you* is to say *I need you*.** And we look in the eyes of our deepest lover, and our deepest beloveds, and we say, *I love you*. Oh my God, *I need you!*

This is not *codependent* need, nor *egoic* need which manipulates for the sake of its own greed—**but we need each other for the sake of the all. We all need each other desperately.** So I want to say clearly, when I say *I love you*, it *always* means I desperately need you. And you desperately need me, and we look at each other and say, *we desperately need each other*.

Do you know how much joy it is to desperately need someone? That's what happens when you're making love. When you're making love you have this sense, *Oh my God, we need each other to go home*. There's a reason we're not self-pleasuring and instead making love.

We are making love because we need each other.

We need each other's touch.

We need each other's tenderness.

We need each other's fierceness.

We can only enter heaven *together*.

Teilhard de Chardin, the Jesuit paleontologist, didn't have the word Unique Self Symphony, but he had the beginning of the vision of it. He writes very beautifully: "There is almost a sensual longing for communion with others who have a large vision. The immense fulfillment of the friendship between those engaged in furthering the evolution of consciousness has a quality impossible to describe."

There is nothing more sensual than sensemaking together, I would add.

There is nothing more sensual than the knowing, the gnosis, the knowing together, and then embodying together as Unique Self Symphony.

We have our historical friends, and those are important; our historical friends are important.

And we have our friends that we interact with historically, and we have our business friends that make our businesses run, and we should love each other and be good to each other.

But the people we can be at home with are our *evolutionary friends*:

- The people with whom we're participating together in the evolution of love.
- The people who are willing—together with us—**to move from the cross to the crossing**.
- The people who are willing—together with us—**to be omni-considerate for the sake of the whole**.

Can you feel that with me?

INFINITY NEEDS YOUR SERVICE

Now, I want to just take us just one more step here.

I love you, I need you—where does that come from, who said that first? What's the source of that great statement, what's the source of it? Who said it first? *I love you, I need you.*

We think *I need you* means there's a lack of power. It's not. It's not. It's not. The most powerful person is able to look in the eyes of his or her beloved, or circle of beloveds, and say:

> *Oh my God, I desperately need you, and I'm powerful enough to tell you that I need you.*

So, who says that first, my friends?

That's the great statement of the Divine.

That's God's great proclamation.

In all of the understanding, when you weave together exterior sciences and interior sciences, we have this realization that at some moment, this world that we live in *manifests the un-manifest:*

- The eternal becomes the temporal, the un-manifest becomes the manifest.
- Infinity discloses itself as finitude.
- In the language of the great traditions, no-thingness becomes thingness.
- And in the singularity, Cosmogenesis explodes.

However it happened, whatever the story is—whether it's a multiverse story, or a single universe story—at some moment, this Reality, this manifest Reality that we live in, *explodes.*

And Infinity turns to us and says:

It's not enough for me to be Infinity. I am. I am Eros itself. I am love itself. I am creativity itself. I am all power. I am the Infinity of Power—but it's not enough for me to be the Infinity of Power because power requires intimacy. I'm only powerful if I'm powerful enough to surrender.

So God Herself, Divinity Herself, the Buddha Herself, the Christed One, the Aboriginal vision of heaven and sky, that vision of the transcendent source of all, turns to us—literally *to us*...

Because where were you at the moment of the Big Bang? You were right there. Where else could you have been? **At the moment of the Big Bang, we were all there together.** We were all there, quite literally, scientifically, in that original singularity. We were there together.

Mathi and Claire, you were sitting there together at the moment of the Big Bang, and that's why you found each other now, to sit and have a drink in Paris together, and to plan a revolution. Brothers and sisters. Kristina, oh my God. Dr. Kincaid. Kristina Amelong. Krista. David. Jacqueline Lee. Zohar. Benjamin. Simona. Jamie. Krista. *All of us.* **No one's outside the circle.** Chahati—we can't do it without Chahati. Every single one of us, we need each other, and we need each other desperately. We desperately need each other.

And so we turn to each other and say: *Oh my God, I love you, I need you.* Because that's what God said to us. God said to us—

> *I can't do this myself.*
> *I want to be not just the Infinity of Power.*
> *I need to be the Infinity of Intimacy.*
> *I need to surrender in order to be alive, and I want to surrender*

to you.
I need to partner with you in creating the most beautiful possible world.
I cannot do it myself.

Immortality turns to mortality, God turns to the human being, and says:

> ## *Let us—you and I, together—create the world in my image.*

There's a great statement of Infinity, from the sixteenth century, from Ibn Gabbai, one of the greatest masters, the great statement of Divinity: *Avodah tzorech gavoha*: God/Goddess needs your service.

God needs your service, quite literally. Without Suzette, there is no game. God needs Suzette. Goddess needs Suzette. Doesn't happen without it. Goddess needs Madea. Goddess needs Mosa. Goddess needs every single one of us—no one's left out.

Uniquely, uniquely, God needs your service.

Your deed, my deed, is God's *need*. We need each other.

MY HOUSE IS YOUR HOUSE

I want to invite—*me*, and *we*, and *thee*—to feel the joy of *She*, of Reality, knowing that we need each other, and knowing the radical joy of needing each other.

My money is your money. My time is your time.

When you're in trouble, I'm in trouble—for real.

Now, God can do that infinitely for 7.8 billion people. We have to do it for fewer people individually. There's X amount of people we can hold—and so we hold as many as we can.

And then we turn towards the whole story, and we actually go to rewrite the source code. Because we need to all take care of each other.

It cannot be a top-down governmental system controlled by a technocracy, where we all have ID numbers, and if we toe the party line, and if we agree with whatever the official dogma is, then we can get health insurance, we can get a job, and we can get food—that's where we're going now.

Now, we cannot go there. We've got to go someplace else. We've got to go to a place where the universe *self-organizes*, where we have more and more local communities, in which we take care of each other.

My house is *not* my house; my house is *your* house.

The Center for World Philosophy and Religion actually just bought a home for the Center, and it's owned by the Center. We wanted to have a place where fellows who are studying could come and work and write. But we also wanted a place where if someone got in trouble, they'd have a place to come. We have five guest bedrooms, and I hope they'll be full all the time. **Because we've got to have a home, a home where people can gather.** We have to take care of each other. We *have* to take care of each other.

Does that make sense? Who can feel that? I need you!

I apologize for being so personal today—but I need you.

And you know what? You need me. And you know what? **We need each other, every one of us.**

We can do this! And the utter joy of making love is the joy of knowing that we need each other to enter heaven.

- We need each other to explode in joy.
- We need each other to scream *Yes*.
- We need each other to scream *Oh, God!*
- We need each other to scream each other's name.

That's what Unique Self Symphony is. That's what a Unique Self Symphony does.

And we have to hold each other's *holy and broken Hallelujahs*. Because, friends, we are *all* holy and broken Hallelujahs. It doesn't matter—we say it every week—*it doesn't matter what you heard, there's a blaze of light in every word. The holy and the broken Hallelujah.*

So I want to just thank you.

WE ARE NOT ALONE IN COSMOS

Just one more thing before we go into prayer: **We are not *alone* in the universe.**

Anyone who thinks we're alone in the universe is not actually examining the information. One could make that statement fifteen years ago, possibly ten years ago. Today, a vast amount of information available tells us:

- We are living in a larger galactic field.
- There are other civilizations.
- There are other life forces in the universe.

This is clear beyond the shadow of a doubt.

I don't know if you've tracked this information. This used to be fringe, hidden from the public eye. It was fringe, a kind of sideshow. No one serious or respectable could talk about the fact that there were clearly other life forces in the universe. But now, at Harvard, in *The New York Times*, at Technion in Israel, the Sorbonne, leading figures in these fields are tracking and gathering information, and writing in the mainstream media. It's very clear that our best explanation for an enormous amount of information is that we're not alone in the universe.

We are in a wild Cosmos. I want you to get that phrase: *It's a wild Cosmos, a galactic Cosmos*. And our role in this wild Cosmos is to demonstrate for the Cosmos:

- What it means *to evolve, to transform.*
- What it means to birth a New Human and a New Humanity.

Whether we participate in a leading role, contributing gorgeously to this wild Cosmos, or whether we end this very short story of humanity, *depends on us.*

Will we birth the new human and new humanity? It begins right here and right now. I am the birth.

I want to ask everyone to do it in the most serious way. I love you, I need you. You have resources, you have time, come work with us. We have a whole editing team, where we are editing texts that we want to download into culture. Let's do this. Friends, let's pour our funds, our resources, our money, our passion, our time. Let's love this open. **This is ours to do.**

And I've just got to say, if you're really here—and you are here, that's why you're here—**if you're here today, it's because this is *your* story. This is *your* revolution.**

Abraham Kook asks a question. He's one of the great thinkers of the twentieth century. He asks, who are the leaders of this generation?

Is it the priests? No, he says.

Is it the great scholars, the academics? No.

Is it the politicians? No.

Is it the titans of industry? No.

So who are the leaders, who's going to take us home, who's going to take us to the next level? Who is going to be Moses in this generation? Who's going to be Buddha?

He says something so insanely beautiful. He says:

> *In this generation, for the first time, the people who are the leaders are the people who choose themselves, who feel this call in their heart.*

Sometimes that call is very faint; they can barely hear it.

Sometimes that call gets covered over by the trauma, pain, and the demands of life. But they *feel* it, they can *hear* it—and because they can hear it, they *self-choose*.

They are not willing just to live lives that are small and ordinary; they're committed to the extraordinary.

We are here to be extraordinary. We are the leaders, and this is ours to do.

In this generation, we are at the center of the band of Outrageous Lovers, that are here literally:

- To love it all open.
- To birth *Homo sapiens* into *Homo amor*.
- To be a beacon to each other and to the galaxy, to this wild Cosmos where we're about to start finding each other in a new way.

It's a wild world we live in, friends, and we have a wildly gorgeous role to play.

She needs us.

She needs us, and we need each other.

What a crazy pleasure that is!

Let us offer that in prayer now. And we offer it in prayer not to an ethnocentric God who is trying to make sure that you don't get too much pleasure, or trying to demand your obedience. **We turn to the cosmocentric force of meaning in the world that is more personal than your most personal relationship.**

God is in us, as us, and through us.

God is the All.

God is the Field of intimacy, and God is also the Field of personhood that knows our name and holds us at the same time.

To that Infinity of Intimacy, we turn and say, *hold me*. Hold all the details of my life. Hold my *holy and broken Hallelujah*. I am here, and I am willing to cross.

I'm going to cross over to the other side.

CHAPTER FIFTEEN

LIVING THE DREAM IN RESPONSE TO THE META-CRISIS: LIBERATING THE SPARKS OF CELEBRATION FROM ANCIENT TRADITIONS INTO A NEW WORLD SPIRITUALITY

Episode 324 — December 25, 2022

ONLY A NEW STORY OF VALUE CHANGES THE VECTOR OF THE REAL

I want to just welcome everyone, and welcome myself, and welcome every part of ourselves, and welcome everyone all over the world, from Europe and Asia and Africa, and all across the United States.

We are, in this moment, in celebration— and celebration really *matters*.

We've spent a lot of time here in the last decade deep in an understanding of the meta-crisis. By meta-crisis:

- We mean existential risk.
- We mean catastrophic risk.
- We mean the ways that we are poised before a **potential dystopia**.

But we also realize that we are poised before a **potential utopia**. We have—in this moment in which these two paths

diverge in the woods—we have the possibility, not just to protest, but to *act*:

- Effectively
- Judiciously
- With discernment
- With precision

Remember, in that epic of modern storytelling, which is the most heard story of the late twentieth and early twenty-first centuries, called *Star Wars*, in episode six, movie three, *Return of the Jedi*, there is a moment in which the Death Star—representing the culture of death—needs to be taken down, needs to be exploded. But the rebels—and we *are* the rebels now—don't have the manpower, don't have the horsepower, don't have enough resources. So how do we do it? The only way to do it is to score a direct hit on the Death Star. What's that direct hit?

That direct hit is to evolve the source code itself, to participate in the articulation of a new Story of Value, rooted in evolving First Principles and First Values that change the vector of history itself.

And for those of you, and those *parts of us*, who feel like: *Oh, we're pragmatic realists, and that couldn't really happen*—well, that's not a realistic approach.

Because actually, the nature of the Real is that—when you understand history—*only* **a new Story of Value is able to consistently change the vector of the Real.**

It's *precisely* the telling of a new Story.

That's exactly what happened, for example, in the Renaissance, in that time between worlds and that time between stories, after the Black Death had swept through Europe, and distended stomachs, and bloated corpses, and rotted flesh littered the streets of Europe and Asia and Eurasia. What a group of people in Florence understood, and what the Medici family understood, was that there is something to be done here. We cannot heal every individual piece of suffering because we don't have the resources, but **we need to heal the root source of the suffering by invoking, telling, articulating a new Story of Value.**

As we've said here many, many times before, that new Story of Value was **modernity**, which:

- Introduced universal human rights.
- Began to heal slavery.
- Introduced the scientific method.
- Gave voice to the feminine.

And as we've said—and say the words with me, because you *know* the words—this is *ours to do*. This is ours together, we are doing this together. We're in Unique Self Symphony together in this think tank, as this band of Evolutionary Lovers, as this Renaissance band. Say the words with me, because you know the next words: **to the precise extent that modernity got the plotline right, they introduced the great dignities of modernity**.

But to the precise extent that modernity got the plotline wrong, that those who followed da Vinci and Ficino in the Renaissance, and began to tell the story of modernity got the plotline wrong, **they missed key pieces of the story**. For example:

- What is intrinsic value, and what's a new theory of value?
- How do we *ground* universal human rights in the values of Cosmos itself?
- How—after we throw out religion, which needed to be, in certain forms, thrown out—how do we articulate a new shared grammar of value that is actually *real*, that we can trust?
- How do we articulate a new vision of human personhood,

human dignity, and human divinity?
- How do we re-understand our relationship to Source?

None of that was done. So much was left out.

The assumption was that we could just:

- Borrow the social capital of the traditional world.
- Explode its underlying assumptions but just *pretend* that we hadn't.
- Assume that the general principles of the Western enlightenment—reason, fraternity, liberty, justice—would be enough. We don't need to root them in an actual *ground of value*. We can just call them "self-evident truths."

Well, **self-evident truths don't cut it.** We actually *need* to articulate a new Story of Value that is worth its salt, a story that's rooted in profound understanding.

We need to reclaim not just the Eye of the Senses and the Eye of the Mind, but the Eye of Consciousness, the Eye of Spirit, the Eye of the Heart, and the Eye of Value.

We need to understand that all of these perceptions need to be woven together, and that the deconstruction of value, the abandonment of the Tao, of the Field of Eros, desire, and value (value that's real) is actually the root cause of the global intimacy disorder.

This is the true cause of the multipolar traps and the rivalrous conflict governed by win/lose metrics, that drive all of existential risks, that drive all of catastrophic risk.

If you want to understand how to heal this, not just to be on a soapbox and scream—although soapboxes have their place—but **if you actually want to heal this, if you want to address suffering, we have to tell this new Story.**

WORLD RELIGION AS A CONTEXT FOR OUR DIVERSITY

THE WORLD ITSELF PULSES WITH JOY

Now, here's the thing: We cannot tell this new Story unless we are in celebration. So, this week is not going to be about meta-crisis issues, economic or political or social. This week is going to be about celebration.

We need the technology of celebration in order to be able to address the meta-crisis. If not, we become bitter, burnt-out, and frayed at the edges.

- We need to reclaim our second innocence.
- We need to reclaim our joy.
- We need to reclaim our capacity to celebrate, in order to be able to take our seat at the table of history and address the meta-crisis.
- We need to be able to sing, and to sit in silence, and to chant, and to be in the holy days, in order to walk through the void.

It's only by bracketing our tendency for *a-void-dance* (dance around the void), **it's only by walking through the void in full celebration, that we avoid the bitterness that cripples all revolutions**—and we can't afford to be crippled now. Remember, Langston Hughes, the wonderful Black poet who wrote a poem called "Harlem," where he says:

What happens to a dream deferred?

Does it dry up like a raisin in the sun?

So today, we're not deferring the dream. Today, we are celebrating.

Welcome, everyone—we're celebrating with the wild, crazy joy of the great traditions.

The great traditions, the great religions, got a lot wrong.

- They did a lot of ethnocentric hijacking: we own the truth, no one else does.
- They didn't understand yet the new methods of science, because premodernity didn't yet understand them.

- They got confused between their rituals that were often surface structures, and their deep depth structures of true knowing.

Yes, that's true, the great traditions and the great religions got a lot wrong—but they also knew, in their deepest interior sciences, how to access the Eye of Spirit, and the Eye of Value that intuits and knows value deep in our interiors, the Eye of Consciousness, and the Eye of the Heart.

And they knew how to celebrate.

Often, the celebration was way too limited, and not everyone was included, and it was *us* and *them*. They made lots of tragic mistakes. But **we need to liberate the spark of the sacred that lived in the old religions, and create together a new world spirituality, a new shared language of Spirit, a universal grammar of value as the context for our diversity.**

Today, we are all about celebration. We are not deferring the dream. **You see, we can only change the world if we are willing to live in the world that's already changed.** Otherwise, we become bitter. Otherwise, we become contracted; something rots in our souls.

When we say *we are committed to the pain*—yeah, we're committed to the pain. But we also have to be *committed to the joy*. We must laugh out of one side of our mouth, and cry out of the other side of our mouth.

I grew up in a family which lost most of its members to the gas chambers, so I know a little bit about crying. I grew up under intense conditions of suffering, so I know a little bit about suffering. And so do you. We all know how to suffer, and we know that there's malevolence, and we know that there are forces in the world operating in ways that need to be roundly challenged, opposed, and exposed.

But, friends—

- There is also massive goodness and massive joy.
- There are billions of people in the world who are filled with

goodness, truth, and beauty.
- There are billions of acts of kindness done every day.

And the world itself pulses with joy.

There's an ode to joy at the heart of the Cosmos.

There's a pulse of joy that lives in Reality itself.

There's a light in the world.

There are structures of allurement that bring us together.

There is an impulse of joy that is the actual fabric of Eros, that animates the CosmoErotic Universe—and we as human beings participate in that CosmoErotic Universe.

So, today, we're in celebration. And if you have a glass, let's raise our glasses. Cheers, everyone! *Salud*!

Celebrating you! Celebrating *we*!

Celebrating the Unique Self Symphony!

Celebrating the joy! Celebrating the dream!

WE ARE WELCOME

Today, we are here to *live* the dream, and we are here to *tell the story* of the dream. We're going to tell the story through the prism of Hebrew wisdom, and we're going to tell the story through the prism of Hanukkah. *Salud*! *L'chaim*, to life! Let's feel, everyone.

Let's feel it across the world.

Let's blow our hearts open.

Let's love this moment open with the joy that's already here, with the goodness, the truth, the beauty of people all over the world.

LIVING THE DREAM IN RESPONSE TO THE META-CRISIS

Joy to the world! Joy to the world! *L'chaim*! *L'chaim*! *L'chaim*! *Salud*!

We are going to begin with Hanukkah. This is our first Dharma today. Welcome! Just welcome each other. Just cry out *Welcome* to each other—because **there's *nothing* deeper than knowing that we are welcome.** Indeed, the most important question in the world is: are we welcome?

We are absolutely welcome.

When someone does something for us, we say, *wow, thank you*.

And what do they say back to us? They say, *You're welcome*. *You're welcome* means that when you say *thank you*, we don't *owe* each other. It is not a manipulative debt or exchange. No, no, thank you for doing that for me. And the other person says, *you're welcome*. You are welcome—it's my joy to exchange with you as lovers, as Outrageous Lovers in this CosmoErotic Universe. By *Outrageous Love*, we don't mean love which is a strategy of the ego, but **love which is the heart of existence itself.**

Love is not mere human sentiment—love is the heart of existence itself, and the heart of existence itself is this quality of Eros, or what we call *Outrageous Love*. As we say so often here, we live in a world of outrageous pain, and we never turn away from outrageous pain—but the only response to outrageous pain is Outrageous Love.

We are a think tank; that's our public guise. And we *are* a think tank, we are acting as a leading-edge think tank in the world, addressing the meta-crisis, with every bit of seriousness, gravitas, and joy—and we need to resource that think tank exponentially to have the right capacity to actually launch what needs to be launched. But right *underneath* the think tank, we are actually something deeper.

- We are a spiritual society.
- We are a political society of joy.
- We are a band of Outrageous Lovers.

As part of that band, with your permission, everyone, I want to say something about Hanukkah, and then we're going to light the Hanukkah candles. Then we're going to say something about Christmas, and then we're going to sing some Christmas songs and do some Christmas Dharma.

But first, the Evolutionary Love Code.

EVOLUTIONARY LOVE CODE: THE UNIQUE SELF OF EVERY RELIGION

Every religion has a Unique Self.

The Unique Self of a religion is the intimate quality of meaning and meeting between the infinite and the finite that is particular to that religion. That unique quality of intimacy is irreducible and utterly needed in the great Unique Self Symphony of Spirit.

The rituals of a religion are not the surface structures of a religion, but rather the unique intimate expressions of that religion's erotic embrace of Divinity.

LIBERATING THE SPARKS FROM HANUKKAH

Today is day seven of Hanukkah, tonight is the eighth night of Hanukkah, and eight always is that which is precisely beyond seven. That's why Leonard Cohen talks about the secret chord in the first stanza of "Hallelujah." The secret chord is always, in mysticism, the *eighth* chord—because eight is beyond seven. **Seven is the law of nature, and eight is the miracle that inheres in nature.**

- Eight is the Eros.
- Eight is the love.
- Eight is the plotline that tilts towards goodness, truth, and beauty.

The story of Hanukkah takes place about 160 years before the Common Era. The way the story is told is, after Caesar dies, the great empire is split into two: part of it is in Greek Syria, and part of it is in Alexandria. In Greek Syria, the Seleucid Empire rules, and they come to conquer Judea, where the Temple lives, the great Temple of Judea, the Temple which has the cherubs above the Ark of the Covenant in the Holy of Holies. The Greek Syrians come, and they defile the Temple. That's the story that's told.

In the Temple, there's a *menorah*, a candelabra, and the candelabra needs to be lit with pure oil. The Greek Syrians come, and they conquer Judea, and they defile all of the oil, so there is no pure oil left. And the Temple is turned into a Greek amphitheater of kinds, and the great interior science of Hebrew wisdom—of goodness, truth, beauty, Eros, and love—is considered to be over. All of those who are in the know, all of those who are culturally sensitive, become Hellenists, meaning that they abandon their lineage. They join this assimilationist trend because they think that power is with the Greek Hellenists; they go where the power is in order to survive.

That's the story.

Then this band from this little village outside of Jerusalem—not the aristocratic priests of Jerusalem, but these country priests—come together and they say, *no*. They have a father. There's a father of five children named Mattathias, and his first son is called Judah, Judah the Maccabee. They say, *no, no, no*.

- We're standing for the interior sciences.
- We're standing for integrity.
- We're standing for truth.
- We're standing for goodness.
- We know that truth is beauty and beauty is truth, and we can't let this go.
- The Greeks have split truth and beauty, and they've split truth and beauty from goodness and from ethos—so **we are going to stand for the lineage which says that what matters in the**

world is kindness, what matters in the world is tenderness, what matters in the world is justice, what matters in the world is integrity.

They rebel against the Greek Hellenist rule, and—the way the story is told is—they succeed in the rebellion. They throw the Greek Hellenists out, and they reconsecrate the Temple with pure oil. We commemorate that miracle by lighting the Hanukkah candles. That's the story.

Okay, what's the problem with the story? The problem with the story is, that's not exactly what happened.

Now, go slow with me, we're going to play with this Dharma just for a couple of minutes. I'm going to raise three problems.

THE MIRACLE OF THE FIRST DAY

One, why is Hanukkah *eight days*?

The reason that the mystics say Hanukkah is eight days long—and we talk about this every year, this is part of our tradition, and it's very beautiful, and let's see if we can find our way here—the reason Hanukkah is eight days long is because, in the classical story, when the Hebrews reclaim Jerusalem, they go to reconsecrate the Temple, and they need to find pure oil. They only find one cruse of oil, with enough oil to last for *one* day, and so they light that oil because that's all they have. In the classical story, that cruse of oil with enough for only *one* day lasts for *eight* days. That's why we light the Hanukkah candle for eight days.

That's the story that's taught in the schools. That's the public story.

Okay, what's wrong with that?

Well, the problem is, if that's true—and I'm going to ask this question as a *koan*, as we would say in Zen Buddhism—if that's true, meaning if there was enough oil for one day and the oil lasted eight days, how long should *the miracle* be?

It should be *seven* days!

Does everyone get that? It should be seven days.

Now again, this is not a real question. This is the way a Zen koan works: you ask a question to provoke a deeper understanding, and you need the *sing-song* of the tradition. Well, if there was enough oil for *one* day, and the oil lasted for *eight* days, so then the miracle should only be *seven* days. So, why do we have Hanukkah for eight days?

What's the miracle of the first day?

The miracle of the first day is our think tank, the Center for Integral Wisdom. It is One Mountain.

The miracle of the first day is as follows.

When everybody got together after the Greek Syrians were defeated, according to the public story, and they found the cruse of oil which only had enough for one day, everybody said,

> Well, we can't start. We can't start lighting the candelabra because we don't have enough resources. We don't have a budget; we don't have everything we need. We only have enough oil for one day, and it's going to give out after one day, so it'd be inappropriate to start. Let's wait till we gather all the resources—it might take a few weeks, or it might take a couple of years—and then we'll start.

That was the dominant opinion, but then there was one priest who stood up and said, *No, we can't wait, we've got to start now.*

In other words, **it's only if you're willing to take the first step, if you're willing to light the first candle, and you're willing to trust that somehow the resources will appear, that somehow the miracles will happen.** If you build it, they will come…

If you build it, they will come—but only if:

- You *believe* if you build it, they will come.
- You're willing to light the candle.
- You're willing to lay it on the line.
- You're willing to believe that somehow resources will appear, somehow possibility *will* appear, somehow emergence *will* happen, somehow people *will* join.

That's the miracle of the first day.

The miracle of the first day is the willingness to take the first step when you have no idea how to take the steps afterwards.

So who's willing, friends? Who's willing to take the first step—even though we know we don't have all the resources, and we know we don't know exactly how to do it, and there's lots of questions, and there's lots of issues, and lots of challenges. We are willing *to leap*.

Leap, and the net will appear! That's Hanukkah. Hanukkah means: leap, and the net will appear!

Can you feel that? Leap, and the net will appear. If you wait for the net, and you don't leap, it's *never* going to happen.

- There's a thousand reasons *not* to take that first step.
- There's a thousand reasons *not* to trust.
- There's a thousand traumas that contract us.
- There's a thousand things that make us bitter, that pollute and corrode our soul.

But still, we're going to leap. We're going to leap, and the net will appear. We're going to trust each other, we're going to trust the Unique Self Symphony, and we're going to trust the CosmoErotic Universe.

And that was the lighting of the first day.

The miracle of the first day is that *they lit the oil at all.*

CAPACITY TO CELEBRATE PARTIAL VICTORIES

Now let's go deeper, friends.

We are reclaiming, as part of our new world spirituality, the intimate understanding of two traditions today: the Hebrew tradition and the Christian tradition. **We are *liberating* the sparks and making them part of this new grammar of value.** So, the first piece in the new grammar of value is: leap, and the net will appear. It's the miracle of the first day. It's *build it, and they will come.* That's what it means to create a field of dreams that people can step into.

But now, let's go deeper. **What's the second miracle of Hanukkah?** The second miracle is even more dramatic.

I am going to tell you a crazy secret, and this is the story that they never quite tell. The way it's told in public, that there's this great victory—that the Maccabees succeed in throwing the Greek Syrians out of Jerusalem, and there's this great triumph—that's only part of the story. Here's what actually happened. There were five Maccabee brothers. Four of them were killed, and the old man died. They won a number of battles and freed Jerusalem, but then, not more than twenty-five years later, they were defeated, and the Seleucids came back, and the Greek Syrians triumphed for a long period of time.

Why don't they tell that story?

Number one, the victory was a partial victory. It was an imperfect victory. It didn't last forever. So, the second value of Hanukkah that we liberate from the ancient tradition into the fabric of our new universal grammar of value is: **the capacity to celebrate all partial victories.**

Can you hear that, friends? It's the capacity to celebrate partial victories. Am I willing to celebrate partial victories?

Because, friends, it's *always* a partial victory. It's always incomplete.

It's always a holy and a broken Hallelujah.

When you wait for the complete and perfect victory, you die waiting. We step in and we live, and we have the capacity to poignantly celebrate the beauty, the richness, the depth of the holy and the broken Hallelujahs—because *there's a blaze of light in every word, and it doesn't matter which you heard, the holy or the broken Hallelujah.* It's a partial victory. And we make a decision: **we're going to celebrate the partial victories.**

That's the second principle of Hanukkah.

THE WAY WE DECIDE TO TELL THE STORY DEFINES EVERYTHING

So, friends, beloveds, brothers and sisters, we could have told the story as the story of a defeat, but we made a decision to tell the story as a story of triumph.

Now, I want you to notice something, and I want to say this gently.

When was the last time that you saw a Greek Syrian Seleucid moving through your neighborhood in Corsica, or Virginia, or Greece, or in New York, or upstate New York, or Holland, or Asia, or Israel? When was the last time you met a Greek Seleucid? When was the last time you saw Hellenism at play in your life? You haven't.

But, friends, all over the world, in these last eight days, holders of this lineage are lighting Hanukkah candles.

LIVING THE DREAM IN RESPONSE TO THE META-CRISIS

In the end, the way we decide to tell the story defines everything.

It's the story that I decide to tell, and when I decide to liberate the spark of joy and to tell that story, and to celebrate the miracle, then what becomes the fabric of history are the Hanukkah candles.

- The Greek Syrian Seleucid Empire has disappeared.
- The Babylonians have disappeared.
- The Roman empire has disappeared.

And yet, Hanukkah candles remain—because a little bit of light dispels a lot of darkness.

It's all in the story we decide to tell. Oh my God!

Friends, I'm just going to take a moment with you, and with your permission, we're going to light Hanukkah candles. Can we see them there? Yes, we can.

We are just going to light some Hanukkah candles together, and we're just going to celebrate.

You don't need to be Jewish. We're creating a new world spirituality in which we actually take the best of all of them. So we're going to light these candles together.

This is the story.

These are the candles.

This is the miracle.

This is the joy.

Happy Hanukkah, everyone. It all started with enough just to light one candle.

LIBERATING THE SPARKS FROM CHRISTMAS: THE BIRTH OF GOD AS HUMAN BEING

We are now going the next step. This is celebration. What happens to a dream deferred—Langston Hughes in his poem "Harlem"—does it dry up like a raisin in the sun?

We are in celebration. We are living the dream.

Merry Christmas, everyone. Merry Christmas, the day that Christ was born. Merry Christmas!

What does that mean? What is this "Silent Night"? What is this beautiful moment?

We are going to go the next step in the Dharma today, and **we're going to liberate the sparks of the great Christian tradition**, and we're going to take a look at "Silent Night," and we're going to hear a rendition of "Silent Night" from a dear friend and new study partner, a student, friend of mine, Jackson, who's going to do a rendition of "Silent Night."

But first, we're going to study together. Let's take a look, everyone.

> *Silent night, holy night.*
> *All is calm, all is bright.*
> *Round yon Virgin, Mother and Child*
> *Holy Infant so tender and mild*
> *Sleep in heavenly peace.*
> *Sleep in heavenly peace.*
>
> *Silent night, holy night.*
> *Shepherds quake at the sight.*
> *Glories stream from heaven afar.*
> *Heavenly hosts sing Alleluia.*
> *Christ the Savior is born.*
> *Christ the Savior is born.*
>
> *Silent night, holy night.*
> *Son of God, love's pure light.*

> *Radiant beams from Thy holy face*
> *With the dawn of redeeming grace*
> *Jesus Lord, at Thy birth.*
> *Jesus Lord, at Thy birth.*

This song was written in 1818 by a young priest in Austria. He's looking at the village, and he's looking at all the pain in Europe, and the Napoleonic wars had just been raging. He feels this breath of Spirit, he feels this breath of possibility. In this song that he wrote, there is both the glory of Christ consciousness, and some of the shadows of early religion.

We are going to read the song, but we are going to read it *as an evolutionary song*, and **understand it in its full evolutionary potential**.

Merry Christmas, everyone.

I was trained as an orthodox rabbi, and I love Christmas. Yeah, I understand the commercialization of Christmas, and I understand the consumerism of Christmas, and I understand how it's been hijacked in all the ways that it's been hijacked. And I also know that:

- Christmas stands for the goodness of the human being.
- Christmas stands for the Possibility of Possibility.
- Christmas stands for the billion acts of kindness that ordinary human beings do every day.

The reason we can stand against the upgrading of algorithms and the downgrading of human beings is because human beings are glorious. Human beings are expressions of goodness, truth, and beauty, of wonder and delight.

> *Silent night, holy night.*
> *All is calm, all is bright.*
> *Round yon Virgin Mother and Child.*
> *Holy infant, so tender and mild.*
> *Sleep in heavenly peace.*
> *Sleep in heavenly peace.*

What is this about? Friends, let's go deep for a second.

This notion of Silent Night is the dream of Metatron in the Hebrew wisdom tradition, and Metatron got translated into Christ. Metatron means apotheosis. It means that the human being is, in Dante's phrase, *a baby-face Divine*.

- Not the God you don't believe in—the God you don't believe in doesn't exist.
- Not the God who is homophobic, ethnocentric, and chauvinistic, not *that* God.
- God which is the spirit of goodness, truth, and beauty.
- God which is hope.
- God which is the Possibility of Possibility that inheres in us.
- God which is the human being, at her most noble, at her most tender, at her most beautiful—quivering joy, filled with Eros.
- God who is expressed as human hands, and human possibility, and human creativity, and human capacity, and human innovation, and human joy, and human tears.

It's this notion that God is born as the human being, that God is *born*, that God becomes Christed, that God becomes *human*—or, said differently, that **Infinity itself desired to clothe itself in finitude**. *Finitude means the mortal, the limited. Infinity desired to clothe itself in finitude.*

God desired to be Christed.

There lives, in the human being, the virgin mother and child. In every human being, there's the virgin—meaning we can *revirginate*. Even after:

- All of the pain
- All of the brokenness
- All of the trauma

We can access second innocence. The mother revirginates. The mother is always holding that quality of compassion, that quality of love, that quality of joy.

The mother lives *in me*, and the mother lives *in all of us*.

We are *all* the virgin.

We are *all* the baby.

We are *all* the mother.

That's who we are: We are all the mother. We are all the virgin. We are all the baby.

That's the first verse. The first verse is, **the birth of God *as* human being—** when I realize:

- I'm not just a skin-encapsulated ego. I am Divinity Herself.
- I am a unique configuration of infinite desire.
- I am a unique configuration of the Infinity of Intimacy that lives in me.

WE NEED THE DEMOCRATIZATION OF THE CHRISTED ONE

Take a look at the second verse.

Silent night, holy night.

Shepherds quake at the sight.

And so we look at each other, and we say: Oh my God, *I see you.*

- I am blown open by your beauty.
- I am blown open by your goodness.
- I am blown open by the glories that stream from heavens afar and live in your face. *Heavenly hosts singing in you Hallelujah.*

The only mistake that Christianity made was that it limited this notion to Jesus.

It's not just about Jesus the Christ. It's about *you* the Christ, about *every one of us* in Unique Self Symphony the Christ. We are *all* the Christed ones.

We are all expressions of silent night, holy night. Son of God, daughter of God, we're all love's pure light, with radiant beams moving from our holy faces.

We all incarnate *the dawn of redeeming grace*, in the third verse. We're all *Jesus Lord at our birth*.

That's Silent Night.

You can feel the virgin, you can feel the mother, you can feel the grace. And the reason you can feel it is because it is you, it is me.

We need the democratization of the Christed one.

We need to move from the elites and the gurus to the democratization of greatness, the democratization of enlightenment.

The Christed one becomes the Unique Self Symphony, in which we each play our instrument, and we liberate that spark from Christianity, and we bring it into the new world spirituality.

Feel that beauty. Feel the stunning moment.

In *Silent Night*, you can feel a prayer for humanity to be blown open like this. Oh my God, everyone.

It's so wild to be together.

It's so gorgeous to be together.

We are the Christ force, and we sometimes need to go into the Temple, and to turn over the money carts, and to:

- Challenge all that needs to be challenged.
- Speak truth to power.
- Become instruments of power ourselves.

We do this in order to respond to this meta-crisis.

But we can't do it unless we stay connected to the Eye of Consciousness, to Silent Night, to Holy Night, to the young virgin mother and child, the Christ that lives in us, so that we can have the capacity to light that candle when everyone says that we don't have resources to light it.

To build that field when everyone says, *but it's not possible.*

> *Silent night, holy night.*
> *All is calm, all is bright.*
> *Round yon Virgin Mother and Child.*
> *Holy infant, so tender and mild.*

We have to create this together.

We have to create this Unique Self Symphony, because that's what glory is all about.

GLORIA IN EXCELSIS DEO ("GLORY TO GOD IN THE HIGHEST")

Right now, let's feel what's called *kavod* in the lineage.

Kavod is *Gloria in Excelsis Deo* ("Glory to God in the highest"). What *Gloria in Excelsis Deo* means is that we can access the divine in our bodies, in our spirit, in our soul. As Krista Josepha sang before we started, *I can feel it in my body and my spirit and my soul, I can feel.*

In Excelsis Deo—I can feel the highest degree of purity, of sincerity, of devotion, of joy, of ecstasy, that's available to me, that lives in my body.

My body is wired for joy.

My body is wired for pleasure, and pleasure is the source of all ethics.

Know what gives you pleasure *for real*—not superficial pleasure, not surface pleasure; the opposite of the sacred is the superficial.

Find what truly gives you pleasure, and you'll find your ethics.

That's *Gloria*, that's *in Excelsis Deo*. Let's feel it, let's play it, let's dance it.

Gloria in Excelsis Deo.

CHAPTER SIXTEEN

TELLING THE EVOLUTIONARY STORY OF CRUCIFIXION AND RESURRECTION

Episode 339 — April 9, 2023

EVOLVING THE SOURCE CODE, THE INESCAPABLE FRAMEWORKS IN WHICH WE LIVE

I am so madly delighted to be with you, during this Easter time, to be in this holy holiday.

We are going to dedicate today to Easter.

We are going to be first talking about Barbara Marx Hubbard, which is going to be exciting and important. It's Barbara's *Yahrzeit*, the anniversary of her passing, and I want to really go deeply into the beautiful Barbara space. We are going to be entering this unimaginably important and critical part of the Dharma, which is Outrageous Love Stories.

I am going to start it today, but first I want to frame where we are—and the particular piece of Dharma we are going to be looking into is the unpacking of **this understanding of Reality as being animated by Outrageous Love**.

Now, that's not nothing.

That's not a casual statement.

That's not a New Age statement.

It's not a religious fundamentalist statement. What we are saying here at One Mountain, Many Paths is something I don't even have words for. I try to re-invoke it every week. It is so pressing, it is so important. It's so *source-code changing*.

People don't even realize there *is* a source code, but there is.

> *There is a source code, the framework which generates the entire system.*

The source code of the program on the computer generates all the applications. All the applications of science, and economics, and business, and law, and psychology, and finance, and sociology, and relationships, and the way we do sports, and the way we do sexuality—all of those applications run on a source code. **The source code is the inescapable frameworks in which we live: the stories that we tell about Reality, and the First Principles we assume Reality is based on.**

If you move to change only the applications, you won't have enough firepower.

But the way the applications are now running, they are driving us literally, at breakneck speed, into a brick wall. That's called the meta-crisis. The meta-crisis is: the way the First Principles are now constituted in Reality are themselves already a form of artificial general intelligence.

There is this big fear about artificial intelligence:

- Why is that a threat?
- Why is that such a fundamental issue?
- Why is there a new ontology in Cosmos, in which intelligence itself is generating more intelligence, in ways that are dissociated from First Principles and First Values, and that will generate a reality in which there'll be a fundamental dehumanization?

THE EVOLUTIONARY STORY OF CRUCIFIXION AND RESURRECTION

Not because artificial intelligence is evil, but because it lacks interiors and empathy, and it lacks a set of human values that would drive it in a certain direction.

The best response to the existential threat of artificial intelligence (and all the other existential threats), the only cogent response, is to evolve the source code. The applications running on the world system today are going to crash the system. The system will not be able to reboot. The global civilization will fall like all the local civilizations did, but this time it's powered by exponential weaponized technologies, and the destruction wrought will not allow for an easy reboot at all. We're talking about all of the unborn, we're talking about all of the future that's at stake.

You can't go up against the Death Star (*Return of the Jedi*). It just can't be done. It's the Death Star; it's too colossal. There is a culture of death at play, and the culture of death is:

- Both **the death of the individual**, from heart attacks, obesity, opioids, mental breakdowns, suicides, lives cut short in so many different ways,
- And the death of Spirit, **the death of humanity**, or the death of *our* humanity—two forms of existential risk.

That's the Death Star. The applications that are running the Death Star are too powerful, they're too guarded. There is too much vested egoic structure. It cannot be taken down—**but what we can do is change the source code itself that's powering all the applications.** *That* **can be done.**

That's what I've meant for the last decade, and what Barbara has meant, when we say: we want to evolve the source code of consciousness and culture. It's not a casual phrase. We understand that you cannot stop the applications.

Their nature is that there's always going to be an update of the same application. It can't change—but we can evolve the source code itself.

WE CANNOT EVOLVE THE SOURCE CODE WITHOUT RELIGION

To evolve the source code means telling a new Story and articulating new First Principles and First Values. It's not a new Story which is a conjecture, but a new Story of intrinsic value. Put those together: what we're saying is that to respond to the meta-crisis, we need First Principles and First Values embedded in a new Story of Value.

And they can't be static; they've got to be *evolving*. That's what we call *Evolving Perennialism*: a new global understanding, a new global Story of Value, rooted in First Principles and First Values, a story of an Evolving Perennialism. In other words:

> *The perennial, eternal, unchanging truths that are evolving—it's that paradox that holds Reality.*

That's the new Story of Value: Evolving Perennialism, which is not just principles, but principles rooted in a storyline, in a *plotline* of value.

That is the game today. That is the move, the change that changes everything.

I spoke to someone this morning who said: "Wow, that is so grandiose, this notion that you're going to change the lives of billions of people by evolving the source code. That's a grandiose notion."

No, it's not grandiose.

It's the core of the prophetic lineage. The prophetic lineage is: *be a light unto the nations*.

To *be a light unto the nations* means to tell a story that can become a world story, that will allow us, as history complexifies, to find our way and not actually *end* history, in a kind of End of Days destruction—but will allow the birth of a new world. That's what the great traditions called *Messianism* or *Messiah*—but **Messiah means a new world, a New Humanity where *Homo sapiens* becomes *Homo amor*.**

- We become *omni-considerate* for the sake of the whole.
- We can actually *feel* the whole: the whole lives in us, and we live in the whole.
- We actually birth a New Human and a New Humanity.

But not in a Marxist way. Marx says: *wow, there's a false consciousness of capitalism, so let's birth a New Human and a New Humanity*. Marx got that right—but he wanted to do it without First Principles and First Values: without individuality, without personhood, without irreducible uniqueness. He tried to birth a New World Order without First Principles and First Values.

Disaster!

We have to birth a New World Order, literally, which is what all the traditions envisioned: that **there would be a moment in history in which we would need to take a new momentous leap in the history of humanity**. We are not going to just go on and on and keep repeating ourselves. What is unchanging is that it always changes. The unchanging nature of Reality is that change always happens, and there are moments of punctuated equilibria, of momentous leaps. **When the system is far from equilibrium, when it hovers on breakdown, a minor fluctuation point in the system can jump it to a higher level of order.**

A direct hit on the Death Star can explode the culture of death. That direct hit is the evolution of the source code. That's what we are talking about.

To evolve the source code, we want to integrate the best of the validated premodern, modern, and postmodern insights of wisdom. That includes religion. **Religion cannot be left out**. We cannot do it without religion—we need religion. We cannot merely do *Human Potential, liberal, academic ways of talking to each other*, which are narcissistic and self-involved. Seventy percent of the world lives in the context of organized religion. We have to take religion seriously—and so we celebrate religion here at One Mountain, Many Paths, hence the name.

This is the place where we are madly committed, with radical audacity and trembling humility, to come together as a band of beloveds—in the language of the lineages, a band of lovers, a band of what we call Outrageous Lovers—to articulate this new vision and tell this new Story together. This new Story has to include the validated insights, not only of modernity and postmodernity, but of the traditional period as well.

WEAVING EASTER AND PASSOVER INTO THE NEW STORY

Today is Easter, and today is Passover. So we want to integrate Easter and Passover.

> *We want to go into Easter, and go into Passover, and integrate their most important, most profound, and wildest insights.*

That's what we want to do today. That's a big deal.

I know it's a big Easter day, and people are at Easter dinners. But I just want to say, your being here at One Mountain *makes* One Mountain. It belongs to us all, and what makes it is:

- Our coming and our showing up.
- Our animating the space.
- Our breathing life into it, our breathing life into this revolution.

Every single week, we keep articulating this new Story of Value. We keep sharpening, we keep clarifying, we keep purifying, we keep rewriting, we keep editing, we keep adding chapters, we keep deepening. This is what we're doing.

We are actually understanding that it's only a new Story of Value rooted in First Principles and First Values that evolves the source code, and we *show up*. We show up week after week. This is our 339th week—and we show up—whether we are listening to a replay, whether we are here in-person. We show up. You might think, it's just going to go on, no matter what I do—that's not true.

- We need each other.
- We need to do this *together*.
- We need all of our energy together to make this happen, to make this come alive.

So I just want to thank everyone, today on Easter, where so many of us decided: *we're going to show up today, we're going to be here today, we're going to tell this new Story today, and we're going to tell a wild new Story today—the story of Passover and the story of Easter—together.*

Today, we're going to integrate the validated realizations and insights from those stories into the larger story of value, the new Story of CosmoErotic Humanism, this new Story of Value rooted in First Principles and First Values—in response to the meta-crisis.

Easter and Passover get woven in today—so Happy Easter, everyone.

The Holy Trinity, Palm Sunday, Lent—all of it. Happy Passover, everyone. Oh my God, Happy Passover. Happy *Pesach*, which is the Hebrew name for Passover.

EVOLUTIONARY LOVE CODE: HOPE IS THE ONTOLOGY OF REALITY

> The holy trinity of cosmic pattern is: order, disorder, higher order.

Hope is in the knowing of this pattern.

Hope is not a Pollyannaish whimsy. Hope is the ontology of Reality.

The crucifixion is never the end; there is always resurrection. Resurrection is the ontology of Cosmos itself.

Hope is a memory of the inevitable future.

REDEMPTION IS A POLITICAL AND ECONOMIC EVENT

Holy Days means that **the sacred lives in time**—so part of this new Story of CosmoErotic Humanism is to begin to *live the calendar*. We need to create a new world religion calendar, which has universal Holy Days. Within the context of that calendar, there can be ten, twenty, thirty, forty, fifty, 100 religions—but there has to be a shared calendar. We have a global reality, and there's got to be a shared global calendar that weaves time together—so that we can do Ramadan here, and we could do Yom Kippur there, and we can do a Christian Easter over there, and we can do a Druid holiday, and we can have an Aboriginal holiday. Those are all beautiful. And we can't skip the Chinese New Year.

We need a shared sacred calendar that we live.

Today, we are in what's called *Paskha*, and *Paskha* means Passover. But *Paskha* is—for example, in the Eastern Orthodox tradition—the name for Easter. In much of Christianity, Easter is called *Paskha*. *Pesach* is the Hebrew for Passover—but Easter also is part of *Paskha*.

There is one sense here, a sense of a larger, complete holiday.

We are not reducing Easter and Passover, they are actually quite distinct—but there are certain themes that each have, which—when you weave them together—are a critical part of the new Story of Value.

THE EVOLUTIONARY STORY OF CRUCIFIXION AND RESURRECTION

The word *pesach* means *peh-sach*: *the mouth that speaks*—that's Luria's interpretation, one of the great interior scientists of the sixteenth century.

And what does the mouth speak? The mouth tells the story. **The lineage practice of these days is telling the story of leaving Egypt.** *Sippur Yetziat Mitzrayim*: telling the story of leaving Egypt.

Now it gets dramatic.

This notion of telling the story of leaving Egypt, this lineage structure is not incidental. It's not once a year—but actually, **the entire Hebrew wisdom lineage, the entire thing, from beginning to end, revolves around a daily telling of the story of leaving Egypt.**

Why? Let us hear and feel this on two levels.

One, it would be very easy to adopt a profoundly despairing story of Reality. For most of history, most people, in most lives, live in injustice. That is true.

Can we get that for a second? For most of human history, most people, most humans, live lives that are unjust—that are not free, that are filled with pain. And within their lifetime, there is no liberation. There are broken vessels, and broken hearts, and broken lives, and broken bodies. Let us just hold this reality for a second. That's been the status quo for much of history. It's a big deal.

And along comes Passover, along comes *Pesach*, and tells a different story.

- *Pesach* says that slaves should be free.
- *Pesach* says that freedom is a fundamental human dignity and right.
- *Pesach* says that the status quo is not unchanging, that the status quo needs to be changed and needs to be challenged.

Pesach, the Exodus event, rejects the status quo. The Exodus event says that:

- The Infinity of Intimacy, the divine voice that suffuses

Cosmos, that divine voice, *Va'ishma Elohim na'aqatam*: **God/Goddess hears their cries, the cries of the oppressed, the cries of the slaves—and responds to them.**

- There is a divine force that lives in us, as us, and through us, that holds us, and that acts and moves to transfigure history.
- Divinity is not *beyond* history;
- Divinity is not an *internal* event, not an internal redemption.

Redemption or liberation is not merely an internal event. It has an interior dimension, but it's not *merely* an interior dimension.

It is a *political* event.

It is an *economic* event.

That was Marx's correct intuition that got hijacked and terribly degraded—his intuition was that **the Messianic idea, liberation, redemption is a political and economic event**, and we need to subject this emergent capitalism—in Manchester, and in other places in England where Marx and Engels were looking at it—to a very profound critique, and usher in a new possibility. As mentioned, he tried to do this without First Principles and First Values, but there was a basic understanding that this new possibility has to emerge.

Now, let's go even deeper.

There is an Exodus event, and that Exodus event means:

- People need to be free.
- We can change the status quo.
- Reality *cares*.

I want to really get this straight:

Exodus says that Reality cares.

That's what this event is about: reality cares. It's a shocking realization!

Reality is not neutral.

Reality is not impartial.

Reality is partial to love.

Reality is partial to Eros.

Reality is partial to justice.

Reality is partial to the cries of the oppressed, to the desperate agony of the needy.

That's the nature of reality. Exodus says: **Reality is partial to love.**

That's what we mean when we say Reality is a love story. It's not an ordinary love story but an Outrageous Love Story, meaning it's an inherent quality of Reality itself. It's what Solomon means when he says, in the Song of Solomon, *tocho ratzuf ahava*: "its insides are lined with love."

EVERYTHING IS ABOUT THE STORY WE DECIDE TO TELL

Now let's take it another step:

The ontology of Reality is story.

There *is* a story we often get caught in—the recursive loops of reviewing certain parts of our personal life story again and again—and that becomes a kind of pseudo-eros that doesn't allow us to actually write the next chapter of our story. So, it is correct that there is a story I need to move beyond—when the ego gets me locked in the story in a way that I cannot liberate myself from the recursive loops of the past. That's true, and that's important.

That's separate self.

That's the pathology of separate self.

However, I can *move beyond* the narrow contraction of the recursive loops of the old story of yesterday, which I'm revisiting not in a way that productively constructs tomorrow, but in a way that keeps me locked in the past.

I need to transcend that, so I go into this larger Field as True Self, which is beyond story, and I am in the realm of being.

But then, *after* True Self, I return to the depth ontology of Reality, which is story. **I re-enter the story, and I reclaim the plotline of my story.** I realize that story is not something I merely move beyond.

Don Juan and Carlos Castaneda, with all due respect, got it wrong when they said that you leave the story behind. He writes, *I remember the day I left my personal history behind.* No, you never leave your personal history behind. You leave the *pathology* of recursive loops of your personal history behind—but then you go to the wider Field, the seamless coat of the universe, True Self, and **then you emerge as your unique story, with your unique plotlines, and you realize that your story matters, that your story is chapter and verse in The Universe: A Love Story.**

Now, let's go deeper.

That means that the invitation of Reality is: *live your story*, not *move beyond* your story. But in order to live your story, you have to *choose* your story, and **you have to choose the *right* story.**

Choosing the right story is a big deal.

I have a book here by James Shapiro, a top geneticist at the University of Chicago, called *Evolution: A View from the Twenty-First Century*. He has one chapter, quite a complex scientific chapter, where he talks about how the DNA code tells multiple stories, and then the receptor cells *choose* which DNA story they're going to activate. So DNA is telling multiple narratives at the same time. I'm not going to do a deep scientific dive, but it's a brilliant chapter. The DNA is telling multiple stories, and then the receptor cells *choose* what story to tell.

THE EVOLUTIONARY STORY OF CRUCIFIXION AND RESURRECTION

Have you ever heard of King Arthur's Round Table? Now, did King Arthur's Round Table work in the long-term, even in the myth? No, it didn't. Why didn't it work? Because Mordred took down King Arthur's kingdom.

But let me ask you a question: Is anybody telling stories about Mordred?

No, no one's telling stories about Mordred.

We are telling stories about Avalon. We are telling stories about Camelot.

Camelot is the story about King Arthur's vision of a round table, and about the devotion to the damsel, and the devotion to the emergence of the Goddess, the feminine and the emergence of the noble masculine. And we put our swords in service together, and we create a holistic hierarchy, where everyone is playing their exact right role, and we create a Unique Self Symphony together. **The Knights of the Round Table were the first Unique Self Symphony.** And we have to be kings together, and we have to be in service and devotion to this new possibility.

Now, in the end, King Arthur's vision didn't work—but *the story worked, the story inspires*. The story created the next generation of knights. It created the next link—

- in the chain of nobility,
- in the chain of rapture,
- in the chain of service,
- in the chain of wild and gorgeous knighthood.

Mordred historically won, but *the story* belongs to King Arthur. It's all about what story we tell.

I'll give you a second example. This is another thing in the Hebrew wisdom lineage that you may remember, a few months ago we mentioned Hanukkah, the eight-day holiday of Hanukkah, when the Hebrews fought the Greek Seleucids.

First, I'll give you the bad news: we lost the war. Twenty-five years later the Greek Seleucids won. There was this one little moment when it was beautiful, and it was Camelot—when they came back to Jerusalem and they reconsecrated the Temple, and there was a miracle: the candlelight that was supposed to last for one day lasted for eight days.

But here's the thing: even though the Greeks later won, when was the last time you saw someone telling a story about the Greek Empire 150 years before the Common Era? No one is talking about the Greek Seleucids. It's a tradition that died. And yet, the tradition of the Hebrews is alive. Why? **Because they are telling the story of the partial victory.**

Life is filled with partial victories. There are no absolute victories in life, my friends. In the world of *samsara*, there are no absolute victories. **But there are partial victories, there are celebrations, and we can live the dream, and we can celebrate, even amidst the tragedy.** Even as I'm living in tragedy, day in and day out—

- I can claim my second innocence,
- I can live the dream,
- I can be part of the new Story,
- I can tell the new Story,
- I can take my seat at the table of history,
- I can give my unique gift in my unique circle of intimacy and influence.

And I do not need to cry tears of resignation.

I can cry tears of ecstasy.

I can cry tears of pain.

I can cry tears of shattering.

I can cry tears of agony.

I can cry tears of joy.

I don't cry tears of resignation. I don't throw in the towel. I don't give up. I don't step off the court. I'm not in the stands but on the court. I'm in the game. That's Hanukkah. It's the story that we decide to tell. Everything is about the story we decide to tell.

LIFE IS A SERIES OF LOVE STORIES

Postmodernity got this insight, but in its pathological form. Postmodernity says:

- There is no Field of Value; it doesn't exist. There's no Tao. We are not in the Tao, in the Field of Value.
- Therefore, says postmodernity, all that's left is *story*.

And then, the pathology of a rivalrous win/lose metrics reality—let's call it *empire*—chooses the story to tell. **The story is with the victors, and so the story itself becomes a made-up mechanism, served up by the victors.** Story becomes propaganda. Story is reduced to propaganda.

No, but story is *not* just propaganda. Story is not just owned by the empire. Story is the ontology of Reality.

So, postmodernity got it—it said: it's all about the story you decide to tell—you are making it up. The only thing left we have is the story we tell, but that story, they claimed, is just made up (my friend Yuval Harari writes this all over the place). All the stories are made up, so we might as well tell a good story. My friend, Werner Erhard—and I spoke to Werner about this deeply—said it's about the meaning you decide to create. None of the other stuff worked, so make meaning that seems to work for you—but none of it is *real*, none of it is *intrinsic*.

No, no, no, that's not right.

Story is the structure of Reality. Story matters.

God loves stories, in the language of lineage—or, in the language of CosmoErotic Humanism, **story itself is a First Principle and First Value of Cosmos.** Reality is written in stories. It's not something we *impose* on

Reality. We are not imposing story on a value-neutral reality, which is desiccated from meaning and from narrative.

No, story is the nature of Reality.

The story I choose to tell is not made up: *Oh, I'm not going to tell a victim story, I'm going to tell a player story.* They both aren't really true, so we might as well tell one that works?

No, no, no. There is the highest, deepest, and best story, which is the one that's most inspiring, and most constructive, and most generative of goodness, truth, and beauty, which most takes me out of my narcissism and allows me to be in service.

- The story that blows my heart open.
- The story that makes me dance.
- The story that makes me sing.
- The story that makes me make love.
- The story that arouses me.
- The story that causes me to throb and pulse as part of, as living Reality.
- The story that fills me with gratitude, delight, and ecstasy every moment of every day.

This is not Pollyannaish—it's not that I turn away from the pain, turn away from the suffering, but rather live in the utter beauty of the story that I've chosen to tell, *which is the deepest ontology, the deepest truth of Cosmos that I'm able to grasp.*

And it is a love story. It's got agony, and it's got ecstasy. My friends, it actually *is* a love story. Because the ontology of Reality is a love story.

It's true that *its insides are lined with love*. It's not made up.

THE EVOLUTIONARY STORY OF CRUCIFIXION AND RESURRECTION

> *From quarks, to atoms, to molecules, to macromolecules, to cells, to multicellular structures—the whole freaking thing is a love story, all the way up and all the way down.*

That's actually true: my story is a love story. It might at times be an agonizing love story, but it is a love story.

My commitment to my son is a love story. The commitment of the father to the son, of the mother to the son—it's a love story. But you can never let one love story exhaust you. **We've all got to live multiple love stories**. We all have to be polyamorous because if you're only living one love story, if your love story is dependent on one person. It doesn't matter whether it's a wife, daughter, husband, sister, grandfather, if you let one love story define you, then you've made that story into an idol.

Our love lists are too short.

Our list of love stories is too short.

We live in a series of love stories. That's what life is. Life is a series of love stories.

That's what it is.

And sometimes, it's not a one-night stand—sometimes it's a three-minute stand, it's a one-minute stand.

I was recently in Austin with Kristina, and we had to get out of the house to get some food. And there was a particular waiter who came to our table, and he looked sad, and we had this incredible, sixty-second exchange. It was completely ecstatic, we just made love in that moment. Our eyes locked, we exchanged—maybe it was two minutes, three minutes at the most.

It's a love story. And he's going to tell that story to everybody. It was so beautiful. I'm not going to tell you the story now, but it was such a beautiful three-minute exchange. We found each other, and the whole world just opened up. Instead of being just another waiter whose name we didn't know, it became a love story.

And it's *all* a love story.

What story I choose to tell is everything—but it's not everything in a postmodern way: making up a story as an arbitrary act, a story with no meaning and no significance and no intrinsic value, so might as well choose a good one.

No, no, no—it ultimately matters.

I am lived by my love story. **My love story is the source code of my life.**

THE EVOLUTION OF LOVE IS THE SOURCE OF HOPE

Now, here is what Easter says: **the story never ends with crucifixion.** Easter says, there is a basic pattern of reality, and the pattern of reality is hope.

Hope is not Pollyannaish.

Hope is not whimsy.

Hope is a structure of Reality itself.

The pattern of Reality is: order, disorder, higher order.

Jesus is born at a particular moment, and he steps into the story, and he gathers people around him, and they begin to tell a new Story together, and a new order is born, and a new possibility is born, and a new love story is born.

THE EVOLUTIONARY STORY OF CRUCIFIXION AND RESURRECTION

That's what we mean by a new order—that love *emerges*, that love *evolves*. A new order of love is born, what Whitehead called "the creative advance of novelty." That's what we call here *the evolution of love*. It's not a slogan but the structure of Reality—and **the evolution of love is the source of hope.**

Reality is radically hopeful—ontologically, in its very nature.

So, there's this new order, the Christ order—and then that order is challenged, that order is crucified, that order is attacked, and that order does not have the possibility, just does not have the possibility of responding.

We have much of that today, in our social media world where people assume what's written on the internet is true. But often what's written on the internet is a set of captured interests. Wikipedia is a great example. Living person pages on Wikipedia are an absolute disaster. They are filled with disinformation, put up there by editors who captured the pages often 15 to 20 years ago, telling stories that are not true. I've met dozens of people in public life, who were just devastated by this. Crucifixion.

- Crucifixion: I've gotten shattered by life.
- Crucifixion: My vessels have been broken.
- Crucifixion: I've been dealt an impossible hand that there's no way I can play without collapsing, without giving up my joy, without giving up my lovemaking, without giving up the quivering tenderness and the trembling of ecstatic aliveness, which is self-evidently good, true, and beautiful.

No, there is *always* Resurrection.

Spring *always* comes after winter.

As above, so below—so says the *Corpus Hermeticum*, translated by Marsilio Ficino at the Plato Academy of Florence, the great Hermetic tradition echoed in the Talmudic tradition. As above, so below. Said in our terminology: as interiors, so are exteriors. As within, so without. Insides and outsides mirror each other.

Spring always comes after winter.

Hope is an ontology of Cosmos.

We reject the status quo—hopelessness is *not* the nature of Reality.

Human beings deserve to be free, and human beings will be free—a higher order will always emerge from the disorder.

She comes in threes, and the third is always the higher order. It's *always* the new possibility.

Sometimes it comes and shows itself, and then it disappears—**so we celebrate, we tell the story of the moment that it showed itself because it was the evolution of love struggling to emerge, but it couldn't yet attain a stable center of gravity.**

What we do, as the ultimate revolutionary subversive act, is tell the story of the new higher order. That's what we do.

We don't tell the story of the Greek Seleucids, in the Hanukkah story.

We don't tell the story of Mordred, in the Round Table story.

We tell the story of the higher order. There was that moment where spring, the first buds of spring emerged, and then there was another winter—but that's okay, we saw those first buds of spring, and we know that they are true, and we know that they are good, and we know that they are beautiful.

Our hope is rooted in the nature of Reality itself.

THIS LIFETIME IS A CHAPTER IN THE STORY

But maybe you'll say: "Okay, that's great. But there wasn't an *actual* resurrection, was there?"

Well, *maybe there was.* Just stay with that possibility for a second. Why are we convinced that there wasn't an actual resurrection?

Now, you're going to say: "Oh my God, Marc has now been revealed, he's been hiding it. He's a fundamentalist!"

No, I'm not a fundamentalist, not in any sense. I grew up deep in a lineage, and I've struggled my whole life to create a new lineage beyond fundamentalism.

But if you look at reality seriously, what do we actually know? I don't *know* whether Jesus was resurrected in this historical story. I just don't know. But would I dismiss it as a possibility? I would have to be a blithering idiot, and I'd actually have to be a fundamentalist to dismiss it.

Why? Well, it's really simple.

In the last 140 years, we've gathered an enormous amount of information, which began with Eleanore and Henry Sedgwick at Cambridge who started the British Society for Psychical Research. Then they wrote to their friend William James in Boston, who started the Harvard Psychical Society, which began to track empirical information on events not accounted for by the classical laws of physics and biology.

The laws of physics and biology are of course real, but most of contemporary science is *selectively* empirical. I am a mad reader of the sciences, in devotion to the sciences, and anyone who knows me knows that. **But much of science today—not in its science from, but in its *dogmatic* form—is *not* empirical**. They don't actually take account of *all* the data. Science is selectively empirical. It looks at data that match the conclusion it's seeking to draw, and that conclusion is often reductionist-materialist, suggesting that reality is empty of any structures of meaning, that the *only* way connections happen is through the classical laws of physics. But of course, this past year's Nobel prize went to research on non-local connection. We are now realizing, more and more deeply, that there are many invisible lines of connection woven throughout all of Reality, and that we cannot account for empirical reality without realizing two things:

- That there is a structure of consciousness that creates

intimacies all through Reality.
- That death is not the end of the story.

Death within one lifetime is not the end of the story.

You cannot live your story within the context of one lifetime—it doesn't work. **This lifetime is a *chapter* in the story.** If you try and work out your lifetime, to be happy within one lifetime, it's just not going to work.

How about being fulfilled, being aligned with value, giving your unique gift within one lifetime? Then—

- As a *byproduct* of being aligned with value,
- As a byproduct of being aligned with the higher plotlines of Reality that live in you,
- As a byproduct of giving your unique gift, living your Unique Self

—you'll also attain a degree of happiness: the highest degree of happiness and joy you could possibly attain. Because:

Joy is a byproduct of living your Unique Self.

But your storyline is never exhausted in the context of one lifetime. It's not true. We have to extend the storyline. This lifetime is one chapter in a larger evolving, almost never-ending story—and that story has direction, and it's got *telos*, and it's got Eros.

It is a telerotic story, and it's moving towards the evolution of love.

My life has order and disorder—and it's moving towards a higher order.

That's the direction of Reality, if I can get out of my temporal myopia, where I am living in this minute. Enlightenment is to feel the larger Field.

THE EVOLUTIONARY STORY OF CRUCIFIXION AND RESURRECTION

CHOOSING TO TELL THE MOST ACCURATE STORY

However, we don't wait for the next lifetime. That's not what we're saying. We move to create heaven on earth. What we are saying is that this story, this movement to create heaven on earth, is living in the context of a larger story. Of course it is.

How do we know? Because we know that **justice is a given**.

We know that justice is a First Principle and First Value of Reality—and most people don't achieve justice in one lifetime. Therefore, we actually know, in our very anthro-ontological existence and our very bodies—*through my body I vision God*—that the story must go on. Because the story is always the story of justice. It's always a story of goodness, truth, and beauty.

But that's not achieved by millions, even billions, of people in one lifetime, so this means there must be a continuity of consciousness. Plus, there's the empirical evidence, gathered by the British and American Psychical Societies over the last 140 years, which actually indicates there's continuity of consciousness.

So, what does Easter say?

- Easter says *no* to death.
- Easter says death is not the end of the story.
- Easter says Crucifixion is not the end of the story. There's Resurrection.

Now, does Resurrection happen three days later? Maybe. Maybe not. Maybe it's a historical myth. But is Resurrection true? Absolutely. Absolutely, without question, Resurrection is true. **Resurrection is a truth of Reality.** It does not end with crucifixion.

Hope is a memory of an inevitable future.

That's the story we're going to tell. That's the story we're *choosing* to tell. Does everyone begin to feel, friends, how this all comes together?

We are choosing to tell that story—

- Not because it's a fanciful story, not because we're making it up, not because it's a conjecture.
- Not because stories are a figment of our imagination.
- Not because stories are mere social constructs.

No, story is the ontology of God. Story is the ontology of Reality. The story—when we put together the best information of the interior and exterior sciences and we tell the most accurate story—*that* is the story that births and continues the evolution of love.

What are we doing here together? We are at this moment of meta-crisis, and we've come together to tell a new Story of Value. This is a da Vinci moment (and Medici's, please come forward and help resource this). We are telling a new Story of Value, which is the single most important thing we could do at this moment in history. It's the overwhelming moral imperative of this moment in history—

- Not to tell a New Age story,
- Not to tell a regressive Pollyannaish story,
- But to tell *the most accurate* story, the most accurate love story that we can tell, grounded in all the sciences, integrated into a plotline which becomes self-evidently clear, that lives in us, as us, and through us.

I'm just going to finish with one thing. Have you ever noticed, friends, that there is music in reality? I love music.

Music is Reality seeking to tell its story. And music has lyrics, which are Reality's attempt to give *words* to the story. Sometimes, the lyrics are truly poetic, but usually they are not. Usually they're telling a story; most lyrics tell a story. Isn't that interesting? Most music has lyrics, and most lyrics tell a story.

And almost every song is a love story. Across culture and time, almost every story is a love story.

- Sometimes it's love of the beloved.
- Sometimes it's love of country.
- Sometimes it's love of God in all Her distressing disguises.
- Sometimes it's love of the earth.
- Sometimes it's love of truth.
- Sometimes it's love of beauty.

But it's always a love story. Why?

Because Reality is not merely a fact—Reality is a story.

And Reality is not an ordinary story—Reality is a love story infused with hope.

Hope is a memory of tomorrow's never-ending love story.

CHAPTER SEVENTEEN

"SHOW ME SOMETHING REAL, TELL ME SOMETHING TRUE": A HERETICAL BLUEPRINT FOR A WORLD RELIGION AS A CONTEXT FOR OUR DIVERSITY

Episode 380 — January 21, 2024

WE DON'T WAIT FOR THE PROPHETS

When I come to One Mountain, I am surrounded by friends, colleagues, students, interlocutors, and co-creators.

- We are looking together towards the future,
- We are responding to the meta-crisis,
- We are living in celebration,
- We are laughing out of one side of our face and shedding tears out of the other side.

Most importantly, at the heart of the revolution, **we are telling the new Story of Value based on a field of First Principles and First Values** because we understand that *only* telling a new Story of Value—out of which we create the future, out of which we articulate the memory of the future—can respond to the meta-crisis.

That's the core of One Mountain: an understanding that we are at this time between worlds, this time between stories. In that time in between, in that space in between, when the old world order is breaking down, it's either going to devolve and collapse, or there's going to be a breakthrough, like that which happened during the birth of modernity, when a new story of Reality was told.

To the extent that they got the plotline right, we birthed the great dignities of modernity, but to the precise extent that they missed pieces of the plotline, the dignities of modernity wound up creating a structure that crossed planetary boundaries. It was a structure driven by rivalrous conflict governed by win/lose metrics, which governed all relationships and created exponential growth curves.

This structure created massive gaps between haves and have-nots and emptied the Field of Meaning—the Field of Value. Everything became but *a social construction* of Reality, and the only story that guided us was a success story, and perhaps a personal romantic story.

That structure of society drove this rivalrous conflict governed by win/lose metrics right off a cliff. We've created complicated, fragile systems. We crossed planetary boundaries, and we now have fourteen or fifteen different vectors where existential risk is more real than you can possibly imagine.

How do we respond? How do we take the meta-crisis seriously? (And some of you are saying, "God, we know that already. Let's get down to the new Dharma this week. Let's not rehearse this again.")

We actually don't look away. That's the nature of One Mountain. We don't look away.

- We look *into*.
- We *feel* into.
- We feel where we are.
- We are evolution feeling itself through us.

- We are the pulse, the throb, the tumescence of *She*, of the Evolutionary Love unfolding itself, feeling herself through us, and we look around and feel the whole.

That's what The Crossing means.

The Crossing means: I don't look away.

The Crossing means: I cross over from the side of *homo sapiens* who's involved in his or her own win/lose metrics—whether it's religion against religion, or a nation against nation, or family against family, or employee against employee, or executive against executive, or company against company.

We step out of that narrow, myopic view of Reality, that *temporally* myopic view—meaning I can only see my narrow short-term dimension of time—and we expand our consciousness. We expand our view.

In this expanded view, we feel the future. We literally feel the future in us.

We are not in this petty contraction, using spirituality to try and emerge out of *my* crisis. We are feeling the suffering of Reality, and we feel the joy of Reality in us. We are *Homo Amor*.

- We are the elite. We don't wait for the elite.
- We are the prophets. We don't wait for the prophets.
- We are the sages and the seers. We don't wait for the sages and the seers.
- We are the revolutionaries. We don't wait for some revolution to happen someplace else.
- We feel it all. We feel it moving through us, and we democratize the capacity to feel that feeling.

That feeling becomes not the feeling just of this narrow sector of humanity dissociated from the larger masses of people—the throbbing, teeming masses of people.

There's not some little group that's looking down on us, and they get it, and they're going to lead us. No, no, no, there is no group like that. There is no room of people like that. They don't exist—not in the halls of the prophets, and not in the halls of the sages, and not in the halls of the intelligence agencies, and not in the different departments of governments around the world. **There is no room that's going to save it.**

What is going to save it—

- What's going to change it,
- What's going to shift it,
- What's going to respond effectively to the meta-crisis and allow us to avoid the death of humanity or the death of our humanity—

is actually generating a new humanity.

The realization that I can become something more.

- I can live a bigger life.
- I can play a bigger game.
- I can participate directly in the evolution of love, and that happens by transforming myself.
- I become something new, but I don't just *feel* a little different—I *am* different.

I am not a better *version* of myself—I'm a new self. There's a new me.

FROM HOMO SAPIENS TO HOMO AMOR

That movement is not a fanciful movement. That's not some strange, weird, impossible, idyllic, fundamentalist vision of a rapture, or a New Age vision of the same.

No, it is actually an inexorable movement of Cosmos itself.

Cosmos moves towards evolution, from matter to life to the depths of the self-reflective human mind. The self-reflective human mind deepens, and deepens, and deepens—until, precisely at a moment of crisis, there is this new birth. The new birth is literally a new emergent—just like matter went through all of its levels and triumphed as life, and life went through all of its levels and triumphed as the depth of the self-reflective human mind.

The self-reflective human mind goes through all of its levels. And then, like always, it hits a crisis. **The crisis is always a crisis of intimacy.** It's a crisis of relationship. The parts of the system don't know each other.

There are billions and billions of people on the planet, but they are all governed by win/lose metrics. There is no coherence. There is no resonance because there's no intimacy.

There is a global intimacy disorder—and so **we restore intimacy through the emergence of a new level of intimacy**—an *evolutionary* intimacy, a new quality of intimacy, a new quality of human being.

Literally, Christ the Savior is born, but Christ the Savior is born *as you, as me, as we.*

- We become the Christed ones.
- We become the new prophets.
- We become the new sages.
- We become the new activists.
- We become the new economists, the new politicians, even the new data scientists that are doing data science in an entirely new way.

We become *Homo Amor*. **We cross to the other side—we shift the way we experience Reality**. I can make that shift, and I can do that crossing—simply right now in this very second. That crossing doesn't mean that I need to go head an intelligence agency; I don't even need to write a book.

I shift something inside of me.

A HERETICAL BLUEPRINT FOR A WORLD RELIGION

That's what The Crossing means: something inside of me shifts.

What shifts? I move from the side of *homo sapiens* who's involved in his or her own win/lose metrics, who loves a very narrow group of people, and I realize that I'm not *homo sapiens*, I'm actually part of the whole:

- I'm related to the whole.
- I'm omni-considerate for the sake of the whole.
- I'm omni-responsible for the sake of the whole.
- The pulsing that pulses in me is the Evolutionary Impulse.
- I feel the whole.
- I participate in the whole.

I'm a unique expression of the currency of Eros, of the currency of Amor, of love that moves through Reality.

I become the New Human, I become *Homo amor*, the New Humanity, the new genus—which means I realize:

- I'm participatory in the Field of Eros.
- I'm participatory in the Field of Desire.
- I clarify my desire, and I clarify my story, and I realize that my story is a love story.
- I clarify my interiority, and I clarify my intention, and I fix my broken vessels because every human being has broken vessels, and I fix my traumas, and I fix my lies, and I fix my delusions one at a time, even in the smallest way I can.

My intention there is no longer psychological.

I'm not fixing myself merely for the sake of my psychology. I realize that **psychology is the metaphysics of the whole**. Psychology is the psyche of the whole. My interiority, my insides, affects everything. *Da Ma LeMalah*

Mimcha, say the interior scientists in the second century: know that which is above (the whole thing) emerges from the depths of your interiority.

That's *Homo amor*.

I know that what pulses inside of me is the heart, the throb, the beating, tumescent, vibratory impulse of Evolutionary Love itself, uniquely beating in me. Therefore, through my shifting, and reshaping, and recasting, and developing, and evolving, and transforming my own interior, I change the whole thing. I literally have the capacity to be a mad lover that changes the whole thing. Not an ordinary lover, but an outrageous lover. Mad lover.

The only sanity is mad love.

In the sixteenth century, Isaac Luria called that *Leshem Yichud. Leshem Yichud Kudsha Brich Hu U'shekhintai*: **Every action I take through my healing the split off parts of myself creates intimate communion**, all the way down and all the way up.

That's who we are. That's the reset.

We are here in One Mountain to become *Homo amor*, to cross to the other side. There's no more insane joy than being on the other side, than knowing:

- I am never powerless.
- Everything that happens inside of me is significant; it is witnessed.
- I'm personally addressed by Reality, by all of Reality, by her personal infinite face, by God who is the Infinite Intimate.
- I have the capacity to personally address Reality.

To cross over is to cross over to the side of love.

That's what we are going to talk about this week. We are going to talk about the side of love.

A HERETICAL BLUEPRINT FOR A WORLD RELIGION

EVOLUTIONARY LOVE CODE: WE ALL STAND TOGETHER ON THE SIDE OF LOVE

There is only one side, the side of love.

What that means about what should be done is a question of impossible complexity, pain, and uncertainty. We stand for a culture of Eros against a culture of death. We stand for intimacy against alienation. This requires us to be both tender and fierce, to stand for Love against all forms of un-love.

Distinctions around value are an expression of Love. Love and un-love are real. But Love and un-love are not an inherent split on racial, national, ethnic, or religious grounds. That kind of thinking itself is an expression of un-love and anti-Value, that in and of itself is the cause of so much horror.

There is only one side, the side of love. We all stand together on the side of Love.

In our formulation, good and evil is discerned simply: to be good is to stand for Love. No one is outside of the circle of Love. To be on the side of Love requires the cultivation of radical discernment within a broken information ecology.

There is only one side, the side of love. We all stand together on the side of Love.

A SHARED STORY OF VALUE IS A COSMIC ANTHEM

The Dharma is the nature of Reality.

Imagine that you are Steven Weinberg (who died recently), who won the Nobel Prize for his work on muons. Imagine your ecstasy when you begin to understand something new about muons because you're understanding something about the core structure of Reality.

There is a structure of Reality, in its exteriors and its mechanics—and there is a structure of Reality in its melody, in its music, in its interiors.

As Nietzsche understood, Reality mocked people who looked at it just as mechanics and not as music.

What we're doing in advancing the Dharma today is **we want to understand, and feel, and even write a new note in the music of Cosmos**—because when I understand, and I can write the note, it means I'm hearing the music. When I can hear the music, I can write the symphony. When I am pressed into Reality, the music clarifies. We understand something new. When the music clarifies, we try and add it to the symphony.

What we want to do is to advance the Dharma, but this music that we're trying to hear and put notes to isn't just another casual symphony. **We're trying to write the cosmic anthem. Not the national anthem, not even the global anthem, but the cosmic anthem.**

What is the anthem of value that unites us? What is the music that we all rally to, so that we feel, "Okay, we're all part of this together?" That's what we mean by a Shared Story of Value. This is our song.

- A couple often have their song—a couple can be two friends, it can be people in a biological bond, it can be people who are creating together, a deep, deep, deep friendship of evolutionary beloved Whole Mates, or it can be a romantic couple. You should always have your song with your friends.
- A country has a song. That's the national anthem.
- Can you imagine there is a *global* anthem?
- Now imagine there's not just a global anthem, but a *cosmic* anthem, because value is not just global—**value is actually cosmic.**

The national anthem expresses the music of the nation.

The global anthem is the music of the globe, the world's spirituality.

But imagine that **the world's spirituality is rooted not just in social conventions of humanity, but humanity is an expression of the universe.**

The universe is a Story of Value. Value is backed by the universe. It's not just a social contrivance. Then, there'd be a cosmic anthem.

My son Zion likes soccer games, and there's a soccer team in San Jose. So we went to a soccer game, and they sang the national anthem. I cannot stop crying to the national anthem. Every time I go with him to a game, I can't get through the national anthem. Everyone stands up—people from different parts of life and different backgrounds. Most people in that particular stadium were immigrants to America, many of them with Hispanic roots. And there's the sense of generosity in the air, and there's the sense of struggle in the air. And then the "Star-Spangled Banner" comes on and people stand up. At that moment, differences drop away.

You can feel the Eros. You can feel the love. You can feel the intimate communion for a moment.

Imagine if we had a cosmic anthem, a song that calls us. **A special song between all of us that calls us to our best. That's what we mean by a new Story of Value.**

The Dharma is the Ring of Sauron. The Dharma is the most alluring, wondrous possibility, but you can't make the Dharma *yours*.

What happens when a particular nation says the ring is mine, I am going to go destroy everyone because I've got some understanding of the ring?

Religious wars—whether the religious wars are communists killing people or classical religious wars in the premodern world, or the Thirty Years War in Europe—take on many guises. The secular ideologies of the twentieth century actually killed more people, because they had more sophisticated weaponry than all the previous religious wars.

But what wars mean is that I actually have this intuition, I understand something that's true. There is a spark of the sacred, but then from that spark I construct a false story. Instead of it being a *cosmological* Story of Value, the Dharma becomes my attempt to take the Ring of Sauron and make it *mine*.

The Ring of Sauron is the ring of power from Tolkien's great trilogy, *The Lord of the Rings*. And whoever tries to own the ring is destroyed. The ring belongs to everyone. We all carry the ring together. The ring is that which should encircle us.

It's the Shared Story of Value.

"SHOW ME SOMETHING REAL, TELL ME SOMETHING TRUE"

The topic of our Dharma for today is to stand on the side of love. This is our third week of talking about standing on the side of love. Our question is: what does it mean to stand on the side of love? We want to deepen that understanding. **What does it mean to cross over and to stand on the side of love?**

I'm going to read you a story from the *New York Times* this morning. It's about being on the side of love. The title is "An Atheist Chaplain, and a Death Row Inmate's Final Hours."[3] It doesn't matter whether you read the article or not. It's a story about an atheist chaplain in Oklahoma, Devin Moss, working with an atheist inmate, Phillip Hancock, who has been condemned to death for two murders he committed in 2001. The *Times* writes:

> There is an adage that says there are no atheists in foxholes—even skeptics will pray when facing death. But Hancock, in the time leading up to his execution, only became more insistent about his non-belief. He and his chaplain were both confident that **there was no God who might grant last-minute salvation, if only they produced a desperate prayer. They had only one another.**

The article begins with the morning of Hancock's execution: he seems focused on his last meal (the guards brought him some white meat chicken instead of dark meat he asked for), and they are still hoping for last-minute

---

3 You can read the whole article here: http://www.nytimes.com/2024/01/21/us/an-atheist-chaplain-and-a-death-row-inmates-final-hours.html.

clemency from the governor Kevin Stitt (who two years ago claimed "every square inch" of Oklahoma for Jesus Christ). Clemency means the sentence of death would be annulled.

> But if the hour of death came to pass, what would the chaplain do? Moss felt viscerally the absence of any higher power on the prison compound that morning. "It's well known that people that really believe, that really have faith, die better," he said. "How can we help people die better that don't have supernatural faith?"

Scholars who examine the phenomenon find that in prison, faith can be a comfort. People are searching for a new identity beyond "criminal," a sense of empowerment, the vocabulary to ask for forgiveness and the feeling of control over their future. Religion answers all these calls: The new identity is that of a convert. The power is in being an agent of God. The route to forgiveness runs through belief, or through proselytizing. And past sins become just steps on the path to God.

Hancock, 59, had the opposite path. He had entered prison as a Christian, with an appetite for reading, learning and debate that he shared with many imprisoned believers. Along the way, he became an atheist.

In his early years in prison, he started to feel abandoned by God. When, in 2007, a court denied the appeal of his death sentence,

> Hancock had a revelation: "I decided, it makes more sense to me to hate a God that does not exist than to be slave to one," he said. "The weight of the world came off of me. Because I wasn't concerned about this maniacal, narcissistic, omnicidal psychopath."

That's the story of Hancock. Now we switch to the story of the Chaplain.

> The chaplain, Moss, grew up in Hailey, Idaho, and jokes that he was born with an existential crisis: Instead of coming out of the womb saying "wah," he came out saying "why?"
>
> His parents sent him to a private Catholic school, but he couldn't bring himself to believe in biblical tales; at the University of

Texas at Austin, he studied existentialism, Friedrich Nietzsche, Baruch Spinoza, Joseph Campbell and Buddhist philosophers.

He realized the existentialists made more sense to him than the Christian teachings of his youth. And he eventually concluded that he did not believe in God, though he still sought a sense of spiritual purpose.

He decided to make a podcast about spirituality and death called "The Adventures of Memento Mori," referring to the Latin phrase: "Remember you must die." During a podcast interview, a Buddhist chaplain, the Reverend Trudi Jinpu Hirsch-Abramson, told Moss: "You'd make a good chaplain." The remark stuck with him.

He joined a newly launched program for humanists at the Meadville Lombard Theological School in 2019. After he graduated, in June 2022, the American Humanist Association heard about Hancock—an inmate who wanted a chaplain who did not believe in God.

They started to communicate by phone (the calls were capped at twenty minutes).

During one of their first calls together, last February, Hancock explained to his new spiritual adviser the conundrum that he faced: "I want more than anything to believe in something other than this," meaning the life he was living, "I just can't do it though, lacking evidence."

Hancock had one request of his spiritual adviser. It was drawn from a set of Bible verses, Philippians 4:7-8. "Show me something real," he said to Moss. "Tell me something true."

In July, Moss began visiting Hancock in person.

"Moss stopped feeling so anxious about what he was offering Hancock. He listened, as Hancock ate vending machine cheeseburgers and drank cans of Mountain Dew. **It became clear to Moss that Hancock did not believe in God, but he did believe in what people can do for each other.** He seemed to believe, in particular, in the relationship he was building with Moss.

In August, Moss decided that he would sublet his Brooklyn apartment and move to Oklahoma for the month leading up to the execution so that he could visit the prison more easily. The time they spent together in person felt more human—the eye contact, the stretches of time uninhibited by the 20-minute phone limit. "Hey Devin, you're blowing me away," Hancock said when he heard about the chaplain's plans. "You're showing me something I haven't seen from—I don't recall anybody really coming through like this."

Meanwhile, the legal case continued. Hancock and his lawyers were asking for clemency because he acted in self-defense. Hancock had said that the two people he killed were giving drugs to his girlfriend that were actually destroying her, and that he got in a fight with them, and that's how they were killed. The board voted 3-2 to recommend clemency, but Gov. Stitt had to make the final decision.

Moss sometimes posed deeper, cerebral questions, the sort he had initially envisioned that he would explore as a chaplain, like where humans should find their moral compass. And Hancock said to Moss, the pastor, "Do unto others as you would have them do unto you," explaining his view of ethics with a biblical passage. "That's it in a nutshell. That's it. You don't have to have all these other things, you don't have to believe in certain things—that God has been and always will be."

"What do you think happens when a person dies?" Moss asked another time. Hancock assured his chaplain he found morsels of comfort in his nonbelief. "Nonexistence didn't bother me before I existed. I don't think it's going to bother me after I'm dead."

And now we get to the final visit. The execution was set for Nov. 30th at 10 a.m. This is really what I wanted to read with you.

That morning, Moss wrote out in a notebook what he planned

to say to Hancock in their final minutes together. Hancock, no longer able to make phone calls, was in his cell listening to music from the heavy metal band Slayer, one of his favorites. Moss arrived at the prison at 7:35 and entered the room where he would wait for a decision from the governor. The minutes moved in a torturous crawl. Soon it was 8:30, then it was 9 a.m. The lawyers and prison staff were waiting together, some making small talk about the rain.

Around 10:10, an aide for the governor called. The execution was to move forward, quickly. Over on death row, the inmates gave Hancock a send-off—kicking their doors and filling the prison with the rumbling sound of a makeshift goodbye. Because of the delay, Moss had to cut short his final minutes with Hancock. He had been told that they would be together for 20 minutes, but instead they got only about 10. "Phil's been shorted again," Moss thought, remembering the fried chicken.

Moss was shuttled to H-unit, where the execution chamber was located. He entered the sparse room where Hancock lay strapped to a gurney, wearing a gray shirt and with a white sheet covering the lower half of his body. Moss was struck by how tiny the space was, and the tightness of the straps slung over the gurney.

He rested a hand on Hancock's knee and recited the words that he had written in his notebook: "We call the spirit of humanity into this space," Moss said. "Let love fill our hearts. We ask that in this transition into peaceful oblivion that Phil feels that love, and although this is his journey that he is not alone. We invoke the power of peace, strength, grace and surrender. Amen."

Moss turned to his final words for Hancock. "In the beginning of this, when I asked what you really wanted out of a spiritual care adviser, it was Philippians Chapter 4," he said, "That you quoted to me." "Show me something real, tell me something true." Moss looked at the face, Hancock's face, that he had come to know well. **"What is real is that you are loved," he told his friend. "What is true is you are not alone."**

It was time for Hancock's final words.

> He thanked his legal team and told the attorney general, who was seated in the front row with his legs crossed, that he had been "hoodwinked." He told his witnesses that he had acted in self-defense, and still hoped to be exonerated after his death.

And finally, they describe the moments after Hancock's death:

> Moss surprised himself by murmuring a spontaneous prayer that came out involuntarily, like a sneeze. He prayed that whatever came next for Hancock, that he would be dealt a better set of cards.
>
> The families of the victims, Jett and Lynch, spoke in the prison's media room right afterward. "I am grateful that justice has been served according to God's will," said Lynch's niece, reading a message from her mother. "I can only hope that he chose to get his soul right with God before his window of opportunity closed for eternity."
>
> Outside the execution chamber, the drizzle had turned into sheets of rain. Moss sat in his car and began to cry. In his hand was the paper where he had written down his final message to Hancock. There were the instructions he had written to himself: "Call the spirit of humanity into this space." And there was a sentence fragment he'd crossed out, following the word spirit: "Of the divine."
>
> Moss had gone back and forth on how to approach those last moments. He knew he wanted his final words to his friend to honor what both of them believed to be true, "God has nothing to do with this."

THE GOD YOU DON'T BELIEVE IN DOESN'T EXIST

What is this story about? This story is about being on the side of love. The story is beautiful. It's heart-wrenching. And it also tells us where we are today, because the truth is that God does have nothing to do with this.

WORLD RELIGION AS A CONTEXT FOR OUR DIVERSITY

> *To cross over to the side of love is to know love's true nature, and to know love's true nature is to include all of the opposites and all of the oppositions.*

The God you don't believe in doesn't exist. The love that creates splits between people, the love that says only we are the loved ones and you are not—that love does not exist. **The rejection of God by Moss and Hancock, the heresy of Moss and Hancock is the highest faith.** I stand with Moss and Hancock.

This is heresy which is faith.

Moss and Hancock are rejecting the small god. Look at the text: "He and his chaplain were both confident there was no God who might grant last minute salvation if only they produced a desperate prayer."

You get that caricature of God? The caricature of God that runs throughout the article is a god who might be willing to give a last-minute salvation if only they would produce a desperate prayer. You get the subtle mocking. It's a mocking of God: "If you'll just give me a desperate prayer, I'll take you through."

Hancock claims that it was in self-defense. We don't know. We weren't there. But that's certainly a possibility. After two decades, he maintains the story, and you can get a sense of his decency, of his goodness. He clearly didn't have enough funds to hire a lawyer that would have done the work to exonerate him. And there's almost no justice in the system if you don't actually have the means, the legal means (which means the finances) to defend yourself, so there is actually a significant possibility that he was innocent. But we don't know.

But the families of the victims say, "I'm grateful that justice has been served according to God's will. I can only hope that he chose to get his soul right with God before his window of opportunity closed for eternity." Clearly, they're fundamentalists. If he doesn't get his soul right with God, then the window closes for eternity, and he is damned forever.

And the governor, who has claimed every inch of Oklahoma for Jesus Christ—he can grant clemency, but he doesn't.

The picture of God in the article is: God is on the side of the fundamentalists. God is the one who's going to give you maybe a last-minute salvation in exchange for a desperate prayer. This God is not on the side of love. This is the God they rejected.

But it is so much more beautiful, and so much more deep, and so much more wondrous and stunning.

What actually happens?

He says, "Show me something real. Tell me something true." And what is real and what is something true? What did they say? "We don't have God, we only have each other."

There is this sense in the article that having each other *matters*. **Having each other matters enormously, unimaginably.**

But of course, there is a confusing word in that sentence: "only." They had *only* one another. "*Only* one another" connotes a separate self that has no eternity, that doesn't participate in the Field of Value.

They had *only* one another. No, they *had one another*. They had one another, and *She* spoke through that, and they were the two cherubs above the Ark, in the Holy of Holies, and the voice of *She* spoke from between them. The prison was the Ark, and the table between them was the Ark of the Covenant, and they were the two cherubs on either side, and the voice of God had emerged from between them.

Moss says, "We call the spirit of humanity into the space." And he wrote "the divine," but he took it out. This divine that he took out was the God we don't believe in. And then he says, "Let love fill our hearts." Let love fill our hearts.

What does that mean? Why does it matter that love fills our hearts?

It's the thing that matters more than anything in the world. And Moss flies down and sublets his apartment to be there for the last month, so he can be with his brother that he found, so he can walk through with him.

He says, "Let love fill our hearts," and he says to Hancock, "And know that you're not alone." And then he talks about this transition into "peaceful oblivion," but if it's oblivion, how can it be peaceful? How can it be anything at all?

The assumption is that you go into nothingness, but that's okay because I wasn't concerned about nothingness before, so why would I be concerned about nothingness now. This is utterly ridiculous, because you're now in the middle, you're now here. You may not have been concerned before, but now you're in this world and wanting to be connected to value that matters forever, and wanting to feel that there is a larger justice, and that things actually work out, and there is a larger karma, and there's a sense that there's a rectification of the violations of God.

He is feeling something. He is knowing something.

This is in the culture, this rejection of the surface God. There is this heresy. This is the *New York Times* writing.

This is the center of culture that has correctly rejected the God of the great religions, who is the God you don't believe in.

The God you don't believe in doesn't exist.

- ◆ The God of the great religions, which hijacked those gods for the sake of cruelties.

- The gods of the great religions who in their external form were fundamentalist gods that condemned you to eternity and hell, as the relatives of the people that he killed thought might happen to him if he didn't get it right with his fundamentalist faith.

"WHAT'S REAL IS THAT YOU'RE LOVED"

But then there is this deeper understanding.

They say, "We're heretics. We reject God."

But what they're saying is: "No, no, after you reject the surface God, after you reject the God you don't believe in, then you begin to know something."

What do you begin to know?

- That we just have each other.
- That somehow a miracle happened, and Hancock found a friend.
- That this friend was willing to come there and to love him.
- That they loved each other.
- And that the friend cried for him after he died.

What do we want? We want a friend who will cry for us in the car after we died—and he found a friend who cried for him after he died. He found a friend who felt him, who hung on to his every word, who exchanged with him in sacred conversation.

In this Conversational Cosmos, the cosmos came awake and alive in that conversation. That conversation was God talking to God.

There is this realization, in the conversation between them—

- that dignity matters,
- that meaning matters,
- that truth matters,

- that integrity matters,
- and that how we hold each other matters.

Moss understands that he's got to wear the right clothes and that he wants to say the exact right thing. He understands that he's going into a sacred moment, and he says, "We invoke the power of peace, strength, grace, and surrender. Amen."

There's this sense of eternity, but as Wittgenstein, the great logical positivist, said, eternity is not everlasting time. It's *beneath* space and time. It's the everlasting space, which is forever.

Then Hancock dies. And almost against his will, Moss prays. He prays that whatever comes next for Hancock, he will be dealt a better set of cards.

This is a sacred text, written without the intention to be a sacred text. It was just released into culture a few hours ago. What does this text tell us?

First, **it tells us that the whole thing is about love**. He says to him, "What is real is that you are loved." That's true. That's the most ultimately real statement.

What does that mean? It means that Reality is Eros. Its insides are lined with love. What's real is that you are loved.

- Not love as a social construction.
- Not love as a made up social contrivance.
- Not, "love isn't real."
- Not, "love is just a human value that was made up," as ChatGPT suggests.

No, there's this deep, intuitive knowing in Moss, even though he can't articulate it, even though he understands it as being *against* God—against the nonexistent God you don't believe in.

What does it mean that the God you don't believe in doesn't exist? The God you don't believe in is the God who would say that Moss and Hancock are not gorgeous incarnations of Himself or Herself.

Actually, God lives as Moss. God lives as Hancock. When they say, "All we have is each other," that's God loving God.

He says, "What's real is that you're loved. What's true is that you're not alone." Moss is stating metaphysical facts of Reality. This is a credo of faith in its most stunning form.

We have to throw out all the metaphysics. We have to throw out all the religious wars. We have to get to the second simplicity—what's underneath everything.

"WHAT'S TRUE IS THAT YOU'RE NOT ALONE"

There's a couple of key things we can learn from all this. Number one: **Reality is Eros, and Eros is the movement of separate parts into larger wholes**, which is the movement of the value of Cosmos itself.

Number two is: **what is true is you're not alone.** It's the beginning of the *Book of Genesis*. And God said, "It's not good for the human being to be alone." God is good, and God stands against aloneness. God doesn't say "I want your desperate deathbed prayer, and I'll give you a quick salvation." No, that's a caricature. That mocks God. That's the God you don't believe in. That's the small god that comes from the small comprehension, from the contracted self. Now what's true is that you're not alone. Sometimes we live lives of quiet desperation, but we never live lives of ultimately lonely desperation. We're not alone. That's two.

Number three: **justice matters**. That's very clear in the article. He wants to be exonerated even *after* his death. He says, "I was innocent. This wasn't true." This was a violation of fairness. Justice matters.

And number four: actually, the journey goes on. **There's continuity of consciousness**. What does Moss say? Against his will, he offers a prayer: "I pray that whatever comes next for Hancock, he'll be dealt a better set of cards." Meaning: justice needs to be rectified. It can't remain unjust. Fairness needs to be restored. And the journey goes on. In the last moments, when he's trying not to pray, he says, "Know that in this journey he's not alone."

He is on a journey. And he's not alone, and love is real, and he needs to be dealt a better set of cards. So we have:

- Justice.
- Intimate communion.
- The Reality of love.
- The integrity of justice throughout worlds.

I think we just got the core of religion itself at its best, didn't we? It's a big deal.

We have to reclaim a language of value. **The language of value intuitively knows that it's not over when it's over. It's not over at the moment of death.** Intuitively, Moss understands it and prays that he'll be dealt a better set of cards as his journey goes on.

We understand that if it's over when it's over, it's a violation of fairness. It is a violation of justice. Moss understands this, and Hancock understands this.

They engage in this fierce, gorgeous, sacred heresy.

They refuse to accept a small god.

They refuse to accept a traumatized contracted god.

They refuse to adopt a superficial or petty faith that will give them petty and superficial comfort.

They want the pleasure of true gnosis, of true knowing, the pleasure of knowing:

- That love is real.
- That what is true is that you're not alone.
- That justice matters.
- That the way we love each other matters.

- That the details matter. It matters that when I ask for my last meal and I want dark meat, but the system ignores me, and they bring me white meat—that's not okay. That's a violation of the Divine.

Dignity matters. Honor matters. Even in the last moments of life.

> *To be on the side of love is to be on the side of God.*

There is no separation between those.

There is no God versus love. *To be on the side of love is to be on the side of God, and to be on the side of God is to be on the side of love.*

That means that we have to let go of the superficial dogmas of fundamentalism and of fundamentalist scientism.

TENETS OF THE WORLD RELIGION

We're going to pray together because what can we do more now than to pray?

The article shows exactly where the intelligentsia of culture is today, which defines the academy, the university, the default assumptions of the decision makers in culture. What it basically says is, you've got fundamentalism on the one side, and the other side is against God—they're good humanists.

In the article, fundamentalism is represented by the governor who claims every inch of Oklahoma for Jesus Christ, but he doesn't give clemency. The fundamentalist god is the god that he learned growing up in school where he was mocked by the assemblies of "god people" for being a sinful, abominate Methodist. The fundamentalist god is a god prayed to by those at the end who celebrate his death, and say that if he didn't get it right with his fundamentalism, he is condemned for eternity. That's the fundamentalist god. That god is rejected by Moss, and it's rejected by Hancock, and it's obviously rejected by the writers of the article. And that's a gorgeous rejection.

But that was never true in the great religions. **The great religions always held a deeper view.** They always had a deeper realization. The great religions themselves, at their best, understood exactly what the writer of the article knows in her body but can't quite express, which is that **there are basic tenets to religion, which is really geared to** *reconnect*.

And what are those tenets of a world religion?

We came together here to be on the side of love and a world religion.

We are on the side of love.

This article gorgeously expresses the core tenets of a world religion, and it does so from Philippians in the New Testament, Chapter 4. What does Philippians say?

"Show me something real, tell me something true."

- Tenet one: What is real is that you are loved.

But we go beyond the article. It's not just because it's a psychological reality in this moment. Even though Moss and Hancock don't have the words to articulate it, they understand this is more than psychology. This is real. Reality is Eros, *Tocho ratzuf ahava*: "its insides are lined with love." It's an amorous cosmos. It's an intimate universe.

This act of intimacy between these two men is an ultimate expression of God. God is the Infinite Intimate. There's a new quality of intimacy between Hancock and Moss that never existed before. It's a stunning quality of the Infinite Intimate.

In Hancock and Moss, a new God is literally born. There's more God to come, and it matters.

- Tenet two: What's true is you're not alone.

So love is real, and you're not alone. Reality is Eros. It's in communion. Everything is connected to everything else.

- Tenet three: justice matters.
- Tenet four: you are on a journey.

In the next stage of the journey, you got to get dealt the right cards. The cards are going to balance out. There is an ultimate coherence through Reality. **There is an ultimate fairness.**

It's actually not true that because Hancock couldn't afford a lawyer, and other people could—that actually guilty people hired the best lawyer and got off, and perhaps an innocent person was sent to his death.

No, that's not true. That's a violation. Hancock knows it, and Moss knows it. And Hancock knows it's important to be exonerated after his death. Justice matters.

Tenet four, **there is a continuity of consciousness**. That's why the prayer emerges from Moss. There is a continuity of consciousness. Death is a night between two days. That is a truth of Reality.

Those are the four tenets of a world religion.

We need to be heretics, my friends. We need to be heretics.

- There is heresy which is faith. That's Moss and Hancock.
- There is faith which is heresy. That's the faith of the fundamentalism, the faith in the small god. That's faith which denies God, which denies love.

There is never a split between God and love. Can't be.

We are the church of Evolutionary Love. It's a religion of love. **Love is religion, and religion is love.** There is no split between them. They are one and the same.

But love is not superficial or insipid.

Love is fierce and makes demands. It rips us apart. It's a holy and a broken hallelujah. It demands everything from us.

What is this force of love?

It's not all sweetness and light. It's not just tenderness. It's fierce, quivering, pulsing tenderness that rips us apart and puts us back together, and somehow we come out more whole. Somehow we come out more God. Somehow we become not merely *Homo sapiens*. We cross over to the other side and become *Homo amor*.

So that was our sacred text for today, and now we're going to turn to prayer. We're going to put on "Hallelujah," and offer our holy and the broken *Hallelujah*. "Even though it all went wrong, Hancock, even though it all went wrong, I stand before the Lord of Song with nothing on my tongue, but *Hallelujah*."

And this is the truth, and I swear by this truth:

We are personally addressed by the Divine.

Sometimes the personal address takes the face and the body of Moss, talking to Hancock. Sometimes it's us talking to each other right now. Sometimes it's somebody reading this text.

And we love each other madly.

And it matters.

And it's not over when it's over—there's a continuity of consciousness.

PRAYER AND WORLD RELGION

CHAPTER EIGHTEEN

ANSWERING THE CALL OF PROPHECY: ENVISIONING NEW POSSIBILITIES & THE DIGNITY OF PRAYER

Episode 196 — July 12, 2020

WE BECOME THE VOICE OF THE NEXT ITERATION OF EVOLUTION

I want to offer something. We are the "Yes."

Can we feel a "Yes" in the space? We are the holy "Yes" at the moment of the Big Bang. Yes! Scream "Yes." If you're sitting on the side and saying, "I'm not going to write 'Yes,' I'm not one of the people who writes 'Yes', I'm one of the people who sits back and listens," you might have done that your entire life in every dimension. So if you're not a person who writes "Yes"—write "Yes" now. This is the moment where you become the Big Bang, you actually become the whole thing, and we begin to actually scream "Yes" together.

That's not a metaphor, that's not a declaration—dear friends, it's the nature of Reality itself.

It's shocking, that Reality itself screams "Yes" through me—and the truth of Reality is that *I am evolution.* What we used to think is that the Universe was kind of a backdrop to this human story.

Science is the revelation of the nature of Reality, and the exterior sciences match the interior sciences of the great traditions—which, of course, need to be evolved and transmuted—and we're bringing them together in a new set of First Principles. What we now understand with complete clarity is that if I think *the Universe is a background and I'm living my life*—that's a mistake. **I am the Universe in person.**

I am the universe in person, and my "Yes" is literally the "Yes" of the Universe.

We're at this moment of incredible peril and incredible promise. We're at this moment of incredible, fabulous potential, potency, fragility, and poignancy, as well as pain beyond imagination—and they're happening together. Literally all of evolution is poised between utopia and dystopia. We're at the first emergence of the Anthropocene, this moment where what we do—this has never been true before in history—as human beings affects the chemical structure of the planet, the atmospheric structure, the molecular structure, the cellular structure. We actually affect the entire thing, and we're a hair trigger away—100 seconds before midnight—before potentially ending the whole thing. And at the same time we're also at the brink of a potential emergence of a new set of First Principles.

We're in a unique time, a time where the old world is breaking down. We're at a phase shift. We've been saying here for the last couple of years. I've called this a time between stories, and I've noticed that people are picking that phrase up in the world, and they're sharing it, which is great. Let's just feel that. We're at a time between stories.

So we are the storytellers. But to be the storytellers we can't just make it up, we can't just declare it. We've got to study, enter, and weave together. What we're trying to do here is swallow it whole—all of the interior sciences, all of the exterior sciences—and let it emerge as evolution seeing with our eyes, evolution speaking with our lips, evolution moving with our hands. **We literally become the voice of the next iteration of evolution.**

THE UNIVERSE: AN EVOLVING LOVE STORY

We're going to tell the new Story—not because it's a declaration but because it's actually a genuine integration in a larger, seamless whole, a larger code of intimacy.

A story is a new configuration of intimacy. That's the language we're developing. We need new language. The old languages won't do. There's not an atom, there's an atomic being. There are not 100 elements that emerged after hydrogen and helium, but there are about 100 elemental beings. What's an elemental being? An elemental being is a configuration of intimacy.

It's not just that *the universe is evolving to more complexity*. More complexity means more interconnectivity whose interior experience is intimacy. **The universe evolves towards more and more coherent intimacy.** The arc of evolution is long, but it's moving towards coherent intimacy. It's going towards more love. Not because we're ignoring all the pain in the world—but rather because *the understanding of pain and evil only makes sense in the context of an intimate universe, of a universe that's moving towards the evolution of love.*

So when Rwanda happens, and 800,000 people are killed in 100 days, or when the COVID-19 pandemic, which should have been handled and prepared for by a group of world leaders in December and January, is ignored—that's a failure of intimacy. In February, there are eight things we could have done, which we didn't do, because we were lost in win/lose metrics. For example, in the United States, probably only five percent of the people who've passed away from Covid needed to pass away. We could have responded in a very different way had we actually been operating out of a different set of First Principles.

But the reason that tragedy even makes any sense, the very reason we can even call it a tragedy is because we live in an intimate universe—because evil is a failure of love, evil is a failure of intimacy.

Let's experience together: it's fifteen billion years ago and the universe explodes. There's this originating Power.

- You might call it the Tao.
- You might call it God.
- You might call it Intimacy, explosions of Infinite Intimacy seeking to evolve.

The Universe explodes. The originating Power of Reality flares forth, and in every droplet of existence there's an intensity of Eros that will never be felt again. It's a singularity, a singular intensity. It's thick with infinite power.

This explosion of the originating creative power ultimately births the first atomic beings—configurations of intimacy—hydrogen and helium. Then it takes a million years of ecstatic turbulence, of relationships that are created for a moment and then broken, until Reality is actually able to find its way to ever greater, more coherent, and stable intimacy. That's what Reality is seeking.

Reality seeks the first elementary particles, the first coherent, stable intimacy of these elementary particles, which are each beings with unique dynamics and unique configurations, held together by allurement, that experience this allurement in their being, which weaves them together into unique dynamic elements that are filled with potency and *potentia*, which are going to literally birth you and me—and which literally live in you and me and everyone else.

Then there are a billion years of night. "*Ve'ha'aretz Hayta Tohu Va'Vohu Ve'Choshech Al Pnai Tehom*" —and there was darkness on the face of the Earth as the Universe was preparing itself for its next transformation, its next transfiguration. And the Universe trembles with immense, infinite creativity disclosed in the finite and the galaxies explode—the Andromeda, Pegasus, Fornax, the Magellanic Clouds that are crowding the galaxy, the Coma Cluster, Sculptor, all of it, the Hercules Cluster, our own Milky Way.

Can you imagine: 100 billion galaxies and each galaxy is a Unique Self: each one a unique form in the universe, each containing its own inherent coherent patterns of intimacy, each bringing forth from its own interior billions and billions of primal stars.

All I did was map just the first millisecond there. That's it. This is the very beginning and the first million years, then the first billion years of the universe seeking intimacies. But that's just the first generation of stars. We didn't even get to the second generation where carbon and oxygen and this whole other set of new configurations of intimacy are born in all of that, all the way through, all that lives in us.

When you're born, literally a star is born, literally *a new, unique configuration of coherent intimacy that takes into account all of matter, all of life, and all of mind.*

I just did the tiniest snapshot with you, just one little snapshot of this magnificence beyond imagination that literally lives in you, that breathes you, that breathes in you. When we place our attention on it, we're blown away.

Our topic is going to be First Principles, and we're going to look at one particular principle, which is the second-person principle of personhood, of the personal, and *how this creates a notion called prayer*—many people think it is some dogmatic idea, but it's not. It's based on the First Principle of personhood.

WE ARE ALL CONNECTED: INVISIBLE LINES OF NON-LOCALITY

The prophet says the lion lies down with the lamb, and somehow, the prophet says, *no longer is there any boundary between the human being and the animal—maybe something else is possible.* What are the First Principles that got us here? When was the last time you ate a steak? Or maybe it was lambchops from a lamb that was in a little torturous, couldn't-move cage for three months in order to create that succulent bite that you were going to enjoy after the lamb got slaughtered? What do you think that does to the structure of the planet?

We currently know scientifically that *there is non-locality*. For example, every cell in our body is in every second in touch with every other cell, but not just every cell. Every element in the universe, every elemental being, every atomic being is in touch in some way with every other atomic being. That's actually true.

That's called non-locality, and it's real.

There's some level of intimate invisible lines of connection that exterior science is disclosing, and that interior science has always been aware of. So what do you think happens in the community of lambs? Do you think the community of lambs is unaware of the human community? Now, I don't mean that they're having lamb gatherings, but I'm saying there's an awareness deep in the structure. The community of lions?

I'm just going to throw at you another wild example, so you can get the idea of First Principles at play—that there are in fact First Principles, and we don't realize they're at play.

IN THE SEPARATE SELF, WE'VE LOST THE FIRST PRINCIPLE OF PERSONHOOD

Everyone knows that there's such a thing as a speed limit. Now, in Germany there's no speed limit. Germany's got a big thing about having no speed limits. In America it varies, but Germany is against speed limits.

Let's say the average speed limit in the world is seventy-five miles per hour. Now, if we lowered the average speed limit to sixty-five or fifty-five miles per hour, do you know that we would save minimally 100,000 lives a year? Does everyone get what we just said? Just let that into your body.

I'm not saying we should or we shouldn't, but what are we saying? We're valuing the experience of speed and the human flourishing that comes with being able to do a lot of things. We're busy—but that busyness is often what Heidegger calls "busy, busy man": we're covering up a fundamental emptiness, because our First Principles have broken down. We've got universal human rights with every human being as a separate self, but in that separation we've grown lonely:

- We've lost a sense of being part of the value proposition of Cosmos.
- We've lost a sense of there being the Good, the True, and the Beautiful that's seeking to emerge through us.

When you talk to someone about *objective values that are not merely social constructions*, they look at you as if you must be totalitarian—and not wrongly, because often totalitarians claimed that they knew the objective values and then imposed them. The great religions had great shadows, we know that. **The rebellion against the old versions of objective values was in some sense correct—but then we left a vacuum.**

We established the universal human rights of the separate-self individual, and then people went into alienation. We differentiated from each other, but then we dissociated from each other, and we dissociated from the larger context of Value. But we needed a story, so we put in a success story with its win/lose metrics, with no genuine Eros in which we participate, and now we're *busy, busy men and women* speeding all around.

Our implicit covenant in culture is that 100,000 people are bloodily dying with the steering wheel going through their chest and puncturing their stomach—and I'm sorry but that's what happens—splattered on the pavement—sorry, but that's what happens. That's what traffic accidents are. It's a horror. If Germany and other countries lowered their speed limit, you would save so many gruesome deaths every year.

Now, I'm not saying we should lower our speed limit to ten miles an hour. I'm saying *why are we going so fast*? Does everyone catch it? This is a First Principle that no one ever talks about it. When have you heard this conversation in the public space? When did we actually have a referendum: *Let's give up 100,000 lives to bloody deaths in order to travel a little faster?*

- We're waking up.
- We're revolutionaries.
- We're trying to envision a new world.
- We're in this time between stories.
- We have to tell a new Story.
- We have to actually reformulate our economies.
- We've got to reformulate the way we do governance.
- We've got to reformulate the way we do medicine.

This a big deal. So I'm just pointing to these two things: the relationship between the animal and the human world and speed limits. Does everyone just see how those are a little bit shocking?

What if this was a First Principle: Its insides are lined with love. That's a phrase that Solomon offered 2,000 years ago, "*Tocho ratzuf ahavah*," in the Song of Solomon. Those first particles that come together, those first 100 elements, they're held together by love, by allurement that creates relationship, which creates a new whole greater than the sum of the parts. *That Eros is the core quality of Reality.*

BEING A PROPHET MEANS ACCESSING YOUR UNIQUE VOICE AND SEEING NEW POSSIBILITY

Prophecy: that's a word you don't hear a lot, right? Do you feel the part of you that cringes? *Prophecy? What are we talking about? That's weird.* But let's go slow with this.

A prophet means someone who sees a new possibility, someone who's participating in the evolutionary field, and in that participation they feel the voice moving uniquely in them.

They surrender ego, they bracket ego, they study. There were actually schools of prophets: there was no attention economy hijacking attention. You actually had many people at certain points participating in schools of prophecy.

Prophecy means the ability to enter into the inner sanctum, to enter into the Inside of the Inside and *to feel the intention of Reality moving through you and envisioning a new possibility*, to reject the status quo and say, "*Wow, maybe the speed limit shouldn't be 85 miles an hour.*"

- A prophet challenges.
- A prophet speaks truth to power.
- A prophet says, "Maybe steaks aren't what we should be eating."
- A prophet says, "Maybe concentration camps for animals aren't great for the morphic resonance of the planet."
- **A prophet speaks new First Principles.**

I want to tell you something incredibly beautiful, which I was teaching intensely twenty years ago. Every human being holds the capacity for prophecy. There's not just an elite prophetic school. *Every* human being holds the capacity for prophecy. You can't just declare it, though. You can't just speak slowly, sound spiritual, and say, "That's how it is. I'm a prophet." That's nonsense.

Prophecy means you pour yourself open, you commit yourself, you're willing to do the journey, you're willing to study, to engage, to open

your heart, to rip your heart open beyond the contraction again and again—to find your unique voice.

Most prophets don't write prophecy. Writing prophecy is not about writing a book. **Being a prophet means that you can access your unique voice and see a new possibility.** The prophet holds the quality of Reality which is the divine quality. That's what we mean when we say that God initiates, that God invokes. In other words, *the prophet is called*. How many people have ever heard a call? We call each other. We're the voice of God often. We might be blown away in a particular moment in our lives where we meet a new quality of consciousness, and we say, *Oh my God, that feels right. I'm called to that*.

So I want to just ask you a question. Are you willing to hear the call? Are you willing to be a prophet? What we want to do, what we want to be—as one church, as the global communion of pioneering souls, as one synagogue, as the anti-church, as one mosque, as one secular humanist center—we want to *be* prophecy. **We want to *be* prophecy, friends.** Meaning: we want to speak truth to power, we want to reject the status quo, and we want to articulate a vision of what's possible, that in fact *justice can roar like a mighty force throughout the land*, that in fact the Good, the True, and the Beautiful lives in every human being yearning to emerge, that the promise will be kept.

Yes, there were great religions in the past, but, friends, we need greater religions in the future. **The great religions in the past had their beautiful moments, but they were disfigured by the structures of consciousness:** structures that rejected the feminine, that rejected the body, that were mutually exclusive, that were ethnocentric in a dominant kind of way, that were homophobic, that were elite while the masses starved.

We need to write a new sacred text. We need to ontologize love. We need new First Principles.

We have a sister initiative called the Center for World Philosophy and Religion. The think tank might not use the language of prophecy because so many will think, *what are they talking about?* But I want to feel with us here together: **can you feel the language of prophecy?** You're called to be a prophet. Can you actually feel that? You're called.

A Unique Self is a prophet.

A Unique Self has a unique voice.

That's what Unique Self means. Every Unique Self is a potential prophet. A prophet means you're holding a piece of the future utopia. Your gift, your voice is needed. Prayer and prophecy are verbs in the divine-human conversation, the endless conversation between the infinite and finitude.

SLOW DOWN, LISTEN DEEPLY, AND BE FILLED UP WITH EROS

I'll just tell you a little story—David and I were looking for the code for today, and completely unbeknownst to me this code just came down and I wrote it down and sent it to him—that's how prophecy works. In other words, *we're listening*. You can do this. But you've got to be listening all the time. You've got to be committed.

So I have one question. Are you willing to be a prophet?

Are we willing to speak prophecy together?

Are we willing to open to prophecy so that this unique voice moves through us when we really open to it? Are we ready to bracket the ego and be madly committed and madly in love, so that voice begins to be the prophetic voice?

But not the one prophet. **We're going to be the prophet together.**

Being a prophet doesn't mean *I'm a mad man on a hilltop*. It doesn't mean *everything I say is true*. It means I'm deeply alive, I slow down, and **I begin**

to let myself fill up with Eros. Not because I'm yelling and screaming all day, no. I'm going deep inside. I might be really busy. *"Slow down"* doesn't mean *"I do less".*

It means whatever I do is filled with spaciousness.

I'm excited. We've declared something today. It's an audacious declaration:

- Prophecy means Isaiah and Jeremiah, and prophecy means Einstein.
- Prophecy means Hafiz, and prophecy means Rumi, and prophecy means Richard Feynman, and prophecy means Freeman Dyson.
- Prophecy means I'm madly committed, fully in, every day and every night, and I'm standing for new possibility, standing for utopia. Utopia begins to live in me. I am the new possibility.

Wilhelm Reich was a prophet. Prophets have many distressing disguises, and they don't look like we think they do—and they live in us. Prophecy lives in us.

We've got to reclaim prophecy from fundamentalism. Prophecy doesn't mean speaking in tongues and then claiming that we're the only people who've got the voice. **Prophecy means radical commitment, radical passion, integrating mind, body, and heart into a new Dharma, a new set of First Principles.** That's what prophets do.

Prophets challenge the old First Principles, and they offer new First Principles. Wow. Da Vinci was a prophet. So the prophet tells a new story. We're at a time between stories. Yay!

Prophecy means *I'm called to my unique voice*, and *when I get quiet enough my unique voice actually speaks the voice of the Infinite*, that the Infinite speaks through the lips of finitude. That's the principle of prophecy.

Prophecy elucidates and articulates new First Principles. Prophecy speaks truth to power. Prophecy articulates the Possibility of Possibility. Prophecy rejects the status quo. That's the first principle of prophecy.

THE PRAYER YOU THOUGHT WAS PRAYER IS NOT PRAYER

Immanuel Kant used to write that *modern man is embarrassed by prayer*. That's true, and we need to understand that. In the world of the New Age, for example, prayer is embarrassing. Prayer is considered fundamentalist: "That's some strange, weird Christian/Jewish/Islamic idea. We're much more sophisticated than that now." It's a big deal.

I had a huge argument with one of the great integral philosophers, and then we came together on this in a really beautiful way. We deeply impacted each other, and we articulated this notion of prayer inside of a system called Integral Philosophy.

Prayer is a very big deal, but it's not the old prayer. The God you don't believe in doesn't exist, and the prayer you thought was prayer is not prayer. We've got to go deeper.

EVOLUTIONARY LOVE CODE: PRAYER AND PROPHECY

> Prayer and prophecy are verbs in the divine-human conversation, the endless conversation between the Infinite and finitude.
>
> We must all pray.
>
> We're all prophets, and we're all messengers, but so often we're messengers that have forgotten our message because we've lost access to our unique voice.
>
> In prophecy, God initiates, the Infinite initiates, and the Infinite invokes.

In prayer, the human being—man, woman, transgender—initiates. The human being invokes.

We pray with our lips, we pray with our hearts, we pray with our arms, and we pray with our feet.

When Abraham Joshua Heschel joined Martin Luther King in Selma and Montgomery in Alabama, he said, "We're praying with our feet."

We pray with our feet, with our bodies.

We pray with our activism.

We're the language of God. We're Her verbs, Her adjectives.

We're even her dangling modifiers.

Man and woman, we're always in search of God, and we're always finding each other and losing each other, searching again. God is always in search of man and of woman, and of the human being.

This is the great conversation.

So I want to talk about this First {rinciple of prayer, to walk through three steps to access the First Principle. It's not a dogma. There's no dogma here. It's actually something you can access in your first-person experience. You actually know it. It lives inside of you. It's a First Principle. **All First Principles you can actually recognize because they live inside of you.**

The First Principle is:

> *In the language of the interior sciences, there are three primordial perspectives, and those perspectives are First Principles of Reality: They are first-person, second-person, and third-person.*

That sounds like nothing, but it's actually wildly exciting. In the original interior sciences of Hebrew wisdom, for example, it's *ani*: I, first-person; *hu*: him or her, they or them, third-person; and *ata*: you, thou, second-person. That is a first principle that lives in the interior sciences. The passage I was just citing comes from a thirteenth-century document which says *there's always I, there's always You, and there's always He and She*, meaning first-person, second-person, third-person. In Kashmir Shaivism the same principle exists. That's what we mean by a First Principle: *I'm not just making it up*.

Wittgenstein said, "Pay attention to language." Derrida said, "Pay attention to language." The interior scientists said, "Pay attention to language"—and they thought they were disagreeing with each other. They weren't. Logical positivism, deconstruction, and the interior sciences are all moving in the same direction, and we've got to bring them together.

They're all pointing to the centrality of language. **When language has a common structure all over Reality, that means language is pointing to a First Principle. It's not just a social construction of Reality.** It's the principle of first-person, second-person, and third-person.

SECOND PERSON: THE PAN-INTERIORITY OF COSMOS

So what's the second-person? The second-person is the Personhood of Reality. **Reality has Personhood.** I was talking to Howard Bloom, a great scientist, the other day, and I was sharing with him this new phrase that occurred to me, which is "the personhood of protons."

Phrase one: Reality has Personhood. Phrase two is the personhood of protons, meaning *Reality has Personhood all the way up and all the way down*. I want to create a new word for that. We're creating a new word here in First Principles: *pan-interiority*, meaning **all of Reality has interiors.** Pan-interiority. That's what prayer is based on: all of Reality has interiors. That's a big deal.

Materialism, which says that *all of Reality is just an exterior*, is not true.

On the other hand, dualism says, *there's spirit and there's material, two separate forces.* That's not true either.

I'm not going to go through the philosophical structures on this. There are a lot of them. We can't do that in this First Principles section. **Materialism and dualism—which is what philosophy talks about—are both limiting.** There are about five or six critiques of each of them.

The best possibility is a third possibility, which matches Reality, which fits gorgeously in terms of evolutionary science, and is what the interior scientists in Kashmir Shaivism like Abhinavagupta picked up on—as well as Alfred North Whitehead.

I'm giving it a new name, and this is the first time I'm saying it in public: **Pan-interiority—meaning all of Reality has interiors; all of Reality has Personhood.** Now, that obviously doesn't mean that all of Reality is a *person*, but it means *there's a feeling quality in all of Reality*. But let's get the phrase: pan-interiority. It means there's always personhood, and importantly:

All personhood participates in the larger field of personhood.

That quality of personhood, of the personal—that's not the ego, that's not the personal or personality (which Buddhism rejected). It's not the separate-self personal. The separate-self personal is pointing towards this but doesn't quite get there.

It can get lost in its own egoic contraction. **There's actually a personal beyond the impersonal; there's a personal that's an expression of the entire Field of Cosmos.**

THIRD PERSON: ALL FIELDS ARE INTERPENETRATING AND ARE AN EXPRESSION OF THE LARGER EROS

When I say the "impersonal" I'm talking about the third-person. The third-person is the field of energy, the field of motion, the electromagnetic field, the strong and the weak nuclear forces, the gravitational field. **All those fields are interpenetrated with each other.**

There is no gravity independent of electromagnetism. The strong and weak nuclear forces are very connected—as Maxwell pointed out—to electromagnetism.

There are currently all sorts of movements now happening towards discovering how the Unified Field works, but we know the fields are all interpenetrating.

The way we would say it in our new set of principles is *all those fields are an expression of the larger Eros*. There's a larger field of Eros, and one of the qualities of Eros is Personhood.

This means that when I hear you talking, the personhood in Marc hears the personhood in you.

Is it at all possible that my personhood is completely separate from the field of personhood in Cosmos? Obviously not—the same way my energy is not separate from the entire field, nor is my Eros separate from the larger Field of Eros, nor is my experience of value separate from the larger Field of Value.

I'm part of the larger Field, a unique emergent of the larger Field—I don't exist without the larger Field. All of the interiors and all of the exteriors of Reality actually live inside of me. I live in the Universe and the Universe lives in me.

I'm part of the larger Field of Personhood.

PRAYER IS WHEN I TURN TO THE FIELD OF INFINITE PERSONHOOD

Prayer is when I turn to the Field of Infinite Personhood. That's what it means. That's a first principle. My dear friend and integral philosopher Ken Wilber, in his book *Up from Eden*, rejected prayer, and so we had a very deep set of conversations, with Brother David Steindl-Rast and Father Thomas Keating. We came to this deeper realization—*wow, the personhood of Cosmos*—and it was beautiful. When Ken and I first met, I said to him, "Let's pray together," and he was delighted. We accessed this new First principle, which is not a dogmatic principle.

It's the principle of personhood. It's the principle of second-person. It's the Infinite Personhood of Cosmos that lives in you; that which lives in you is part of the larger Field of Personhood. **So if I can hear you, then clearly the infinity of personhood, which is the Infinity of Intimacy, can of course hear you.**

Now, that's more than just a feeling. It's more than just *every feeling I have goes out as prayer*. Not quite. Then I would never pray. There'd be no such thing as prayer. It's actually *the way in which I direct my intention, the way I speak into the Field, the way I focus my attention on the Field*.

Another way to say it: "attention blooms Reality." Love is attention, so prayer is an act of love.

I am placing my attention, my intimate attention.

I am offering up my deepest self in prayer.

That's what prayer does. **Prayer is an act of love. It's an act of attention. It's radical attention.**

I'm turning my attention to the field of the Mother, to the field of the Father, to the field of the Beloved, all the qualities of the Infinity of Intimacy, and I'm saying, "Let's be in communion. I want to be in communion. And I want you to hold me, because you're Father and Mother, and I want You to enter me and love me open, because You're my Beloved, and I want you to feel every feeling I have and hold that feeling with me."

It's the principle of the Christ energy, and it's the principle of the Buddha that holds the 10,000 petals of every feeling, and it's the principle of *Adonai Elohim*, and it's the principle of the Great One.

It's the experience of the Personhood that holds me because just like we can hold each other—just like your beloved can hold you at her or his breast, just like Mother can hold you—even if your individual mother didn't—Friend can hold you, Father can hold you, Teacher can hold you, Student can hold you. We hold each other, in that quality of holding each other in this un-fuckwith-able way: **we're radically present for each other, we hold each other, we take care of each other—that's the Infinity of Personhood that holds me**.

Everyplace I fall, I fall into her hands, and I'm never alone.

I may live a life sometimes of quiet desperation, but there's never lonely desperation because *I'm never alone and I'm always held*.

That's that story of footprints in the sand that has entered culture from this notion of the Infinity of Personhood. The person is walking along the beach and he says, *I'm walking and I see footprints behind me*. Then he sees a second set of footprints because *I'm not alone and I'm always with the Infinity of Intimacy that loves me*. Then I get in trouble and I look behind me and I see no footprints and say, *Oh my God, how could you abandon me?* And the voice speaks and says, *No, I didn't abandon you. I'm carrying you on My shoulders.*

Rumi is all about the Beloved, about falling into the arms of the Beloved. That's the quality of Personhood. That quality of Personhood is not a dogma of the old religions. It is a First Principle of Reality—the Infinity of Personhood that knows my name, and **everyplace I fall, I fall into the arms of the beloved.**

Prayer is not a cosmic vending machine where you put in the right formula and Reality gives you a new car. That's not what prayer is.

> *Prayer means that I'm never alone, that I'm always held, and that it always matters.*

My Beloved is holding it with me, witnessing it with me, and acting in my life intimately.

Prayer means there's an Infinity of Intimacy, who is an infinity of power, who holds Reality, who partners with us in Reality, who moves Reality towards ever deeper levels of the Good, the True, and the Beautiful—and **who acts in our lives in a thousand ways but doesn't always step in and save us in the way we think we should be saved.**

The Infinity of Intimacy is part of the wider Field of Reality, and that wider Field of Reality is beyond this lifetime, and it's beyond this particular incarnational frame of existence. It's a much wider field.

We stand always at the edge of mystery.

Anyone who tells you they've worked it all out defaces Spirit, degrades Spirit. We stand always dancing in the certainty of what we know in our interiors *and* on the edge of uncertainty—but we know that we can pray.

God is the Infinity of Intimacy that holds my hand, that hears my prayer, that receives my prayer more intimately than my beloved does, more intimately than the ultimate mother does, the ultimate father, the ultimate brother. That's the realization of Rumi. It's not a dogma. It's a realization.

- Prayer is not a dogma.
- It's a First Principle.
- It's the realization of the Infinity of Personhood that knows your name.

ENVISIONING NEW POSSIBILITIES & THE DIGNITY OF PRAYER

Let's practice a meditation. I hear your voice. Our hearing is part of the Field of LoveIntelligence. We know that Field of LoveIntelligence is personal.

Just as I hear you in my unique quality of personhood, my unique quality of personal LoveIntelligence, so does the entire Field of LoveIntelligence in which I participate and which I'm emergent from—which in terms of evolutionary science, complexity theory, and systems theory I'm an ineradicable and indivisible part of. **Clearly, that entire field of the second person hears every word I say. So every prayer is heard.**

We just cut through 2,000 years of dogma, 2,000 years of sophistry, and 2,000 years of argumentation. It's actually a First Principle.

We hear each other. Our hearing comes from our personal LoveIntelligence and our personhood, which is part of the larger Field of Personhood, part of the larger Field of Intimacy, part of the larger Field, the Infinity of Intimacy, the Infinity of Personhood that hears every word we speak. **When we place our intention, when we place our attention on the Field and we open our hearts, when we pour out our deepest longing and our deepest yearning, we're speaking prayer, we're doing prayer.** In other words:

When we pray we affirm the dignity of personal need.

We don't only pray for that which is beyond us. We pray for everything that's personal. We pray for every need that we have—but *we clarify our needs*: "What do I really need?" Prayer demands the clarification of personal needs. Then I expand my identity beyond my personal self and pray for my nation, my people; we clarify the needs of the community and the nation. Then we expand our prayer beyond the ethnocentric, and we pray for the world. We are the world. We clarify and ask, what are the genuine needs of the world? Then we expand to the cosmocentric, to every atomic being and every elemental being and every cellular being.

We experience the personhood, the pan-interiority that animates the Whole, and we pray as the Whole and for the Whole—and we pray to the Whole that holds us in every second.

We feel and experience the paradox of both participating in the Whole and being held.

Everyplace we fall, we fall into She, we fall into Mother, and we fall into Father, and we fall into the arms of the Beloved.

THIRD-PERSON REALIZATION IN PRAYER

In this moment we deepen in our meditation, and we feel the field of third-person: the field of all the laws of chemistry, all the laws of physics, all of the billions and billions of light years, and the quintillion sets of particles all held together in unique inner dynamics of coherent intimacy. It's uncreatable: a billion supercomputers couldn't manifest it.

We feel the super, infinite, gorgeous, stunning, unimaginable, dazzling Beauty, Goodness, Truth, complexity, immense beyond imagination, a shuddering of divine creativity that blows open mathematical formulas and layers and layers and layers and layers that can only be mapped by supercomputers that are only getting the bare edges of it, of all of Spirit in the Third-Person, Creative Eros in the Third-Person, all of that through all of time from the beginning to the end and then beyond and then into the next cycle of time, all of that beyond.

Spirit in the third-person, in this moment, is sitting on a chair looking at you right now—that's the realization—looking at you and loving you madly, beyond any and all imagination, blown open by your beauty, yearning to be intimate with you, yearning for your own transfiguration, for your own transformation.

And in fact, Spirit in the second-person manifested all of Reality for you. You were there. You were part of that Spirit that manifested it all for this emergence of you, this individuated-beyond-ego, essence-of-Spirit-uniquely-voiced-as-you.

Your transformation and your deepening and your joy and your pleasure, the pleasure of your transformation, the pleasure of your intimacy, *is* **the intention of Reality itself.**

So it is. And it's true.

This God in the second-person, this originating power in the second-person, this Spirit in the second-person, is looking at you and knows your name and loves you beyond any and all imagination. Wow.

It's to this Spirit that we turn and pray.

CHAPTER NINETEEN

PRAYER: THE PERSONHOOD OF COSMOS—RESTORING THE DIGNITY OF PERSONAL NEED

Episode 202 — August 23, 2020

WE ARE ALLURED TO EACH OTHER IN A NEW CONFIGURATION OF INTIMACY

Who are we? We are a band of Outrageous Lovers. That is the highest bar of admission. And what do we say? OLATT. Outrageous Love All The Time.

A band of Outrageous Lovers means that we are committed to being revolutionaries. We're committed, we come together like Marsilio Ficino and Leonardo da Vinci—in that time between worlds, in the Renaissance—came together.

- How many people were involved in the Renaissance? There were maybe a thousand people, total, who were at the core of the Renaissance. They were a band of Outrageous Lovers.
- There's a famous text, the *Mahabharata*, from ancient India. Who wrote the *Mahabharata*? A small band of Outrageous Lovers.
- There's the U.S. Declaration of Independence. Who wrote the Declaration of Independence? A small band of Outrageous Lovers.

That's always how it happens: there's an evolutionary communion where people come together.

It's the elite. But not the financial elite—that's a passing, ephemeral elite without substance and without eternity. Not a superficial power elite in the sense of pseudo-pathological power-over, where *I've climbed and become an apex predator in the win-lose metrics of the success story.*

Not the old *Homo sapiens*.

It's those of us together, all of us here, who feel the call of the imaginal cell that wants to turn the caterpillar into a butterfly.

When the caterpillar hangs itself up in a chrysalis, what initially happens biologically is that the immune system attacks each imaginal cell. What has to happen next is that the imaginal cells have to bond together. They have to find each other, and they have to literally feel their allurement to each other.

We're allured to each other. As imaginal cells we bond together. It's only when we actually feel that allurement that we create a new configuration of intimacy, rooted in the actual felt experience of Outrageous Love.

We love each other.

We're here not just for our own personal fulfillment—although we're personally addressed and addressing each other. But we have a wider intention. We have a deeper intention.

Our intention is to participate directly in this moment, in this time between worlds, in this time between stories, to participate directly in the evolution of love.

We find each other and we want to feel each other, so we ask each other, "Are you ready?" Are you ready to find the other imaginal cells? Are you ready to become part of the new DNA of the New human and the new humanity? Are you ready to take upon yourself the burden, the joy, the ecstasy, and the responsibility of knowing that Reality needs your service?

Now we're going to go from "Are you ready?" to "Are we ready?" Yes, we're excited. We're gently excited, and we're ecstatically excited, and we're quivering, and we're tender, and we're ecstatically trembling before evolution and *as* evolution.

And we ask, "Are we ready to play a larger game?" Yes!

Let the *yes* resound. Let it become a cacophony. Let it become rivulets moving into streams and streams moving together into rivers and rivers moving together into the great ocean of She, the shimmering deep of She that lives in us, as us, and through us.

"Are we ready to participate in the evolution of love?" **A river of yes, a cacophony of yes, the yes of the original Big Bang is *yessing* right now,** not just as the radiation of the Big Bang that actually lives as the ancient celestial Reality in our world—that radiance is unimaginable.

The radiance, the shimmering of the Big Bang is also here today. Because we understand in cosmology that the Big Bang is not over.

It's banging.

It's loving.

It's alive.

YOU ARE THE RADIANCE OF THE BIG BANG INCARNATE

You are the radiance of the Big Bang incarnate. Here's the wild thing, friends. That's not a declaration, or some nice metaphorical comment. No, that's actually the truth. That is actually the nature of Reality, based on the best interior sciences and the best exterior sciences.

The radiance of the Big Bang literally directly birthed its unique configuration as Reality having the experience of you. You are *Amor*—love itself, but not ordinary love. *A band of Outrageous Lovers* means not just our personal ordinary love, not just our romantic stories to cover up the pain—but the largest romance.

We're being romanced by Reality itself.

And romance lives through us uniquely.

Rapture lives through us uniquely.

We are power uniquely incarnate as the Radiance being us. Wow! *Amor.*

Solomon talked about it. Solomon from the Temple in Jerusalem *Raiders of the Lost Ark*, first spoke of *Amor*. Solomon who built the temple in Jerusalem where the Ark of the Covenant stood. Solomon, whose wisdom is aligned with the best of exterior complexity science, systems theory, and chaos theory, which understands that the insides of Reality are lined with love.

All of Reality is kissing each other in every second.

That's the essence of systems theory. It's not just a bunch of interconnected "its." That's a bad read of systems theory and a superficial understanding of systems. Every "it" is actually a "Thou."

- It has an interior.
- It's alive.
- It's pulsing.
- It's yearning to touch and to connect.

So wrote the great interior scientists. So wrote Alfred North Whitehead. But you can feel it yourself. It's the essence of a First Principle, a First Value. **All of Reality yearns to touch, desires to be intimate.**

So, *Amor*: its insides are lined with love. *Amor* is our chant every week. It's a verse from the Song of Solomon: *Tocho ratzuf ahava*. Its insides are lined with love—not figuratively, not metaphorically, not declaratively. Literally.

Its insides are lined with love.

> *Allurement, or desire, holds Reality together and evolves. Love evolves until it becomes you, until it becomes me.*

That's the core First Principle, First Value.

PRAYER: THE SEVEN STEPS OF THE STAIRWAY TO HEAVEN

When you think about the word "prayer," what do you think? What comes up for you?

- "I stopped doing it that way a long time ago."
- "Obligation."
- "Prayers not answered."
- "Asking for stuff."
- "It doesn't mean anything."
- "Petitionary prayer."
- "Pray to something outside of me."
- "Reciting impenetrable text."
- "Affirmative prayer."

Okay, good. Affirmative prayer is something else. Affirmative prayer is not asking for anything. In affirmative prayer you'll say, for example, "The healing power is moving through the Universe right now, and we are one with that power. The healing is happening right now—it's already done."

Affirmative prayer removes the request, it removes the asking, so affirmative prayer is actually a form of meditation. It is a statement, it's a kind of affirmation. It affirms the healing power of Reality, but it refuses to ask. Contemplative prayer is not really prayer. It's really meditation. There's no ask.

But prayer always has an ask.

Fundamentalism misunderstands prayer as a kind of cosmic vending machine: you put in a prayer, with the right words to the right God. They say, "My God is the only real God who can answer prayer." You say, "Please give me this or that." If you say the right words and you're a good boy or girl, you might get it. Prayer is not that. It's not a cosmic vending machine. But it is an ask.

So what is prayer? **Prayer is a First Principle and a First Value.** Let's lay down these tracks.

I want to see if we can go seven steps together.

STEP ONE: FACES OF GOD

A person I care deeply about says, "I can't really think about God, but if I do I think about the laws of nature and the laws of physics and all of that—that's God to me."

Now, is that God? Is that right? Well, yes, it is. That's a dimension, that's a face of Divinity. In the *Zohar* that face of Divinity is the face of God you might call: It, Him, Her, She, or Outrageous Love.

There are parallels in all the interior sciences:

- It's a force that moves through Cosmos.
- It's the laws of physics.
- It's the laws of chemistry.
- It's the four fundamental forces: the electromagnetic, the gravitational, the strong and weak nuclear.

- It's those forces animated by Eros that drives all of Cosmos, the Evolutionary Impulse—this incessant creative force. It's a third-person force.

That's one face of the Divine. That's the third-person force.

Then there's a first-person force: the She who lives in me. She lives in me. *Tat tvam asi.* Thou art that. The *ani*, the I, is *ayin*, which is infinite no-thing-ness. The infinite no-thing-ness lives in me, my small I. When I wake up I realize I-Am, and the same I-Am that lives in me lived in Abraham, in Buddha, in Thomas Jefferson, in Confucius, and in Lao Tzu. That's I-Am. That's the God/Goddess that lives in me. **That's the first face of God: God in the first-person who lives in me.**

But then at the center of everything is the personhood of Reality, and **we call that God in the second person.** If we begin to understand that Reality is an Intimate Universe, we realize that Reality is sourced in the Infinity of Intimacy:

- That knows my name and responds, that is deeply aware of the particulars of my life.
- That lives in my disappointment and lives with my heartbreak.
- That holds my broken heart.
- That holds my *holy and my broken Hallelujah.*

In this intimacy my *hallel*, my praise, is also my *holelut*, my brokenness. That word *Hallelujah* that Leonard Cohen uses, drawn from the original Hebrew lineage, means *drunken intoxication*, and it also means *pristine praise. The holy and the broken Hallelujah*—She holds it all.

The first, second, and third face of the Divine.

God in the first-person, second-person, and third-person—that's the first step.

STEP TWO: REALIZING THE PERSONHOOD OF DIVINITY

This is the personhood of Cosmos, the personhood of protons, the personhood between you and me, the interior, the interiority that lives all the way up and all the way down.

I want to coin a new phrase that I'm using a lot in writing now. We live in a world which has "pan-interiority." It's interiors all the way up and all the way down. The nature, the feeling of this interiority is intimacy.

> *God is the Infinity of Intimacy that knows my name, and wants me, and desires me, and holds my holy and broken Hallelujah.*

That's step two. This is not information. We're not learning a new idea. We've studied this deeply together over the years, but we're bringing this all together and grounding it in practice.

STEP THREE: PRAYER IS ALWAYS HEARD BY DIVINITY

Does the Infinity of Intimacy hear my prayer? We'll talk about what the prayer is and what the ask is, because we've already said there's an ask in prayer. We're bringing all of ourselves, and there's an ask.

But before that, let's find step three. Does the Infinity of Intimacy hear my prayer? How do we answer that? We do that with a pointing-out instruction. Let's meet on the inside.

Let's say I'm hearing someone talking. How do I hear her? I hear her through my ears, but it's not just my ears technically, biologically. It's not just a technical structure in the ears. It's my heart, but what else is it? It's my intelligence. **It's the unique intelligence that is me that hears her.** In meeting the intelligence that she is, she can step up and give her unique contribution; she can be open and have her heart flowing.

The intelligence that lives in me hears her.

Now, does that intelligence which lives in me live *only* in me? Is it just *my* intelligence? Obviously not. Marc's intelligence obviously is not limited to Marc. **I'm participating in the larger field of cognition, the larger field of intelligence.** That's what cognitive theory is beginning to understand. It's what all the interior sciences understand. It's what the exterior sciences of systems theory understand. I'm part of a system, but even my intelligence doesn't live just in me. It accesses all sorts of inputs, and it's animated every second by the larger system of intelligence. My intelligence participates in the larger field of intelligence.

So if I can hear her when she prays, when she talks, is there any possibility that the larger Field of Intelligence, the Field of Infinite LoveIntelligence, Infinite LoveIntimacy, and Infinite LoveBeauty cannot hear her? No. It absolutely can.

I hear her through my matrix of intelligence, which is part of the largest Field of LoveIntelligence. The Field of LoveIntelligence hears and holds preciously every word.

Notice what happened, friends, in this pointing-out instruction. It goes to what you already know directly and all the way through. It completely changes Reality. We're not doing 2,000 years of theology, obtuse reasoning, and sophistry on prayer.

You can actually find it and access it directly in your first-person experience.

That's the third dimension of prayer. It's *heard*.

STEP FOUR: THE MOVEMENT OF PRAYER

What do we do when we pray? What are we doing when we pray? What's the action of prayer? What's the movement of prayer?

The movement of prayer has two dimensions. **The first movement of prayer is erotic.** The erotic movement is towards union: being held, being loved, being nourished, being caressed, being entered, being blown open by the Infinity of Intimacy that holds me, knows me, and wants to penetrate me with all of its fire, with all of its tenderness, with all of its trembling, with all of its quivering.

That's union.

Prayer is a movement towards union.

I turn to the Infinity of Intimacy and I say, "Take me. Take all of me. Receive all of me. Hear all of me. Lick all of me. Kiss all of me. Hold all of me. Let me fall into you."

We fall into union in the sense of being held. We realize we're part of and not separate from, *and yet we're held* by that which is so much larger than us. That's the erotic movement to union.

The second movement of prayer is existential. Existential means *I need things*, and prayer affirms the dignity of personal need. I need things. I need everything. My Uncle Morris needs things, and my cousin Joanna needs things, and my aunt and my second cousin and my friend and my sister— my sister needs so much. I've got so many sisters with broken hearts, the ones who are closest to me and the ones who are farther away.

I have needs, and those needs are real, and they're beautiful, and they're holy.

Prayer affirms the dignity of personal need.

So when I pray I ask for everything. Nothing's left out.

STEP FIVE: FEELING THE INFINITY OF POWER

In the first part of this meditation, we can feel and reach for the immensity of power which is the Infinity of Power. This is God in the third-person—power beyond imagination. When we do push-ups, that is power, when we lift weights, that is power. But that power doesn't even begin to compare to the power of a diesel engine.

Then imagine that we are at Cape Canaveral in Florida as Apollo 11 is launching. It's incredible to see that launch, those engines, the rocket fuel. Liftoff is achieved. That's power. But that power is absolutely nothing—it doesn't even exist compared to the gravitational power, the power of the strong and the weak nuclear forces, and the electromagnetic power.

Then feel the power of the galaxy, the galactic power that forms stars, the power of supernovas, the power of hundreds of billions of galaxies across Reality, the power that drives Cosmos, **the incessant, self-actualizing, self-organizing creativity of Cosmos manifesting myriad complexity**, so dazzling beyond all imagination that we faint in rapturous ecstasy and can't begin to grasp even the pale reflection of what it is.

All of that is Divinity, is Spirit in the third-person.

STEP SIX: THE INFINITY OF POWER IS RIGHT HERE WITH YOU

Imagine the Reality of all of that energy, that force, that complexity, that intelligence, that desire. **Imagine all that God, Spirit in the third person, is now sitting in a chair right next to you.**

Look with the Eye of the Heart, the Eye of the Spirit at the Infinity of Intimacy sitting in a chair, looking at you, loving you madly, loving you beyond imagination, knowing every detail, every jot and tittle. Nothing is left out of your life.

Every thought. Every gesture. Every flutter. Every fear. Every fantasy. Every glimmering of greatness. Every gorgeousness. All of the *holy and broken Hallelujah.*

She knows it all.

And She's loving you madly and holding you. And you know She'll never let you go. **That's God in the second person—knowing you, looking at you, tenderly holding you beyond imagination in this very second.**

STEP SEVEN: THE FEELING OF GOD

Imagine one more step. What does the interiority, the inside of God sitting on that chair, knowing you, *what does She/He feel?* The transgendered God, the beyond-gender God, the Unique Gender God, the He/She God, the beyond, the before.

What does God/Goddess feel on the inside, looking at you?

Imagine your most tender moment of holding, of nourishing, of protecting, of quivering commitment beyond imagination. It might be for a son or for a daughter or for a beloved or for a friend or for the face of a little boy or girl. Just imagine the deepest tenderness you ever felt and allow that tenderness to be doubled and tripled and quadrupled, ten and twenty and a hundred times over—so much tenderness and quivering, nourishing care. And then continue: a thousand times and hundred thousand and a million and a billion and a hundred billion times exponentialized tenderness—*ad infinitum.*

That is the first quality of the Infinity of Intimacy that's sitting in that chair and knowing you and looking at you in this second.

Then imagine your deepest yearning, your most wanton, raw, holy, lustful yearning, this urge to merge, to become part of, to be penetrated, to be loved open, and to penetrate. Quivering, trembling your body in fierce, burning desire unlike any other, and then double it, triple it, times ten, times a hundred, times a thousand—and we're now searing and melting and disappearing—and a billion and a hundred billion times exponentialized *ad infinitum.*

Then take, as the alchemist, that infinite, wanton, raw desire, together with the most quivering, beautiful, soft tenderness, and merge them together until they become purely one.

And feel all of that literally looking at you, holding you, and blowing you open, holding infinite tenderness and passion together, in this very second. You're participating on the inside of Divinity in this very second.

What does She want?

- She wants everything from you.
- She wants you to reach out your hand, to hold Her hand and be Her partner.
- She wants to receive all of my and all of your holy and broken Hallelujah.
- She wants to lick every prayer.
- She wants to kiss your heart.
- She wants to hold everything.

She wants you to know that She's there even when She seems to be silent and that Her silence is always a Silence of Presence and never a silence of absence. She says to you, "My child, my lover, my sister, my brother, my mother, my father, my deepest, most wondrous friend, you're all of these to me. Ask for everything."

Let's hold that as we go inside to the *holy and broken Hallelujah,* holding all of these seven stages on the stairway to heaven.

From there we'll pray. Leonard Cohen, thank you for being with us, *the holy and the broken Hallelujah.*

CHAPTER TWENTY

PRAYER: THE PERSONHOOD OF COSMOS—RESTORING INTIMACY THROUGH PRAYER AS PROTEST

Episode 203 — August 30, 2020

THE URGENCY OF A WORLD WITHOUT FIRST PRINCIPLES AND FIRST VALUES

I want to first set our intention. Who are we? What are we doing here? Why are we here? We're not here for entertainment, although entertainment is great. It's not even wisdo-tainment—wisdom as entertainment. What are we here for?

We're here to make a fucking revolution!

The world is on the brink of suffering beyond imagination, or on the brink of a potential utopia, a flowering and flourishing of humanity beyond imagination—we're poised between those two places. **What we do here can literally make all the difference as to what road we take.**

That's why we're here. That's the reason to be here.

We're not doing cute Sunday services. Cute Sunday service is great. We love cute Sunday service, but that's not what we're here for. We're here in this place, poised between utopia and dystopia, to feel evolution awakening in

us, as us, and through us, to feel our capacity to gather the best knowledge that exists in the world—not just what's called merely "subjective" knowledge, not just *fictions that are social constructions of reality*—but knowledge based on First Principles of Value that undergird everything and tell us something about:

- Who we are
- The nature of the Universe
- The Universe Story
- Our narrative of identity
- Why we're in this Cosmos
- Why every decision we make is so urgent
- Why we're desperately needed by all of Reality.

It's only those First Values and First Principles that can respond to a pandemic, and respond to the meta-crisis.

We get used to Reality so fast. How many people were here four months ago when we did "one breath" because people were dying and couldn't breathe in the pandemic? Here's the crazy thing. It's happening right now. So let's do it again, because we forget. How many of us have almost forgotten that it's happening because we get used to it?

How many people remember—this is going to date us—being a little kid and watching on television in the mid-1970s the Phalangist War in Lebanon between the Christian Phalangists and the Islamic parties, such a horrific war. Lebanon, and Beirut particularly, which was the jewel of the Middle East in many ways, was being utterly and radically destroyed. Does anyone remember the mid-1970s, as that was going on in Beirut? I remember watching it as a little kid, and I remember seeing that during this war, there were weddings and birthday parties and romances and theater. So in the middle of bazookas, Howitzers, and explosions around the city, you had this kind of normal life—and if you lived a few blocks out of the war zone you kind of went on as normal.

I remember being shocked by it.

We can get used to anything, friends. "Getting used to it" is exactly what we don't want to do.

We want to break that sense of the regular, of the routine in which we're dead, in which we're asleep. We want to step into the center, and we want to have a seat at the table; we're demanding a seat at the table. You can do that today.

We're demanding a seat at the table. We're saying:

- We're going to be so committed.
- We're going to open our hearts so deeply.
- We're going to be such Outrageous Lovers.
- We're going to read day and night.
- We're going to integrate.
- We're going to make that da Vinci move in Florence at that time between worlds and time between stories.
- We're going to do it because it needs to be done.

We're self-appointed: There is no one to appoint us. There's no one to say, "I bless you, children. This is yours to do."

No one appointed da Vinci. No one appointed any set of iconoclasts and revolutionaries in the world.

We do it because we feel the ecstatic urgency of it; it gives us great pleasure to have this privilege.

What are we doing? We're here to articulate a set of First Principles and First Values. They're not doing it at Oxford, where I did my doctorate. My partner, Zak, did his doctorate at Harvard. They're not doing it there. They're not doing it at Stanford. They're not doing it at the Sorbonne. That's why we're not there. **Universities today have become bastions of** mediocrity, repeating old dogmas. They've become bastions of the alt-left, just like certain other institutions have become bastions of the alt-right.

You've got secularism on one side, which is devoid of Spirit, and you've got Spirit hijacked by all forms of regressive and fundamentalist religion on the other side—neither of those is going to take us home.

> *We have to articulate the next move.*
> *Friends, we are Spirit's next move.*

I know that's an audacious thing to say, but I want to say it. We are Spirit's next move.

A secularism devoid of Spirit in which all ultimate values are "social constructions of Reality"—that is not Spirit's next move.

A regressive fundamentalism—that is not Spirit's next move.

IT'S A FUCKING REVOLUTION

Someone just wrote in the chat box: Wow, how could we use the word "fuck?" That's a very funny question. The word actually is an intensifier. It captures an intensity, and occasionally we use it to capture that intensity.

It's not a degraded word. There's an intensity to it

It's about the fierceness of Cosmos.

So, yes, I'm going to say again: *it's a fucking revolution*. Not a degraded revolution—that's not what it means. Those of you who've studied with us, we wrote a 15,000-word essay on the etymology of that word, what it means, and how it actually intensifies a moment and captures a moment. It's got nothing to do with sexuality. That's a later usage of the word, but that's a different conversation.

I want you to get the intensity of it. That's what I'm trying to say. This is not ordinary. This is not like a New Age gathering. This is not *let's get together and pat each other on the back.* There's an insane urgency of people who can't breathe all over the world. There's an insane agony of people who can't breathe all over the world. I want to feel this with you.

Let's go play. Let's get all the way in.

Anyone who can't get all the way in, that's totally fine, too. We're all good. Everyone will find their way in at the right time in the right way. **I'm glad there's a challenge, because when there's no challenge we can't wake up. Feel the discomfort, feel the disconnect, and then go deeper and find it again deeper.**

> *What's the urgency? The urgency is a world without First Principles and a world without First Values.*

That's what the urgency is about. Can we find that urgency? Can we feel that urgency? That's why I borrow that word: because it holds the urgency.

It's important to occasionally deploy that word in order to engage the discomfort, to get out of our routine, to get out of the regular, to find our place. So let's find it—yay!—again, with so much tenderness. When someone's uncomfortable, we hold that person with tenderness and love, and we thank them, whoever it is—and we're all uncomfortable at different times. Then after the tenderness, there's a fierce commitment—a fierce da Vinci commitment—to articulating a new and gorgeous vision of Reality.

Together, I know—with a thousand percent, a billion percent certainty—that we can become evolution, that we can turn this around, that we can articulate these First Principles.

EVOLUTIONARY LOVE CODE: THE GOD YOU DON'T BELIEVE IN DOES NOT EXIST

The god you don't believe in does not exist.

God is not only as She has been described by the great traditions as the Infinity of Power, but more profoundly as the Infinity of Intimacy.

God is the Infinity of Intimacy desiring finitude. And prayer is intimate communion between the Divine and human.

It is true that human beings participate in Divinity. This is the first person of the Divine that lives as us.

It is no less true that we are held by Divinity in every moment. Every time we fall, we fall into She. This is the second person of the Divine. Prayer is intimate communion between the Infinity of Intimacy and the intimacy of finitude.

Divinity is the force of Eros always seeking deeper coherence and wider intimacies, from quarks to culture and beyond. This is the third person of Divinity.

REALITY IS THE PROGRESSIVE DEEPENING OF INTIMACIES

We do our chant practice, which is *Amor*. Amor means *its insides are lined with Love*. It's a verse from the Song of Solomon. It's a description of the nature of Reality.

The nature of Reality is *its insides are lined with Love*. Reality is moving towards deeper and deeper Love. But Reality is held together by Eros in every second; it's bonds of allurement that hold separate parts in larger wholes. It's true on the molecular and atomic levels, on the level of biology, all of the life world, all of the world of matter—and it's true in the world of mind, in the human world.

All of Reality is seeking more and more coherent intimacy. That's the plotline of Reality.

> *Reality has a plotline, it's not just moving from simplicity to complexity, which is the exterior understanding of Reality. The plotline also means more, wider, deeper coherent intimacies.*

The subatomic particles come together—a hadron, a proton, a quark, a lepton. They come together and form an atom. When they do, the subatomic particles don't disappear; they form a new whole, a new configuration of intimacy deeper than the sum of the parts. Here's the sentence, and it's a First Principle: **Reality is a progressing deepening of intimacies.**

Isn't that shocking? Whenever we feel not intimate for a second, we'll now say, "Oh, I've got to get intimate again."

Reality is the progressive deepening of intimacies. Evolution is the evolution of intimacy. It's not just simplicity to complexity. It's the progressive deepening of intimacies, that movement of Reality towards deeper intimacy—that's *Amor*.

That's the Love that lines Reality.

PRAYER ITSELF IS A FORM OF PROTEST

I now want to talk about prayer as protest. Protest happens in many ways. Protest happens through humor, through laughter, and protest happens through demand. But there's a revolution in prayer. When we're protesting, there's a protest that challenges Divinity.

> *We don't only come to prayer as supplicants asking, pleading. In the interior sciences, prayer itself is a form of protest.*

My colleague Sam Harris wrote a book called *The End of Faith* in which he essentially caricatures the shadows of the great religious traditions, accurately, but it speaks only of the exterior, superficial dimensions—he misses the depth of the interior sciences that the great traditions held.

In the great traditions, there were two forms of protest where *I challenge God*. I challenge God as part of the revolution. **I both partner with the Divine—I'm Divinity's evolutionary partner—***and* **I'm protesting. So I partner and protest at the same time.**

PROTEST, LAUGHTER, MYSTICISM, AND PARADOX

One form of protest—and these are deeply related—is laughter, so I'll tell you a joke. It's a deep joke. This man dies, and he's super righteous—so righteous, so good, such a great master, that he literally goes straight to the highest heaven. There he is before God, and God says, "What can I do for you?" He says, "Can I tell you a joke?" God says, "A joke?" No one had ever said that to God, so God says, "Sure, I guess tell me a joke." This righteous man then tells God a Holocaust joke. When he finishes God doesn't laugh and says, "I don't get it." Then the guy says to God, "I guess you had to be there."

Do you get how many layers there is to this? God doesn't get the Holocaust joke, so the master says to God, "You had to be there."

Let's get the paradox in this. We're deep in this together here. We're in this revolution, and we're going to add a piece. Sam Harris and his whole gang—Chris Hitchens, Yuval Harari, Richard Dawkins, and all the rest—

they caricature religion. Yes, religion has many shadows—but Spirit is much more subtle than that.

The great traditions at their best had an enormous amount of subtlety that we need to transcend *and* include.

- We need to create a new language of Spirit.
- We need to create new subversive vocabularies that are First Principles.
- We need to weave together premodern, modern, and postmodern into a new larger whole, but we can't just throw out premodernity. They didn't just get it wrong.

The great traditions had and still have something wildly important, which is this notion of paradox. Whenever you've had a mystical experience—which means a genuine, direct access and experience of the absolute, self-evident Truth and Beauty and Goodness of Reality itself, the truth of Love—**whenever you have a mystical experience, one of the characteristics of a mystical experience is paradox.** So how could you use the word "fuck" in the middle of a holy conversation—how could "fuck" be holy? It's paradoxical.

What's the difference between a paradox and a contradiction? In a contradiction, A is the opposite of B, and either one or the other is right. In a paradox, we hold both of them together—there is no split. We're holding it together. So in this joke we just told, both A and B are true at a higher level of consciousness. That's a paradox.

THE PARADOX OF CHOICE AND CHOICELESSNESS

I'll give you an example. Here's a paradox: How many people who are here made a decision, *I could have done ten things this morning, but I made a decision to be here*? How many people feel like, *I made a decision to be here. I didn't have to be here, but I decided to be here*. That's true.

There's obviously a great truth to that, but here's another truth. Another truth is you didn't decide at all. You were being *lived* by Reality.

This is yours to do. It's the place where you need to be. All of your life and all of my life brought us together in this revolution this morning.

> *This is what we can call choicelessness: It decided me.*

So, on the one hand, I decided. Obviously I decided. I had many choices, I'm an autonomous being, a separate self with free will, and I made a decision.

But at some deeper level the reason we know each other—the reason we're together, the reason we're in this revolution, the reason we're the ones making this commitment, the reason we're taking responsibility—is because something larger than us is living us, and it's beyond choice. We actually have no choice at that level. We *have* to do this. We can't walk away, even when we're exhausted and we feel like, *Oh my God, I can't do this.* But there's this larger mystery in which we're beyond choice.

Can you feel that? That's a first-person moment of enlightenment.

On the one hand, there's a contradiction. What's the contradiction? "Either I chose to be here or I didn't choose to be here. One or the other—you can't have both." That's the level of contradiction.

But then in a mystical experience, I reach a deeper level of consciousness where I'm actually holding contradiction. I both chose *and* I didn't choose.

If you look at the most important moments and movements in your life, you begin to realize, *Every place I've been I needed to be there.* It couldn't have been any different.

And I also chose to be there. That's the paradox.

LAUGHTER HOLDS PARADOX

So what is this joke holding? That's what laughter does: laughter holds paradox. This is big. It's a deep principle.

We generally think of there being five senses in Reality, but actually in the First Principles of the interior sciences there are twelve senses. What is a sense? A sense gives you access to a dimension of Reality that the other senses don't give you. So, fragrance/smell tells me something about Reality. Touch tells me something else about Reality. Auditory tells me something else, giving me access to a different layer of Reality. Sight gives me access to another layer of Reality, tasting—the five senses.

But there are more than five senses. We have other ways of accessing Reality.

A mystical book written about 100 years before the Common Era called *The Book of Creation* has about 450 words—and it's one of the most important texts ever written. It talks about these twelve senses, the highest of which is laughter. Wow! So laughter is a faculty that allows me to access Reality in a way that nothing else does.

Now, what's the paradox in this joke? That joke has so many levels. It's so subtle. It's so good. What's the paradox in the joke? This righteous man, this master, ascends to the highest heaven. He's talking to God. Then he tells a Holocaust joke, which is ultimately not cool. Holocaust jokes are not cool—they're just not funny. I have one friend who I'm very close to—I won't say his name—who once told me a Holocaust joke, and I said, "If you ever do that again I'm never talking to you again." Some things you don't joke about.

But he's there before the Divine and decides, *Okay, there's nothing else I can do, I've got to tell a joke.* Then God doesn't get it. So he says, "I guess you had to be there."

What's the joke about? The joke is about evil. It's about how can there be an infinitely good God and there's a boy hanging on the gallows in Auschwitz every day, and 12,000 people were gassed every day in 1944? How can those hold together?

On the inside of the inside we don't explain suffering. We never do. We can never explain suffering. We can't. If anyone tells you they can explain suffering—and there are a thousand traditional and New Age explanations of suffering—that they're going to work out the contradiction between infinite goodness and human suffering, just walk away. Don't trust them. You can't explain suffering.

> *But when you're in the relationship, when you're on the Inside of the Inside, your heart is ripped open, you can actually be speaking to God directly and say, "You had to be there."*

Now, that makes no sense. It's a paradox. That's mystical realization. It's gorgeous. It's a mystical understanding. It's super subtle. It's everything. It's this joke about a master who goes to God and says, "You had to be there." Wow!

WHEN WILL YOU COME ALREADY? WE'RE WAITING FOR YOU

So there's a dimension of prayer which is protest. God, where are you? Where are you? One of my favorite prayers, just a very subtle prayer, is:

Mim'kom'cha malkeinu to'fiah	God, from your place, appear
V'tim'loch aleinu	And be the king.
Ki me'chakim anachnu lach	Because we're waiting for you.
Matai tim'loch?	When will you come already?

Can you feel that? There's a protest in that. We're waiting for you. *Where are you?*

GOD, SHOW UP, BE HERE

I'll give you another prayer, a famous prayer that many people have written major essays about. You may have heard about it. Leon Wieseltier wrote a couple of gorgeous essays on Kaddish. It's called the Kaddish Prayer, a prayer in Aramaic which is said when a person has died. It's a mystical prayer. The only thing is: the Kaddish Prayer doesn't say anything about death.

Kaddish is this prayer you say when a person dies, but it doesn't talk about death. The words of the prayer are:

> *Yit'gadal v'yit'kadash*   *Magnified and exalted*
> *sh'mei raba.*   *will be Your name in*
>   *the future.*

Isn't God's name magnified, exalted, and perfect right now? Why is it in the future? Because death is in some sense a violation of Divinity.

Death is painful. Death rips our hearts out. Yes, there's life beyond death, and, yes, there's continuity of consciousness, but death itself, in some profound way, contradicts Divinity.

I've got to hold the contradiction and turn it into paradox. That's what prayer does.

Can you feel that? I hold the contradiction. I turn it into paradox.

Yitgadal v'yitkadash sh'mei raba. In the future, God, your name is going to be magnified, but now in the face of death there's something empty about your name. So, God, show up, be here. Turn your Silence of Presence into a full presence of speech. We demand your partnership.

So prayer is audacious. Can you feel it?

This is an important dimension of prayer.

GETTING BENEATH THE SPACE-TIME CONTINUUM AND RECONFIGURING THE PAST

Let's go even deeper in. I want to really get this dimension of prayer. Once a year, in the lineage tradition of Hebrew wisdom—out of which Christianity emerged and Islam emerged, and which has had an enormous impact on Reality—there is a day of the year which is called Yom Kippur. The Day of Atonement.

It's the day where everyone comes and prays. People pray for hours and hours and hours. It's a twenty-five-hour kind of prayer fest. It's ecstatic prayer for twenty-five hours—complete joy. Again, this doesn't need to be your tradition. I'm borrowing this from the Hebrew lineage tradition to model something, to demonstrate something. It doesn't matter whether this is your tradition or not. That's not the point. This is a universal principle.

People are completely brokenhearted on Yom Kippur, but they know that they can meet the Infinite Love of Reality and literally—this is one of the most profound ideas in the world—**the reason it's so completely joyous is because you know that you're already forgiven.**

On Yom Kippur, you can actually get underneath the space-time continuum and recommit your life to your Unique Self.

Simply by recommitting your life and regretting any past mistake that any of us have made with true regret and by making a true commitment into the future, there's a mystical formula that places you literally underneath the space-time continuum and actually obliterates the past.

It doesn't exist anymore.

You've reconfigured the past.

That's the joy.

It's a very deep idea—what does it mean to get underneath the space-time continuum? It's not just a woo-woo idea. It's a very profound idea in physics now. We're actually realizing the space-time continuum is just one dimension of Reality; we can actually go deeper, and consciousness is underneath the space-time continuum. That's what Yom Kippur is about.

GOD, I'M DONE—LET ME KNOW IF WE HAVE A DEAL

With that context for prayer, I'll just tell you a short story. It's Yom Kippur eve, and everyone's gathered at the prayer hall of the great Hasidic master named Levi Yitzchok of Berditchev. Derrida, the great postmodern deconstructive thinker, loved Levi Yitzchok of Berditchev and wrote about him.

So Levi Yitzchok of Berditchev is at the prayer hall. It's packed. Everyone's there in full joy. They're there ready to offer up their prayers.

In the middle of all this, in walks this man who everyone knows never comes to the prayer hall. He pushes his way through, goes to the front, stands by the holy ark. Then he grabs the curtain and mumbles a few sentences. Then he says, *I'm done. Let me know if we have a deal*, and then just walks out. Everyone wants to grab him. They're utterly furious with him.

So this man has now walked out and everyone is trying to grab him to stop him. He's violated the sanctity of the day, and they can't understand. You know the word *chutzpa*, meaning arrogance? What kind of arrogance is this? How can he walk in on the holiest day of the year, pray these few sentences and then say, "Do we have a deal?"—whatever that meant—and just walk out? So people are naturally furious with him.

Twenty-five hours later, at the end of the holy day, the great master Levi Yitzchok of Berditchev says, *Get me that man. I desperately need to talk to him.* Everyone is like, *Why does he want to talk to this arrogant man who came in and violated the sanctity of the day?* But they go and find him, and they bring him before Levi Yitzchok. Friends, open your hearts. Let's open our hearts together. Levi Yitzchok says to this man, *You've got to be my teacher. I have never seen anyone pray with the confidence that you prayed. You must tell me your prayer.* Wow.

The man says to Levi Yitzchok, *I'll tell you my prayer. It's very simple. I said to God, "God, you know, I've made some mistakes this year. There were a couple of weights and measures I didn't do exactly right, and there were times I got angry that I shouldn't have, and I got a little contracted, and I'm sorry for that. And I didn't always get to fulfill all of the rituals. There are times I should have been a tad sweeter. God, I want your forgiveness, but, God, you've had a terrible year. The woman who lives two doors down from me, her husband died in the middle of the night, and she's left with four children. Two blocks over, there's the woman who lives by herself with three children, and one of them is sick. She can barely put food on the table, and she's wracked with anxiety every day."* This man went through the entire list of people suffering intensely in Berditchev. Finally, he says, *God, you've had a terrible year, but you know what? I'm willing to work with you. Let's make a deal. You forgive me, and I'll forgive you. Do we have a deal?* And then he walked out. Wow!

Levi Yitzchok looks in his eyes and says, *Never has a more holy prayer ever been prayed, but, my friend,* he says with tears in his eyes, *you made only one mistake. You prayed only for yourself and not for the whole world. Had you prayed for the whole world, the whole world would have been instantly liberated in one moment.*

Can you hear that, friends? That's prayer as protest. That's demanding something from God. Prayer as protest—and it's a complete paradox.

We come before God with our holy and broken *Hallelujah*.

THE PARADOX OF HALLELUJAH

We're going to do one little thing before we pray, and we're going to offer prayers together. If you listen deeply to the holy and the broken *Hallelujah*, you'll actually feel the protest.

> *Hallelujah is a joke. The word Hallelujah means—as we've shared here before, but now you'll get the paradox in it—on the one hand pristine praise of the perfect God, but Hallelujah also means drunken, wild laughter, revelry, and the great joke.*

So I come to God in the laughter and in my broken Hallelujah, and as in Leonard Cohen's song, *even though it all went wrong, I stand before the Lord of Song with nothing on my lips but Hallelujah.*

IN GENUINE INTIMACY WITH GOD THERE IS PROTEST

We fall into the arms of Divinity who holds us in every second, the second-person of Cosmos. The First Principle is the Personhood of Cosmos.

- God is third-person: the laws of physics.
- God is first-person: the God who lives in me.
- But God is also the Personhood of Cosmos, the Infinity of Intimacy that knows my name.

But in that intimacy there's protest. In genuine intimacy there must be protest.

No, God, it can't be this way.
God, we're so intimate.

God, I love you so madly I can't allow for this pandemic.
God, you've got to heal it.
God, you've got to fix it.
And, yes, God, we're going to be revolutionaries.
And, yes, we're going to be activists.
And, yes, we're going to evolve the source code.
And, yes, we're going to articulate the new First Principles, but you've got to be there with us—we demand your presence.
We demand that you hold our hands.
We demand that you heal the world.
We demand that you partner with us.
We can't do it without you, and you can't do it without us.
We are protesting every tear, and we're protesting every person who can't breathe.
God, we are with you—one breath—and let your name be magnified and exalted, because in this moment right now you are absent.
God, you didn't get the joke because you weren't there.
Be there, God.

Of course, in that moment of the void, we know that the silence is a Silence of Presence. We know that as we scream those words, Divinity is speaking through us—and God is more present in the apparent absence than He/She/It, the Infinity of Intimacy, ever was.

It's not a silence of absence. It's a Silence of Presence.

The voice of protest is the voice of the Divine speaking through us. Evil is a failure of intimacy, and it's only when we restore the intimacy in the act of protest that we can be revolutionaries. So we're not revolutionaries in the Marxist sense, where we're stepping away from the Divine. We're revolutionaries in this new sense in which our lives are a protest.

We offer our lives as protest, prayer as protest, prayer as holy audacity, prayer as: "God, let's make a deal—and, God, this is a deal you can't refuse, because we need you, you need us, and the time is now. *Ad matai?* Until when? It's got to end now." We protest.

You know what Divinity does when we protest? Smiles. God laughs. God gets the joke, and we get the joke—and **in the power of our laughter, together we move to transform Reality.**

So let's step inside to the holy and the broken *Hallelujah*. Then we're going to come together, and we're going to pray. For just a couple of minutes we're going to offer up prayers, but we're going to find this new chord in the symphony of the First Principle of Prayer—prayer as protest. Let's go all the way inside, into the holy and the broken *Hallelujah*.

Now, before we pray, I just want to ask: can you feel that dimension of protest in Cohen? You can't understand the song without it. It's impossible to understand. You can't understand Cohen without it. Cohen is in this tradition of protest. He's in this lineage of Levi Yitzchok of Berditchev. It's where he's writing from.

So let's pray as protest.

"Hallelujah," by Leonard Cohen.

Just feel in the prayer, it's not so much the words—it's the energy of it, meaning *it's the God in us.* **It's the Divine voice itself that's protesting through us.**

We've added this subtle dimension to prayer. Thank you, everyone, deepest bow. We lift these prayers to the sky.

We protest, we demand, and we say, "Now." We ask for everything, and we demand everything. It's only that kind of relationship with Divinity that can avoid the emptiness of secularism and its empty dogma, and that can avoid the dogmatism and emptiness of a fundamentalism that always has all the answers.

There are two dogmas: a dogma of secularism that ignores an enormous amount of evidence, and a dogma of fundamentalism that ignores an enormous amount of mystery. So we've got to bring those two together.

We're up there in the highest heavens.

WORLD RELIGION AS A CONTEXT FOR OUR DIVERSITY

We're with the Divine.

We're madly in love.

We speak of our love in the morning, and we trust Her in the night—we protest, and we act.

We act as God.

We protest to God even as we're madly in love with the Divine, as She lives in us and as She holds us in every moment.

CHAPTER TWENTY-ONE

PRAYER AWAKENS US TO THE APPROACHABILITY OF THE INFINITE

Episode 251 — August 1, 2021

INTENTION SETTING: RATZON AND HOLY SEDUCTION INTO OUTRAGEOUS LOVE

We think, friends, that "will" always means, *I'm strong, I'm using force*—but "will" in Hebrew is *ratzon*. It's an erotic word, and it comes from the Song of Solomon. In chapter one, the text reads: *Mash'che'ni a'charecha, na'rutza.* "Draw me after you, seduce me, and my will is yours."

We're not talking here about unholy seduction. Unholy seduction is when we go to seduce someone to break their appropriate boundary for the sake of our greed. We're talking about what the great interior scientists called holy seduction. **And holy seduction means we invite someone to seduce us, or seduce someone else to their own highest gorgeousness, to their own deepest wonder.**

We turn to those around us, to ourselves, and we say, *I wish that I could tell you, when you are lonely or in darkness, the astonishing light of your own beam.* That's *ratzon*. "Will" means, *I trust Reality. I trust myself. I trust you, and I'm going to surrender my will, be intoxicated and*

on fire in service and joy. I'm going to embrace all of the brokenness, but from that broken place, we're going to live into a new Reality.

- We're aware of the existential risk landscape and we're also aware of the gorgeousness of human possibility.
- We're aware that the human being is Divinity incarnate.
- We're aware that we are divine miniatures.
- We're aware that we are participating in the evolution of love.
- We're aware that we are ourselves quite literally the memory of the future.

It's all about madly rejoicing, but it's madly serious. Rumi said, *Love mad*. We can't do ordinary love.

Ordinary love is not going to take us home.

We live in a world of outrageous pain; the only response to outrageous pain is Outrageous Love. We've got to get mad with love.

We're here to be mad with love. But that mad love has to translate into profound, careful, discerning wisdom around policy, around articulating a new vision, a new Universe Story, a new narrative of human identity.

- It has to include footnotes.
- It has to include deep writing and deep communication.
- It has to include the wisdom of long-term planning.
- It has to include steadiness.

It has to include an insane amount of hard work because that's the only way to be sane. But it's hard work that is so animated with joy, so animated with light, so animated with human dignity, that the line between the human being and infinity blurs.

Infinity and finitude blur into each other as the New human and the new humanity emerges.

EVOLUTIONARY LOVE CODE: PRAYER IS INTIMATE COMMUNION WITH THE INFINITY OF INTIMACY

The God you don't believe in does not exist.

God is not only as She has been described by the great traditions, the Infinity of Power—but more profoundly, the Infinity of Intimacy.

God is the Infinity of Intimacy desiring finitude.

Prayer is intimate communion between the Divine and the human.

It is true that human beings participate in Divinity; this is the first person of the Divine that lives as us. It's no less true that we are held by the Divine in every moment.

Every time we fall, we fall into She; this is the second person of the Divine. Prayer is intimate communion between the Infinity of Intimacy and the intimacy of finitude.

Finally, Divinity is the force of Eros always seeking deeper coherence and wider intimacies, from quarks to culture and beyond. This is the third person of Divinity.

PRAYER: TURNING TO THE INFINITY OF INTIMACY

We're going to move into prayer. One of the things we want to reclaim together is this notion of prayer. As we've talked many times, in order to effect a planetary awakening in Love through Unique Self Symphonies, we need to integrate the best of traditional consciousness and its deepest insights, the best of modern consciousness and its deepest insights, and the best of postmodern consciousness and its deepest insights. One of the things that the traditional world understood was prayer.

We need to up-level the consciousness of prayer.

Prayer is not a diluted version of the law of attraction that attracts a car—which is how prayer has been translated in some of the public space.

Prayer is not the turning to appease a vengeful God and to placate and beg in a way that effaces our essential dignity as human beings.

Prayer is rather the child turning to Source, the son to the Mother, the daughter to the Father, the lover to the Beloved, and saying:

> *Hold me.*
> *I can't do it myself.*
> *I need you.*
> *I need you to hold it all with me.*
> *I throw myself before you, and at the same time I rise before you and hold your hand.*
> *I'm willing to partner with you.*
> *I'm willing to do everything with you.*
> *I'm willing to literally be your partner in making this world what it desperately yearns to be.*

It yearns in us. **We feel the desire of Reality rising us.**

But we know that as separate self, a small self, we're not big enough to do it. We know that the value in the yearning and the desire that lives in us is bigger than us.

We participate in the Field of Desire.

We participate in the Field of Yearning and in the Field of Longing. And our deepest heart's desire is the desire of She. It's the desire of evolution itself. And so we turn to you, Divine, we turn to you who are not only the Infinity of Power but the Infinity of Intimacy, and we say, *Hold us. Hold it all.*

And we pray.

We're going to share a new prayer by our blind friend who sees beautifully, Andrea Bocelli. Let's hold the space, open our hearts, and feel into the power of evolutionary prayer where *I'm both powerful and yet I can turn to Source—Source that lives in me and that holds me at the same time.*

Céline Dion and Andrea Bocelli, take us inside prayer.

Often when we pray, there's not a big crowd.

We pray in the broken places.

We pray when there's no one around.

We pray when we feel completely abandoned, when we feel there's no one left to hold us.

PERSONHOOD OF PRAYER: FIRST PERSON

One of the First Values and First Principles of Cosmos is the infinite dignity of the three faces of Reality. This is how we know that prayer is real, that prayer is heard. Let's open the space if we can.

We know there's a first-person experience, which means, *I am consciousnesses aware of itself.*

We have the experience of being self-reflective. We know that we can take perspectives on Reality; we can look at ourselves and look inside ourselves; we can feel our own experience. We can feel pain, and we can feel joy. That's the miracle of consciousness—which makes no sense from the perspective of materialism.

It's the quality of Reality.

It's not just *I exist*, but *I experience my existence*. It's huge.

That's first person, and it's an absolute structure of Reality itself. First-person reality is the interior experience. We have good information that there's some level of first-person experience all the way up and all the way down, at all levels of Reality. Alfred North Whitehead talks about *prehension*. He talks about a *proto-interiority* that exists even at the molecular level, the experience of allurement or longing between a proton and electron 380,000 years after the Big Bang.

It's not that the proton and the electron are Romeo and Juliet. They're not Montagues and Capulets. It's not a human experience of longing. There's discontinuity, but there's also continuity. We're part of the same Field of Desire. We're part of the same Field of Longing.

PERSONHOOD OF PRAYER: SECOND-PERSON

Then there is the second-person experience, which means:

> *There's space between us*
> *and I want to be seen by you,*
> *and I want to see you,*
> *and I'm so lonely if you can't see me.*

If, somehow, you're my person and you don't quite understand me, I'm desperate to have you understand me. When you do see me, when you feel me, you liberate me from loneliness and my life takes on self-evident meaning.

And I'm willing—if I'm Tom Hanks, in a movie called *Castaway*, living on a beautiful island in the South Pacific with full capacity to survive and even thrive, filled with beauty and food—I'm willing to cast myself into the ocean with a virtually zero percent chance of survival in order to have the remote possibility of looking into the face of another again and being heard.

That experience lives all the way up and all the way down.

And so, in the precise same way that you can hear me talking right now. In the precise same way that I heard Krista singing *Amor*, David resonating the code, and Kristina doing the Dharma recapitulation—why did I hear? Not because I'm a technical, artificial-intelligence structure. I didn't just register it; it didn't just become data in my field of machine intelligence. I *felt* David resonating the code, I *felt* Kristina doing the Dharma recapitulation, I *felt* Krista singing *Amor*, and her pleasure and joy. My full field of feeling intelligence heard.

So if Marc's field of feeling intelligence could hear, say Kristina—is Marc's field of feeling intelligence the entire field? Obviously not.

Marc's feeling of LoveIntelligence is part and parcel, actually scientifically indivisible—in terms of both interior and exterior science, unique but indivisible—and participatory in the larger field.

So if I could hear Kristina talking because my intelligence could hear her, could it be that the Field of LoveIntelligence that animates me and you and all of Reality, and mitosis and meiosis, this intelligent, non-random Cosmos—could it be that the Field of LoveIntelligence couldn't hear Kristina? Of course not. That's what prayer means.

> *Prayer means that every word is heard, that no word is lost.*

Imagine what it means to speak words knowing that they'll be absolutely heard. Imagine you were before the most powerful human being in the world now and you could speak words.

This human being said:

I love you madly, and I want to do anything I can to meet you—within the parameters of the possible—and be there with you.

What would you say? That's prayer.

In prayer, we ask for everything because prayer affirms the dignity of personal need. We ask for everything for ourselves. We ask for everything for Cosmos.

In prayer, we turn not just to the Infinity of Power; we turn to the Infinity of Intimacy that knows our name, and we ask for everything. So let's pray. No prayer is lost.

Amen.

Let's lift these prayers to the sky. Oh my God. Let's deepen into prayer, friends. We are going to enter into the world of prayer and expand our knowing in some new and magical way.

THE BUTCHER'S PRAYER

I want to tell you a story, with your permission. It's a beautiful story about the butcher in a Eastern European town called Košicein, a story about Yankele.

So you fully get the story, I've got to tell you a little bit about how classical Hebrew wisdom practice works. Every day, there are these three silent prayers with eighteen blessings and the spiritual leader of, let's say, the congregation usually prays the longest. When I was in that world as the leader of a congregation, what happens is everyone prays at the public prayer service these quite long prayers, but the assumption is that the leader of the congregation is praying with hyper-intense seriousness. So everyone waits for him to finish his prayer, and when he takes three steps backwards, he's done, then we go on with the service.

Now, of course, that becomes a little complicated because it's a little bit of an egoic game. Rabbis are demanded to pray the longest to demonstrate their extreme piety. Religion always has the places where it can get corrupt, and there's no ulterior motive like the ulterior motive of piety. I used to laugh at this game. Sometimes I would, with a bit of an impish smile, quickly end my prayer before anyone instead of after everyone, which made people aghast. It was shocking and scandalous, not helpful to my reputation as a heretic, but that's the subject of a different tale.

There was a butcher in the town of Košice, who would go to the prayer service of the great rabbi of Košice. The rabbi would, of course, pray for quite a long time, and he was truly a great human being, but no matter how long he prayed, the butcher would always pray longer than him. *Wow!* The butcher would always pray longer than him, no matter what he did.

PRAYER AWAKENS US TO THE APPROACHABILITY OF THE INFINITE

The butcher was not a particularly pious man. He wasn't a deep philosopher, and he didn't really give a lot of philanthropy. He never really went overboard and never really tried hard enough. This great rabbi of Košice couldn't understand: *How is it that this simple butcher is always praying longer than me?*

One day, the rabbi can't take it anymore, so he asks his assistants to demand that the butcher come for a private meeting. The butcher arrives, and the rabbi asks his attendants to leave. It's only him and the butcher because *who knows what this man's going to say*, and he doesn't want to impugn his reputation. Finally, he says, quite exasperated, when they're by themselves: *What is going on here? What are you doing? I can't understand how could you possibly pray that long.*

The butcher says to him, *When I walk by you in town, when I say hello, Shalom Aleichem, you say hello. You're polite and nice and you walk on. Occasionally, you stop and ask me, in a somewhat perfunctory way, how's my wife and the children. When I pass by the philanthropists in town and I say hello, they also say hello, and if they need a choice piece of meat, they might spend an extra minute talking to me, but they don't pay me much heed—and, really, no one does. Everyone's nice and polite enough. I have one or two friends and even they get a little bit exasperated with me.*

Yet, the butcher says, *when I come before God—the Infinity of Intimacy; the King of all Kings; the Queen of all Queens; the mode of force and the animating presence of all Reality and all worlds, all the way down and all the way up—for as long as I'm willing to stay and talk, She is willing to listen intently to every single word.*

That's what prayer is.

Prayer is about the approachability of the infinite, the intimacy of the infinite.

She's right next to you.

She's whispering in your ear.

She knows every jot and tittle, every detail, that took place in your life today.

She's holding every flutter of your heart, every shutter of your soul, every desire of your body and your mind.

She's with you in all of it, and all She wants is for you to reach out, hold her hand, and be her beloved, radical, wild partner.

She wants to give you everything She can within the context of your highest, most wild and radical emergence. That's what prayer is.

PERSONHOOD OF PRAYER: THIRD PERSON AND SECOND PERSON

Prayer is an affirmation of the personhood of Cosmos. Just like personhood exists between you and I, personhood is the nature of one face of Cosmos.

- Yes, there are laws of physics, and they're real.
- Yes, the four forces are real: the strong and the weak nuclear, the electromagnetic, and the gravitational.
- Yes, dark matter needs to be taken seriously.
- Yes, that's all true and, yes, the Eros, which is the animating force that animates all the four forces, is a third person force that drives Cosmos forward. That's all true.
- Yes, my own consciousness is real, and I can feel myself and that's first person.

But personhood is utterly real as well.

The personhood between you and me, the personhood that you felt in your most deep and profound intensity participates in the personhood of Reality.

PRAYER AWAKENS US TO THE APPROACHABILITY OF THE INFINITE

Your most intimate moment—your most erotic moment, your most tender moment, your moment filled with the most fierce and wild passion—is but a glimmer, a pale expression of the Infinity of Intimacy desiring you and knowing you.

Let's practice together now. Let's do an enormously important meditation together. Imagine and feel with me Reality in the third person: God. Not the god you don't believe in. Remember: The god you don't believe in doesn't exist.

Imagine God as the Infinity of Power:

- All the laws of physics, integrated
- All the principles of mathematics
- All the underlying structures that animate the infinite algorithms of an infinitely complex and dazzlingly true and beautiful Cosmos
- All the force in Reality
- All the speed, beyond the speed of light
- All of the galaxies—a hundred billion galaxies, and in each galaxy at least a hundred million stars

Imagine all of that beauty. You can't. Let your imagination fall into rapture, just yearning for a glimpse, a picture of that God in the third person stretched out across all of Reality, governed by an algorithmic complexity of dazzling brilliance that no human mind can barely wrap around.

Just feel into all of that.

All of its power.

All of the glory of the dazzling brilliance beyond any and all comprehension.

All of God in the third person is now sitting in a chair—right now, in this very second, sitting next to you, holding your hand, or sitting at your bedside this evening looking deeply at you as you sleep and kissing your eyelids awake as you awaken—**looking at you, loving you madly.** That's God in the second person. Unimaginable.

Now take the next step with me, friends.

What is God in the second person—sitting in that chair—feeling?

You might ask, *Well, how do you know what God feels?* Recall the sacred text from 3,000 years ago: *Vayomer Adonai El Libo,* "And Spirit spoke to Her heart." So the masters of interior science say, *How do we know what Spirit said to her heart?* My guide in interior science, Mordechai Leiner of Izbica, writes, *We know what is in the deepest recesses of the divine heart, of divine desire, because our desire, in our heart, participates in the divine heart and participates in divine desire.*

- There's one desire.
- There's one love.
- There's one heart.

In the original Hebrew, the actual word for "attention"—and I'm quoting directly from a 3,000-year-old text—is *simat lev,* "the placing on the heart." Attention is *the placing of attention on my heart.*

When I place attention on my heart, I disclose ontology. I discover what's real.

We call it "Anthro-Ontology." When I find the inner heart of my unique anthro-expression— "anthro" meaning human. When I find and feel the pulse of my uniquely beating heart, then I know something about Reality. Our hearts share their beating.

Your heart beats in mine, and my heart beats in yours. I can feel your heart beating inside of mine. **We can hear and feel the divine yearning because we can hear and feel the murmurings of yearning, the inconsolable longing, that lives in us.**

PRAYER: TENDERNESS AND FIERCE PASSION EXPONENTIALIZED

Find the most tender love that ever lived in you:

Quivering tenderness, dripping in your heart, tumescent, alive, awake.

Multiply that tenderness by 10, and then exponentially multiply that tenderness by 100, and 1,000, and 100,000, and a million until you are the platonic form of tenderness; infinite, dripping, mad tenderness is you.

Then feel the fierce desire, passion, and urgency throbbing inside you—the fierce, sensual, urgent throbbing. Then double it, then triple it, and then 10 times over, and then exponentialize, and then go to 100, and 1,000, and 100,000, a million until you are pulsing, yearning, unimaginable.

Then—in the third step of this meditation—**bring together your quivering tenderness with your pulsing, dripping, throbbing, yearning. Bring them together and exponentialize them again into infinity. Then you'll know what that God in the second person**—all of the third person sitting in second person on that chair, looking at you waking up in the morning—that's what She feels for thee, that's what Infinity feels for you.

To know that is to wake up. That's the shock of awakening. And you'll never be the same again.

It's not a dogma. It's a realization. The mysteries are within us.

Find that moment of your infinite tenderness, that moment of your infinite throbbing, dripping desire, and merge them together in a larger synergy exponentialized into infinity—there's no polarity between tenderness and throbbing; they're part of the larger Field of Eros.

You participate in Infinity. You know what She—what God, what the Infinity of Intimacy—feels like on the inside.

You participate in Cosmos itself, awake, uniquely alive in you.

CHAPTER TWENTY-TWO

THE THREE FACES OF GOD = THE THREE FACES OF LOVE: REWEAVING THE UNIVERSE: A LOVE STORY

Episode 281 — February 27, 2022

EXISTENTIAL RISK PRESSES US INTO THE REALIZATION THAT THE EVOLUTIONARY IMPULSE IS LIVING IN US

We're here, poised in this moment between utopia and dystopia, to tell the new Story. We're talking about the new Love Story of Reality—because Reality is always a Love Story. We're always telling love stories. We come together in this moment, this time between worlds, this time between stories, between utopia and dystopia. But for real. It's the genuine experience of Reality if we understand what's going on.

About ten years ago, I was talking about existential risk and about this realization that we've actually hit the second shock of existence. Many of you already know the vocabulary.

The first shock of existence is the experience that the human being dies.

It's not the biological, rational, factual knowledge of death.

It's the *existential experience* of death, which completely transforms me.

Death presses me into life.

When a human being encounters the first shock of existence, that ultimate *No* of death, it turns all of life into a *Yes*.

Once all of life is a *Yes*, I have this deeper realization that there's also a *continuity of consciousness*. (And there's an enormous amount of empirical information that talks about a continuity of consciousness, but that's a different discussion.)

The second shock of existence is the realization not just of the death of the individual human being as an inevitable milestone in our journey that we have to confront—and we do have to confront the first shock of existence—**but actually, there's also the potential, not just of death of the human being, but the death of humanity.**

People say to me, *Marc, why are we talking about this? I love the teachings that you're doing, but what am I supposed to do with this? I don't even know how to hold it.* That realization, that "it's not too big to fail," is a shocking realization.

But just like the first shock of existence presses me into life as an individual human being, as humanity, *the realization of the second shock of existence looming on the horizon presses us into joy, into life, into creativity*. It presses us into the realization that *in this very moment, the Evolutionary Impulse that animated and drove and exploded at the moment of the first singularity, that same Evolutionary Impulse is living in you and me and in we.*

That capacity of creativity, that capacity to stand on the abyss of darkness and say *let there be light*, lives in our We, our collective.

THE NARRATIVE ARC OF THE STORY OF REALITY

After all, where were we at the moment of the Big Bang? We were there! Because where else could we have been? Now we're here, at a moment in which we need to move from what we've called the Third Big Bang to the Fourth Big Bang.

The First Big Bang is the singularity: the emergence of the physiosphere, the cosmological Reality.

Then, after billions of years, we get to the Second Big Bang, which is the emergence of the biosphere: the world of life from matter.

Then we get to the Third Big Bang, which is the emergence of the depths of the self-reflective human.

But one of the things that we're understanding in this new Story is, number one, *that it's a story*. **First Big Bang, Second Big Bang, Third Big Bang; there's a narrative arc to Reality.**

It's not, as many religions claim, *that the world is a precursor to some future heaven*. It's not as scientism claims—science not in its true science, but scientism that turns science into its dogmatic shadow form—*the world is random and meaningless and pointless*. NO!

The world is a Story. There's a narrative arc: a First Big Bang, a Second Big Bang, and a Third Big Bang. What we're understanding in this new Story is that we're at the precipice of what needs to be a Fourth Big Bang.

In this moment between utopia and dystopia, we have to turn towards utopia; we have to be pulled by a memory of the future.

As in classical psychology, where we turn to a memory of the past in order to animate the present and allow us to actually engage, we need to also turn to a memory of the future, because the memory of the past is insufficient to heal.

Healing cannot be done only through the tools of classical psychology. We need to actually expand psychology to include Unique Self: Unique Self means recovering a memory of my future. We need to integrate the memory of my past *and* the memory of my future.

I need to do the same thing that I do in the personal but at the level of the collective. **We need not only to learn from history**—because, as Santayana said, *Those who do not learn from history are doomed to repeat it*—**but we need to also be pulled by the evolutionary memory of the future.**

The memory of the future is the Fourth Big Bang.

It's the emergence of the New human and the new humanity.

It's the emergence of *Homo amor*. It's the new Love Story.

It's not about a transhumanist cyborg human being who lives in a pseudo-erotic metaverse—although there may well be a metaverse. **But the metaverse has to be grounded in Evolutionary Love and First Principles and First Values.**

We need to realign with the Field of Value, and then enact a data science that is actually enmeshed in First Principles and First Values and Eros and Evolutionary Love.

We need to enact a blockchain that's an expression of Evolutionary Love, of the Intimate Universe.

We need to move from the Third Big Bang to the Fourth Big Bang.

I PARTICIPATE AS THE UNIVERSE IN PERSON, IN THE FIELD OF LOVE

What we're doing here in this moment is participating as the Universe: we are the Universe in person. We are the Evolutionary Impulse in person.

Our choice is world propaganda or world spirituality, a new Story that animates Reality with a memory of the possible human, the future human that has to become awake and alive in us. We have to cross to the other side and actually become that future human.

Are we willing to become the future human? There's a Hebrew phrase *Avraham ha'Ivri*: Ibrahim/Abraham, the Hebrew. What does the word Hebrew mean? *Iver*: the one who crossed to the other side. That's what Abraham is about; Abraham is about crossing to the other side.

So we're crossing to the other side; we can see the Promised Land. *I may not get there with you*—said Martin Luther King Jr.—*but I can see the Promised Land*; we can see the Promised Land together. The Promised Land is a world in which every man, woman, and child knows:

> *I participate in the Field of Love.*
> *And I count.*
> *And I matter.*
> *And my story matters.*
> *And my life matters.*
> *I need to be celebrated.*
> *And I need to celebrate you.*
> *My life is infinitely valuable and I'm not subject to value only if I've managed to commodify myself.*

If I haven't managed to self-commodify or self-productize, the reality of today tells me I'm not valued. But no, *you're infinitely valuable*. And I'm in devotion.

WE'RE HERE TO TELL THE BEST LOVE STORY EVER TOLD

We actually can enact together a new world. So we've got to tell the best Love Story ever told, and that's what we're here to do.

We take this seriously! We're lost in footnotes. So we're not doing this just as declaration—although we need to do it as declaration as well—but we're doing this in the most serious, rigorous, painstaking, agonizing, ecstatic way we can, day and night.

To come together, and together become da Vinci. But da Vinci in the best sense, not da Vinci lost in modernity, in all the structures of the Renaissance that didn't allow for the full potential of humanity to emerge.

> *Let's take the best of the Renaissance, and then let's weave together the best of the last 500 years—all of the validated insights and all the major streams of wisdom and science—and tell this new Story.*

Let's shout it from the rooftops.

Let's speak it in every language.

Let's speak it in every country.

Let's speak it in every place, so that there's no corner of the Earth where this shared music isn't felt. **This music is not a homogenizing music. It's not a homogenizing Story. It's a context for our diversity.**

I could not be more excited to be with you. We're trembling with joy. And we're trembling with trepidation. We're trembling with the realization that we need to go forwards; we can't go back to imperialism.

We've got to tell the best Story. Putin is telling a love story. He's telling a love story about Mother Russia. But he's telling a distorted love story:

- It's a degraded love story.
- It's a corrupt love story.
- It's not the love story we need to tell.

The Russians are gorgeous and beautiful, and they're all loving each other today in a thousand different ways. But he got lost in a distorted ethnocentric love story, in which *I only experience us loving each other by placing you outside the circle. I'm only in Eros if you're outside the circle.* That's not Eros, but pseudo-eros.

> *We've got to tell a Love Story in which no one's outside the circle, and everyone gets to have autonomy, and everyone gets to choose.*

It's not the mother who embraces and suffocates. It's not the mother who says: *Ukraine, you've got to be with me and part of me, and if you're not with me, I'm going to smother you.* We've got to take the "s" out of "smother" and embrace "mother":

- The mother loves the child so much that the mother allows the child to choose even when the child chooses against the parents.
- The mother stands for the individuation of the child.

It's mothering, not smothering. It's not an ethnocentric embrace—which stifles the autonomy and free choices that were made in 2002 and 2014, at great expense, by Ukraine—after an incredibly painful history.

Ukraine has had such a painful history. Two hundred years under the Tsar, and a brief moment of independence that was then crushed by the Tsarist army. Then Ukraine was subject to the Holodomor famines in 1932–33, in which five to seven million Ukrainians died of starvation because there was a famine intentionally created by Stalinism. It's tragic!

Stalinism was a tragic inversion of what should have been a love story. Communism was meant to be a love story, but it didn't make it there: anyone who was in violation of what it thought was going to be a world love story needed to be killed—"for the sake of love," of course.

Love stories can go bad.

Then, after the Holodomor famines, finally, Ukraine had this moment—after the fall of the Soviet Union—this possibility of becoming independent, and no one thought that it could do it, no one thought democracy could take place in Ukraine. But it did. Ukrainians have stood—in this quite incredible way—for the possibility of a new future. So we're with Ukraine today in this moment. And we're here to talk about real love stories.

OUTRAGEOUS LOVE CODE: IN THE GREATEST LOVE STORY EVER TOLD, NO ONE AND NOTHING IS OUTSIDE THE CIRCLE

We are never not telling a love story.

The question is, "What love story are we telling?

What is the plotline of the love story?" There are good love stories, and there are bad love stories. We need to tell the greatest love story ever told, where no one, no thing, and not one part of ourselves is split off.

In the greatest love story ever told, no one and nothing is outside the circle.

Rather, everyone and everything is in the circle.

I want to establish something which is a really big deal:

In telling this new Love Story, we have to establish First Principles and First Values.

Part of the new love story is to integrate the best of the traditional modern and premodern world, the traditional modern and postmodern world—to take the sparks of truth, the sparks of realization, the sparks of validated insight in the exterior and interior sciences—and weave them together in a new Story. That's what we need to be doing.

WE CAN'T LEAVE GOD OUT OF THE STORY

Now, I want to say something very radical. (Radical comes from the Latin *radix*, meaning root or essence.) In that Love Story, there's no room for a god who is dissociated from the Cosmos—a god who stands outside the Cosmos, a god who is a kind of Cosmic vending machine, a god who says: "Be obedient to me, and if you're obedient to me, I'll reward you." I don't want to live in a Cosmos like that.

Thomas Nagel, who is one of the best analytic philosophers in the world, wrote in his book *The Last Word*: I don't want to, in any way, be part of a Cosmos with god, and I want to be right about my denial of god because I don't want to participate in a world where god is in it."

It's an incredible quote.

David Ray Griffin, who is probably the best Whiteheadian philosopher in the world, sent me that quote a couple of weeks ago, and I went and looked it up in *The Last Word*. Of course, Nagel has a caricature of god, and I agree that I don't want to have anything to do with this caricature either.

But we can create a story that's a Love Story, in which no one is left out, in which nothing is left out. If we leave out the interiors, we leave out the non-arbitrary basis of Cosmos.

That's a new way to say it:

- There's a non-arbitrary basis of Cosmos; Value is intrinsic.
- There's an infinity of Value.
- And that's what we mean by God.

See, my dear friend, Thomas Nagel, *the god you don't believe in doesn't exist*, so don't worry about it.

THE THREE FACES OF GOD = THE THREE FACES OF LOVE

I remember many years ago, at the beginning of my path when I was functioning in a more formal role within the world of organized religion, someone came into my office and said: *I can't have anything to do with God; God is just nonsense.* So we worked together for a few weeks, and in the end, he told this story of his mother chasing him with a broom after beating him downstairs. He ran upstairs to the attic—it was one of those three-storey houses—and there was a bathroom in the attic, and he locked the door. He heard his mother banging on the door with a broom in her hand saying: *God is going to get you in there too, even if I can't get in!*

So I said to him, *the god you don't believe in doesn't exist.* In your mind, God is that god your mother said was going to beat you in the bathroom when she couldn't get in. That's a traumatized understanding.

I don't think we can abandon the word God. I get the New Age move: "Let's not talk about God, it's getting uncomfortable here." But actually, sixty to seventy percent of the world engages with the energy called God. Are they all completely wrong? No. So we need to evolve the word.

I want to say something audacious: **We need to *participate* in the evolution of God**. As Nikos Kazantzakis wrote, we're "the saviors of God." So we absolutely need to evolve that term.

We need a Love Story in which God is not left out. We need a Love Story in which nothing can be split off from that Love Story: no idea, no person, no thing, no part of ourselves. Nothing can be split off from the Love Story, or the Love Story gets desiccated and destroyed. So God has to be part of the Love Story.

THE THREE FACES OF GOD WHICH ARE FIRST PRINCIPLES AND FIRST VALUES

God has three faces or three personas, and these three personas are First Principles and First Values of Cosmos. They're not made-up. It's part of the structure of Cosmos.

> *A First Principle and First Value of Cosmos means it's inherent and structural to Cosmos, and you can't think of Reality without it.*

It's one of the core projects of the Center for Integral Wisdom, which began as the Center for World Spirituality—we need to embrace all wisdom.

So there are these three inexorable faces of Reality, which are First Principles and First Values.

And one of our major missions at the Center is to articulate the Evolving First Principles and First Values of Cosmos. It's a major idea, we're calling it the **evolving perennialism**. It's exciting!

So we have to identify what these First Principles and First Values are. I'm going to give you just one set right now. There is first person, second person, and third person; there are three primordial perspectives.

There are many ancient texts that talk about this, and there's an enormous amount of modern and postmodern literature that talks about this, each in their own languages.

But I'll just take one example from thirteenth century. There's *Ani*, I; *ata*, you; and *hu*, him/her/it—first person, second person, and third person.

THE THIRD-PERSON PERSPECTIVE OF REALITY

I can look at Reality through a third-person perspective. What's the brilliant body of knowing that's working on that today? Science. **The sciences are looking at the world through a third-person perspective—both the hard sciences and the soft sciences.** That's critical, it's important, it's vital, and we need to do it.

What are the laws?

What are the patterns that organize Reality?

Reality has an inherent set of patterns, waiting to fulfill themselves. That's the core of science: the trust, the knowing, and the love of those patterns—and their disclosure.

So let's call that *Reality in the third person*, but you could just as well call it *God in the third person*.

THE FIRST-PERSON PERSPECTIVE OF REALITY

First person is *Reality moving through me*. That's the experience of consciousness.

What's the experience of consciousness? *The experience of me*—that's a good way to cut through. Thomas Nagel wrote about this beautifully, twenty-five years ago: *The experience of me.*

I'm being me; I'm experiencing me. That's the experience of consciousness.

Now, when I go deep into that experience and clarify that experience, I have this realization that *I'm not merely*—as Albert Einstein pointed out—*an isolated separate self.* That's an "optical delusion of consciousness." Instead, I understand that *I am indivisible from the larger Field*, the seamless coat of the universe.

But that seamless coat of the universe is *seamless*, not *featureless*. It lives *uniquely* in me.

- I participate in the whole Field, and I'm not separate from the whole Field.
- When I go deeper, I have an experience that the whole Field is alive in me.
- When I go even deeper, I have an experience that I'm irreducibly valuable and that the entire Field is valuable.

- When I go even deeper, I find myself in devotion to the whole Field.
- When I go even deeper, I actually realize the Field is in devotion to supporting me.

Those are all interior experiences, subject to verification through the practices of the interior sciences. Some people would call it enlightenment. But it's not enlightenment in the old sense, where I just have awareness. *I'm aware of my awareness.* That's beautiful. That's important. That's critical. It's huge. But it's insufficient.

I'm aware that Love is moving through me, and Love is moving through me uniquely, and that I am actually being lived as Love. I am not going to apologize for being excited about this! This is the new narrative of identity; this is the first-person Divine:

> *The LoveIntelligence of Cosmos, the LoveIntelligence of Reality, or, if you will, the LoveIntelligence of God, lives in me, as me, and through me, and I can actually be lived as Love.*

It's shocking, it's insanely beautiful, and it's validated by all the interior sciences in whatever languages they use. **They used many different languages, and they all fought with each other not realizing that they were saying the same thing.** But actually, all the esoteric traditions or the great traditions have different versions of this: *I'm being lived as Love*, and that's my actual identity.

Who am I? I'm lived as Love. I'm lived as a unique expression of Love.

Tat tvam asi: Thou art that. But it's not just Thou art awareness; **Thou art Eros.**

CosmoErotic Humanism—the CosmoErotic Universe lives in you uniquely, and it's a humanism because *it affirms the inherent goodness of humanity*. It's not *natural* goodness; goodness has to be trained and activated. Just like when I work out, I'm activating my muscle structure.

That's Reality in the first person; that's the first-person perspective. That's the feeling of me.

THE THIRD-PERSON AND FIRST-PERSON PERSPECTIVES OF COSMOS ARE NOT ENOUGH

But that's not all. If I'm actually being scientific—what William James called "radical empiricism"—I realize that there's also a second-person perspective of Reality. That second-person perspective of Reality is a very big deal. And in telling a new Love Story, you've got to include a second-person perspective.

So it's not just that I'm telling the story of the evolutionary Eros and Evolutionary Love as a third-person force: animating the incredible unfolding that takes place in embryology, the incredible unfolding of the sixteen kinds of quarks that reign in gazillions at the beginning of the first nanoseconds of the Big Bang. It's not only that Evolutionary Love, Evolutionary Eros, animating the stories of molecular biology and the stories of molecular physics. That's all Evolutionary Love in the third-person.

Evolutionary Love, Eros, or what we sometimes call Outrageous Love, is a third-person force that animates the four forces: the strong and the weak nuclear, the electromagnetic, and the gravitational. They are all animated by Eros; there's a self-actualizing principle of Cosmos, a self-organizing Universe, which is another way of saying the inherent Eros, which Stuart Kauffman not incorrectly called the *ceaseless creativity of the Universe*. Wow.

- That's love in the third person.

- That's Eros in the third person.
- That's Evolutionary Love.

Thou art that actually means *Thou art a unique expression of the Field of Eros*, a field of third person—and it animates everything.

This is fundamental. We're telling this fundamental new Story.

But then there's love in the first person: *I'm being lived as love*, and *I'm a unique expression of Outrageous Love.*

- I'm a unique individuated expression.
- I'm in individuation beyond separate self,
- I'm in individuation beyond ego.
- I am the higher individuation of the irreducibly unique configuration of Evolutionary Love that lives in me, as me, and through me.
- I'm lived as Love.

That's first person.

THE SECOND-PERSON PERSPECTIVE OF REALITY

But what's second person? Second-person perspective is: **I desperately want to know you.**

I want to know you.

I want to meet you.

I want to be intimate with you.

I want to realize that I have some level of shared identity and shared pathos with you. This is our definition of intimacy in CosmoErotic Humanism, or at least one piece of it.

I want my interior to speak to your interior.

If the interior of one human being is not speaking to the interior of another human being, our experience is that life is actually valueless; it's not worth living. As the good book originally said 3,000 years ago, *it's not good for the human being to be alone*. In fact, this means it's not good for the human being to be lonely. If I have everything, but I can't share it with the interiority of another being, then I have nothing.

That's second person, the desire for intimacy; in that sense, that's the experience of the personal.

God is the exponentialized infinite Field of Personhood.

So we might call God not just the Infinity of Power, or the Eros that drives the third-person Cosmos, and that lives in me, first-person—**but God is also the Infinity of Intimacy that knows my name, just like we know each other's names.**

God is not just the Infinity of Power—and the god you don't believe in doesn't exist, and the god that Thomas Nagel is describing of having wanting nothing to do with, we want nothing to do with either. But that's the caricatured cosmic vending-machine god.

If we want to create a world Story, then we can't split off any part of ourselves, and God is a part of ourselves. So we actually have to participate, and *we have to become the saviors of God.*

In other words…

Medicine has moved on from the sixteenth century. Can you imagine if you went to a doctor today and you had a serious—God forbid—illness, and you went to a sixteenth-century or seventeenth-century doctor? You'd be out of your mind! **We don't go to seventeenth-century doctors, but somehow, most organized religion in the world today is teaching seventeenth-century religion.**

What are we doing? **We have to participate in the evolution of consciousness, which is the evolution of love, which is the evolution of God.**

God is not a cosmic vending machine. **God is, or, if you will, Reality is**—God equals Reality, and Reality equals God—**the Infinity of Intimacy that knows your name,** no less than we know each other's name.

ENACTING THE NEW STORY THROUGH LIVED, DIRECT EXPERIENCE: THE PRACTICE OF PRAYER

Let's practice this, because we can't enact the new Story unless we know it in our bodies. It has to be a lived, direct experience. We do have to know it in our minds, and we have to be able to conceptualize it. But there's an infinite field of experience that's non-conceptual: I can't reduce *I love you* to concepts; I can't reduce *I feel you* to concepts.

> *The Universe lives in me, and the Universe feels, and the Universe feels Love. I am the Universe in person.*

So let's try and get this non-conceptually in a set of pointing-out instructions. And I want to read this through and then pause to practice with your eyes closed, so we can find it on the inside.

We're in the Field of Imagination—but not made-up imagination—but what the Sufi master Ibn Arabi called *the imaginal field*; we're entering into the inside of Reality. Here we go.

Let's say I heard David talking. So when I heard David talking, what in me heard David talking, or what in you heard David talking? You might say *your ears*. Well, that's true. You did need the structure of your ears, absolutely. There's this dazzling structure called the ear, which is shockingly beautiful.

But it wasn't only your physical ears: it was this *whole interior system within you*, which has both exteriors and interiors, which has *telos,* and which has inherent interior design, which means it has inherent interior intelligence.

That's a simple scientific given if you're thinking clearly in science. There's an inherent interior *telos* of the body, and it has direction of moving towards life. So it wasn't your ears that heard me, it was actually your intelligence. *You heard me with your intelligence.*

Now, I know there's crazy intelligent, beautiful people here. But are you the most intelligent person in your whole state? Maybe not. In the whole country? Probably not. There's other intelligent people, and there's other intelligences.

So for example, even before human intelligence, there was photosynthesis. I've spent a lot of time studying photosynthesis and the chlorophyll molecule. Anyone who tells you there was no intelligence before the human is mistaken—**there clearly was pre-human intelligence, before the human cortex. Reality is self-evidently intelligent. It has meaning structures, it exchanges information.** As James Shapiro at University of Chicago has pointed out in his work on natural genetic engineering, *a cell is self-evidently intelligent*—if you understand the cellular structure.

So your intelligence heard me, and my intelligence heard you. But **your intelligence is not the only intelligence**. It might not even be the greatest intelligence. And is your intelligence separate from the larger Field of Intelligence? Absolutely not! **So if you heard me talking—meaning your intelligence heard me talking—and you're not separate from the larger Field of Intelligence, is it in any way possible that when I talk, the larger Field of Intelligence doesn't hear me? Not a chance. It absolutely does.** Wow.

So that's a pointing-out instruction, if I can borrow that phrase from my Tibetan Buddhist brothers and sisters. **Let's cut through 2,000 years of sophistry on prayer. The prayer you don't believe in doesn't exist, and the god you don't believe in doesn't exist.**

So what prayer means at its core, its original intention before it got distorted and hijacked, is: **when I speak—bringing my holy and broken *Hallelujah* before the Infinity of Intimacy that lives in me and holds me—that Intelligence hears me**. Just like you hear me and you're also part of the larger Field of Intelligence, it couldn't be that only your intelligence hears me but the larger Field doesn't. So when I speak or when you speak, the larger Field of Intelligence hears you.

Don't think about this, just feel it. Go underneath. We always think. (And I'm all about thinking.) But *you've got to feel. [Pause reading, close your eyes, and feel this.]*

We're participating, in this moment. This is not a personal transformation seminar. This is not self-help.

We're trying to transform Cosmos. We're trying to participate in the evolution of God.

It's shocking, isn't it? It's like, *wow*. It changes everything.

All of a sudden, *I'm not alone.*

Imagine what it might mean to know that *I speak and Infinity hears me*. So after knowing this, I don't turn to my partner and say: "*If I shared something with you, and you didn't get it immediately and instantly, in the exact way I needed you to get it, I'm devastated, distraught, and destroyed.*" Well, no!

Of course, there's a love story between me and my Beloved. It might be the person I live with. It might be a sister, a brother, or a friend. There's a field of Beloveds, of course. **But that Field of Beloveds participates in the larger Field of Eros, in the larger Field of Intimacy.**

It's not just a larger Field of Consciousness, with all due respect to much of classical enlightenment teaching. *It's a Field of Consciousness whose interior is Love, Eros, intimacy, desire.*

I've spent a decade critiquing those classical teachings as they appear in many places, including Integral Theory. It's a field of Love and Eros. It's not just about awareness. **It's about the Field of Eros itself.** Wow, that's a big deal. That's exciting.

THE FIELD OF EROS HAS A PERSONAL QUALITY

The field of Eros has a quality that's personal.

I didn't make that up; it's a primordial structure of Reality: first person, second person, and third person. It makes no scientific sense for any kind of person who's a serious radical empiricist, to dismiss the second-person part of the Field of Reality.

Now, it's not a love story in which I get absorbed by the second person; I'm in dialogue: *diálogos* with the second person.

Prayer is when humanity speaks to the Infinite, and prophecy is when the Infinite speaks to humanity. Prayer is when finitude turns to the Infinite, and prophecy is when the Infinite overflows into the finite. Prophecy has many forms, from the eureka of scientific disclosure to the revelations of the interior sciences. We have to get this. It changes everything!

My relationship with the Divine is not—this is where Spinoza got it wrong in his *Tractatus*—it's not that I'm an obedient child. No, that's the god that Nagel doesn't want any part of—nor do I, and nor do we.

It's rather the experience of Divinity as the Mother, as the Lover, as the Queen, as the Sister, as the Daughter. And as the Son. And as the best Friend. **That's the Infinity of Intimacy. It's the lover's model.**

She knows me. She knows my name. She cares about me infinitely.

ATHEISM: THERE'S HERESY WHICH IS FAITH

I have to participate as a partner, which means that sometimes the partner needs to step back to allow me room to breathe, to act, and to choose. I can only do that if I'm not smothered. Now here's the shocking thing. **The Love Story is not a Love Story if there's not a part in you which can deny the Love Story.** If there's not a part of me that can step out of the Love Story and see me independently of the Love Story—and even at moments, I can deny the Love Story, only to come back to it—then it's not a Love Story.

So we would call that, in the collective consciousness, *atheism*. Atheism is also part of the Love Story because atheism is the possibility where *I can't see it for a moment*. In other words:

> *The uncertainty—the mystery—is part of the Love Story. It's not a fundamentalist explication of why and how everything happens. It's a Love Story that dances with the mystery.*

So when I look at a world aflame with joy, a world aflame with suffering, I don't turn to the god that doesn't exist to fix it.

No. She turns to us and says: *To speak of your love in the morning, and to trust you through the nights.* These are the words of Solomon's father, David, who is called "the one who is beloved." The word David means *Djavida*: the one who is beloved by Source. She turns to us and says: *Be Me, and don't rely on some caricatured version of Me.*

For a moment, you've got to be an atheist. That's heresy which is faith.

Then there's faith which is heresy: the small version of a caricatured god, the cosmic vending-machine god who we're going to rely on to make it all okay.

The heresy which is actually faith is not believing in the small caricatured god, but in God as the Infinity of Intimacy. And, in fact, I don't *believe* in it—I actually *experience* it and *feel* it.

It's a direct knowing. That's second person.

PRAYER IS THE EXPERIENCE OF THE PERSONHOOD OF COSMOS THAT KNOWS MY NAME

So we can't leave second person out of the love story. Let's look at our code one more time:

We are never not telling a love story.

The question is, "What love story are we telling?

What is the plotline of the love story?" There are good love stories, and there are bad love stories. We need to tell the greatest love story ever told, where no one, no thing, and not one part of ourselves is split off.

In the greatest love story ever told, no one and nothing is outside the circle.

Rather, everyone and everything is in the circle.

That means that I can bring my holy and broken *Hallelujah* into the circle; nothing's left out. We're going to end with what we call prayer. Not to the cosmic vending machine; this is evolutionary prayer, second-person prayer.

Me and my friend Ken Wilber talked about this intensely in 2002–2004, in conversation with David Steindl-Rast and Thomas Keating. They thought about prayer more as meditation, as contemplative prayer, which is important. There is absolutely a meditative dimension to prayer, but that's not what prayer is at its core. I was excited to share this with Ken from deep in the lineage.

> *Prayer is when I experience that You're right there and I'm right here, and that the Personhood of Cosmos knows my name.*

Just as when I'm talking directly to you, and you're talking directly to me—and we know each other infinitely personally—I'm talking directly to the Infinity of Personhood, the Infinity of Intimacy that knows my name, and that's both holding me and is held by me.

That's a Love Story.

That's the holy and broken *Hallelujah*.

As the song is playing, just feel what you want to ask for, and we're just going to ask for everything.

Who are we asking from? The Infinity of Intimacy that's us and that holds us. The holy and the broken *Hallelujah*, Leonard Cohen is telling a love story.

Let's listen to "Hallelujah," by Leonard Cohen.

Pray not in a way that's emasculating.

Pray with the fullness of your presence as an irreducibly unique expression of the LoveIntelligence and the LoveIntimacy of Reality. We bring our holy and our broken *Hallelujah*, and we ask for everything.

When we pray, we ask for everything. Prayer affirms the dignity of personal need. And when we pray, we know that we're heard. We don't give up our autonomy for a second; autonomy and communion dance together.

THE THREE FACES OF GOD = THE THREE FACES OF LOVE

What we did today is we participated literally, directly, in the evolution of Love, which is the evolution of God. There are tears in my eyes—these are the most beautiful prayers in the world!

They're lifting like a prayer to the sky, into the depth of the depth.

INDEX

Abhinavagupta 356
Achok Rinpoche 84, 85
Adonai Elohim 54, 359
affirmative prayer 368, 369
algorithm 31, 104, 281, 407
Allah 41, 42
Allahu Akbar 40, 41, 42, 44, 52, 54, 178
All-That-Is 12, 13, 16, 20, 27, 67, 73, 165
Amelong, Kristina 187, 257
Amorous Cosmos 53, 193, 224
Anthro-Ontology 24, 89
Anthropocene 143, 342
Ark of the Covenant 191, 199, 273, 329, 367
Armageddon 123, 126
artificial intelligence 108, 125
atheism 149, 430
attention 78, 80, 217, 239, 250, 345, 349, 355, 358, 361, 408
The Avengers 222
axis mundi 80

Bach 167
Be Here Now (Dass) 12
Big Bang 8, 9, 10, 18, 116, 118, 119, 257, 341, 366, 367, 401, 411, 412, 413, 423
   Fourth 10, 412, 413
   Second 412
   Third 412, 413
biosphere 7, 8, 9, 66, 412
Bocelli, Andrea 5, 11, 74, 400, 401

Bohm, David 152
Book of Judges 198
Book of Life 74
Branigan, Laura 69, 72, 74
British Society for Psychical Research 307
Browning, Robert 76
Buddhism 15, 32, 51, 167, 171, 189, 257, 261, 274, 356, 359, 370

Castaneda, Carlos 298
Castaway (movie) 402
catastrophic risk 21, 23, 31, 57, 64, 75, 100, 123, 139, 142, 182, 249, 264, 267
chanting 78–91, 138, 213, 220, 221, 224, 268, 368, 382
Christianity 13, 15, 17, 25, 28, 34, 38, 49, 51, 53, 58, 59, 61, 70, 74, 82, 83, 112, 126, 167, 170, 178, 181, 183, 188, 189, 209, 227, 277, 280–285, 294, 305, 316, 323, 324, 329, 335, 353, 359, 378, 390
Christmas 2, 56, 57, 58, 59, 70, 182, 183, 189, 272, 280, 281
clarification of desire 129, 361
Cohen, Leonard 20, 79, 90, 161, 162, 210, 221, 272, 370, 376, 393, 395, 432
commons 100, 107, 116, 125, 186
Common Sense Sacred Axioms 96
complexity 5, 7, 13, 18, 45, 59, 72, 319, 343, 361, 362, 367, 374,

INDEX

383, 407
Confucianism 61, 167, 189
Conscious Evolution 18, 124, 141
contemplative prayer 369
continuity of consciousness 13, 308, 309, 333, 337, 338, 389, 411
conversational Cosmos 118
cosmocentric structure of consciousness and intimacy 15, 26, 30, 79, 262, 361
CosmoErotic Humanism 41, 53, 56, 96, 103, 113, 134, 139, 143, 144, 147, 155, 159, 195, 293, 294, 301, 423, 424
CosmoErotic Universe 270, 271, 276, 423
Cosmos
 interior face of 78, 149, 152
 personhood of 137, 184, 358, 371, 406
creativity 4, 5, 6, 42, 45, 102, 147, 158, 192, 254, 257, 282, 344, 362, 374, 411, 423
crisis
 as birth 186
 as crisis of intimacy 186, 316
Crosby, Stills, Nash & Young 61
crucifixion 227, 228, 251, 252, 253, 294, 309

Dalai Lama 84
Dante 148, 164, 282
da Vinci, Leonardo 39, 71, 75, 76, 89, 94, 142, 199, 218, 243, 266, 310, 364, 379, 415
Dawkins, Richard 384
death 23, 139, 140, 141, 217, 218, 219, 265, 289, 291, 308, 309, 315, 319, 322–327, 333–335, 337, 389, 410, 411
death of humanity 139, 217, 289, 315, 411
death of our humanity 139, 140, 141,
289, 315
deepest heart's desire 129, 131, 134, 135, 207, 208
Derrida, Jacques 355, 391
Devi Prayer 82
Divine Will 130
DNA 298, 366
Don't Look Up (movie) 71
doomerism 166
Dune (movie) 80
Dyson, Freeman 352

Easter 182, 287, 292, 293, 294, 304, 309
ego 12, 37, 80, 114, 161, 231, 233, 234, 235, 239, 271, 283, 297, 349, 351, 356, 363, 424
egocentric structure of consiousness and intimacy 26, 30, 79, 106, 164
Egypt 33, 34, 251, 295
Einstein, Albert 152, 352, 421
Elisha 79
Eros and ethics 151
Eros equation 132
eternity 8, 53, 129, 256, 290, 327, 329, 331, 332, 335, 365
ethnocentric level of consciousness and intimacy 15, 16, 26, 28, 30, 46, 48, 49, 50, 54, 79, 84, 97, 101, 103, 104, 126, 154, 169, 175, 189, 262, 268, 282, 350, 361, 416
evangelism 23, 24, 25, 26, 27, 28, 29, 30, 31, 35
Evolutionary Impulse 5, 12, 15, 18, 20, 69, 92, 134, 172, 223, 317, 370, 410, 411, 413
Evolutionary Love 2, 20, 122, 144, 155, 156, 168, 173, 194, 208, 236, 250, 272, 314, 318, 337, 413, 423, 424
evolutionary psychology 22

Evolutionary Unique Self 27, 114, 134, 135
Evolution: A View from the Twenty-First Century (Shapiro) 298
evolution of love 3, 79, 80, 128, 149, 151, 154, 158, 251, 255, 304, 305, 306, 308, 310, 315, 343, 365, 366, 398, 426
existential risk 21, 22, 23, 36, 37, 38, 57, 64, 69, 75, 76, 100, 102, 120, 123–126, 139, 140, 164, 179, 182, 217, 222, 239, 249, 264, 289, 313, 398, 410
exterior sciences 21, 66, 89, 155, 164, 256, 310, 342, 367, 372
Eye of the Heart 45, 46, 77, 267, 269, 374
Eye of the Mind 45, 77, 267
Eye of the Senses 44, 45, 77, 267
Eye of the Spirit 45, 77, 374
Eye of Value 77, 78, 80, 89, 267, 269
Ezekiel 48

family
  biological 62, 63, 64, 67, 68, 69, 71, 73
  evolutionary 64, 65, 68, 69, 72, 73
Father Thomas Keating 358
feminine, the 4, 94, 191, 193, 194, 266, 299, 350
Feynman, Richard 352
Ficino, Marsilio 76, 94, 142, 218, 266, 305, 364
Field of Cosmos 356
Field of Desire 317, 400
Field of Divinity 176, 177
Field of Eros 81, 244, 267, 317, 357, 409, 424, 428, 429
Field of Infinite Personhood 358
Field of Intimacy 361, 428
Field of Prayer 221
Field of Value 77, 79, 86, 89, 99, 186, 222, 301, 313, 329, 357, 413

finitude 2, 111, 256, 282, 351, 352, 353, 382, 398, 399, 429
First Principles and First Values 30, 57, 77, 86, 96, 103, 104, 105, 106, 109, 117, 124, 127, 128, 143, 147, 167, 168, 180, 224, 265, 288, 290, 291, 293, 296, 379, 413, 417, 419, 420
Frischmann, Brett 141
fundamentalism 25, 57, 70, 195, 209, 244, 288, 307, 315, 331, 335, 336, 353, 380, 430

Gandhi, Mahatma 39
Genesis 73, 333
global coherence 125, 179, 187
global coordination 125, 179
global intimacy disorder 124, 125, 182, 186, 267, 316
global resonance 125, 179, 187
Gloria 1, 5, 10, 11, 13, 14, 15, 16, 68, 69, 70, 72, 73, 74, 285, 286
gnosis 26, 81, 93, 109, 165, 187, 188, 195, 209, 211, 255, 334
God
  as Infinity of Intimacy 13, 19, 90, 111, 136, 137, 138, 161, 184, 185, 195, 221, 224, 257, 263, 283, 295, 358, 359, 360, 361, 370, 371, 373, 374, 375, 382, 393, 394, 399, 400, 403, 405, 407, 409, 425, 426, 428, 429, 431, 432
  as Infinity of Power 19, 111, 138, 195, 257, 374, 382, 399, 400, 403, 407, 425
  as the Infinite Intimate 41, 161, 166, 175, 176, 177, 179, 180, 184, 185, 195, 221, 318, 336
  as the Possibility of Possibility 116, 117, 120, 223, 281, 282, 353
  first person 13
  glory of 4, 5, 6, 14

INDEX

in the second person 13, 18
in the third person 18, 407
more God to come 4, 5, 10, 11, 13, 336
Personhood of 13, 18
the god you don't believe in 4, 18, 327, 382, 407, 418, 419, 425, 427
three faces of 401, 419
will of 130, 131, 327, 328
Goddess 2, 74, 82, 89, 131, 138, 184, 191, 192, 258, 296, 299, 370, 375
Goodness, Truth, and Beauty 95, 112
grammar of value 89
Great Library 68, 127, 144, 146, 243
Griffin, David Ray 418
Gyoto monks 84

Habermas, Jürgen 94
Hafiz 13, 352
Hallelujah 13, 19, 20, 58, 90, 161, 162, 185, 196, 210, 211, 216, 221, 223, 225, 226, 260, 263, 272, 278, 283, 338, 371, 375, 376, 392, 393, 395, 428, 431, 432
  holy and the broken 13, 90, 185, 210, 211, 223, 225, 226, 260, 338, 376, 393, 395, 432
Hancock, Phillip 322, 323, 324, 325, 326, 327, 328, 330, 331, 332, 333, 334, 336, 337, 338
Hanukkah 270, 271, 272, 273, 274, 275, 276, 277, 278, 279, 299, 301, 306
Harari, Yuval 301, 384
Harris, Sam 384
Hebrew wisdom 13, 33, 183, 189, 270, 273, 282, 295, 299, 355, 390, 404
Hegel, G.W.F 103
Hinach Yafah 88
Hinduism 51, 81, 183

Hitler 149
Homo amor 17, 27, 38, 39, 52, 53, 54, 55, 56, 61, 67, 74, 91, 124, 126, 128, 134, 165, 213, 243, 251, 262, 291, 317, 318, 338, 413
  as new human and new humanity 38, 53, 61, 74, 91, 123, 126, 129, 147, 165, 213, 243, 251, 261, 291, 317, 366, 398, 413
Homo armor 27
hope is a memory of the future 129
Hubbard, Barbara Marx 2, 17, 18, 115, 120, 122, 127, 158, 216, 287, 289
Hughes, Langston 35, 268, 280
humanism 3, 17, 70, 350
Hume, David 46, 96
Huxley, Aldous 170, 174

Ibn Arabi 426
Ibn Gabbai 258
imaginal cells 365
Implicate Order 178
Infinity of Intimacy 13, 19, 90, 111, 136, 137, 138, 161, 184, 185, 195, 221, 224, 257, 263, 283, 295, 358, 359, 360, 361, 370, 371, 373, 374, 375, 382, 393, 394, 399, 400, 403, 405, 407, 409, 425, 426, 428, 429, 431, 432
in-group 17
Integral Theory 25, 42, 47, 52, 58, 86, 124, 141, 171, 174, 181, 275, 353, 420, 429
interior sciences 18, 21, 89, 129, 130, 155, 164, 196, 256, 269, 273, 342, 354, 355, 367, 369, 372, 384, 387, 418, 422, 429
Internal Family Systems 99
intimacy
  evlolving 122
  evolution of 9, 383

unique configurations 7
intimacy equation 150
Intimate Universe 21, 190, 192, 221, 232, 244, 248, 370, 413
Isaiah 48, 202, 352
Islam 25, 32, 40–43, 45, 49, 50–54, 61, 70, 112, 167, 183, 188, 189, 353, 378, 390
its insides are lined with love 332, 348, 368

James, William 307, 423
Jeremiah 352
Jesus 28, 74, 79, 281, 284, 304, 307, 323, 329, 335
Jobs, Steve 25, 223
Judah the Maccabee 273
Judaism 12, 15, 17, 18, 25, 32, 49, 51, 53, 70, 126, 167, 181, 183, 189, 279, 353

Kabbalah 17, 61, 93, 172, 185
Kaddish 389
Kafka, Franz 136
Kant, Immanuel 45, 87, 353
Kashmir Shaivism 81, 183, 355, 356
Kauffman, Stuart 42, 66, 423
Kempton, Sally 181
Kincaid, Kristina 27, 257
King Arthur 299
Kook, Abraham 202, 261
Krishna and Radha 122

Lao Tzu 370
laughter 383, 384, 387, 393, 395
Leibniz 168
Leshem Yichud 318
Levi Yitzchok of Berditchev 391, 392, 395
Love
 as real 17, 45, 78
 as religion 4, 5, 10
 evolution of 3, 37

politics of 10, 12
LoveIntelligence 20, 27, 67, 144, 164, 166, 184, 196, 361, 372, 403, 422, 432
Luria, Isaac 172, 295, 318

Mahabharata 364
Mao 149
Martin Luther King Jr. 414
Marxism 291, 394
Mary Magdalene 83, 190
materialism 16, 106, 149, 153, 401
mathematics 45, 66, 77, 78, 166, 244, 407
matzah 33, 34, 35
Merkavah Adonai 48
Messiah 15, 74, 80, 81, 126, 291
meta-crisis 107, 139, 141, 168, 177, 186, 201, 211, 218, 243, 248, 264, 268, 271, 285, 288, 290, 293, 310, 312, 313, 315, 378
Mizmor Shir 87
modernity 21, 22, 31, 52, 57, 101, 126, 169, 178, 181, 187, 190, 201, 251, 265, 291, 353, 385, 399, 417, 420
Molinard, Claire 134
monogamous polyamory 218, 219, 220
Mordechai Leiner of Izbica 408
Moss, Devin 322, 323, 324, 325, 326, 327, 328, 329, 330, 332, 333, 334, 336, 337, 338
Mozart 90, 167
music 3, 78, 79, 80, 81, 85, 86, 125, 128, 150, 159, 166, 175, 179, 189, 216, 241, 253, 310, 311, 319, 320, 326, 415
mystery 130, 190, 191, 245, 360, 386, 395, 430
mysticism 33, 40, 48, 272, 384
myth 198, 232, 299, 309

INDEX

Nachman of Breslov 136
Nagel, Thomas 418, 421, 425, 429
Neem Karoli Baba 12
New Age 3, 10, 25, 30, 97, 109, 111, 181, 218, 220, 229, 287, 315, 353, 381, 388, 419
Newton, Isaac 66

O'Connor, Sinéad 58, 60
olam (world) 34, 91
orgasm 137, 178
Orwell, George 201
out-group 17
Outrageous Acts of Love 20, 35, 152, 154, 155, 156, 157, 159, 160, 162, 208, 231, 232, 233, 236
Outrageous Love 2, 20, 27, 28, 38, 39, 57, 60, 61, 62, 65–68, 70, 88, 114, 144, 147–152, 155, 156, 160–165, 207, 208, 212, 216, 223, 226, 229–232, 242–246, 253, 271, 287, 297, 364, 365, 369, 398, 423, 424
Outrageous Love Letters 60
Outrageous Love Story 155, 156, 297

pan-interiority 355, 356, 362, 371
paradox 30, 220, 290, 362, 384, 385, 386, 387, 388, 389, 392, 393
Passover 33, 34, 292, 293, 294, 295
perennial philosophy 32, 46, 168, 169, 170, 171, 173, 174, 175
Phenomenology of Eros 131, 190, 192
Philippians 324, 326, 336
photosynthesis 427
physiosphere 5, 6, 7, 412
Planetary Awakening in Love through Unique Self Symphonies 20, 122, 158, 165
Plato 109
postmodernity 21, 31, 57, 178, 187, 251, 291, 304, 385, 391, 399, 417, 420

post-tragic 88, 116, 117
prayer 18, 81, 90, 106, 136, 137, 138, 161, 162, 171, 184, 195, 196, 201, 209, 210, 211, 221, 223, 224, 226, 260, 262, 322, 327, 328, 329, 333, 337, 338, 345, 353, 354, 355, 358–362, 368–373, 376, 382–384, 388–395, 399–406, 409, 426–433
  as affirming the dignity of personal need 225, 226, 361, 373, 403, 432
  as erotic 373
  as existential 373
premodernity 15, 21, 22, 31, 32, 46, 57, 78, 92, 95, 96, 101, 102, 103, 106, 109, 169, 178, 187, 189, 244, 251, 268, 291, 321, 385, 417
Process and Reality (Whitehead) 93
prophecy 48, 54, 55, 57, 123, 290, 312, 314, 315, 316, 349, 350, 351, 352, 353, 429
pseudo-eros 56, 57, 98, 100, 104, 107, 220, 227, 228, 297, 416
pseudo-value vii, 97, 98
psychedelics 137, 214, 215, 223, 224
Pythagoras 66, 78

Radical Kabbalah (Gafni) 17
radical uniqueness 9
Rama and Sita 83, 122
Ramadan 41, 44, 52, 61, 126, 189, 294
Ramana Maharshi 134
Ram Dass 12, 13
Ratzon HaShem (will of God) 130
Reality
  as Eros 332, 333, 336, 337
  as Love Story 410
Reality needs my service 20
Rebbe of Belz 56
Re-Engineering Humanity (Frischmann) 141

Reich, Wilhelm 352
religion 3, 4, 5, 10, 15, 16, 17, 26,
   32, 33, 40-55, 59, 62, 81, 92,
   101-112, 117, 119, 120-124,
   136, 155, 165-181, 188, 189,
   192, 266, 272, 281, 290-294,
   314, 334-337, 380, 419, 425
depth structures 32, 47, 58, 180, 269
ethnocentric 16
surface structures 32, 42, 47, 51, 52,
   58, 59, 168, 173, 174, 180, 269,
   272
unique 41, 48, 55
Renaissance 36, 75, 76, 92, 94, 106,
   109, 142, 143, 166, 169, 190,
   195, 218, 243, 265, 266, 364,
   415
Resurrection 287, 294, 305, 309
revelation 46, 49, 50, 51, 52, 54, 169,
   193, 195, 209, 211, 323, 342
ritual 47, 51, 53, 178, 181, 182, 183,
   199, 201
Rosh Hashanah 183, 189, 190, 192,
   194, 197, 198, 201, 203, 204,
   205, 206, 209
Rumi 13, 44, 352, 359, 360, 398
Russell, Bertrand 129, 149, 153

Schelling, F.W.J. 113
Schmachtenberger, Daniel 40
Schuon, Frithjof 174
Schwartz, Richard 99
scientific method 94, 266
second simplicity 59, 333
Seder 33
seduction 128, 131, 132, 133, 134,
   135, 136, 397
   holy 128
   unholy 128, 135, 397
self-organization 9, 20, 140, 158, 374,
   423
separate self 22, 95, 107, 133, 134,
   135, 136, 169, 170, 175, 213,

   216, 297, 329, 346, 347, 386,
   400, 421, 424
Shakespeare, William 24, 63
Shapiro, James 298, 427
shared grammar of value 111, 115,
   117, 118, 125, 130, 146, 177,
   182, 266
shared identity 19, 93, 118, 150, 193,
   424
Shekhinah 184, 191
Sheldrake, Rupert 181
shofar 194, 195, 196, 197, 199, 200,
   201, 204, 210
Silence of Presence 376, 389, 394
Silent Night 57, 58, 59, 60, 280, 282,
   284, 285
Silicon Valley 30
Skinner, B.F. 200, 201
Smith, Adam 40
Solomon 60, 79, 85, 88, 131, 190, 191,
   196, 199, 222, 297, 348, 367,
   368, 382, 397, 430
Song of Solomon 60, 88, 131, 132,
   222, 297, 348, 368, 382, 397
source code of culture 17, 18, 37, 39,
   40, 55, 67, 68, 71, 74, 105, 110,
   141, 142, 144, 145, 146, 147,
   158, 167, 177, 180, 186, 187,
   222, 227, 259, 265, 287, 288,
   289, 290, 291, 293, 304, 394
Spinoza, Baruch 324, 429
Stalin 149
Star Wars 219, 265
St. Augustine 49
Steindl-Rast, David 358, 431
Stein, Zak 127, 201, 379
Story
   new 10, 12, 17, 20, 21, 29, 31, 37,
   39, 40, 41, 53, 57, 65, 67, 68,
   71, 74, 76, 77, 84, 89, 92, 93,
   94, 95, 100, 103, 109, 117, 127,
   136, 142, 143, 145, 187, 195,
   218, 219, 222, 225, 239, 253,

265, 266, 267, 268, 290, 292, 293, 294, 300, 304, 310, 312, 321, 343, 410, 412, 414, 415, 418, 424, 426
Story of Value 57, 76, 77, 84, 93, 95, 96, 98, 99, 100, 101, 102, 103, 107, 109, 117, 127, 142, 143, 167, 168, 177, 179, 180, 182, 187, 188, 195, 211, 218, 219, 222, 225, 239, 243, 253, 265, 266, 267, 290, 292, 293, 294, 310, 312, 320, 321, 322
success story 22, 65, 98, 100, 102, 104, 107, 112, 313, 347, 365
Sufism 61, 183
sunyata 170, 174
symbiogenesis 31

Tagore 148, 149
Talmud 59, 305
Tantra 246
Tao 22–24, 28, 29, 30, 32, 53, 84, 222, 267, 301, 344
Taoism 51
tears 183, 188, 192–201, 205–217, 225, 227, 235, 282, 300, 312, 392, 433
TechnoFeudalism 31, 222
technology 11, 26, 81, 95, 100, 101, 102, 139, 268
 ecstatic 26, 30
Teilhard de Chardin, Pierre 255
telos 151, 156, 164, 308, 427
Thanos 222
the Good, the True, and the Beautiful 16, 79, 81, 86, 167, 172, 347, 350, 360
theology 19, 42, 372
The Origins of Order (Kaufman) 66
The Theory of Moral Sentiments (Smith) 40
The Universe: A Love Story 253, 298
The Wealth of Nations (Smith) 40

tikkun (repair) 172
Torah 127, 180, 182
trauma 37, 107, 108, 114, 136, 164, 241, 249, 250, 262, 282
trialectics 101, 103
True Self 134, 135, 170, 174, 175, 298

unique circle of intimacy and influence 157, 229, 232, 233, 234, 235, 236, 300
unique gift 11, 113, 300, 308
Unique Self 9–12, 18, 20, 27, 29, 33, 34, 36, 39, 42, 44, 47, 52, 53, 54, 57, 58, 61, 70, 74, 90, 107, 114, 122, 123, 127, 134, 135, 136, 138, 144, 145, 146, 155, 156, 158, 159, 165, 168, 173, 175, 178, 179, 180, 183, 187, 188, 189, 208, 210, 216, 229–235, 239, 246, 247, 250, 252, 253, 255, 260, 266, 270, 272, 276, 284, 285, 299, 308, 345, 351, 390, 399, 413
 Evolutionary 27, 114, 134, 135
Unique Self Symphony 20, 42, 52, 53, 54, 70, 74, 123, 127, 134, 135, 136, 144, 145, 146, 158, 159, 165, 168, 173, 175, 179, 183, 188, 189, 208, 216, 230, 233, 239, 246, 247, 250, 252, 253, 255, 260, 266, 270, 272, 276, 284, 285, 299
Universe Story 39, 40, 76, 155, 378, 398
Up from Eden (Wilber) 358

Walden Two (Skinner) 201
Whitehead, Alfred North 93, 129, 150, 305, 356, 368, 401
Whitman, Walt 156
Whole Mate 158
wholeness 24, 108, 119, 132, 163, 195, 209

Wilber, Ken 32, 108, 181, 358, 431, 432
Winnicott, Donald 204
worldcentric structure of consciousness and intimacy 26, 30, 79
world religion 15, 53, 58, 61, 92, 97, 103, 104, 106, 108, 110, 112, 115, 117, 119, 120, 121, 124, 136, 163, 166, 167, 168, 175, 177, 178, 179, 188, 189, 192, 264, 294, 312, 335, 336, 337, 420
  as context for our diversity 112, 117, 120–123, 145, 167, 247, 269, 415
world spirituality 53, 58, 61, 108, 112, 264, 420

Yiddish 56, 57, 58
Yom Kippur xiv, 183, 190, 191, 192, 194, 197, 198, 200, 201, 294, 390, 391
Your Unique Self (Gafni) 18, 134

Zohar 158, 257, 369
Zuckerberg, Mark 86

VOLUME 17

LIST OF EPISODES

1. *Episode 168 — December 28, 2019*
2. *Episode 174 — February 9, 2020*
3. *Episode 233 — March 28, 2021*
4. *Episode 237 — April 25, 2021*
5. *Episode 272 — December 26, 2021*
6. *Episode 278 — February 8, 2022*
7. *Episode 289 — April 25, 2022*
8. *Episode 290 — May 1, 2022*
9. *Episode 292 — May 15, 2022*
10. *Episode 310 — September 18, 2022*
11. *Episode 311 — September 27, 2022*
12. *Episode 312 — October 2, 2022*
13. *Episode 313 — October 9, 2022*
14. *Episode 320 — November 27, 2022*
15. *Episode 324 — December 25, 2022*
16. *Episode 339 — April 9, 2023*
17. *Episode 380 — January 21, 2024*

PRAYER AND WOLRD RELIGION

18. *Episode 196 — July 12, 2020*
19. *Episode 202 — August 23, 2020*
20. *Episode 203 — August 30, 2020*
21. *Episode 251 — August 1, 2021*
22. *Episode 281 — February 27, 2022*

www.ingramcontent.com/pod-product-compliance
Lightning Source LLC
Chambersburg PA
CBHW032028150426
43194CB00006B/190